Applied Environmental Economics

The complex real-world interactions between the economy and the environment form both the focus of and the main barrier to applied research within the field of environmental economics. However, geographical information systems (GIS) allow economists to tackle such complexity head on by directly incorporating diverse datasets into applied research rather than resorting to simplifying and often unrealistic assumptions. This innovative book applies GIS techniques to spatial cost-benefit analysis of a complex and topical land use change problem – the conversion of agricultural land to multipurpose woodland – looking in detail at issues such as opportunity costs, timber yield, recreation, carbon storage, etc., and embracing cross-cutting themes such as the evaluation of environmental preferences and the spatial transfer of benefit functions.

IAN J. BATEMAN is Professor of Environmental Economics at the School of Environmental Sciences, University of East Anglia, and Senior Research Fellow at both the Centre for Social and Economic Research on the Global Environment (CSERGE) and the Centre for the Economic and Behavioural Analysis of Risk and Decision (CEBARD), University of East Anglia. His previous publications include *Economic Valuation with Stated Preference Techniques* (2002, with Richard Carson *et al.*), *Valuing Environmental Preferences* (1999, edited with Ken Willis), and *Environmental Economics* (1993, with R. Kerry Turner and David Pearce). He is Executive Editor of the journal *Environmental and Resource Economics*.

ANDREW A. LOVETT is Senior Lecturer at the School of Environmental Sciences, University of East Anglia. His research focuses on the application of geographical information systems, and he has previously published articles in *Risk Analysis*, *Social Science & Medicine*, the *Journal of Environmental Management*, and the *International Journal of GIS*. He is currently chair of the Geography of Health Research Group of the Royal Geographical Society–Institute of British Geographers.

JULII S. BRAINARD is Senior Research Associate at CSERGE, University of East Anglia. Her research background includes GIS, benefit transfer, outdoor recreation and environmental equity.

APPLIED ENVIRONMENTAL ECONOMICS

A GIS Approach to Cost-Benefit Analysis

IAN J. BATEMAN
ANDREW A. LOVETT
JULII S. BRAINARD

CAMBRIDGE
UNIVERSITY PRESS

PUBLISHED BY THE PRESS SYNDICATE OF THE UNIVERSITY OF CAMBRIDGE
The Pitt Building, Trumpington Street, Cambridge CB2 1RP, United Kingdom

CAMBRIDGE UNIVERSITY PRESS
The Edinburgh Building, Cambridge, CB2 2RU, UK
40 West 20th Street, New York, NY 10011-4211, USA
477 Williamstown Road, Port Melbourne, VIC 3207, Australia
Ruiz de Alarcón 13, 28014 Madrid, Spain
Dock House, The Waterfront, Cape Town 8001, South Africa

http://www.cambridge.org

First published 2003

Printed in the United Kingdom at the University Press, Cambridge

Typeface Times 11/14 pt   *System* LATEX 2$_\varepsilon$ [TB]

A catalogue record for this book is available from the British Library

Library of Congress Cataloguing in Publication data
Bateman, Ian.
Applied environmental economics: a GIS approach to cost-benefit analysis / Ian J. Bateman,
Andrew A. Lovett and Julii S. Brainard; foreword by David W. Pearce.
p.   cm.
Includes bibliographical references and index.
ISBN 0 521 80956 8
1. Environmental economics.   2. Environmental economics – Research.
I. Lovett, Andrew A.   II. Brainard, Julii S.   III. Title.
HD75.6 .B38   2002
333.7 – dc21   2002067360

ISBN 0 521 80956 8 hardback

For Fiona, Ben, Freya and Natasha: my world. With love, Ian.

For Mum and Dad. With love and many thanks, Andrew.

For Isabel, Dan and John. Con cariño, Julii.

Contents

Plates

Figures

Tables

Foreword

Much of environmental change is driven by land use change. To some, the whole history of economic and social development reflects the exchange of one form of asset – 'natural' landscape – for another form of asset – man-made capital. Certainly, viewed from a global perspective, there is a one-to-one relationship between the decline of forested land and the increase in land devoted to crops and pasture. The factors giving rise to land use change are many and varied. But one of the most powerful is the comparative economic returns to 'converted' land relative to the economic returns to 'natural' land. In short, the issue is conservation versus conversion, and this is a conflict that is invariably resolved in the favour of conversion. This systematic erosion of the natural capital base is what worries environmentalists, a term I take to embrace anyone with the slightest modicum of concern about what humankind is doing to its own environment and its fellow species. Acting on that concern takes several forms, as everyone knows. Some want to lie down in front of the bulldozers, protest to their Members of Parliament, write to the newspapers, appeal to some moral principle or other. For the most part quietly, environmental economists have sought a different route. First, they observe that the bias towards conversion arises from all kinds of incentive systems, including, for example, subsidies to agriculture or monocultural forestry. Second, some of those incentive systems are far more subtle, and arise from the fact that many of the functions and services provided by natural systems have no market. At the end of the day, and like it or not, the financial balance sheet drives land conversion. It pays to convert land because the financial returns from conversion exceed those from conservation. The same bias works in reverse: existing land is not converted back to, say, woodland because some of the woodland benefits have no market.

But this is a result that derives from a perversion of economics – markets 'fail' to allocate resources properly because many of those resources have no price, even though they have potentially substantial economic value. Markets are the medium through which prices materialise. If there is no market in the carbon stored in forest biomass, then markets will ignore the fact that the carbon has an economic value. In turn, that value derives from carbon dioxide being 'fixed' by growing biomass or from the fact that it is stored rather than released as carbon dioxide, the main greenhouse gas.

These observations define the first stage of the economic argument for correcting the economic system's biases. This stage consists of 'demonstrating' that economic value resides in natural systems and estimating how much it is. The second stage is partly addressed in this volume, but it involves the redesign of institutions so that the 'missing' economic value is captured and represented as a financial flow. There are many examples of such capture mechanisms – environmental taxes, tradable pollution and resource permits, payments for ecological services, and so on. If there is an encouraging trend in the environmental world it is that, gradually, these capture mechanisms are expanding. Sometimes aided by policy initiatives, and sometimes spontaneous, they help shift the bias of conversion back towards more conservation than would otherwise be the case. In terms of this volume, Ian Bateman and his colleagues look at how farm incomes would change if only the non-market value of land (e.g. stored carbon, recreation) was 'monetised' and added to some of the market values from changed land use (e.g. timber).

Determining economic values has become 'big business' for environmental economists, and few can match the authors of this volume for ingenuity and application of the various techniques that have evolved for finding these values. But 'valuation' is expensive, or, at least, that's how policy-makers like to see it. Millions may be spent on engineering design and legal fees in the context of policy or investment projects. A few tens of thousands of pounds on a valuation study often produces the cry that it is 'too expensive'. In the absence of a saner approach, environmental economists have to live with the very limited resources allocated to valuation. That means that short-cuts are unavoidable. Results from one study have to be 'borrowed' and applied to another study area. But a much understudied issue is the reliability of making these 'transfers'. Transferability requires that the conditions at the 'new' site should at least be similar to the conditions at the previously studied site. Often they are not. A few attempts have been made in the past to adapt transferred values to account for different site characteristics. With hindsight, it seems almost obvious that the logical way to handle variability in site characteristics is through geographical information systems (GIS). But it wasn't done, and the dominant attraction of this volume is that it shows how to do it in the context of a detailed case study. The final analysis is a mix of 'transfer' estimates, modulated by the GIS, and validation of those transfers against actual data for their geographical focus, Wales.

Ian Bateman and his colleagues have successfully pushed back the frontiers in several ways. First, they have 'married' economic valuation with GIS. Second, they have taken a very broad area for their application – the whole of Wales. Third, they have hypothetically reconfigured land use in Wales under the assumption that currently non-market land services and changed market values are integrated into farm incomes. This amounts to a cost-benefit analysis because they compare the costs of this change with its benefits. They are far more modest than I would be about the power and importance of cost-benefit analysis. It is fashionable to criticise the economic approach for all kinds of supposed ethical aberrations, but it has an ethical force of its own. It is democratic in that it allows individuals' preferences to rule rather than those of unelected 'stakeholders' and experts. It reminds us all the time that all decisions involve costs as well as benefits. While these may seem small claims, the reality is that actual decision-making all too often reduces to choices by an elite with little reference to cost. It is worth remembering that cost always reduces to a taxpayer's burden: there is no such thing as 'government money'. Finally, cost-benefit analysis is itself changing. Recent work on valuing the long distant future and on allowing for irreversibility and uncertainty (effectively making rigorous sense of the otherwise ill-defined 'precautionary principle') means that it is time to rewrite the cost-benefit textbooks. In so doing, we would overcome many of the criticisms advanced against it.

So, I would make greater claims for the approach adopted in this book than the authors make for it themselves! But what cannot be disputed is that we have a fine example here of economic valuation being put to an imaginative and unique use by some of the most exciting practitioners of the art of economic valuation.

David W. Pearce

Preface

This book concerns the application of environmental economic analysis to real-world decision-making. In particular it seeks to demonstrate a number of ways in which geographical information systems (GIS) can be employed to enhance such analyses. We have written it because, in our opinion, GIS techniques can considerably improve the way in which the complexities of the real world can be brought into economic cost-benefit analyses (CBA)[1], so reducing the reliance upon simplifying assumptions for which economists are infamous.

As we are primarily interested in demonstrating the flexibility and applicability of GIS techniques to a diversity of situations, we assume no prior knowledge of such techniques and avoid unnecessary technicalities wherever possible by referring the interested reader to related academic papers throughout. In so doing it is our objective to appeal to students, researchers, academics and, in particular, decision-makers and analysts across a broad spectrum of disciplines including economics (especially environmental, agricultural and resource economics), geography, land use planning and management, environmental science and related policy studies.

The application of GIS to environmental economic analyses is introduced gradually through the use of a diverse land use change case study. This concerns the potential for converting surplus agricultural land to multipurpose woodland in Wales. However, neither the specifics of this case study nor its location need be of particular interest to the reader as the study is designed primarily to demonstrate the flexibility of the underlying approach. The book opens by reviewing some basic economic ideas concerning value and CBA (Chapter 1), focusing in particular upon methods for valuing individuals' preferences for non-market goods such as those provided by the environment (Chapter 2). Previous studies of the recreational value of open-access woodland are reviewed and some new applications presented (Chapter 3) through which we first introduce the use of GIS techniques as a means

---

[1] Or benefit-cost analysis, depending upon which side of the Atlantic/Pacific you reside.

of enhancing valuation methods. This approach is then extended to the estimation of the numbers of visitors arriving at existing or potential future woodland recreation sites (Chapter 4). We then turn to consider certain other forest benefits starting with the value of timber (Chapter 5). Again GIS techniques are used to bring together a host of diverse datasets to permit modelling of timber yield and its net value (Chapter 6). These techniques are then extended to conduct an analysis of the carbon sequestration value of woodland, combining models of carbon flux in live trees, timber products and forest soils (Chapter 7). The opportunity cost of converting agricultural land to woodland is then examined, with GIS providing the medium for undertaking assessments of the principal farming sectors in the case study area (Chapter 8). All of these sub-analyses are synthesised through our GIS to undertake a spatial CBA considering, for each location across our entire study area, what the consequences of land use change from agriculture to woodland would be (Chapter 9). Finally we summarise the strengths and weaknesses of our particular application and consider the wider conclusions to be drawn from the approach set out in this volume (Chapter 10).

We hope that readers will find this book interesting and enjoyable and that it might contribute to what we believe would be a timely infusion of realism into economic analyses.

Acknowledgements

The inherently interdisciplinary nature of this project involved a lot of help from a lot of people. In particular we wish to thank Stavros Georgiou, Phil Judge, the late (and much missed) Ian Langford, Frances Randell, Gilla Sünnenberg and Kerry Turner at the University of East Anglia and Chris Ennew and Tony Rayner at the University of Nottingham.

We are also tremendously grateful to the Farm Business Survey of Wales (in particular to Nigel Chapman, Tim Jenkins and the surveyors at FBSW, Aberystwyth), to the Soil Survey and Land Research Centre (in particular to Ian Bradley and Arthur Thomasson) and to the Forestry Commission (in particular Chris Quine and Adrian Whiteman at the Commission's Northern Research Station, Roslin) for provision of, and advice concerning, the data used in this analysis. Quite simply this work could not have been undertaken without their support.

The research contained in this volume was funded in part by the Economic and Social Research Council (ESRC) as part of the Centre for Social and Economic Research on the Global Environment (CSERGE) Programme in Environmental Decision Making.

The publisher has used its best endeavours to ensure that the URLs for external websites referred to in this book are correct and active at the time of going to press. However, the publisher has no responsibility for the websites and can make no guarantee that a site will remain live or that the content is or will remain appropriate.

1

Introduction

The nature of value: differing paradigms

Perhaps the most often quoted definition of an economist is of someone who knows the price of everything and the value of nothing.[1] However, it is an awareness of the distinction between value and price which separates out the true economist from the glorified book-keepers and accountants who so often masquerade under such a title. Recent years have seen a growth of badge-engineering in which so-called new disciplines such as environmental or ecological economics have risen to prominence. However, whilst these are appealing titles, in essence they represent not a radical departure but rather a very welcome return to the basic principles and domain of economics – the analysis of true value.

It is one of these basic principles which underpins this study: namely the assumption that values can be measured by the preferences of individuals.[2] The interaction of preferences with the various services provided by a commodity generates a variety of values. Many economists have studied the nature of these values; however, a useful starting point is the concept of aggregate or total economic value (TEV) (Pearce and Turner, 1990; Turner, 1999; Fromm, 2000).

Figure 1.1 shows how TEV can be broken down into its constituent parts and illustrates these with reference to some of the values generated by the principal commodity under consideration in this study; woodland.

The bulk of economic analyses concentrate upon the instrumental or use values of a commodity. Most prominent amongst these are the direct use values generated by private and quasi-private goods (Bateman and Turner, 1993) which are often partly reflected by market prices, and those indirect use values associated with pure

[1] This is an appropriation of Oscar Wilde's definition of a cynic in *Lady Windermere's Fan* (Act III). However, given the perceived similarity between the two groups, it is easy to see how such a confusion may have arisen (with thanks to Olvar Bergland, Colin Price and others regarding this.)

[2] Speculations upon this issue and, in particular, about whether individuals have definite preferences are presented by Sugden (1999a).

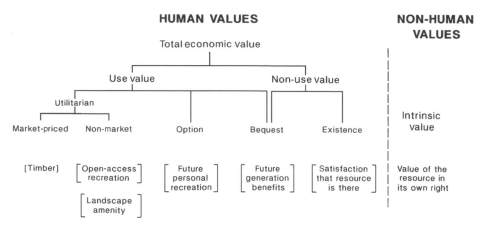

Figure 1.1. The total economic value of woodland. (*Source:* Adapted from Bateman, 1995.)

and quasi-public goods (*ibid.*) which generally have no market price description. A unifying characteristic of these values is that they are all generated via the present use of the commodity by the valuing individual. An extension of the temporal frame allows for the possibility of individuals valuing the option of future use (Weisbrod, 1964; Cicchetti and Freeman, 1971; Krutilla and Fisher, 1975; Kriström, 1990). Related to this is the notion of bequest value wherein the valuing individual gains utility from the provision of use or non-use values to present and/or future others. Pure non-use values are most commonly identified with the notion of valuing the continued existence of entities, such as certain species of flora and fauna or even whole ecosystems. As before, this is generally both an intra- and intergenerational value and because of the lack of an instrumental element has proved problematic to measure. Nevertheless, the theoretical case for the 'existence of existence value' is widely supported (e.g. Young, 1992).

   Wider definitions of value have been argued for. An important issue concerns the extent of the 'moral reference class' (Turner *et al.*, 1994) for decision-making. One question here involves the treatment of other humans (both present elsewhere and future) while another is whether animal, plant and ecosystem interests should be placed on an equal footing with human preferences. The modern origins of such a view can be traced to O'Riordan (1976), Goodpaster (1978) and Watson (1979) who take the Kantian notion of universal laws of respect for other persons and extend this to apply to non-human others. Watson feels that those higher animals such as chimpanzees (which he argues are capable of reciprocal behaviour) should be accorded equal rights with humans. Hunt (in Perman *et al.*, 1996) and Rollston (1988) build upon the land ethic of Leopold (1949) to extend this definition of moral reference even further to include all extant entities, an approach which

Singer (1993) defines as the 'deep ecology' ethic. Such a paradigm argues that these entities possess an 'intrinsic' value separate from anthropocentric existence values. A further departure from conventional utilitarianism is proposed by Turner (1992, 1999) who argues that all the elements of TEV can be seen as secondary to a primary environmental quality value which is a necessary prerequisite for the generation of all subsequent values. Side-stepping the theoretical case for such philosophical extensions, a practical problem with these non-TEV values is that they are essentially beyond the scope of conventional, anthropocentric, preference-based economic valuation. If, as in this study, we constrain the moral reference class to present humans alone, TEV is the appropriate extent of value definition. However, this still leaves the problem of how such values should be measured.

One solution to the problem of valuation might be to abandon conventional neoclassical economic analysis in favour of modified or alternative appraisal and decision-making strategies. One such alternative is to base decisions upon expert judgement and restrict the role of economics to the identification of least cost methods for achieving stated aims (see, for example, Organisation for Economic Cooperation and Development, 1991). Such a cost-effectiveness approach may be optimal for a resource-rich risk-averse society faced with high risk, high uncertainty, irreversible problems such as the treatment of highly persistent pollutants (Opschoor and Pearce, 1991). Here a useful decision guide is provided by the precautionary principle advocated by 'ecological economics' (see, for example, Costanza and Daly, 1992; Toman, 1992; Turner *et al.*, 1995). However, in other, arguably more general, situations where the precautionary principle does not apply, a cost-effectiveness approach may entail avoidable and, in some cases, major net welfare losses compared to a solution based upon cost-benefit analysis (CBA). Such a position is adopted by those who argue for an 'environmental economics' paradigm (see, for example, Pearce *et al.*, 1989; Department of the Environment, 1991; Price, 1997a; Pearce, 1998; Griffin, 1998; Pearce and Barbier, 2000). Supporters of this view accept preference-based values as the basis of decision-making but argue for full assessment of TEV as opposed to the concentration upon market-based measures which appears to dominate much present practical decision-making.

This choice between ecological and environmental economics could be characterised as one between principle and pragmatism. The argument for an ecological economics approach is that nothing less will preserve the environmental integrity which is vital if the present, resource-exploitative, 'cowboy economy' (Boulding, 1966) is to attain a state of sustainable development. The environmental economic critique is that such a rigid approach fails to recognise the mechanisms through which present-day decision-making operates and thereby risks being ignored by those in power. In the absence of hindsight it is impossible to know which strategy is most likely to influence the presently unsustainable course of economic growth.

Our own position is that the two paradigms need not be in conflict and that a modified precautionary principle can be used to assess the most appropriate approach for any given decision situation. Furthermore, we see a role for public preferences within this process. In cases where expert assessment and/or informed public opinion identifies high potential risks or uncertainties from a given strategy or decision then a precautionary, ecological economics approach would appear justifiable. For situations where this is not the case then an environmental economics analysis seems likely to be optimal. From a sustainability perspective, both are significantly superior to simple market-based appraisals.

The theoretical and methodological basis of the study

We therefore need to select the appraisal paradigm which is most appropriate for the subject under analysis. This study examines the economic potential for conversion of land from conventional agriculture to multipurpose woodland in Wales. Two points are immediately important here. First, we are interested in the full range of economic values generated by such a change in land use. Second, following initial review (Bateman, 1991a,b, 1992), it has become apparent that large-scale unquantifiable risks or uncertainties are not a major factor in such an analysis. Given this, the adoption of a CBA paradigm appears defensible.

CBA is generally thought of as an appraisal of the worth of a project from a social perspective. That does not mean that CBA tells us about what is good or bad. Rather, it provides information, going beyond simple market-based assessments to a more complete analysis of value, which, if correctly employed, should improve decision-making (Adler and Posner, 1999). In our consideration of the social value of woodland we have attempted to be reasonably comprehensive although our main foci of interest are timber production, open-access informal recreation, and the value of carbon sequestration (i.e. global warming abatement). This is compared to the social value of agriculture. In both cases we consider items such as the differing subsidies currently paid by society to those who produce agricultural and forest products. However, while such a CBA assessment is of use in informing decision-makers and shaping optimal policy change, it cannot alone predict land-owners' and farmers' responses to that change unless the impacts upon farm incomes are also known. Consequently, the study also examines farm-gate incomes under present and future policy scenarios.

The ultimate objective of this study, therefore, is to provide a policy analysis tool. However, whilst the theoretical CBA framework of the research is conventional, the extent of application and the methodology employed is innovative and unique.

The role of geographical information systems

One distinctive feature of our research is the extensive use of geographical information systems (GIS) throughout our study. A GIS is commonly defined as 'a system for capturing, storing, checking, integrating, manipulating, analysing and displaying data which are spatially referenced to the earth' (Department of the Environment, 1987: p. 132). From an organisational perspective, a GIS typically involves computer hardware, software, data and operating personnel. The origins of what we now regard as a GIS can be found in the 1960s, but use has only become widespread in the past ten years (Burrough and McDonnell, 1998; Longley *et al.*, 1999, 2001). Technologies such as computer-aided design (CAD), image processing, database management systems and automated mapping have all contributed to the development of GIS, but the last of these represents a distinct advance in terms of the capacity to integrate data from different sources (e.g. relate point measures of timber yield to environmental characteristics of areas) and undertake a wide range of analytical operations. Examples of the types of questions that can be investigated using a GIS are given in Table 1.1.

The use of GIS in environmental economics is a relatively recent innovation[3] and in many ways their application could not be more overdue. The unrealistic assumptions, implicit or otherwise, made by economists in order to implement their analyses have often attracted critical comment, but GIS provide a means of avoiding many of the worst simplifications (Lovett and Bateman, 2001). For instance, studies using travel cost techniques to estimate the recreational value associated with open-access countryside locations have often assumed that all trips take place in straight lines between origins and destinations, and ignored much of the spatial heterogeneity within study areas (see discussions in Bateman *et al.*, 1996a, 1999a). With a GIS, travel costs can be calculated in a manner which is far more sensitive to the nature of the available road network and much greater account can be taken of spatial variations in the socio-economic characteristics of populations or the availability of substitute destinations (Brainard *et al.*, 1999). Another example where the application of GIS has already proved beneficial involves hedonic pricing techniques which aim to isolate the influence of environmental characteristics on property prices. In the past, efforts to examine factors such as views of parks, water features or industrial areas from properties have required considerable fieldwork (and involved appreciable subjectivity). The combination of high-resolution digital map databases and GIS, however, now makes it feasible to determine the composition of viewsheds from far larger numbers of properties in a more objective and cost-effective manner (Lake *et al.*, 1998, 2000a,b; Bateman *et al.*, 2001a).

---

[3] Among the few studies to date, not otherwise mentioned, to combine GIS and environmental monetary valuation are Eade and Moran (1996), Bhat and Bergstrom (1997), Geoghegan *et al.* (1997) and Powe *et al.* (1997).

Table 1.1. *Typical questions that a GIS can be used to answer*

Type of question	Example
Identification	What is at a particular location?
Location	Where does a certain type of feature occur?
Trend	Which features have changed over time?
Routing	What is the best way to travel between two points?
Pattern	Is there a spatial association between two types of feature?
What if	What will happen if a particular change takes place?

Source: Based on Rhind, 1990; Kraak and Ormeling, 1996.

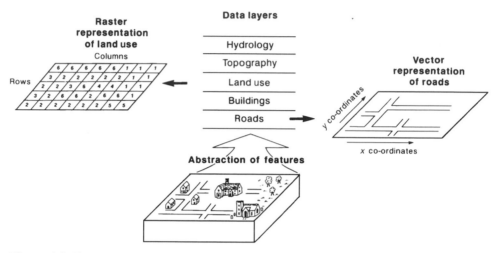

Figure 1.2. Representing real-world phenomena as raster or vector data layers. (*Source:* Based on Lovett, 2000.)

It needs to be emphasised that GIS are no universal panacea for improving data analysis. The quality of the results obtained depends on factors such as the accuracy of the input information and the appropriateness of the data structures used to store digital representations of real-world phenomena. Different types of features are most commonly held in a GIS as separate layers, usually in the form of either raster grids (where values are assigned to cells) or vector structures (where the positions of entities such as points, lines or areas are defined by sets of co-ordinates). Figure 1.2 illustrates these two main approaches. Other methods of data storage are possible (Laurini and Thompson, 1992), but the key principle is that data structures should be selected to minimise distortion when creating a digital representation of reality and maximise analytical or presentational options given the intended use of the data (Berry, 1993; Martin, 1996a; Burrough and McDonnell, 1998).

Notwithstanding the above caveats, by using GIS in this research we hoped to overcome many of the limitations in data handling and modelling which have restricted previous research. With such computing facilities we were able to combine environmental and other spatial data in the form of digital maps and satellite imagery with more conventional variables to enhance the stochastic economic models which are central to this study. As we demonstrate in the contexts of modelling timber yield, carbon sequestration, recreational demand and agricultural productivity, the ability to integrate diverse datasets substantially improves our capacity to understand and predict such variables. However, equally important is the scope for querying and visualising model output (e.g. in the form of maps), so permitting the decision-maker readily to comprehend the impact of alternative policy choices. It is this dual capability to improve modelling and display which we feel allows GIS significantly to enhance many aspects of economic analysis. (For a parallel example in the context of land use, see O'Callaghan, 1996.)

Costs and benefits of woodland: limitations of the study

Forestry has long struggled to compete financially with other land uses (Green, 1996) but has also been a consistent focus of attention regarding its non-market attributes (Hodge, 1995; Mather, 1998). Figure 1.3 illustrates the complexity of internal and external costs and benefits which are generated by woodland. In this diagram the internal costs and benefits are shown in shaded boxes. These items all have market prices from which shadow values, defining the value to society of these goods,[4] may be derived. Certain external items also have related market prices from which values may again be estimated; these are shown in the dotted line boxes of Figure 1.3. However, the remaining externalities do not have related market prices, thereby making valuation problematic; indeed such items are typically excluded from appraisals (Pearce, 1998; Hanley, 2001).

Our study sets out to provide a relatively comprehensive assessment of the values associated with the proposed conversion of agricultural land into woodland. However, we have to recognise certain limitations in the research. First, methods for the monetary evaluation of preferences for non-market goods and services are not uniformly developed for all types of value. In particular, methods for the evaluation of non-use benefits, such as existence values, have been the subject of sustained criticism during recent years (see Chapter 2). Our study reflects these reservations by concentrating upon use values. Second, time constraints and data availability

---

[4] Shadow values adjust market prices (which may be zero for unpriced goods) to provide estimates of the value to society of such goods. Typically this involves adjustments to allow for market failures, such as non-competitive markets, and transfer payments such as grants and subsidies which are funded by society. Chapter 8 provides an example of how shadow values may be derived from market prices.

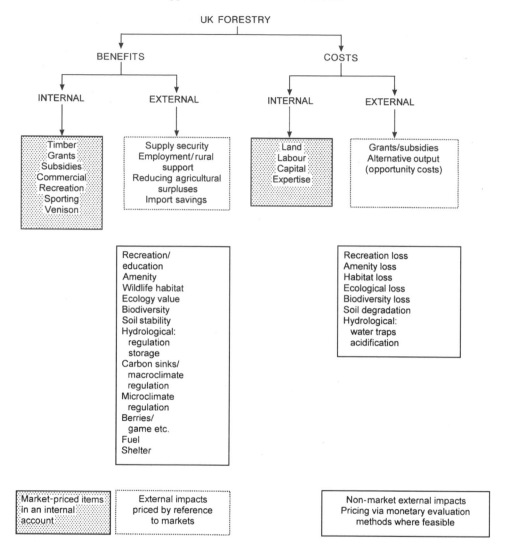

Figure 1.3. Costs and benefits of woodland. (*Source:* Bateman, 1992.)

problems mean that even our treatment of all use values is somewhat uneven. Third, we are only considering conversions from agricultural land to woodland and not to any other alternative use. Strictly speaking, this contravenes the principles of CBA, which state that the appraisal of opportunity costs should include the assessment of a wide range of feasible alternative resource uses (Pearce, 1986; Bateman *et al.*, 1993a; Price, 2000; Hanley, 2001). A fourth issue is that of equity – and its root: ethics.

Ethical questions[5]

Ethics and economics have often been presented as strange bedfellows. Indeed, many proponents of the 'positive economics' which has dominated so much of twentieth-century economic analysis argue that the two concepts cannot be related 'in any form but mere juxtaposition' (Robbins, 1935: p. 148). However, this has not always been a widely held belief. Indeed the early great economists were explicitly concerned with morality and ethics.[6,7]

Two ethical positions which have had a major impact upon the development of economic thought are the libertarian and utilitarian schools of thought. The libertarian view, which may be traced from John Locke and Adam Smith to Robert Nozick (1974), emphasises respect for the rights of individuals. A fundamental concept here concerns the just acquisition of property. This has been interpreted as emphasising both the rights of ownership and also the requirement of appropriate payment or transfer in return for acquisition. However, libertarianism makes no prescriptions concerning the outcome of any trade or transfer. In particular, such a view would almost always condemn any redistributive policy, whether between present-day populations or to future populations (intra- and intergenerational transfers) unless they are freely entered into by all groups including donors.[8] This focus upon processes rather than outcomes differs from the utilitarian view (which derives from the writings of David Hume, Jeremy Bentham and, most notably, John Stuart Mill (1863)), which explicitly highlights the ethical consequences of actions. Classical utilitarianism judges actions according to whether they are 'good' for society, with 'good' being defined (by Mill) in terms of happiness or utility. Actions which promote utility are therefore good and should be judged by the amount of utility created. However, for utility to be cardinally measurable, individuals must be able to express it in terms of a numeric value. Furthermore, in order to assess the social utility of an action we have to assume that we can compare and add utilities across individuals.

These strong assumptions make classical utilitarianism of little use for the practical economic analysis of projects. The neoclassical utilitarianism (Kneese and Schulze, 1985) which underpins modern welfare economics involves rather weaker

---

[5] This discussion relies heavily on Perman *et al.* (1996), Kneese and Schulze (1985) and Pearce and Turner (1990). Relevant discussions are also presented in Beauchamp and Bowie (1988) and Sen (1987).

[6] Interestingly Adam Smith's post at the University of Glasgow was Professor of Moral Philosophy.

[7] Reviews of the work of Marx, Marshall, Pareto, Keynes and others are presented in Schumpeter (1952).

[8] This would conventionally rule out any governmental action towards the enforced provision of such transfers.

assumptions (Layard and Walters, 1978; Varian, 1987). In particular, a common assumption underpinning CBA is that the marginal utility of consumption is equal
across all individuals. If this is so we can ignore distributive issues (which are vital
under classical analysis) since any action which creates net benefits unambigu-
ously raises social welfare. However, in reality, such an assumption seems unlikely
to hold, prompting some users of CBA to consider explicitly the equity implications
of their analyses (e.g. Squire and van der Tak, 1975). For many years such views
were held by an inconspicuous minority within the profession of economics. However, since the 1960s, concerns regarding the effects of environmental degradation
on present and future generations, together with the issue of North/South inequality,
have meant that discussions regarding the ethical basis of economics have grown.
These arguments over the need to consider equity as well as economic efficiency
have recently coalesced within what has been termed the sustainable development
(SD) debate (WCED, 1987; Pearce *et al.*, 1990; Perman *et al.*, 1999).

Both intra- and intergenerational equity issues are central to the SD debate which
has, in essence, proposed an alternative to utilitarianism as a new ethical basis for
economics. Pivotal to this has been the work of Page (1977) and, in particular, Rawls
(1972). Rawls' theory of justice can be seen as a direct development of Kant's
universal laws. Here the individual enjoys common liberties compatible with equal
rights for others, while valid inequalities result only from personal qualities which
are attainable by all (e.g. inequalities arising from diligent work or learning as
opposed to those based upon sex or creed). This latter prescription has important
consequences for equity, as Rawls argues that under such a system the optimal allocation of resources is one that is made behind a 'veil of ignorance' as to their intra-
and intergenerational distribution. This can be seen as being in direct conflict with
the individual maximisation principle of utilitarianism.[9] Such a contrast is perhaps
most clearly demonstrated in the recent literature regarding sustainability. Turner
and Pearce (1993) identify four alternative positions ranging from 'very weak' to
'very strong' sustainability. Each definition moves further from a conventional utilitarian towards a Rawlsian position on equity, steadily imposing more constraints
upon resource use (most notably, natural capital).

The ethical position adopted in this study
There are a number of ethical positions which could be adopted in this research. Despite some considerable personal sympathy with the Rawlsian/'strong

---

[9] The economic implications of classical and neoclassical utilitarian and Rawlsian ethical positions can be expressed through consequent social welfare functions (SWF). Classical utilitarianism implies an additive SWF of
the form: $W = \beta_1 U^A + \beta_2 U^B$ where W = social welfare; U^A, U^B = the total utility enjoyed by individuals A
and B respectively; β_1, β_2 = weights used to calculate W. Neoclassical utilitarianism relaxes the assumption of
additivity such that $W = W(U^A, U^B)$. Finally, following Solow (1974a), the Rawlsian position can be expressed
as the maxi-min function in which we maximise $W = \min(U^A, U^B)$. Note that Perman *et al.* (1996) suggest
that Rawls may have strongly objected to the latter utilitarian reformulation of his work.

sustainability' view, our self-assessment is that this study is essentially neoclassi-cally utilitarian in its ethical basis. The definition of values inherent in the TEV concept remains anthropocentric and is therefore consistent with the extended util-itarian view discussed by Perman *et al.* (1996, 1999). The most non-Rawlsian characteristic of this study is the absence of an explicit incorporation of any pre-cautionary principle or equity constraint. It might be argued that the sensitivity analysis across various discount rates (discussed in Chapter 6), which we include in our CBA, effectively addresses the issue of intergenerational equity. However, as Hanley and Spash (1993) highlight, such an approach will not ensure equality of well-being across generations. Similarly, we do not include explicit considerations of distributional effects nor do we include any analysis which could be construed as compatible with a Rawlsian maxi-min criterion. Our approach is therefore con-ventional in terms of both theory and the ethical basis of such theory. It is only in the practical implementation of our analysis that we have attempted to improve upon convention.

This theoretical standpoint should not be taken as implying a wholesale rejec-tion of the Rawlsian or 'strong sustainability' positions. Rather it is a pragmatic extension of accepted decision-analysis practice.

Selection of the case study and data sources

While the fundamental objective of this study is the comparison of woodland with agricultural values, a supplementary goal is to see how such differences vary across areas of differing environmental character. The country of Wales consti-tutes one of the most diverse areas of the UK with altitudes ranging from sea level to heights above those found in neighbouring England. While smaller than its neighbour,[10] the entirety of Wales represents a very much larger area than has been considered in virtually any CBA to date.[11] Furthermore, from the perspective of land use change, Wales provides a more interesting case study in that its di-verse and relatively more adverse environment means that agricultural production is limited to sectors such as sheep-breeding which have been in long-term decline (see Chapter 9) and are therefore potentially more likely to be suitable for conver-sion to woodland (which has expanded throughout the past century; see Chapter 5). Wales is also interesting from an environmental point of view. While other areas

---

[10] The final CBA results presented in Chapter 9 are given in terms of 1 km square cells. The land area of Wales comprises some 20,563 such cells.

[11] Consideration was also given to extending the analysis to include England, which is considerably more populous than Wales. However, at the time our research commenced, agricultural census data for England were only available down to the parish level. Such resolution fails to identify individual farm locations thus rendering accurate production modelling infeasible. More recently the parish data have been interpolated to a grid cell basis that is available from the University of Edinburgh Data Library (see http://datalib.ed.ac.uk/EUDL/agriculture/). However, even these data do not report certain key profitability variables vital to our analysis of the opportunity costs of converting land from agriculture to woodland.

of the European Union (EU) have responded to falls in the real price of sheep by diversifying into other sectors, Welsh agriculture has seen an intensification of sheep-rearing with steadily increasing stocking densities (Fuller, 1996; Woodhouse, 2002). This in turn has raised concerns regarding overgrazing and its impacts upon wildlife (*ibid*.). A number of economic and environmental factors therefore single out Wales as a particularly suitable subject for our case study.

Data sources

Our research draws upon data from a number of sources. All data were provided free or for a reasonable handling charge. We are very grateful to a number of people and organisations for this co-operation without which the research could not have been undertaken (see Acknowledgements to this volume). Detailed descriptions of the various datasets are provided in subsequent chapters, but a brief summary is given here.

Data on farm-level agricultural activities, costs and revenues were obtained from the Farm Business Survey in Wales (FBSW). We are indebted to the enlightened attitude of the FBSW which, by being prepared to enter into a confidentiality agreement whereby no farm-level results were reported, allowed us to use grid-referenced farm data which could be linked to local environmental characteristics, so facilitating a substantial improvement in the ability to model agricultural production and its value.

Environmental data were provided in the form of the LandIS database, kindly loaned by the Soil Survey and Land Research Centre (SSLRC), Cranfield. This is the premier repository of land information data for England and Wales. When used in conjunction with the FBSW data, LandIS provided the highest-quality combination of information possible for modelling agriculture in the study area.

Our other principal data source was the Forestry Commission's (FC) Sub-Compartment Database (SCDB). This is the most extensive and comprehensive source of woodland data in the UK and is again geographically referenced to a high degree of accuracy, permitting integration with the environmental data contained in the LandIS database.

A number of other sources were employed to provide specific variables. These included Bartholomew's 1:250,000 digital map database made available to UK universities under a CHEST agreement, 1991 Census data purchased for academic research use by ESRC/JISC, details of windiness provided by the Forestry Commission and digital maps of Environmentally Sensitive Area boundaries supplied by the Ministry of Agriculture, Fisheries and Food. The project also involved surveys and interviews which are described later in this book, the structure of which we now consider.

Context and structure of the book

The majority of the research presented in this book was undertaken for a Ph.D. thesis (Bateman, 1996).[12] A number of journal articles discussing individual aspects of the research have since been published and are referenced in appropriate chapters, but this book brings these elements together allowing the integrated results to be considered in detail.

Many of the data used refer to the early 1990s and, given, in particular, the constantly changing context of agriculture and to a lesser extent forestry, we are wary of asserting that all findings are directly transferable to the present day. However, it remains our strong contention that the methodology adopted is still relevant and capable of wider application. At appropriate points in the text we have sought to provide some updating of the economic and policy context and to comment on the applicability of the substantive findings in the light of this.

As discussed above, the book considers the application of environmental economics using GIS through a case study concerning woodland, agriculture and a CBA comparison of land use change between the two. We begin with a consideration of the recreation value of woodland. This is subdivided into an appraisal of methods for the monetary evaluation of woodland recreation (Chapter 2), a review of previous valuation studies and presentation of our own studies (Chapter 3) and GIS-based analysis transferring results from these various evaluations to the case study area through predictions of the latent demand for visits (Chapter 4). The focus of attention then shifts to timber and a further evaluation model is constructed (Chapter 5) and applied to newly estimated timber yield models (Chapter 6). Our analysis of woodland values is concluded by extending the definition of values to include the net benefits of carbon sequestration (i.e. counteracting the greenhouse effect of global warming) provided by forests (Chapter 7).

We then turn to consider the opportunity cost of converting land to woodland, which in the case study area of Wales involves losses of agricultural production. Models of both the farm-gate and social values of such production are presented for the dominant farming types of the area (Chapter 8).

The preceding analyses are finally synthesised through cost-benefit analyses of potential conversions of land from agricultural to woodland use (Chapter 9).[13] Both market and social-perspective assessments are presented and the results clearly demonstrate the sensitivity of findings to whether analyses are restricted to consideration of market prices alone or extended to include non-market values. Further

---

[12] Further details of this thesis can be obtained by navigating from the CSERGE website at http://www.uea.ac.uk/env/cserge/ or by going directly to Ian Bateman's personal home page at http://www.uea.ac.uk/~e089/.

[13] The analysis also indicates, by default, whether conversions from existing woodland to new agriculture are justified, although our results indicate that this is rarely the case.

sensitivity is found regarding which agricultural sector is considered for conversion, the choice of discount rate, choice of woodland tree species and many other policy variables. Perhaps most markedly, our GIS-based methodology highlights the spatial dimension of CBA decisions, showing that the same policy decisions yield social and market gains or losses depending upon the location chosen for policy application (Chapter 9). This analysis therefore identifies a number of interesting results from which policy implications and conclusions are drawn and presented (Chapter 10) along with an assessment of the methodology adopted in the research and consideration of the scope for further extensions, certain of which are ongoing.

2

Recreation: valuation methods

Introduction

At the heart of cost-benefit analysis (CBA) theory lie two basic principles (Pearce, 1986; Hanley and Spash, 1993): first that, as far as possible, all the costs and benefits arising from a project should be assessed; and, second, that they should be measured using the common unit of money. While these seem common-sense precepts, in application both principles raise highly complex problems. The issue of complete appraisal is, when taken to the extreme, ultimately insoluble in a world ruled by the laws of thermodynamics where, as noted by commentators such as Price (1987a, 2000) and Young (1992), everything affects everything else. For real-world decision-making, practical rules regarding the limits of appraisal are needed. Such rules are the stuff of numerous project appraisal guidelines, for example the Treasury's 'Green Book' (H.M. Treasury, 1991), whereas the research described here focuses on the second principle – of monetary valuation.

In discussing approaches to the monetary evaluation of environmental preferences we can first identify a wider global family of monetary assessment methods (see Figure 2.1). This comprises both the formal 'valuation' (or demand curve) methods discussed below and a quite separate group of *ad hoc* environmental 'pricing' techniques (see the review in Bateman, 1999). In theoretical terms valuation and pricing approaches are quite distinct. Whereas the former are based upon individuals' preferences and yield conventional, neoclassical, welfare measures (hence the term 'valuation methods'), the pricing techniques are much more akin to market-price observations. For example, the shadow project pricing approach uses the costs of hypothetical environmental asset replacement, restoration or transplantation schemes (Buckley, 1989) to yield prices for the environmental costs of a proposed project. While it has been argued that such methods provide useful information for the appraisal of projects, policies or courses of action (Turner *et al.*, 1992), pricing techniques reflect the costs of protecting or providing environmental

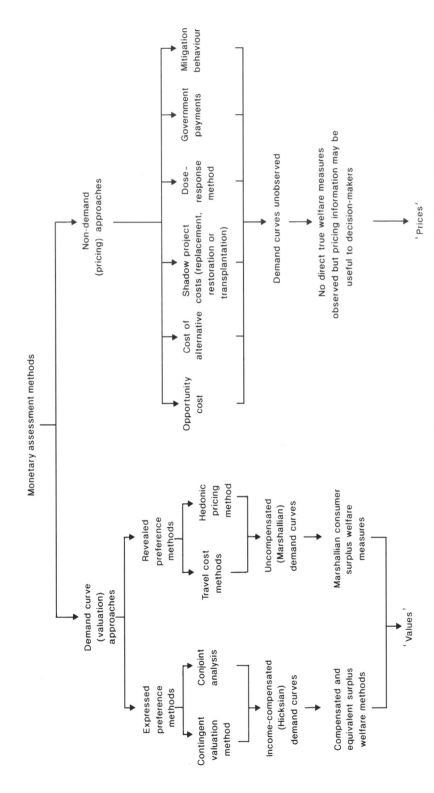

Figure 2.1. Methods for the monetary assessment of non-market and environmental goods. (*Source:* Bateman, 1999.)

assets but not the benefits of doing so. In considering only prices rather than values, decision-makers are in danger of making incorrect choices.[1] Certainly such information is insufficient for adequate CBA appraisals. We therefore reject the use of pricing techniques and turn to consider the more theoretically rigorous valuation methods.

The valuation methods all ultimately rely upon individual preferences. However, within this genre two distinct categories of approach can be defined: methods based upon preferences which are revealed through purchases by individuals of market-priced allied goods; and methods which rely upon expressed preferences elicited through questionnaire surveys. Both of these variants provide measures of value which are valid according to economic theory. However, the same theory shows that these measures need not be identical even when the same change in provision of a non-market good is considered (further discussion of this issue is provided in any basic microeconomics text, for example Laidler and Estrin, 1989; a simple overview is given here).

Revealed preference techniques typically cannot be applied directly to the valuation of environmental goods because of the lack of an observable market price. One solution is to investigate a surrogate market and this approach is adopted by the travel cost (TC) method. Here the costs of a visit to a recreation site are calculated as some combination of any entry charge (typically zero for UK forests), travel expenditure (e.g. petrol costs) and the opportunity cost of travel time (i.e. the value of the time devoted to travelling to the site; this might be wages forgone or the lost opportunity to enjoy some other activity during that time).[2] By comparing these travel costs with the number of visits, we observe that as costs increase (e.g. the further an individual has to travel to a wood), fewer visits are made. This negative relationship maps out a 'demand curve', the area under which provides an estimate of the value of visits to the site which is known as the 'consumer surplus'.[3] While this is a useful measure it is in fact the sum of two components: the substitution effect (which measures the increased consumption of any good when its price falls) and the income effect (which shows the change in consumption due to the increase in purchasing power or 'real' income which occurs when the price of a good falls). While the substitution effect is positive[4] for a reduction in travel costs, the income

[1] As an interesting example of how pricing methods may give little practical guidance to a decision, Medley (1992) refers to the Department of Transport's pricing of a motorway tunnel to avoid a cutting through the Twyford Down Site of Special Scientific Interest in Hampshire. At £70 million this was considered too expensive and abandoned without any appraisal of the benefits of such an alternative being undertaken.

[2] Brief discussion of how these travel costs are estimated is provided subsequently.

[3] In essence the reader can think of the consumer surplus value being estimated as the sum of what the individual visitor would pay, if required, for each of the visits to a woodland. In an attempt to widen readership we have avoided various technicalities in this and subsequent descriptions. References to further reading are provided below.

[4] Strictly speaking this effect is non-negative rather than absolutely positive.

Table 2.1. *Welfare change measures obtained from expressed preference measures*

	Change in provision	
	Gain	Loss
WTP measure	WTP to ensure that the proposed gain occurs	WTP to avoid the proposed loss occurring
WTA measure	WTA compensation if proposed gain does not occur	WTA compensation if proposed loss does occur

effect of such a cost reduction may be either positive or negative depending upon how the individual varies their consumption of the good as the purchasing power of their income changes. Given this uncertainty, consumer surplus might provide an imperfect estimate of the 'income-compensated' welfare provided by a given recreational site.

This problem is at least in theory addressed through the application of expressed preference approaches such as the contingent valuation (CV) method. Here respondents are directly asked to state the change in income which would just offset a proposed change in the provision of the good under investigation. Respondents might be asked to consider either a gain or loss over the present level of provision and in either case be asked questions concerning how much they might be willing to pay (WTP) or willing to accept in compensation (WTA) to just offset the relevant welfare change. Table 2.1 illustrates the four welfare measures so defined.[5]

The income-compensated values estimated by the expressed preference methods can therefore claim some theoretical superiority as welfare measures compared to the consumer surplus estimates provided by revealed preference approaches. However, expressed preference methods have been the subject of considerable criticism regarding the ability of respondents to articulate values for complex goods such as those provided by the environment (Kahneman and Knetsch, 1992; Hausman, 1993; Diamond and Hausman, 1994). In practice there is evidence that both TC-based consumer surplus estimates and CV-based WTP values are reasonably similar,[6] and our research uses both methods, as they are, respectively, the most commonly applied revealed and expressed preference techniques for valuing woodland recreation benefits.[7]

[5] For further discussion see Just *et al.* (1982), Johansson (1987) or any similar intermediate microeconomics text. For an empirical comparison of all four measures, see Bateman *et al.* (2000a).

[6] Carson *et al.* (1996) review 83 studies from which 616 comparisons of CV to revealed preference (RP) estimates are drawn, yielding a whole sample mean CV:RP ratio of 0.89 (95 per cent confidence interval = 0.81 to 0.96). This suggests that, while statistically different from each other (and, as we will see subsequently, on occasion strongly dissimilar), revealed and expressed preference measures do on average produce estimates which fall within the same broad range.

[7] For applications of the hedonic pricing revealed preference method to the valuation of woodland landscape amenity, see Garrod and Willis (1992a). In our own recent research we have examined the potential for improving

The remainder of this chapter presents brief reviews of the CV and TC methods, concentrating on areas of particular interest to this study. Given the focus of this research, these reviews are far from exhaustive and are deliberately written in a non-technical and introductory style. For further reading concerning the CV method, see Mitchell and Carson (1989), Bjornstad and Kahn (1996), Bateman and Willis (1999) and Bateman *et al.* (2002), while for the TC method, see Hufschmidt *et al.* (1983), Bockstael *et al.* (1991), Freeman (1993) and Herriges and Kling (1999); an introduction to all non-market valuation techniques is given in Champ *et al.* (forthcoming).

The contingent valuation method

Introduction: applying the CV method

The implementation of a CV study involves a number of distinct stages. In the first, preparatory, stage a 'hypothetical' or 'contingent' market is set up in which individuals are asked how much they are either WTP or WTA in respect of the proposed change in provision of the good under investigation. These questions may be framed using a variety of elicitation methods. In a WTP study the major alternatives are: (i) *open-ended* (OE), in which the respondent is asked 'how much are you willing to pay?', an approach which produces a bid response which is truncated at zero but is otherwise continuous;[8] (ii) *dichotomous choice* (DC), where respondents are asked 'are you willing to pay £X?', the amount X being systematically varied across the sample to test individuals' responses to different bid levels. This approach produces a discrete bid response variable and may be iterated using higher or lower bid amounts depending upon the respondents' replies to previous amounts;[9] (iii) *iterative bidding* (IB), in which a series of DC-type questions are followed by a final OE question; (iv) *payment card* (PC), in which respondents select their maximum WTP amount from a list of possible sums presented on a card to them.[10]

The respondent also requires information regarding the nature of the good under evaluation, the proposed quantity/quality change in provision of the good, who will pay for and who will use the good and how payment will be collected (the 'payment vehicle', for example higher taxes, entrance fees, donation to a charitable trust, etc.).

hedonic pricing models of landscape and noise disamenity values through the application of GIS techniques (see Lake *et al.*, 1998, 2000a,b; Bateman *et al.*, 2001a). Expressed preference methods other than CV (such as choice experiments, contingent ranking, etc.; see Champ *et al.*, forthcoming) have not to date been widely applied to the study of woodland recreation values. An exception is provided by Hanley *et al.* (1998) who present a choice experiment study of forest landscape values in the UK.

[8] Bateman *et al.* (1995a) provide a comparison of OE, DC and IB formats.

[9] See, for example, Hanemann *et al.* (1991); Langford *et al.* (1996); Bateman *et al.* (2001b).

[10] See, for example, Rowe *et al.* (1996).

With the questionnaire complete, the process moves to the survey stage to obtain responses. In so doing the relevant population of either users or non-users, or a mix of the two, must be determined. User surveys may be conducted either on or off site while non-user surveys are restricted to the latter locations. In both cases either face-to-face or mail/telephone surveys may be used, each of which has its own merits and drawbacks.

Once responses have been collected, data analysis can commence. This has the dual objective of both obtaining the required welfare measures and assessing the validity of responses. Validation testing is complex and multifaceted (see discussions in Mitchell and Carson, 1989 and Bateman *et al.*, 2002); typically, however, considerable emphasis is placed upon the consistency of responses with theoretical expectations, this being assessed through the estimation of bid curves linking valuation responses to the characteristics of respondents (e.g. their income, use of the good, etc.), and upon assessing the extent to which CV estimates converge with those obtained by other valuation methods.

The final stage of the study is to derive aggregate welfare measures by linking sample responses to the relevant underlying population.[11] Providing that validity tests are satisfactory, these aggregate measures may then be incorporated within project appraisals.

Focal methodological issues

We now concentrate on topics which are central to our woodland recreation work.[12] The general issue under consideration here is the extent to which design issues affect elicited values. However, to set this in context, we begin by considering the process by which individuals form stated responses to CV questions. This discussion allows a consideration of the impacts which choices regarding survey design may have upon valuation responses. Areas highlighted for subsequent research include the effect of varying the elicitation method and changing the payment vehicle, the impact of asking respondents to consider budget constraints and the effect of varying the order of questions within a survey instrument. Some of these issues are tackled through non-woodland applications, results from which are presented in this chapter. Findings from woodland studies are presented in the following chapter.

---

[11] This is rarely as straightforward as it may appear. See discussions in Bateman *et al.* (2000b, 2002).
[12] This approach precludes discussion of a number of CV issues which we address in other contexts, including the ability of respondents to distinguish adequately between a conglomerate good (e.g. all natural areas) and its constituent parts (just one of those areas) (see Bateman *et al.*, 1997a) and the role of 'reference points' of prior provision in influencing the commonly observed asymmetry between WTP and WTA measures of the same change in provision (see Bateman *et al.*, 1997b, 2000a). This is of course far from an exhaustive list of current CV issues, for which the interested reader should consult the literature cited previously.

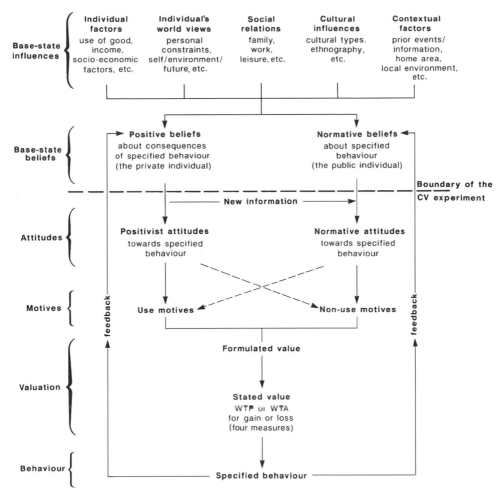

Figure 2.2. The value formation process.

The valuation process and its influences

Consideration of the process through which respondents derive valuation responses to CV questions can be traced back to the beliefs–attitudes–behaviour models proposed by Fishbein and Ajzen (1975) and Ajzen and Fishbein (1977). Recent research has suggested that this process may be highly complex, reaching beyond the somewhat simple models of self-interested rationality underpinning much economic theory. Figure 2.2 draws upon a number of sources to summarise recent thinking in this area.[13]

---

[13] This section draws upon a variety of sources including Fishbein and Ajzen (1975); Hoehn and Randall (1987); Brown and Slovic (1988); Mitchell and Carson (1989); Dake (1991); Harris and Brown (1992); Bateman and Turner (1993); Schkade and Payne (1994); Marris *et al.* (1996); Hanemann (1999).

The model presented in Figure 2.2 emphasises the pre-survey base-state as a vital determinant in the valuation process irrespective of the good under investigation. A variety of base-state influences are identified. These include the individual-level factors emphasised by traditional economic models of preferences, as well as world views (for example, whether individuals see the relationship between the economy and the environment as ultimately benign or degrading[14]), social factors (such as work and family influences), cultural influences (such as the typologies identified in recent empirical studies: Dake, 1991; Sjöberg, 1995; Marris *et al.*, 1996; Langford *et al.*, 2000) and contextual factors which may distinguish otherwise identical changes in provision of public goods. These elements combine to yield the base-state positive and normative beliefs which any individual brings to a valuation experiment.[15]

It is tempting to see the schism between so-called individual and citizen preferences (Blamey, 1995, 1996) as being reflected in differences between positive and normative beliefs and there is some evidence to support such a definition (Peterson *et al.*, 1996). However, the complex and uncertain nature of this argument prohibits us from taking the matter further. Rather we can see these beliefs as the base-line points of reference from which the individual enters the CV experiment. Here the respondent is presented with new information which will be used to update the belief set. These beliefs will then form the individual's attitudes and norms concerning behaviour. Information, beliefs and attitudes all subsequently feed into motivation. It is arguable that non-use (existence and bequest) values arise from non-use motives such as altruism (Randall, 1987) drawing upon normative beliefs, whereas use values arise from positivist beliefs and attitudes. However, while these are likely to be the main routes of influence, we can also imagine norms concerning instrumental goods and positivist ideas concerning non-use values.

These use and non-use motives combine and are expressed as the WTP sum within the CV valuation process. This statement of value and the CV experience itself then feed back either via behaviour (an actual payment) or, more usually, directly into the individual's positive and normative beliefs, such that values for the same good may change if a CV study is iteratively repeated using the same respondents (see Coursey *et al.*, 1986). As a simple investigation of the impact of use and non-use motives upon stated values it was decided that an initial and preliminary objective of our empirical woodland research would be to examine variations in WTP values between users and non-users of woodland recreation as well as to examine the WTA compensation levels demanded by the potential providers of

[14] These views relate, respectively, to O'Riordan's (1976) technocentric man and ecocentric man.
[15] Interestingly, Spash (1997) argues that individuals may also hold beliefs about the valuation process itself and that these may result in the preferences of those opposed to the valuation process being systematically under-represented.

woodland recreation (farmers) who were together the target of the wider research described in this volume.

The transition from formulated to stated value is the subject of theoretical analysis by Hoehn and Randall (1987) and Carson *et al.* (1999). Here the CV respondent is seen as undertaking a two-stage task of (i) value formulation and (ii) value statement. In moving from formulated to stated value the respondent has the opportunity to engage in a variety of strategic behaviours including both understatement and overstatement of formulated WTP. Hoehn and Randall and Carson *et al.* see these various strategies as being chosen according to the elicitation method being used (OE, DC, etc.) and so we consider this issue in some detail.

Elicitation effects

Different elicitation methods may either be neutral (i.e. they have no impact upon stated WTP) or lead to either under- or overstatement of values. Reasons for such effects are diverse and there is considerable debate regarding the impact which the differing strategic incentives and psychological effects of each elicitation method have upon stated values and the consequent validity of those values.[16] If methods are neutral in their effect, the elicitation issue can be ignored. However, both theory and empirical investigation suggest this is not generally the case and so we begin this consideration of potential bias by first considering issues surrounding value understatement, then overstatement, after which empirical evidence is examined and some conclusions drawn. For convenience we shall consider WTP measures throughout the following discussion.

Understatement of WTP

If an individual feels that a good will be provided irrespective of his response to a WTP question, or that the payments of others will be sufficient to secure provision, then, given the ability to freely vary his stated valuation (e.g. in an OE elicitation format), the individual will 'pretend to have less interest in a given collective activity than he really has' (Samuelson, 1954) and will understate his WTP for that good, i.e. he will 'free-ride' (Marwell and Ames, 1981; Brubaker, 1982). A similar result will be obtained when respondents feel that actual payments will (or should) be related to cost shares rather than to WTP (Hoehn and Randall, 1987). Here respondents will state the expected cost, if this is less than WTP, or zero otherwise.

Mitchell and Carson (1989) review a variety of studies for priced goods in which hypothetical OE bids were subsequently compared to actual prices paid. These studies indicated that, where a relatively weak free-rider incentive existed (e.g. where respondents were informed that a group threshold WTP was required in order to

---

[16] See, for example, Carson *et al.* (1999) and Bateman *et al.* (2001b, 2002).

secure provision), then a reasonably close correspondence between hypothetical and actual payments was found (OE bids were between 74 per cent and 96 per cent of actual payments in the studies cited). However, where a strong free-riding incentive existed (e.g. by guaranteeing provision as long as respondents stated some non-zero sum), divergence was consistently greater (OE bids being 61 per cent to 71 per cent of actual payments).

Overstatement of WTP

Bateman *et al.* (1995a) identify five factors which may induce a respondent to overstate WTP in a CV experiment, each of which we discuss below:

  (i) Strategic overbidding (all elicitation formats)
 (ii) 'Good respondents' (all elicitation formats)
(iii) Upward rounding (DC formats)
 (iv) Anchoring (DC formats)
  (v) Starting point effects (IB formats).

(i) Strategic overbidding. In an important empirical paper, Bohm (1972) argues that, contrary to the prediction of free-riding, respondents may overstate their WTP in hypothetical markets. Such 'strategic overbidding' may occur where respondents feel that the amount they will actually have to pay will be related to some sample measure, such as mean WTP, rather than their own statements. In such a case, if formulated WTP exceeds expected mean WTP, the respondent may inflate stated WTP (up to the expected mean) in an effort to improve the probability of provision.

Carson *et al.* (1999) extend this theoretical analysis in the context of OE format responses noting that in a case where there is uncertainty over the provision of a good, individuals have a strategic incentive to overstate their willingness to contribute to subsequent costs of provision, as the very nature of an OE response tells respondents that these amounts are unlikely to bind them subsequently. Empirical support for such a model is provided by Foster *et al.* (1997) who compare CV responses to actual donations for public goods, in this case the preservation of various UK bird habitats. This study found that while OE CV bids were on average not significantly different from those which could be expected in the real payment context, individuals presented with a hypothetical market were significantly less likely to opt out of making a bid than those faced with making real donations.

Contrasting these findings with the evidence for understatement in OE WTP responses (reviewed above) suggests that, in practice, some people respond to the OE elicitation method by free-riding, while others strategically overstate.[17]

---

[17] Further evidence for such a view can be gleaned from the relatively low degree of fit attained by statistical models of OE CV responses. If individuals are responding in diametrically opposed ways to these questions, then models are inevitably going to struggle to explain such data.

However, meta-analyses of CV studies commonly report that OE-format analyses record significantly lower WTP amounts than do those using other elicitation methods (see, for example, Brouwer *et al.*, 1999, and the study presented subsequently in this volume). Therefore, on balance, OE formats appear to result in under- rather than overstatement and may, in the absence of superior measures, be justified as providing conservative estimates of underlying values.

(ii) 'Good respondents'. Orne (1962) points out that the relationship between analyst and respondent is an interactive process with the interviewee seeking clues as to the purpose of the experiment. If this purpose is inadequately conveyed then the respondent may react in one of two ways: either she will not give the questions due consideration or she will attempt to guess the 'correct' answers, i.e. she will try to be a 'good respondent' and give the answers which she feels that the analyst wants. The problem of limited involvement may be assessed by recording and analysing both the numbers of respondents who refuse to take part in the survey and the length of interview. The good respondent problem may be exacerbated where the interviewer is held in high esteem by the respondent (Harris *et al.*, 1989), resulting in responses which differ from true WTP. Desvousges *et al.* (1983) found little evidence of such a bias but it should be noted that this study employed professional interviewers, a potential solution to such problems. Tunstall *et al.* (1988) further recommend that interviewers follow the wording of the questionnaire exactly and that respondents be presented with a choice of prepared responses so as to minimise over- or understatement of true evaluations.

In our own empirical work considerable emphasis has been placed upon minimising such sources of bias at the design stage. Experienced practitioners (including several of those cited above) were consulted regarding the construction of questionnaires and execution of surveys.

(iii) Upward rounding. Bateman *et al.* (1993b) argue that respondents in a DC format survey may have an incentive to accept bids which are in excess of true WTP if the difference between the two amounts is relatively small. The deviation caused by such an effect will only operate in an upward manner, i.e. the respondent will not refuse to pay a bid level which is just below their true WTP. However, provided that the respondent believes in the payment obligation (i.e. she does not engage in strategic overbidding) this should be a relatively minor effect.

(iv) Anchoring. Kahneman *et al.* (1982), among others, have argued that respondents faced with an unfamiliar situation (particularly where the good is also poorly described) will interpret the DC bid level to be indicative of the true value of the good in question (Kahneman and Tversky, 1982; Roberts *et al.*, 1985; Kahneman, 1986; Harris *et al.*, 1989; Green *et al.*, 1998). Here the introduction of a specific bid level raises the probability of the respondent accepting that bid. Proponents of this idea argue that this 'anchoring' effect may occur where a respondent has not

previously considered her WTP for a resource (which is likely with regard to public or quasi-public goods) and/or is unclear in her own mind about the true valuation. In such cases the proposed bid level may provide the most readily available point of reference onto which the respondent latches. There is no *a priori* presumption about the direction of such an anchoring effect.[18]

(v) Starting point effects. Several studies have suggested that the use of an initial starting point in iterative bidding (IB) games may significantly influence the final bid; for example, the choice of a low (high) starting point leads to a low (high) mean WTP (see Desvousges *et al.*, 1983; Roberts *et al.*, 1985; Boyle *et al.*, 1985; Navrud, 1989a; Green *et al.*, 1990; Green and Tunstall, 1991). While the use of starting points may reduce non-response and variance, commentators argue that such an approach may lead respondents to take cognitive short-cuts to arrive at a decision rather than thinking seriously about their true WTP (Cummings *et al.*, 1986; Mitchell and Carson, 1989; Loomis, 1990). It has also been noted that informing respondents as to the construction costs associated with a proposed environmental change may affect resultant bids (Cronin and Herzeg, 1982). One approach to this problem is to allow the respondent to choose a bid from a range shown on a payment card (Rowe *et al.*, 1996). However, in some instances the choice of payment range on a card may affect reported WTP bids (for example, if respondents assume that such a range implies information about the 'correct' valuation response; see discussions in Kahneman and Tversky, 1982; Roberts and Thompson, 1983; Kahneman, 1986; Harris *et al.*, 1989; Dubourg *et al.*, 1997).

In summary, we can see that different elicitation formats may in theory result in either understatement or overstatement of values. We now consider empirical evidence concerning elicitation effects.

Elicitation effects: empirical evidence

Our own studies of elicitation effects have been conducted for both woodland and other resources. Three elicitation methods (OE, DC and IB) were assessed[19] in a CV study examining users' WTP for environmental preservation in the Norfolk Broads, a unique wetland area located in East Anglia, UK (Bateman *et al.*, 1995a, 1999b). Following a pilot survey (discussed subsequently in relation to payment vehicle effects), a main survey sample of about 3,000 visitors was obtained through face-to-face on-site interviews. This sample was divided up to permit sufficient

---

[18] A related problem in DC (and potentially other) formats is the phenomenon of 'yea-saying' or 'nay-saying', whereby the respondent decides *ex ante* to answer positively or negatively irrespective of the actual bid presented (see Kanninen, 1995; Alberini and Carson, 2001).

[19] An iterated exercise, in which an initial DC question was supplemented with two follow-up amounts, was also conducted; see Langford *et al.* (1996) and Bateman *et al.* (2001b). This latter analysis supports the existence of anchoring effects within iterated DC designs.

Table 2.2. *WTP for preservation of the Norfolk Broads using various elicitation methods*

Elicitation method	Mean WTP (£ per annum)	95% confidence interval (£ per annum)
DC	144	75–261
IB	75	70–81
OE	68	60–75

responses to test the various elicitation formats under investigation. WTP results from these formats are summarised in Table 2.2.

Inspection of Table 2.2 shows that the results conform to our prior expectations concerning potential elicitation effects. The overstatement and understatement incentives inherent in the DC and OE formats, respectively, seem to be reflected in the ordering of derived valuation measures with mean DC WTP being more than twice the OE estimate. Of course, it could be that while OE responses were downwardly biased by free-riding (of which some, although not pervasive, evidence was found), DC responses were unbiased. However, statistical analysis of the determinants of WTP amounts provided evidence of a strong link between the starting point in the IB bidding game and the final valuation amount stated. This in turn suggests that DC bid levels might well be interpreted in a similar fashion, i.e. as anchoring points which respondents used as heuristic indicators of the 'correct' valuation of the good under investigation.

This analysis shows that we cannot reject the hypothesis that all elicitation formats are, in one way or another, biased instruments for obtaining WTP values. Which, if any, should be used in our subsequent research on woodland values? The answer to such a question is still unclear and the subject of considerable ongoing research within the CV community world-wide. For the purposes of the research described here we have adopted a simple rule that, wherever possible, we should employ lower-bound assumptions and conservative techniques, thus enhancing the robust nature of derived results.[20] As a consequence, in most of the woodland evaluation research presented in Chapter 3, we adopt an OE elicitation format for our CV studies (with a comparison against a payment card approach in one study) on the grounds that such a choice is likely to produce conservative estimates of WTP.

---

[20] Such an objective accords well with the practice of H.M. Treasury with regard to its evaluations of non-market woodland recreation values. The guidelines for best practice in CV studies given by the US NOAA Blue Ribbon Panel (Arrow *et al.*, 1993) also emphasise conservation design although notably they recommend the use of DC-style referendum elicitation formats because of their desirable theoretical incentive properties.

Table 2.3. *Payment vehicle analysis results*

Payment vehicle	Sample size	Zero WTP (%)	Mean WTP (£)	S.E. mean	Median WTP (£)	Coeff. of variation (%)
DONATE	157	46.5	25.60	3.18	10.00	156
FUND	65	23.1	47.60	17.40	10.00	296
TAX	211	11.8	89.22	9.98	40.00	162

Payment vehicle effects

The idea that the way in which a payment is made is liable to affect an individual's willingness to make that payment (and implicitly the size of payment) is self-evident from the expansion of credit and payment options schemes within modern Western society. That such payment vehicle effects should arise in the purchase of public goods is therefore not surprising and indeed can be seen as evidence that CV respondents act as if hypothetical markets are binding. Payment vehicles can usually be described in terms of two characteristics: collection mechanism and temporal extent.

Considering first the commonly adopted approach of asking survey respondents annual payment questions a number of tax-based and donation-based collection mechanisms appear in the CV literature. The impact of varying these was studied through an earlier survey of visitors to the Norfolk Broads (Bateman *et al.*, 1993b). Here a sample of over 400 respondents were presented with one of three payment vehicles: (i) an unspecified charitable donation (the DONATE vehicle); (ii) a payment to a hypothetical charitable fund specifically set up to facilitate flood defence work in the Norfolk Broads (FUND); and (iii) payments made via direct taxation (TAX).

All payment vehicles were applied using an OE WTP elicitation method. Results, which are detailed in Table 2.3, show that both the DONATE and FUND vehicles elicited large numbers of zero WTP bids (46.5 per cent and 23.1 per cent respectively), which contradicts prior expectations regarding a sample of visitors to the Broads who are expected to derive considerable value from the area. In contrast the TAX vehicle produced by far the lowest zero-bid rate (11.8 per cent) and also performed better in terms of bid variability than the FUND vehicle, and about as well as the DONATE vehicle. As no vehicle produced excessive evidence of strategic bidding (large numbers of unreasonably high bids) this was not deemed a problem.

All respondents in the Broads study were asked why they had responded in the way they had. Many of those presented with the FUND and (especially) DONATE vehicles commented that they were unhappy that such a vehicle would not be binding upon all and that they were not confident that payments via such vehicles would be fully channelled towards preservation work (trust funds were not to be trusted!). Conversely, many of those responding to the TAX vehicle commented that, while they disliked paying extra taxes, they had confidence that such money would be spent efficiently upon any flood defence scheme.

In both the Norfolk Broads and woodlands studies a tax-based vehicle also has the advantage of being the most likely method by which changes in the provision of these quasi-public goods would be funded. This and the advantages outlined above made such a payment vehicle the preferred approach for our subsequent woodland studies. However, a remaining issue concerned the advantages of local taxes relative to national ones, a topic which is discussed in Chapter 3.

Turning to consider variation in the temporal extent of payment vehicles, a number of researchers have experimented with per visit measures for which entrance fees had been used. Several studies have noted differences in implicit values when both per annum taxation and per visit entrance fee measures were obtained for the same good (see, for example, Rowe *et al.*, 1980, on landscape values; also Desvousges *et al.*, 1983; Brookshire and Coursey, 1987; Navrud, 1989b). Given this result we felt it would be interesting to examine whether such a result was obtained when applying the same design to UK woodlands, and if so why. Consequently, such a comparison was made a further objective of our woodland valuation research.

Questionnaire design impacts: budget constraint and ordering effects

An area of particular interest was the impact which changes in the questionnaire might have upon stated values when the valuation question itself was kept constant. This was assessed through a joint consideration of two design issues: (i) the inclusion or exclusion of a question (prior to the valuation question) asking respondents to calculate their relevant annual recreational budget; (ii) the impact of changing the order in which per annum and per visit valuation questions were presented to respondents.

The relevant economic theory concerning the budget constraint issue is presented in the mental accounting literature (Deaton and Muellbauer, 1980; Tversky and Kahneman, 1981; Kahneman and Tversky, 1984) where total income is initially allocated to various broad categories of expenditure (e.g. housing, food, recreation, etc.), and then, in a second stage, subdivided among the specific items which constitute each category (e.g. the recreation category budget is allocated among forest recreation, water recreation, etc.). Because of the hypothetical nature of the CV market a potential problem may arise if respondents fail to consider all relevant material such as the relevant category budget. Evidence on the impact of explicitly asking respondents to consider income constraints prior to stating WTP sums is mixed (Burness *et al.*, 1983; Schulze *et al.*, 1983; Willis and Garrod, 1993; Loomis *et al.*, 1994) and consequently it was decided to make this an objective of subsequent empirical investigation.

Question-ordering effects are considered by Brookshire *et al.* (1981), Tolley and Randall (1983) and Hoevenagel (1990) who note that a good will elicit a higher WTP response if placed at the top of a list of goods to be evaluated than if it is positioned lower in the order. Similar evidence is presented by Kahneman and Knetsch (1992) as part of a series of tests examining the extent to which CV responses are the product of moral satisfaction (i.e. the 'warm glow' of contributing to a good cause) rather than being linked to the characteristics of the good under evaluation. This paper has triggered a wide empirical debate and stimulated theoretical research arguing that, as the consumption of a given good in isolation is not identical to the consumption of the same good as part of a larger set (because the other goods in the set may be substitutes for, or complements to, the good under question), then this phenomenon need not violate economic theory (see Carson *et al.*, 1992, 1998; Randall and Hoehn, 1992, 1996; Carson and Mitchell, 1995; Rollins and Lyke, 1998). While not attempting to establish whether variation is due to moral satisfaction, warm glow or theoretically expected effects,[21] we do use ordering effect tests and simpler sensitivity analyses to establish the extent of such variation in values. Furthermore, by combining the budget constraint and question-ordering investigations within a split-sample design, a further analysis of the interactions of these effects could be undertaken to see whether design effects might multiply through a study.

Summary of woodland CV research objectives

CV is a widely applicable and widely applied monetary evaluation method with a consistent basis in economic theory. Given the breadth of the current research debate, we have deliberately focused our empirical investigations on a subset of related issues which together examine the impact of differing designs upon elicited values. The issues addressed in our subsequent woodland CV studies are:

(i) variations in WTP values between users and non-users of woodland recreation
(ii) the WTA compensation levels demanded by farmers for providing woodland recreation opportunities on their land
(iii) elicitation effects (specifically, a comparison between OE and payment card approaches)
(iv) the choice of payment vehicle (in terms of both local versus national tax payment collection mechanisms and annual versus per visit temporal extent of payments)
(v) budget constraint impacts
(vi) question-ordering effects.

---

[21] Our recent research on the relationship between study design and such effects is reported in Bateman *et al.* (2001c).

Taken together it was intended that these studies would provide some insight into the variability of valuation responses with changes in CV study design. These values could then be compared to those derived from the travel cost method, to which we now turn.

The travel cost method

Introduction

Like the CV method, the travel cost (TC) approach relies upon a survey to gather data. However, whereas a CV survey can, in principle, be applied in almost any situation, a TC survey must involve at least a high proportion of users of the recreational asset in question. Most typically this involves on-site surveys in which a questionnaire is used to collect data on users' place of residence; necessary demographic and attitudinal information; frequency of visit to this and other sites; trip information such as purpose, length, associated costs, etc. From these data, visit costs can be calculated and related, with other relevant factors, to the frequency of visits in a 'trip generation function' (TGF) from which a demand relationship may be established (for details see Freeman, 1993; Champ *et al.*, forthcoming).[22]

As discussed by Bockstael *et al.* (1991), the literature can be divided into random utility models (RUM), which examine the probability of a visit to a site given information on all possible visit sites, and more basic TC models which predict visits to a given site by utilising data collected from a survey of visitors at that site. While theoretically more elegant, RUMs require more data than were available to this research and so the more basic approach is employed here.

Two variants of this style of TC model can be identified depending on the definition of the site visits variable (Bateman, 1993). The 'individual travel cost' (ITC) method focuses on the number of site visits made by each visitor over a specific period, say one year. The 'zonal travel cost' (ZTC) method, on the other hand, partitions the entire area from which visitors originate into a set of visitor zones and then defines the dependent variable as the visitor rate (i.e. the number of visits made from a particular zone in a period divided by the population of that zone). In both cases an uncompensated demand curve can be derived and consumer surplus estimates of recreational value obtained.

The UK woodland recreation literature includes examples of both ITC and ZTC applications which we review in Chapter 3. Results obtained from applying the two

---

[22] Note that Randall (1994) provides a fundamental caution to those who assume that the revealed preference nature of the TC approach gives it automatic ascendancy over expressed preference methods such as CV. He notes that the TC method relies upon researcher-assigned visitation cost estimates rather than observable visit prices and argues that these are inherently subjective, such that the method yields only ordinally measurable welfare estimates. In essence, while the CV method at least presents respondents with hypothetical costs, visitors never see the implicit travel costs used to calculate consumer surplus estimates in TC studies. An empirical assessment of 'Randall's Difficulty' is given by Common *et al.* (1999).

Table 2.4. *ZTC/ITC consumer surplus estimates for six UK forests*

Forest	ZTC Travel cost coefficient	ZTC CS/visitor (£)	ITC Travel cost coefficient	ITC CS/visitor (£)	CS ratio: ZTC/ITC
Brecon	−0.384	2.60	−0.358	1.40	1.86
Buchan	−0.444	2.26	−0.996	0.50	4.52
Cheshire	−0.525	1.91	−1.259	0.40	4.78
Lorne	−0.694	1.44	−0.327	1.53	0.94
New Forest	−0.702	1.43	−0.215	2.32	0.62
Ruthin	−0.396	2.52	−0.386	1.29	1.95

Notes: All coefficients produced via OLS techniques and significant at 5% level; travel cost defined as full running costs; consumer surplus estimates at 1988 prices; $n = 21$ for all forests.
Sources: Garrod and Willis, 1991; Willis and Garrod, 1991a.

variants to the same data have been shown to be substantially different. Table 2.4 illustrates this point with regard to a joint ZTC/ITC study of six UK forest sites. Using the same estimation procedure and cost assumptions throughout,[23] estimates of consumer surplus produced by ZTC ranged from almost 40 per cent smaller to almost five times larger than those produced by ITC. As all the cost coefficients produced by both methods are statistically significant this indicates some serious problems for one or both of these approaches.

One limitation of the ZTC approach is the difficulty associated with the use of an average value as a dependent variable. Employing a zonal visitor rate means that it is impossible to use individual-specific explanatory variables. For example, membership of an environmental or outdoor pursuits association may well be a highly significant predictor of recreational visits. However, information on such individual characteristics cannot be used in the ZTC approach and a constructed zonal average for such variables is likely to be highly inefficient (Brown and Nawas, 1973). Similarly, intrazonal variation is to a considerable degree lost in the ZTC approach, as interzonal average effects dominate in curve-fitting. An extreme case of this occurs where concentric, circular travel time zones are used with no distinction being made within the resultant circles for other variables such as socio-economic or substitute availability measures.[24]

While concentric zones are common in earlier ZTC applications,[25] other approaches to zonal definition are perfectly feasible. The definition of the width

[23] See table notes for details. Cost definition and estimation issues are discussed briefly later.
[24] For an illustration, see Bateman (1993).
[25] Furthermore, zones may be cut off at some finite distance although the outer band may be infinite. Englin and Mendelsohn (1991), in their study of rainforest tourism, analyse visits from all countries.

and number of zones is typically either arbitrary or influenced by the availability of demographic data; for example, Böjo (1985) uses county boundaries to define zones. In effect, each possible definition of zones implies a different aggregation of population and, in practice, almost certainly a different visitor rate. This, in turn, will imply changes in the estimated demand curve and thereby different consumer surplus estimates. Therefore, in reality, it is almost certain that an analyst could respecify zones so as to either inflate or reduce valuation estimates as required. This is an example of the more general phenomenon known as the modifiable areal unit problem (MAUP) (Openshaw, 1984). The extent to which valuation results may alter is uncertain[26] and there is active research into statistical aspects of the MAUP issue (e.g. Batty and Longley, 1996).

A further problem for ZTC, which again does not afflict the ITC method, is that R^2 statistics will always be upwardly biased. This arises as a natural consequence of aggregating individual responses across zones and so reducing the number of curve-fitting points to the number of zones. Consequently the very high R^2 values recorded in many ZTC studies should be treated with extreme caution. Their only real validity is as indicators of which model has relatively higher explanatory power within any particular functional form; their absolute value should be disregarded (and even not reported as it may well be misleading). This criticism does not apply to the ITC for which goodness-of-fit statistics are, in this respect, unbiased.

Given these problems, Brown and Nawas (1973) argue that the ZTC method is inefficient and therefore prefer the use of ITC, a sentiment echoed in early applications by Gum and Martin (1975) and Bowes and Loomis (1980). Indeed the US literature over the past two decades has slowly moved from the use of ZTC to employing ITC. However, the ITC approach is not without problems.

Dobbs (1991) points out that most ITC studies to date have incorrectly estimated consumer surplus, in that they have ignored the inherently discrete nature of the dependent variable. In such cases the integration of a smooth demand function may lead to significant bias in consumer surplus estimates. However, Dobbs develops a programmable approach to the computation of discrete dependent variable benefits which overcomes this problem.

A more fundamental problem with ITC occurs where a high proportion of visitors make only one visit per annum or are first-time visitors (Freeman, 1979; Bowes and Loomis, 1980). In such cases, statistical techniques commonly used in ITC analyses may not have a sufficient spread of observations to make the approach operational. In recent work we have addressed this problem through the application of Poisson distribution models,[27] details of which we present in Chapter 4.

---

[26] See also Christensen (1985) and Price *et al.* (1986).
[27] However, a Poisson regression will have problems of underdispersion with large numbers of low counts.

In conclusion, the decision to use either zonal or individual TC approaches may have a substantial impact upon the results obtained. While there are a number of methodological problems associated with the application of both, these seem more tractable in the case of the ITC approach, which also has theoretical advantages over ZTC (Bockstael *et al.*, 1991). Consequently we adopt the ITC method for use in the valuation studies presented in Chapter 3. However, the recently developed literature on benefits transfer has used the ZTC approach as a readily tractable technique for estimating the numbers of visitors arriving at a given site (Loomis *et al.*, 1995). The area visit rates used in the ZTC provide as much information regarding which areas do not yield visitors (e.g. those which are distant from the site, are socio-economically disadvantaged, etc.) as those which do. Therefore the technique yields demand functions which can readily be applied across a study area of which the site distance, socio-economic and other characteristics are known to yield defensible estimates of the number of arrivals expected at a site.

As a consequence, while we use the ITC approach to estimate the value of a recreational trip to a woodland, our model of the number of trips made to woods and the latent demand for trips to potential new woodlands (presented in Chapter 4) owes more to the zonal-based approach of the ZTC method.

Focal methodological issues

As before, our methodological review focuses exclusively upon those issues which are addressed in our subsequent empirical work, with the interested reader being referred to the previously cited literature for wider discussions.

Calculating travel costs

Travel costs are composed of two principal elements: direct travel expenditure (e.g. petrol costs) and the opportunity cost of time.

Travel expenditure

Two issues are pertinent here: measurement and valuation. Accurate measurement is a vital ingredient of valid welfare estimation. However, we have shown elsewhere that a number of questionable simplifications are commonly adopted in the distance calculations underpinning expenditure estimates (Bateman *et al.*, 1996a, 1999a; Brainard *et al.*, 1999). For example, rather than using the actual point from which a visitor starts their journey, many ITC studies use centre points or 'centroids' of cities (Rosenthal *et al.*, 1986) or counties (Mendelsohn *et al.*, 1992) as outset origins.[28] This may cause a systematic error given that the very basis of the TC method

---

[28] Note that we are referring here to a problem with ITC studies, although all ZTC studies, by their very nature, also use zonal outset areas.

is that individuals are mindful of costs in determining their choice of recreation, i.e. we would expect, *ceteris paribus*, that within any area there would be more visitors from outset locations nearer to the study site than from further away. The use of a centroid will partly mask that variation as all visitors within the boundary of the outset area will be assumed to travel from the common central point. This should, on average, lead to an overestimation of the travel costs faced by visitors from a given area as, within that area, most visitors come from locations which are closer to the study site than is the centroid point. The larger the outset area used, the greater we would expect any resultant error to be. A further measurement issue concerns assumptions regarding routing. The use of constant road speeds or straight-line distances ignores the extent and quality of the road network which underpins true travel distances and times (Rosenthal *et al.*, 1986). We address all of these aspects of the measurement issue directly in our empirical studies through the application of GIS techniques.

Turning to the valuation issue, a variety of alternative approaches can be identified; for example Bojö (1985) simply refers to the economy class rail fare. However, such a simple approach is less applicable to car travel, where three cost calculation options exist:

(i) petrol costs only (marginal costs)
(ii) full car costs: petrol, insurance, maintenance costs, etc.
(iii) perceived costs as estimated by respondents.

Clearly, using option (ii) will raise visit costs above that of option (i) and ultimately increase consumer surplus estimates, a result confirmed in comparisons of these approaches undertaken by both Hanley and Common (1987) and Willis and Benson (1988). Price (1983) and Christensen (1985) argue that the correct cost measure is that which visitors perceive as relevant to the visit. It may well be that visitors are poor at perceiving daily insurance and maintenance cost equivalents or that they see these as sunk costs which do not enter the TGF, i.e. they only consider the marginal cost of a visit, equating this with marginal utility. As a result of this apparent conflict we adopt a sensitivity analysis approach in our empirical work, testing all three of the above cost definitions.

Time costs
Time enters the visit cost function through the travel time and on-site time variables. However, theoretical analysis (McConnell, 1975, 1999; Freeman, 1979; Wilman, 1980; Johannson, 1987; Shaw and Feather, 1999a, 1999b; Berman and Kim, 1999) shows that the relevant opportunity costs per hour need not be the same for these two items. Furthermore, determination of these opportunity costs raises considerable problems.

Travel time values are particularly difficult to analyse in that, as noted previously, we have no definite *a priori* notion of whether travel time utility is positive or negative. If travel time has positive utility, then using some general travel time cost as a price will overestimate the consumer surplus of a visit. This will be the case for 'meanderers' who gain utility primarily from the journey itself (Cheshire and Stabler, 1976). Bojö (1985) does not include a travel time cost (i.e. implicitly he gives such time an opportunity cost of zero) on the grounds that 80 per cent of survey respondents expressed a positive utility for travel time to the site under analysis. This approach assumes that ignoring residual travel time costs only leads to a minor underestimate of the true consumer surplus.[29] However, this approach is far from standard. Indeed static optimisation of any conventional utility function (subject to income and time constraints) would indicate that the marginal rate of substitution between labour and leisure (i.e. the value of recreational travel time) is equal to the wage rate. However, when individuals are not able completely to vary the number of hours worked the substitution of time for money becomes constrained and the direct relation between the value of time and the wage rate breaks down (Johnson, 1966; McConnell, 1975).

Early applied investigations of the relationship of wages to travel time were undertaken by Cesario (1976) and Cesario and Knetsch (1970, 1976). These papers examined commuters' choice of transport to and from work (and relevant costs) to estimate an implicit value of travel time. Cesario (1976) concludes that, 'on the basis of evidence collected to date, the value of time with respect to nonwork travel is between one quarter and one half of the (individual's) wage rate' and subsequently uses a value of one-third the wage rate to price travel time.[30] However, this analysis only considers commuting time and there is no necessary reason why the marginal utility obtained should be applicable to recreation travel time.

Common (1973) and McConnell and Strand (1981) use an iterative process whereby successive time values are substituted into the TGF, the final choice being determined where the explanatory power (R^2) of the model was maximised. Desvousges *et al.* (1983) apply the value of time results of Cesario (1976), McConnell and Strand (1981) and a full wage rate assumption to an ITC model of individual visitation patterns at twenty-three water recreation sites in the USA. Testing at the 10 per cent confidence level, Desvousges *et al.* (1983) reject the McConnell and Strand (1981) approach, while the Cesario (1976) and full wage assumptions perform equally well, both being rejected in approximately seven of the twenty-three cases. On the basis of these results Smith and Desvousges (1986)

---

[29] Johansson (1987) points out that if time costs are ignored, then 'the estimated curve will be located inside and be less steep than the "true" one, except possibly for those living very close to the recreation site, since the underestimation of costs increases in relation to distance from the visitor's zone of origin'.

[30] An alternative approach is that of Nelson (1977) who calculates a marginal implicit price of proximity to the central business district with housing data for Washington, D.C., from which he derives a value of time which, when related to wage rates, falls within the Cesario range.

conclude that 'for practical purposes, there is no clear-cut alternative to... using the full wage rate as a measure of the opportunity cost. Even though it may overstate the opportunity costs... none of the simple adaptations are superior.'

Similar results are obtained in a completely different cultural setting by Whittington *et al.* (1990) in a study of the value of time spent collecting water in Kenya. Here two separate approaches are employed, both of which indicate a value of time approximately equivalent to the wage rate for unskilled labour. However, activities such as collecting water are qualitatively different from those associated with recreation. In their TC study of UK forest recreation, Benson and Willis (1992) employ three wage-rate-based value of time assumptions:

(i) 0, which assumes that visitors would not benefit from some alternative recreation activity
(ii) 25 per cent, the UK Department of Transport's value of non-working time used in CBA assessments of road proposals up to 1987
(iii) 43 per cent, the value of time used by the UK Department of Transport following its review of non-work time in 1987 (Department of Transport, 1987).

While the Cesario approach is, on the surface, theoretically and practically appealing, a deeper analysis of the complexities of the work/leisure relationship highlights some important problems. In a thorough analysis, Bockstael *et al.* (1987) note two major issues: (i) wage rates may vary with work hours; for example, a second job may pay a lower rate than the primary one; (ii) individuals face uneven time constraints, i.e. they may be restricted to working specific hours in particular jobs. As a result the wage rate may be an appropriate measure of time costs for those (at interior solutions) who can fully vary their work hours, but it will be inappropriate for those who cannot (at corner solutions). While Bockstael *et al.* provide a theoretically plausible approach to the valuation problem by incorporating time and income constraints into a utility function, the empirical application of such a technique is problematic. In particular the data requirements of such a model, including information regarding each individual's time constraints, are exacting. For these reasons such complex approaches have not been widely adopted and no published UK study has attempted such an analysis.

Shaw (1992) provides a number of suggestions as to how the value of time problem might be addressed in a practical study. One suggestion is to use CV-type questions to elicit WTP for recreation time,[31] while another is to accept that there is likely to be some rather unclear link with wage rate and therefore to use a sensitivity analysis approach with a wide range of wage fractions.

---

[31] We have employed a similar approach in a TC study of the Norfolk Broads (unpublished). Here respondents were asked WTP to reduce travel time. However, many gave a zero response indicating that the journey contributed positively to trip utility. Further direct questions confirmed this finding.

As far as the unit value of on-site time is concerned, if the length of time spent on site were a constant for all visits to a particular site, then such costs could effectively be ignored as they would imply only an increase in absolute visit costs but not a change in marginal relationships. Furthermore, in an empirical analysis, Bojö (1985) finds no evidence to refute an assumption of constant on-site time costs, while Bockstael *et al.* (1987) omit on-site time from their empirical analysis because of its potentially ambiguous effect upon demand arising from its inclusion within both the utility function and the constraints.

Summary: treatment of travel costs

The treatment of travel and time costs within the TGF is one of the most crucial issues in operationalising the TC method. The approach we have adopted in this study is as follows.

Measurement. One fundamental issue concerns the measurement of linear and temporal distance. We believe that the use of GIS to analyse digital road networks (incorporating road length, quality and average travel time by individual road segment) in certain of our TC studies considerably enhances the accuracy of measurement compared to that in most other published research.

Travel expenditure. Following the above review we adopt three definitions of monetary travel costs: petrol only; petrol plus standing charges (insurance, depreciation, etc.); and respondents' perceived travel cost.

Time costs. We adopt the suggestion of Shaw (1992) and perform a wage rate sensitivity analysis upon travel time. Four wage rate values are employed: 0 (following the argument of Benson and Willis, 1992); 43 per cent (the UK Department of Transport's value of time); 100 per cent (following the empirical findings of Smith and Desvousges, 1986); and the variable wage rate percentage which provides the best fit to the data (our preferred option). We recognise the limitations of such an approach and that the labour supply method of Bockstael *et al.* (1987) is theoretically superior. However, such an analysis is both complex and demanding in terms of data requirements. Given limited resources our approach should provide a reasonable approximation, while yielding an analysis which is more rigorous than other contemporary UK studies. In line with such research, we have omitted on-site time from the cost function (although such data were collected and analysed), following the argument that this may not significantly affect consumer surplus.[32]

Total travel costs. Given that travel and time costs are both functions of distance, their inclusion together within the TGF is likely to create significant problems of multicollinearity. Accordingly (and for additional reasons reviewed subsequently) we use the common approach seen in studies from Cesario and Knetsch (1970)

---

[32] Following the analysis of McConnell (1992a), who shows how on-site time may, in certain circumstances, be a significant factor (and proposes a solution to its treatment), we intend to incorporate this into future studies.

to the present day by adding together travel and time costs to produce total visit costs.

Where pertinent we then multiply the total visit cost by the respondent's stated proportion of the total day's enjoyment attributable to the site in question, thereby allowing for that share of the day's utility derived from other sites and the journey itself. This adjusted visit cost is then entered as an explanatory variable within the TGF.

Other explanatory variables

Demand for site visits is likely to be a response to the quality and attributes of a site, yet multicollinearity problems may make the incorporation of numerous such attributes within a single function difficult. Early TC studies tackled this issue through the construction of single-variable quality indices (Ravenscraft and Dwyer, 1978; Talheim, 1978). However, such an index cannot be adequately defined without full knowledge of the functional relationship between demand and site attributes. As this relationship is dictated by individual preferences for different attributes, the creation of a truly representative index is impractical.

Subsequent research has attempted to tackle the problem via multisite studies (Vaughan and Russell, 1982) or by adopting two-stage estimation procedures in which collinear quality attributes are omitted from the first stage (an otherwise conventional TGF) but then used as explanatory variables in a series of second-stage models which predict each of the independent variables used in the initial analysis (Smith and Desvousges, 1986). Such a two-stage procedure is modified for use in our models of agricultural value presented in Chapter 8.

In our own analyses we initially omit consideration of site quality impacts, concentrating instead on the development of improved measures of the principal explanatory variable, travel cost, through use of GIS techniques. However, in our discussion of ongoing work presented in Chapter 4, we detail recently developed models which use these same GIS techniques to incorporate detailed site quality variables into our TC models. A similar approach is taken to the issue of substitute sites, consideration of which is omitted from the models presented in Chapter 3 but included in Chapter 4, where we show how GIS techniques can produce highly detailed variables quantifying accessibility to alternative sites, measures which are readily incorporated into TC models.

Functional form

Analysts are faced with a variety of functional forms under which the TGF can be specified (typically linear, quadratic, semi-log, double-log and Box–Cox). None of these has strong theoretical ascendancy over the others. However, specification of a linear form produces a first derivative which will be a constant and is therefore theoretically problematic, implying as it does non-diminishing marginal utility for additional trips to a site and thus that the individual cannot decide how many trips to make in total. Log forms may be useful for elasticity estimates and have the advantage of avoiding negative values for the dependent variable.[33] However, the double log form may also be criticised on theoretical grounds as its asymptotic properties imply infinite visits at zero cost, an attribute which is particularly unlikely for demand curves for on-site experience (see Everett, 1979).

An altered functional form (even if it has similar explanatory power) can have a highly significant impact upon the demand curve and resultant consumer surplus estimates. In an early TC study of recreational fishing in Grafham Reservoir (UK), Smith and Kavanagh (1969) found that both semi-log (dependent variable) and double-log functions fitted the data very well ($R^2 = 0.91$ and 0.97 respectively).[34] However, when the resultant demand curves were examined it was found, at a zero admission price, that the semi-log form predicted 54,000 annual visits while the double-log form estimated over 1,052,000, with obvious consequences for consumer surplus estimates. Subsequent re-estimation made little difference to this divergence.

From a statistical viewpoint the most appropriate functional form may be evaluated by examining relative degrees of explanation. However, R^2 tests are strictly non-comparable where the dependent variable changes. A more valid test is to compare visitor rates predicted by the model with observed visitor rates using either a large sample, Wilcoxon signed rank test[35] or a Mann–Whitney U test[36] as appropriate.[37]

Because of its large potential for disturbing consumer surplus estimates, we see the functional form issue as one of the most serious problems affecting the TC approach (as pointed out, it may potentially have far more impact than substitute site or congestion effects). Consequently we have made this a priority issue in our applied research. We investigate a variety of functional forms[38] and estimation procedures (see below) with regard to both the valuation models detailed in Chapter 3 and the prediction of arrival numbers discussed in Chapter 4.

Estimation procedure

Pearce and Markandya (1989) point out that a truncation bias may be introduced where ordinary least squares (OLS) estimation techniques are employed with ITC

---

[33] See, for example, Ziemer *et al.* (1980); Vaughan *et al.* (1982); Desvousges *et al.* (1983); Smith and Desvousges (1986); Hanley (1989); Benson and Willis (1990).

[34] This was a ZTC study, for which R^2 figures are, as previously discussed, upwardly biased.

[35] Wilcoxon (1945); see Mendenhall *et al.* (1986: p. 806).

[36] Mann and Whitney (1947); see Kazmier and Pohl (1987: p. 496).

[37] Box–Cox approaches to fitting functional forms are arguably superior to standard form approaches.

[38] The use of various functional forms such as log models also partially addresses the issue of heteroscedasticity (Maddala, 1988).

data. The normal error distribution inherent in this technique does not allow for the fact that in such studies the dependent variable can only take positive values. This problem has been tackled through the use of procedures such as maximum likelihood (ML) estimation, where the function can be specified so as to explicitly allow for this truncation.

Empirical studies come to differing conclusions regarding the extent of variance between OLS (truncated) and ML (non-truncated) estimates of consumer surplus. While some find relatively small differences (Balkan and Kahn, 1988), others find that benefit estimates differ substantially (Smith and Desvousges, 1986; Garrod and Willis, 1991). Given this debate we have employed both OLS and ML estimation techniques in our ITC studies although valuation estimates from ML models are preferred and only these are used in the CBA presented at the end of this volume.

Although the theoretical case against OLS methods still applies for ZTC models, in practice such an approach should produce accurate results where the definition of zones is such that all have a substantial positive visitor rate (e.g. when relatively few, often large, zones are used). However, if this is not the case then truncation effects will again make OLS techniques inappropriate (e.g. where many, often small, zones are used, some having zero visit rates). While we do not include a ZTC model in our valuation studies, such an approach is applied to our models of visitor arrivals at unsurveyed sites (Chapter 4), with OLS techniques being adopted in a study with relatively few large zones and a Poisson regression model (allowing for truncation) being implemented in a study with many small zones.

Summary of woodland TC research objectives

The TC method is a potentially useful valuation tool producing uncompensated consumer surplus estimates of use value. While the zonal (ZTC) approach is seen as providing a useful basis for prediction of the number of individuals expected to visit an existing or proposed woodland site (an approach which is developed in the potential demand models presented in Chapter 4), a review of the literature indicates an increasing preference for the use of the ITC variant for valuation purposes. Consequently the TC-based valuation studies presented in Chapter 3 use the ITC method. The above review has identified a number of research objectives for these studies which we summarise as follows:

(i) to investigate the impact of different strategies for measuring travel time and travel distance upon resultant consumer surplus estimates; in particular, utilising the analytical capabilities of a GIS, we examine the impact of improving the resolution of the defined journey outset location and the effect of moving from simple to sophisticated approaches for modelling journey routing

(ii) to conduct a sensitivity analysis across a variety of definitions of travel expenditure and time cost

(iii) to examine the impact of various estimation procedures and functional forms upon resulting consumer surplus estimates.

The research objectives outlined above are in harmony with those defined previously for our CV applications in that all of these analyses essentially examine the impact of varying study design and execution upon derived values. Convergent validity testing via comparison of CV and TC results provides a further research objective for our valuation studies.

3

Recreation: predicting values

Introduction

While typically unpriced, recreational time is often the most valuable part of any day (Broadhurst, 2001). This chapter discusses applications of the CV and TC methods to the valuation of unpriced, open-access recreation in UK woodlands. The following section presents a review of the existing literature, after which we describe analyses undertaken as part of this research. We conducted three separate woodland recreation valuation studies, all in the UK: two in Thetford Forest, East Anglia, and one in and around Wantage, Oxfordshire. These are subsequently referred to as the Thetford 1, Thetford 2 and Wantage studies. The design of these studies reflected both the previous findings and research objectives set out in Chapter 2 (i.e. to investigate the validity and sensitivity of measures) and the desire to obtain values which were of use within our wider CBA. In Chapter 4 we consider the transferability of these findings to our wider study area of Wales.

Review of the literature

In the UK there have been more applications of the CV and TC methods to the evaluation of woodland recreation than of any other open-access recreational good.[1] A review of the literature identified over forty relevant papers containing over a hundred monetary evaluation estimates (see details in Bateman, 1996). These included studies calculating national-level values, estimates based on household once-and-for-all payments and various other measures which were of little use in our wider study. However, a smaller number of studies provided per person per visit values which can be readily utilised in valuing the woodland visit numbers

---

[1] We have excluded non-UK studies as we believe that the uncertainties surrounding relevant cultural and socio-economic differences between countries such as the USA (where the majority of evaluation work has been conducted) and the UK make such extrapolations of highly dubious value. Loomis (1996) provides a review of non-UK evaluations of forestry preservation benefits conducted using the CV method.

estimated in Chapter 4. Our review of previous studies is categorised according to the various valuation methods employed (ITC, ZTC and CV).

ITC studies

Prior to the present research, the work of Willis and Garrod (1991b) was the only ITC study giving per person per visit estimates of UK woodland recreation benefits. This study provided estimates for six sites across the UK. However, problems concerning sample size and functional form (detailed in Bateman, 1996) mean that we have reservations about the transferability of these particular results to a wider context and prefer our own ITC measures discussed later in this chapter.

ZTC studies

Table 3.1 presents results from three separate ZTC studies[2] but is dominated by the multisite analysis of Benson and Willis (1992). The figures reported for this particular study are from their 'Standard Model' where travel expenditure is calculated using full costs of 33p per mile and travel time is valued at 43% of wage rate (see the discussion of travel cost definitions in Chapter 2). Consumer surplus values are given for both the study year and as a 1990 equivalent, the latter being the base year for our wider CBA study.

   The utility of these findings for estimating recreation benefits at other sites is discussed later in this chapter.

CV studies

The majority of potentially useful UK woodland recreation studies have been conducted using the CV method. All of the results summarised in Table 3.2 were derived from WTP questions concerning per person per visit recreation values. These studies all employed an entrance fee payment vehicle, although a variety of elicitation methods were used as were both direct 'use' and 'use + option' value formats (see Chapter 1), as indicated.

Benefits transfer

To what extent can the results summarised above (and indeed those from our own studies) be applied to other woodland areas? This issue of transferring benefit

---

[2] The study by Christensen (1985) is reviewed in Bateman (1996) but is not included here because of problems, highlighted by Christensen, regarding the quality of data employed.

Table 3.1. *Forest users' per person per visit recreation values from ZTC studies*

Forest	Study-year value (£)	Study year	1990 value (£)
Benson and Willis (1992)			
New Forest	1.43	1988	1.69
Cheshire	1.91	1988	2.26
Loch Awe	3.31	1988	3.91
Brecon	2.60	1988	3.07
Buchan	2.26	1988	2.67
Durham	1.64	1988	1.94
North Yorkshire Moors	1.93	1988	2.28
Aberfoyle	2.72	1988	3.21
South Lakes	1.34	1988	1.58
Newton Stewart	1.61	1988	1.90
Lorne	1.44	1988	1.70
Castle Douglas	2.41	1988	2.85
Ruthin	2.52	1988	2.98
Forest of Dean	2.34	1988	2.76
Thetford	2.66	1988	3.14
mean (all forests)	1.98	1988	2.34
Hanley (1989)			
Aberfoyle	1.70	1987	2.14
Everett (1979)			
Dalby	0.41	1976	1.30

estimates has in recent years developed into a major area of research.[3] The advantages of a rigorous approach to benefits transfer are clear. The costs, both financial and temporal, of conducting individual valuation exercises at each site involved in a policy decision would be prohibitive. Consequently the US Environmental Protection Agency and, more recently, several UK government organisations, including the Department of the Environment, Food and Regional Affairs and the Environment Agency, have shown considerable interest in this avenue of research. However, as several eminent researchers acknowledge, the problems involved in formulating and conducting a successful benefits transfer are numerous and formidable (Desvousges *et al.*, 1992, 1998; Atkinson *et al.*, 1992; McConnell, 1992b; Smith, 1992; Downing and Ozuna, 1996; Kirchhoff *et al.*, 1997; van den Bergh *et al.*, 1997; Brouwer and Spaninks, 1999).

We can identify two basic approaches to benefits transfer: unit value transfer and function transfer (discussed subsequently). At the extreme, unit value transfer may simply involve assuming that, say, a per visit value estimated at one 'source' site

---

[3] Loomis (1992) actually traces research into benefits transfer back to 1962. However, it was only in the late 1980s that this became a major focus of research. See the review by Bateman *et al.* (2001d).

Table 3.2. *Forest users' per person per visit recreation values from CV studies*

Forest	Value type[1]	Elicit. method[2]	Study-year value (£)	Study year	1990 value (£)
Whiteman and Sinclair (1994)					
Mercia	use	OE	1.00	1992	0.93
Thames Chase	use	OE	0.71	1992	0.66
Great Northern	use	OE	0.81	1992	0.75
Hanley and Ruffell (1992)					
various	use	OE	0.93	1991	0.88
Hanley and Ruffell (1991)					
Aberfoyle	use	OE	0.90	1991	0.85
Aberfoyle	use	IB	1.21	1991	1.14
Aberfoyle	use	PC	1.39	1991	1.31
Aberfoyle	use	DC	1.49	1991	1.41
Bishop (1992)					
Derwent Walk	use	OE	0.42	1989	0.46
Derwent Walk	use+option	OE	0.97	1989	1.06
Whippendell	use	OE	0.54	1989	0.59
Whippendell	use+option	OE	1.34	1989	1.46
Willis and Benson (1989)					
New Forest	use	OE	0.43	1988	0.47
Cheshire	use	OE	0.47	1988	0.51
Loch Awe	use	OE	0.50	1988	0.55
Brecon	use	OE	0.46	1988	0.50
Buchan	use	OE	0.57	1988	0.62
Newton Stewart	use	OE	0.73	1988	0.80
Lorne	use	OE	0.72	1988	0.79
Ruthin	use	OE	0.44	1988	0.48
mean	use	OE	0.53	1988	0.58
New Forest	use+option	OE	0.88	1988	0.96
Cheshire	use+option	OE	0.72	1988	0.79
Loch Awe	use+option	OE	0.76	1988	0.83
Brecon	use+option	OE	0.66	1988	0.72
Buchan	use+option	OE	0.79	1988	0.86
Newton Stewart	use+option	OE	1.18	1988	1.29
Lorne	use+option	OE	1.02	1988	1.12
Ruthin	use+option	OE	0.63	1988	0.69
mean	use+option	OE	0.82	1988	0.90
Hanley (1989)					
Aberfoyle	use	OE	1.24	1987	1.53
Aberfoyle	use	PC	1.25	1987	1.55
Willis et al. (1988)					
Castle Douglas	use	OE	0.37	1987	0.46

Table 3.2. (*cont.*)

Forest	Value type[1]	Elicit. method[2]	Study-year value (£)	Study year	1990 value (£)
South Lakes	use	OE	0.39	1987	0.48
North Yorkshire Moors	use	OE	0.53	1987	0.66
Durham	use	OE	0.31	1987	0.38
Thetford	use	OE	0.23	1987	0.28
Dean	use	OE	0.28	1987	0.35
Castle Douglas	use+option	OE	0.80	1987	0.99
South Lakes	use+option	OE	0.86	1987	1.06
North Yorkshire Moors	use+option	OE	1.03	1987	1.27
Durham	use+option	OE	0.56	1987	0.69
Thetford	use+option	OE	0.41	1987	0.51
Dean	use+option	OE	0.63	1987	0.78

Notes: [1] Valuation categories investigated are as follows: use = use value; option = option value (the extra WTP to ensure conservation of the site for future use).
[2] Elicitation methods are: OE = open-ended; IB = iterative bidding; PC = payment card; DC = dichotomous choice.

can be applied to the 'target' or 'policy' site for which values are required. This is clearly very crude and so a considerable literature has developed applying the principles of 'meta-analysis' to benefit estimates.[4] Here researchers have related measures such as the mean benefit value reported in each of a set of source site studies to a series of simple (usually binary) explanatory variables detailing, for example, the evaluation method employed, the type of resource studied, the measurement unit and the elicitation method used (see, for example, Smith and Kaoru, 1990; Walsh *et al.*, 1992; Rosenberger and Loomis, 2000). Our benefit transfer study of reviewed articles derives directly from such a meta-analysis approach. Given that we are only considering woodland recreation studies, we do not need to define variables detailing the type of good evaluated,[5] and other explanatory factors are incorporated by defining relevant binary variables as in the studies cited above.

Before considering results from our meta-analysis we need to consider the alternative benefit function transfer approach, which in many ways is more theoretically appealing. Here, as before, a set of source site studies are gathered together, but

---

[4] For an introduction to the principles of meta-analysis, see Glass *et al.* (1981) and Wolf (1986). Note that these sources show that the form of analysis found in the benefit valuation literature and in this volume is, strictly speaking, only a partial meta-analysis dictated by the constraint of studies which were not designed with such cross-study analyses in mind (e.g. definitions of variables typically vary between benefit studies). Guidelines for a common standard of design and reporting for future studies to facilitate such meta-analyses are set out in Bateman *et al.* (2002).

[5] In a separate study we present a simple analysis of valuations across differing recreational experiences, noting that the results were logically related to both the substitutability of the environmental resource concerned and the magnitude of the change in provision considered (Bateman *et al.*, 1994).

rather than using summary results, such as mean values, the raw data are used to estimate a general benefit value function. This is then used to estimate values for the target site by holding the estimated coefficients of the function constant and changing the explanatory variable values in line with the characteristics of the target site. So, for example, if the benefit transfer function estimated from source sites included a coefficient linking recreational values to the size of a site, then one of the elements in predicting values for the target site would be to multiply its size by the estimated coefficient in the transfer function. Undertaking this operation for all the explanatory variables in the transfer function provides the overall estimate of values for the target site.

This approach need not be confined solely to the estimation of values, and in Chapter 4 we apply it to the estimation of visitor numbers, showing that the method works quite acceptably in such an application. However, in empirical trials, the function transfer approach does not fare so well in the estimation of values for target sites (Loomis, 1992; Bergland *et al.*, 1995; Downing and Ozuna, 1996; Brouwer and Spaninks, 1999). In a study combining data from a single survey questionnaire applied at source sites in five countries, Brouwer and Bateman (2000) find that the function transfer approach yields higher benefit value estimation errors for target sites than does a simpler, meta-analysis style, unit value transfer. One possible cause of such findings is that benefit value functions differ more substantially between sites than do functions predicting arrival numbers (which the results presented in Chapter 4, as well as ongoing research, suggest are comparatively simple).[6] Value functions may differ in terms of which explanatory variables are pertinent and/or in coefficient estimates for those variables (i.e. what influences benefit values, and how, varies across sites). While these effects may not be that profound when viewed as a whole (making simpler unit benefit value transfers reasonably valid), the function transfer approach may give undue weight to these differences, leading to unreliable value estimates.

Given the above, we adopt a function transfer approach for estimating the number of arrivals to target sites (see Chapter 4), but a simpler meta-analysis transfer approach to the estimation of values. Consideration of the ZTC studies reviewed above (ITC studies being discarded for the reasons given) indicated that these results were not suitable for entry in such a meta-analysis both because of a lack of observations and because our own TC work (see discussion of the Thetford 2 study later in this chapter) suggested that the travel expenditure and travel time cost assumptions used in the Benson and Willis (1992) 'Standard Model' were liable to produce overestimates of benefit values. Given our desire to emphasise defensible lower-bound values, the estimates given in Table 3.1 were not used for further

---

[6] This work has been carried out at a variety of woodland and non-woodland sites (e.g. waterways, beaches, built attractions, etc.) and is funded by the Forestry Commission, British Waterways and others.

analysis.[7] Thus we argue that only the CV studies detailed in Table 3.2 provide a suitable concentration of observations for further cross-study analysis.

A meta-analysis of previous CV studies

Our meta-analysis of previous UK CV studies yielding per person per visit values for woodland recreation follows the approach of Smith and Kaoru (1990), Walsh *et al.* (1992) and Rosenberger and Loomis (2000). Table 3.2 lists seven studies yielding forty-four estimates. To this we have added one compatible value from the Thetford 2 study discussed later in this chapter.[8] While this list represents the largest set of estimates for any UK natural resource, it is still considerably smaller than those used by Smith and Kaoru (77 studies of which 35 were used to yield some 400 estimates) and Walsh *et al.* (120 studies yielding 287 estimates of which 129 were obtained using the CV method) in their meta-analyses of US resources. This underlines the difference in available, comparable studies in the US and UK and reinforces our opinion that the major barrier to successful benefit transfer in the UK is the lack of sufficient, high-quality valuation studies. The analysis we conducted here was therefore intended to be illustrative rather than definitive.

Our database of valuation estimates yielded the following simple explanatory variables:

$$WTP = \text{study mean willingness to pay (£/person/visit)}$$
$$OPTION = 1 \text{ if the study asked WTP for use plus option value; 0 if the study asked WTP for use value alone}$$
$$ELICITAT = \text{elicitation method (categorical variable): } 1 = \text{open-ended; } 2 = \text{iterative bidding; } 3 = \text{payment card; } 4 = \text{dichotomous choice}$$
$$OE = 1 \text{ if open-ended elicitation method; 0 if other elicitation method}$$
$$AUTHOR = \text{authorship (categorical variable)}$$

Following Glass *et al.* (1981) an early concern was to ensure the comparability of studies. A number of reviewed studies were excluded from Table 3.2 due to design, implementation or gross reporting problems (see Bateman, 1996). To some extent, further design effects are incorporated within analysis of the AUTHOR variable, which identified individual study designs. Although a generalised linear model[9] (Aitken *et al.*, 1989) analysis did reveal some differences, these were highly correlated with the OPTION and OE variables and the AUTHOR variable had to

---

[7] Such analysis is given in Bateman (1996) which concludes that these results are upper-bound values for woodland recreation.

[8] This value is obtained from the sample in the Thetford 2 study who faced an entrance fee question not preceded by budget or tax questions. This sample is comparable with the other studies examined in Table 3.2.

[9] The estimated model was specified so as to explicitly permit the use of categorical variables such as AUTHOR within linear regression models with each level of the variable being treated in a manner analogous to the use of individual dummy variables.

be omitted from further analysis. Analysis of unusual design effects was therefore conducted by identifying statistical outliers (as discussed below).

Clearly the variables ELICITAT and OE cannot be included within the same model, as one is derived from the other. Analyses of variance showed that the numbers in categories 2, 3 and 4 of the ELICITAT variable were too small to allow for meaningful individual treatment. However, when these categories were amalgamated to form the OE variable, a significant difference (at the 5 per cent significance level) between results from these and the open-ended studies was observed. Following these preliminary analyses we concluded that the most conservative approach was to investigate a simple model of WTP, relating it to just the OPTION and OE variables.

Estimation of this model identified two statistical outliers, which may indicate the presence of unusual design effects.[10] These observations were excluded and the final model was:

$$\text{WTP} = 1.3525 - 0.7571 \text{ OE} + 0.3120 \text{ OPTION} \qquad (3.1)$$
$$(14.04) \quad (-7.28) \qquad (5.02)$$
$$R^2 = 61.1\% \quad R^2(\text{adj.}) = 59.2\% \quad n = 43$$

Figures in brackets are *t*-statistics

A number of interesting observations arise from Equation (3.1). The overall fit of the model is good (given that we are dealing with socio-economic data) with about 60 per cent of total variation explained. However, the strongest explanatory variable is the constant, a finding which may reflect a common perception among respondents regarding an appropriate response to a per visit WTP question. Responses may be reflecting a mixture of respondents' notions of a socially fair level of WTP and prior experience of payments for comparable goods (entrance fees, car parking fees, etc.). Such motivations move bids away from the underlying value they are intended to measure. In effect, such measures may be more akin to prices than values.

The sign and significance of both of the explanatory variables is as anticipated. Relative to other approaches the use of an OE elicitation technique results in lower-bound WTP sums, while asking respondents to assess both their use and option value produces higher bids than when use values alone are considered. By combining these two factors we can use the coefficients of Equation (3.1) to predict cross-study estimates for the four types of per person per visit values shown in Table 3.3. Furthermore, by referring to information regarding the number of persons in an average visitor party we can infer the various per party per visit values also shown

---

[10] The Bishop (1992) OE use + option value for Whippendell Wood and the Hanley (1989) OE use value for Aberfoyle. For further details, see Bateman (1996).

Table 3.3. *Woodland recreation values from a cross-study analysis of CV estimates*

	Per person per visit values (£, 1990)		Per party per visit values[1] (£, 1990)	
Value type	OE elicitation method	Other elicitation method	OE elicitation method	Other elicitation method
Use value	0.60	1.35	1.82	4.12
Use + option value	0.91	1.66	2.78	5.06

Note: [1] Assuming a mean party size (from Thetford 2 study) of 3.05 persons per party.

in the table (sensitivity analysis on these estimates is given in the summary at the end of this chapter).

Conclusions

Our review of UK monetary evaluations of woodland recreation suggests that, while the literature is developing fast, the body of consistent, high-quality papers necessary for advanced benefit transfer does not exist to date (although it is arguable whether this is even true of the more advanced US literature). Consequently we have conducted a fairly simple cross-study meta-analysis concentrating on results from just one valuation method, the CV approach. While this is sufficient to demonstrate our wider methodology, it does mean that the results should be treated with some caution. We attempt to remedy this in the following sections, which examine a number of methodological and theoretical issues across both chosen valuation methods, as well as providing further benefit estimates for the wider study.

The first Thetford CV/TC study

Our initial woodland recreation study was conducted in Thetford Forest, East Anglia (providing the user sample) and the city of Norwich (about twenty-five miles distant; providing the non-user sample) in the summer of 1990 (hereafter referred to as the Thetford 1 study). The research consisted of both CV and TC analyses. The CV study involved a split-sample design examining payment vehicle and elicitation effects across both users and non-users, while the TC study (which used the ITC variant) concentrated on visit cost assumptions and the impacts of varying functional form. On account of space constraints, only principal results are presented here, with full details being given in Bateman (1996).

The Thetford 1 CV study: elicitation, payment vehicle and user versus non-user effects

The CV study asked respondents for their WTP for the recreational services and facilities available at Lynford Stag, a major woodland recreation site within Thetford Forest. In total seven subsamples were gathered. These can be divided into two groups:

 (i) whether respondents were users or non-users
 (ii) whether an annual tax or per visit payment vehicle was used.

In all the annual tax payment (but not entrance fee) treatments it was decided to inform respondents, prior to any WTP question, of the current average level of annual per household payments to support the Forestry Commission, which was estimated at approximately £2.60 per annum.[11] This approach followed contemporary practice in UK CV studies, particularly as pioneered in the work of Turner and Brooke (1988), a study which had recently been approved (as part of a wider CBA) by H.M. Treasury. However, subsequent studies, such as that reported by Baron and Maxwell (1996), indicate that cost information provided to CV respondents may be construed as indicating the value of the good in question (see subsequent results regarding payment card effects and the discussion of starting point bias in Chapter 2). This suggests that in the Thetford 1 study, cost information may have anchored WTP responses towards this sum. Consequently we must treat the absolute level of WTP results from this experiment with some caution although relative differences remain of interest (the subsequent study in Wantage abandoned this approach and so provides some evidence of the magnitude of the anchoring effect). Table 3.4 details WTP results across the three annual tax format samples.

Per annum WTP responses were elicited using an OE question while per visit responses were obtained using a payment card. While this precludes strict comparability across samples (study resource constraints meant that further subsamples could not be gathered at that time), such an approach was chosen to facilitate further testing of design effects as follows:

 (i) For the tax format, while both users and non-users were presented with a general tax payment vehicle, a further subsample of non-users was presented with a community charge (poll tax) vehicle. At the time of the study the imposition of a poll tax was the major political issue of the day and this vehicle was deliberately chosen to examine the potential magnitude of payment vehicle effects. Non-users were identified as the group who might have the most ill-defined preferences and so provide the most extreme responses to such effects.

---

[11] Based upon Forestry Commission (1985a).

Table 3.4. *Summary WTP responses for the Thetford 1 CV study*

Payment period	Payment vehicle	Sample	Elicitation method[1]	Mean WTP (£)	95% C.I. (£)	Median (£)
Per annum	General tax	Users	OE	5.14	1.48–8.81	2.00
Per annum	General tax	Non-users	OE	3.51	1.13–5.88	0.70
Per annum	Poll tax	Non-users	OE	7.09	2.68–11.50	0.00
Per visit	Entrance fee	Users	PCL	1.21	0.99–1.43	1.00
Per visit	Entrance fee	Users	PCH	1.55	1.19–1.92	1.25
Per visit	Entrance fee	Non-users	PCL	1.45	1.15–1.75	1.25
Per visit	Entrance fee	Non-users	PCH	2.37	1.98–2.76	2.00

Note: [1] OE = open-ended; PCL = payment card (low range); PCH = payment card (high range).

(ii) For the per visit format two payment cards were used, the first showing a payment range from £0 to £3 in increments of 50p and the second ranging from £2 to £5 using the same increments. Both cards also explicitly stated that respondents were free to select any other amount.

All samples were collected using face-to-face interviewing of randomly selected respondents.[12] Sample size was fifty for most subsamples falling to a minimum of forty-six. While not large, the continuous nature of the valuation responses meant that these samples were generally sufficient to perform rudimentary statistical and validity analyses. Summary WTP statistics are reported in Table 3.4.

Because of the differences in elicitation method (and the use of existing payment information in the per annum questions) we cannot meaningfully compare per annum with per visit results and must confine ourselves to comparisons within these subgroups. Considering the per annum results we can see that, as expected, when all other factors are held constant (i.e. when a general tax vehicle is used), both mean and median WTP is higher for users than for non-users (although the high response variability typical of OE studies combined with relatively small sample size means that these differences are not statistically significant in this case). Analysis shows that, although all non-user samples are socio-economically similar, the user group enjoys significantly higher income levels, a finding which somewhat complicates the interpretation of this result. However, comparison of these findings with results obtained using the poll tax vehicle shows that the latter has a clear and strong effect on univariate WTP measures. The first point to note is that while refusal to pay rates are similar across the two general tax subgroups (both about 15 per cent), just over 50 per cent of those faced with a poll tax vehicle refuse to pay. Just as interesting are

[12] The authors wish to thank Joanne Wall (formerly of the University of East Anglia) for managing the survey.

the findings that, despite this, the poll tax sample recorded the highest mean WTP amount. In effect, while most respondents reject the use of poll tax as a suitable vehicle for funding the public good under evaluation, a minority are strongly in favour of such an approach and state comparatively large WTP sums, resulting in a relatively high mean.

Consideration of the per visit values detailed in Table 3.4 shows that for both user and non-user samples the higher-range payment card results in higher mean and median WTP sums (although these differences are not statistically significant in the present samples). Both the non-user samples record higher WTP sums than their user group counterparts. One plausible explanation of this finding is that non-users see the use of entrance fees as a method of moving funding costs away from themselves and onto users; we therefore have to discount the validity of such responses as indicators of underlying values.

A number of socio-economic variables were collected in all surveys so as to facilitate regression analysis of underlying bid functions (full results are reported in Bateman, 1996).[13] These functions[14] suggested that a consistent set of factors underpinned valuation responses across formats, with higher WTP values being associated with higher incomes,[15] clear knowledge of, or living near, the area under evaluation. For those facing per annum questions, WTP was positively associated with the number of visits made to Thetford annually, while for those facing per visit questions, regular visitors stated relatively lower amounts. However, for this latter group, when the number of annual visits is considered, this equated to a higher than average total WTP. These findings conform to prior expectations. However, it was noticed that bid functions for all the per visit subsamples were dominated by a highly significant intercept term, suggesting that responses were subject to some prior notion of a 'correct' (or 'social norm') answer, most probably influenced by experience of entrance fees at comparable attractions (for example, car parking fees at National Trust sites). While this again conforms to prior expectations, it undermines the validity of these particular answers as a source of valid valuations.

In conclusion, while the CV exercise carried out as part of the Thetford 1 study produces a number of results which conform to prior expectations, its major findings highlight the potential impact of design effects, so providing valuable pointers

[13] In the case of the on-site interviews with forest users, variables collected included: home address; sex; age; employment; whether the interviewee was a pensioner; income; precise interview location; preference for natural or urban recreation; history and frequency of visits to the specific site and forest entirety; time spent on site; and use-value WTP. Similar variables were elicited from the non-user samples with the addition of questions regarding respondents' knowledge of the forest and integral visitor sites.

[14] In each case a log (dependent) functional form satisfied an n-scores normal distribution test. All functions fitted the data to an acceptable degree, with R^2 values ranging from 0.15 to 0.50.

[15] This relationship was proxied in some cases by a negative association between reported WTP and the respondent being a pensioner.

towards improved study design. In particular, the highly significant impact of changing the payment vehicle indicates that considerable care is needed if future studies are to elicit usable estimates of recreation value (rather than estimates of how respondents perceived the payment vehicles themselves). Furthermore, results from the entrance fee experiment suggest that payment cards have the potential to impact upon stated values. The possibility of entrance fees themselves causing respondents to resort to simple heuristics rather than to preferences in determining values also arose but could not be adequately assessed and so was made an objective of subsequent work.

We now turn to consider the ITC analysis carried out as part of the Thetford 1 study.

The Thetford 1 TC study: functional form effects

Responses from the 129 parties of visitors (comprising almost 400 individuals) interviewed at Thetford Forest were used to undertake an ITC study of recreational values. In addition to the variables discussed previously, data regarding the distance, cost and duration of visits, substitutes and further socio-economic variables which might explain visits were collected. OLS estimation techniques were employed (a comparison with maximum likelihood techniques was conducted as part of the Thetford 2 study described subsequently) and initial analysis considered the correct specification of the dependent variable for our trip generation function (TGF). A series of correlation and regression tests confirmed that a log dependent variable was clearly superior. This decision was not so clear-cut when specification of the cost variable was considered. Following the discussion in Chapter 2, three definitions of travel expenditure cost (marginal (petrol only); petrol plus insurance; full running costs) and three definitions of travel time cost (zero (respondents enjoy travelling); the Department of Transport (DoT) wage rate; full wage rate) were investigated. All linear and logarithmic permutations of these costs were considered in defining total travel costs, and statistical tests indicated that a cost function using the full running cost estimate of travel expenditures and a zero travel time cost assumption provided the most significant travel cost variable. A considerable advantage of using a cost function which is not (via time costs) linked to wage rates is that the visitor's income may be entered as a separate explanatory variable without inducing collinearity problems.

Further explanatory variables were investigated through stepwise regression analysis of the full range of socio-economic variables collected in the survey. Of these, only the respondents' household income proved significant. This finding again echoes the results of earlier UK TC studies (Willis and Benson, 1988, 1989) which report TGFs relating visits to cost and some indicator of socio-economic status.

Table 3.5. *Thetford 1 TC study: consumer surplus estimates for three functional forms*

Functional form	R^2 adj. (%)	Travel cost coefficient. (*t*-ratio)	CS per party per visit (£, 1990)	CS per person per visit (£, 1990)		
				1 child = 1 adult	1 child = 0.5 adult	children omitted
Double-log	44.2	−0.9422 (−8.41)	3.37	1.07	1.19	1.34
Semi-log (dep.)	39.9	−0.0009490 (−7.42)	7.40	2.40	2.67	3.00
Linear	21.0	−0.026719 (−3.96)	27.42	8.88	9.87	11.10

The impact of changing the functional form was investigated[16] and Table 3.5 reports summary findings and consumer surplus estimates per party visit and per individual visit. The latter results are subdivided to consider different treatments of child visitors.

Inspection of Table 3.5 shows the double-log functional form gives the best fit to the data[17] and resultant valuation estimates accord well with prior expectations. Clearly misspecification of functional form leads to substantial error in consumer surplus estimates (e.g. adopting a linear form very substantially overestimates recreation values). The final four columns of Table 3.5 consider the issue of whether to report per party or per person values. These are highly responsive to the treatment of children within the sample. Our proposed solution, which we adopt in subsequent work, is to concentrate upon the party as the basic unit of valuation, thereby avoiding subjective decisions regarding individual level values.

In conclusion, this study was generally satisfactory and provided useful guidelines for our future TC studies. At first glance it also generated a defensible valuation of woodland recreation benefits. However, during the course of this analysis we became increasingly conscious of the theoretical problems associated with applying OLS estimation techniques to ITC data and therefore made an analysis of potential estimation effects a feature of our subsequent TC work, reported in the Thetford 2 study.

---

[16] These are all parametric functional forms and so impose corresponding assumptions upon our analysis. Cooper (2000) considers non-parametric and semi-parametric approaches to TC analysis.

[17] This function yields higher explanatory power than both those reported in the Willis and Garrod (1991b) ITC studies of UK woodland recreation and higher than all but two of the twenty-two comparable OLS estimated functions reported by Smith and Desvousges (1986) in their ITC studies of water-based recreation in the United States.

The Wantage CV study: households' WTP and farmers' WTA compensation for a community woodland

This project consisted of two CV surveys examining issues related to the provision of open-access, recreational woodlands on land currently used for farming.[18] Two specific aims were to determine:

 (i) the willingness of the local community to pay for the provision of such a woodland
(ii) the willingness of local farmers on whose land the proposed woodland could feasibly be located to accept compensation.

The study was motivated by the introduction of the Forestry Commission's (FC) Community Woodland Scheme (CWS), a policy intended to promote open-access woodlands 'within 5 miles of the edge of a town or city and in [areas] where the opportunities for woodland recreation are limited' (Forestry Commission, 1991). Results from the research permitted cost-benefit assessment of the CWS. The study examined valuations of a proposed (hypothetical) community woodland scheme near Wantage, Oxfordshire. Full details of this study are presented in Bateman *et al.* (1996b).

Household WTP survey

Study design

Benefits from the proposed community woodland were assessed through a face-to-face CV survey of 325 randomly selected households in and around Wantage. A number of questions were designed to elicit information which might explain differences in valuations, although the main focus of the survey concerned WTP issues. The survey interview opened with a 'constant information statement' which informed households about the size (100 acres) and facilities (recreational walks and car parking) of the proposed wood and its open-access nature. Respondents were then asked whether or not they would be prepared to pay towards provision of the wood. Such a 'payment principle' question was included mainly as a way of validating zero bids as it was felt that directly presenting respondents with a WTP question might intimidate those who held zero values (Harris *et al.*, 1989). Respondents who answered 'no' to this question were asked to state their reasons for such a response whilst those who answered positively were asked the WTP questions.

Two WTP questions were used in the study. First, respondents were asked how much they were WTP per household per annum in extra taxes (referred to subsequently as the 'per annum question'). Second, respondents were asked how much

---

[18] Further details regarding this study are given in Bateman *et al.* (1996b).

Table 3.6. *Summary WTP results: per annum (WTPpa) and*
per visit (WTPfee) formats

Format	n	Mean (£)	95% C.I.[1]	Truncated mean[2](£)	Median (£)	Lower quartile (£)	Upper quartile (£)
WTPpa	325	9.94	8.92–11.14	8.85	10.00	2.00	15.00
WTPfee	325	0.82	0.75–0.89	0.68	0.75	0.05	1.00

Notes: [1] Bootstrapped confidence intervals calculated by the BCa percentile method (Efron and Tibshirani, 1993). See text for definition.
[2] Omits potential warm-glow bids. See text for definition.
All values in 1991 prices.
Minimum bid is zero for both formats (included in calculation of mean, median, etc.).

they would be WTP per adult per visit as a car parking fee (referred to subsequently as the 'per visit question'). Therefore all respondents who were WTP some amount were presented with, in turn, both the per annum and per visit format questions.[19] In all cases an OE elicitation format was used in line with our previous findings (and a desire to produce defensible, lower-bound values) and the entire design was successfully tested using a pilot sample of thirty respondents.

WTP results

Considering first the payment principle question, just under 25 per cent of respondents stated that they were unwilling in principle to pay for the proposed recreational woodland. This rate is very similar to that obtained for almost identical services in the Thetford 2 study discussed subsequently, and somewhat higher than that recorded for larger, high-profile environmental resources such as National Parks (Willis and Garrod, 1993; Bateman *et al.*, 1994). When asked, well over three-quarters of those refusing the payment principle cited income or related economic constraints as the main factor underlying their answers and none said that they were objecting to the principle of valuation *per se*. Such responses give us no cause for rejecting the application of CV techniques to this issue.

Table 3.6 gives summary WTP statistics for responses to the two formats used in this study. To guard against the potential non-normality of the response distributions we report bootstrapped 95 per cent confidence intervals, calculated via the BCa percentile method (Efron and Tibshirani, 1993) using 999 simulations. This method is based on a refined normal approximation which corrects for bias and skewness in the distribution of mean WTP and is hence an improvement over the basic

[19] Ideally we would want to either use separate samples for each format or vary the order in which questions are presented so that any ordering or anchoring effects might be assessed. Such an analysis is undertaken as part of our second Thetford CV study, reported subsequently.

non-parametric bootstrap. This is of importance with the samples of WTP values considered, which are skewed and truncated at zero.

A within-format comparison with over thirty on-site (user) CV studies of a variety of outdoor recreation resources (ranging across woodlands, wetlands, National Parks, etc.) using per annum WTP measures (Bateman *et al.*, 1994) showed that estimates obtained from the Wantage survey were logically related to the characteristics, substitutability, uniqueness and provision-change factors inherent in the contingent market presented to respondents. Given this result it is interesting to note that the Wantage WTP per annum (WTPpa) measure lies considerably above that estimated for the Thetford 1 samples, suggesting that the inclusion of information on average annual tax support for the Forestry Commission (£2.60) in the latter study had downwardly biased WTP bids. Similarly, while the Wantage WTP per visit (WTPfee) amount falls within one standard deviation of the mean of all other comparable UK studies (as reviewed at the start of this chapter), it lies well below the per visit measures recorded in the Thetford 1 study (Table 3.4), indicating that the latter were upwardly biased by the use of payment cards. On both these counts therefore, results from the Wantage study appear more valid and generally applicable than those from the Thetford 1 study.

The Wantage WTP responses were investigated for evidence of a number of the biases identified in Chapter 2 including warm-glow bids, free-riding and strategic overbidding (see Bateman *et al.*, 1996b, for details). No conclusive evidence of free-riding or strategic overbidding was found; however, limited indications of warm-glow effects were detected. Warm-glow giving (Kahneman and Knetsch, 1992) occurs where respondents purchase moral satisfaction rather than the good on offer in the contingent market (i.e. they see the CV market as a donation to a good cause and offer some, typically small, amount which is not related to the specific characteristics of the good and therefore contravenes the assumptions of the CV method). In order to investigate the sensitivity of welfare measures to such a bias the distributions of bids under both formats were examined for evidence of any appropriate amounts which respondents might choose to give under warm-glow bidding. For the annual format, a strong assumption was made that the relevant bid threshold was £5 per annum whilst for the per visit question, a threshold of £0.50 was assumed. Mean WTP was then recalculated by setting all bids up to and including these thresholds to zero to yield the truncated means listed in Table 3.6. Inspection of these truncated means indicates that, for both formats, even under such strong assumptions, warm-glow bidding makes relatively little difference to the estimated mean, which declines 11 per cent for the annual payment format and 17 per cent for the per visit format (medians remain constant throughout). We would suggest that such assumptions are too strong as they omit some genuine, low-value bids. We conclude then that although warm-glow bidding may be a feature of this

Table 3.7. *Stepwise regression of lnWTPpa on significant predictors*

Step	1	2	3	4	5	6
Constant	−5.397	−5.335	−5.096	−4.418	−4.214	−4.374
lnINCOME	0.755	0.726	0.683	0.683	0.647	0.630
	(9.79)	(9.56)	(9.06)	(9.16)	(8.54)	(8.33)
lnRURVIS		0.165	0.160	0.140	0.156	0.131
		(3.78)	(3.74)	(3.25)	(3.61)	(2.98)
lnPKVIS			0.246	0.227	0.239	0.235
			(3.69)	(3.43)	(3.62)	(3.59)
PREFTOWN				−0.590	−0.560	−0.520
				(−2.90)	(−2.75)	(−2.58)
AGE17–25					0.167	0.173
					(2.32)	(2.42)
lnVISWOOD						0.140
						(2.34)
R^2	0.288	0.261	0.292	0.310	0.321	0.333

lnWTPpa = natural logarithm of household's annual WTP (£)
lnINCOME = natural logarithm of household's gross annual income. Income was recorded on an eight-point scale (see Bateman *et al.*, 1996b, for details).
lnRURVIS = natural logarithm of number of visits made by household to rural sites per annum
lnPKVIS = natural logarithm of number of visits made to parks
PREFTOWN = 1 if prefers town-based recreation; = 0 otherwise
AGE17–25 = number of persons in household aged 17–25 years
lnVISWOOD = natural logarithm of household's predicted visits to proposed wood per annum
Figures in brackets are *t*-statistics.

and other CV surveys, with regard to this study the impact of any such tendency is not severe.

Validation: bid curve analysis

Responses to both WTP formats were subjected to theoretical validity testing via bid curve analysis. For the WTPpa bids, analysis showed that a log-linear functional form provided the best fit to the data. Table 3.7 reports results from a forward-entry stepwise regression analysis relating the log-linear dependent variable, lnWTPpa, to significant explanatory variables. These models provide a good degree of explanation (easily satisfying the fit criteria discussed in Chapter 2) with bids being linked in the expected manner to a number of explanatory variables. In essence the models show that higher WTP bids were associated with richer households, containing young people, which enjoyed outdoor rather than urban-based recreation. Tests for multicollinearity suggested that the variables lnRURVIS and lnVISWOOD should probably not be included in the same model and so we identify the model given at step 5 of Table 3.7 as providing the best explanation of per annum WTP responses.

Unlike the per annum bids, analysis of responses to the per visit WTP question showed them to be much less firmly linked to standard explanatory variables. While a log-linear dependent variable provided the best fit of the data, the resulting bid curve model, detailed in Equation (3.2), achieved only a low degree of overall explanatory power ($R^2 = 5\%$) and failed to satisfy the fit criteria discussed previously.

$$\text{lnWTPfee} = 0.595 - 0.135 \text{ PENSION} - 0.00175 \text{ VISWOOD} \qquad (3.2)$$
$$(25.33) \quad (-3.94) \qquad\qquad (-2.26)$$

where:

    lnWTPfee = natural logarithm of stated WTP per visit
    PENSION = number in household aged 65 years or over
    VISWOOD = predicted number of household visits to the proposed wood
                per annum
  Figures in brackets are *t*-statistics.

Comparison of Equation (3.2) with those obtained from the Thetford 1 per visit format (detailed in Bateman, 1996) showed that all were dominated by the intercept term. This observation, we suggest, may be reflecting the 'social norm' concept discussed with respect to our cross-study analysis of the UK CV literature.

Aggregation

The procedure used to calculate aggregate WTP varied according to the question format used. The per annum format question elicited a mean WTP (including those who refused to pay as zeros) of £9.94 per household. At the time of the study the town of Wantage had an adult population of about 11,500. Therefore, even if we take an extreme upper-bound estimate on household size (so as to derive a lower-bound estimate on household WTP) of 2.57 (Central Statistical Office, 1991)[20] this would give an estimate of some 4,473 households in Wantage which would, in turn, imply an aggregate WTP of £44,450 per annum for the woodland.

For the per visit measure we elicited a WTP of £0.82 per adult visit (again including those who refused to pay as zeros). The mean estimated number of visits (including those who would not visit) was just under fifteen per annum, implying a total annual entrance fee expenditure of £12.29 per adult. Grossing up across all adults[21] implies a total annual willingness to pay entrance fees of £141,252.

---

[20] This figure refers to average UK total household size (including adults and children) rather than the average number of adults per household. If the latter were used this would increase our estimate of household WTP, i.e. we have employed a conservative, lower-bound assumption.

[21] Note that we have already accounted for non-visitors in the annual per adult visit rate.

Table 3.8. *Farm characteristics and farmers' willingness to accept compensation for transferring from present output to woodland*

Farm	Land use	Tenure	Profit/acre (£)	WTA/acre (£)	Allocation (acres)	Reason for non-allocation
1	Mainly arable	Owned	100	250	0	Land should be used to produce food
2	Mainly arable	Owned	—	20,000	0	Does not like government policy
3	Mainly arable	Owned	125	300	0	Does not want public access to the farm
4	Arable	Owned	30	200	5	—
5	Arable	Owned	105	250	30	—
6	Arable	Owned	45	150	2	—
7	Mainly arable	Owned	130	—	0	Does not want public access to the farm
8	Arable	Owned	—	—	0	Land not suitable to grow trees upon
9	Dairy	Rented	85	—	0	Does not want public access to the farm
10	Arable	Owned	116	300	0	Farm too small for the scheme
11	Mainly arable	Owned	100	—	0	Does not want public access to the farm
12	Mainly arable	Owned	186	100	125	—
13	Mainly arable	Owned	186	200	100	—
14	Mainly arable	Owned	163	250	20	—
15	Mainly arable	Rented	150	250	0	Does not want public access to the farm
16	Arable	Owned	280	600	3	—
17	Arable	Owned	145	150	0	Farm too small for scheme
18	Mainly arable	Owned	140	—	0	Farmer too old to undertake long-term project
19	Set-aside	Owned	—	250	0	Unwilling to undertake alternative to set-aside
Mean[1]	—	—	130	250	15	—

Note: [1] Excludes Farm 2.

However, we are sceptical that respondents would actually visit as often as stated (stated visitation rates considerably exceed the actual rates which we have observed at other woodland sites; see Bateman, *et al.*, 1999c and Chapter 4) and so regard this as an overestimate of the likely annual value of such a site. Further comment on these findings is given in our conclusions to this study.

Farmers' WTA survey

Design

Farmers around Wantage were interviewed in order to obtain information concerning likely participation in the Community Woodland Scheme (CWS) and associated compensation requirements. Data on a variety of factors which might determine WTA levels were collected. Table 3.8 lists several of these factors, together with stated WTA sums and the amount of land farmers were willing to allocate to the CWS, for the nineteen survey participants.

WTA results

Twelve farmers (63 per cent) initially stated that they were unwilling to allocate land for public access recreational woodland.[22] Amongst these the most commonly stated reason for refusal was that the farmer did not want to allow public access to the farm (five farms, or 42 per cent of those refusing to enter the scheme). Such concerns may be well founded, as repeated public use of footpaths within a wood may lead to their classification as public rights of way. Furthermore, subsequent interviews with senior Forestry Commission staff revealed that land-owners would not be granted felling licences unless equivalent areas of replanting were agreed.[23] In other words, the decision to allocate a certain area of agricultural land to recreational forestry may, in practice, be difficult to reverse. Such irreversibility may, perversely, prove to be a considerable block to the extension of farm-forestry although the small sample size precludes any firm conclusion being drawn.

Seven farmers (37 per cent) were initially willing to allocate land to the recreational woodland scheme, the mean allocation being just over 40 acres per participating farm. Uptake among participating farms appeared to be bimodally distributed, with two farms willing to allocate 100 acres or more to woodland and the remainder only willing to undertake small-scale afforestation projects. Whilst grant aid is available for small-scale schemes, if the objective is to provide a viable, discrete recreational area then such small pockets (unless they can be combined) may not be suitable. Nevertheless the willingness to undertake large-scale planting

---

[22] This general unwillingness to participate in such schemes is also reported in a similar study in France by Noel *et al.* (2000).

[23] Interview with Chief Forester, Santon Downham, Thetford Forest. See also Chapter 5, this volume.

by two farmers is encouraging, particularly where the objective (as under the CWS) is simply to ensure that the local community has access to a nearby woodland recreation site.

The majority of interviewees (fourteen farms; 74 per cent) stated a sum which they would be willing to accept in annual compensation for allocating land out of agriculture and into public access woodland (WTApa). This included seven (58 per cent) of the farmers who initially rejected the principle of such allocation. This latter result seems to indicate that, if the price was right, such farms would consider a move out of conventional agriculture. However, there was one very noticeable 'protest bid'[24] amongst this subsample which, at £20,000/acre, was not only more than 150 standard deviations above the mean of the remaining sample and more than thirty times larger than the next highest bid, but also of approximately equal magnitude to the entire annual net farm income. It is possible that this respondent had in mind a discounted total net present value sum for the entirety of the project, in which case such a response would be reasonable. However, given that no other respondent gave an answer within the same order of magnitude, we feel that such an explanation is unlikely and a protest strategy seems much more probable.

Excluding this one outlier, the mean stated WTApa was £250/acre. Almost all farms required higher annual subsidy compensation rates than they currently achieved under agriculture. This seems reasonable given that woodland is an unknown quantity to most farmers, who consequently require a risk premium compared to standard activities.

Validation: bid curve analysis

Analysis of responses showed that stated compensation levels were strongly related to both existing profit levels and the overall size of the farm. No further significant explanatory variables were identified and the best-fitting regression model for WTApa is:[25]

$$\text{WTApa} = 94.04 + 1.48 \, \text{PROFIT} - 1.93 \, \text{ACRES} \qquad (3.3)$$
$$(1.81) \quad (4.04) \qquad\qquad (-3.37)$$

where:

PROFIT = Farmers' required compensation (£/acre) for
entering the woodland scheme
PROFIT = Level of profit under existing agriculture (£/acre)
ACRES = Area in acres which the farm is prepared to allocate
into the woodland scheme

Figures in brackets are *t*-statistics.

---

[24] The authors dislike the general application of this term to anyone who does not give an expected answer to a bidding (WTP or WTA) question. However, this particular respondent seemed to satisfy all relevant requirements of an archetypal 'protester'.

[25] The previously identified outlier was excluded from this analysis.

The model presented in Equation (3.3) fits the data well (although sample size is clearly a problem), satisfying fit criteria ($R^2 = 70\%$) and indicating logical relationships between the dependent and explanatory variables. Farmers with higher profit levels from existing activities demanded higher levels of compensation for entering the woodland scheme. Furthermore, those who were only willing to consider small-scale planting required higher per acre payments. This implies, logically, that large-scale plantations, which presumably will benefit from economies of scale, are considered viable alternatives at relatively lower per acre subsidy rates than small-scale woodlands.

Aggregation

To allow comparability with our household WTP survey, aggregate farm WTA needed to be calculated for a similar 100 acre site. Using the mean stated WTApa of £250/acre produced a total compensation requirement for such a woodland of £25,000 per annum.

Comparison of household WTP and farm WTA measures

Both measures of aggregate household WTP exceeded our estimate of aggregate farm WTA to a considerable degree. In the case of the annual format we have a simple[26] benefit/cost ratio of 1.78 whilst the entrance fee format yields a ratio of 5.65. Such results point strongly in favour of the establishment of Community Woodland Schemes. However, we prefer to retain a cautious approach to the WTP sums. Another way of examining these is to consider the minimum number of payments needed to meet the required aggregate compensation level. Using the per annum format and our estimated household size implies that some 2,515 households (i.e. 56 per cent of all those in Wantage) would need to pay the £9.94 mean WTPpa for the scheme to break even. Alternatively, all the households in Wantage would have to pay £5.59 per annum for the scheme to again break even.[27] Using the per visit mean WTP of £0.82 implies that 30,487 individual visits per annum would be required to pay for the forest, i.e. each individual in Wantage would need to make 2.65 paying visits per annum for the site to break even.

The Wantage study: conclusions

The Wantage study provides a number of findings which are of use to our overall research objectives. First, it gives a number of recreation benefit estimates which, compared to our earlier Thetford 1 study, appear relatively unbiased. Second, the

---

[26] The term 'simple' refers here to the fact that this study represents only a partial cost-benefit analysis of such a scheme.

[27] Note that this is considerably less than the mean WTP excluding suspected strategic overbidders detailed in Table 3.6.

WTA experiment suggests that, given appropriate compensation, sufficient farmers are prepared to countenance entry into the CWS to make the scheme viable. The strong bid function estimated from WTA responses implies that familiarity with the concept of compensation makes farmers adept at determining appropriate threshold compensation levels, these levels being linked to current profitability and postulated involvement with the scheme. Third, aggregate benefit sums considerably exceed estimates of farmers' compensation requirements suggesting that the implementation of such projects could result in the creation of substantial net public benefits. The magnitude of the implicit benefit-cost ratio is also sufficient to overcome any residual concerns regarding the precise value of estimated welfare measures.

The second Thetford CV/TC study

This study consisted of a joint CV/TC on-site survey of recreational visitors to Lynford Stag, the site previously used in the Thetford 1 study. The overarching objective was to examine how responsive benefit estimates were to changes in study design and analytic methods. We will discuss the CV study first (further details can be found in Bateman and Langford, 1997a).

The Thetford 2 CV study: budget constraint and question-order effects

The CV study used a split-sample design to address two principal issues arising from the literature review presented in Chapter 2:

(i) the impact of explicitly asking respondents to consider their budget constraints prior to stating WTP
(ii) question-ordering effects.

In addition to these effects, payment vehicle impacts were again investigated through use of both per annum taxes and per visit entrance fees.

Study design

The study objective required a split-sample design in which respondents were divided into two groups, each of which was further divided into two subgroups as follows:

Group B: Prior to any WTP question, respondents were asked to calculate and state their annual recreational budget.
Group NB: No budget question was asked prior to any WTP response.
Subgroup 1: WTP per annum (tax payment vehicle) was asked prior to WTP per visit (entrance fee payment vehicle) question.
Subgroup 2: WTP per visit (fee) was asked prior to WTP per annum (tax) question.

The above design gave us four subsamples (B1, B2, NB1 and NB2), each of which provided both per annum (tax) and per visit (fee) WTP responses for which we defined a series of testable hypotheses concerning the effects under investigation. Testing used various approaches. Simple comparisons of means and standard (normal) confidence intervals were undertaken. However, while of interest, such statistics are potentially biased by necessary distributional assumptions. To combat this, non-parametric confidence intervals for mean WTP were calculated via the BCa percentile bootstrap method (Efron and Tibshirani, 1993) as discussed previously.

In line with preceding studies an OE elicitation format was used throughout. In addition to the valuation responses the survey also elicited information regarding relevant visit, socio-economic and interview condition variables necessary for subsequent validity analyses. The questionnaire was tested with a pilot survey of thirty-two respondents. This resulted in marginal changes to the questionnaire which was then applied to the main survey from which a sample of 351 respondents was collected.

WTP results

As in previous designs, prior to the budget and WTP questions, respondents were asked a 'payment principle' question enquiring whether or not they were willing to pay anything at all. Some 96 respondents (27.6 per cent of all respondents;[28] a rate in line with previous results)[29] stated that they were not prepared to pay at least some amount for the recreational facilities provided at the site, leaving 255 respondents to answer the budget and WTP questions. To prevent overstating sample WTP (and avoid problems caused by somewhat uneven numbers in each subsample accepting the payment principle), in later calculations these refusals were allocated evenly between the four subsamples and treated as zeros.[30]

Those who agreed to the payment principle were (unbeknown to themselves) then randomly allocated to one of the four groups defined above and asked the relevant WTP questions, results from which are described below.

WTP per annum (tax) responses

Table 3.9 presents mean WTP per annum (via taxes) for each of our four subsamples. For notational simplicity we can refer to the subsamples described in the upper row as $NB1_a$ and $NB2_a$ (left- and right-hand cells respectively; subscript a indicates per annum (tax) response) and those on the lower row as $B1_a$ and $B2_a$. Below each mean (in rounded brackets) we report 95 per cent confidence intervals calculated

---

[28] Reasons for refusing to pay were mainly related to economic factors and are analysed further in Bateman and Langford (1997a). At most only 2 per cent of the sample gave refusal reasons which can be interpreted as in some way protesting against the valuation process.

[29] See, for example, Bateman *et al.* (1995a).

[30] The inclusion of such zeros reinforces the need to conduct non-parametric testing.

Table 3.9. *Mean WTP (tax) per annum and 95 per
cent confidence intervals for each subsample
(including payment principle refusals as zeros)*

	Payment ordering scenario	
Budget question	1 (tax then fee) (£)	2 (fee then tax) (£)
NB (not asked)	12.55 (8.94–18.47) [8.11–16.99]	7.62 (4.36–15.77) [2.87–12.37]
B (asked)	32.60 (23.18–45.89) [21.76–43.43]	16.37 (11.78–22.12) [11.19–21.55]

Note: Figures in round brackets are 95% C.I.s calculated by
the BCa percentile method, as discussed previously, while
figures in square brackets are conventional 95% C.I.s.

via the BCa percentile bootstrap method, while below these (in square brackets) we report standard normal 95 per cent confidence intervals for comparison.

Table 3.9 indicates that the inclusion or exclusion of the recreational budget question, and/or changes in the ordering of payment vehicle presentation, results in apparently consistent and major impacts upon stated WTP. For ordering scenario 1 (tax then fee), the inclusion of the budget question (i.e. moving from cell $NB1_a$ to cell $B1_a$) raised mean annual WTP (tax) by a factor of 2.60, while for ordering scenario 2 (fee then tax) inclusion of the budget question (i.e. moving from cell $NB2_a$ to cell $B2_a$) raised mean annual WTP (tax) by a factor of 2.15. However, examination of BCa confidence intervals shows that only the first of these differences is clearly significant (i.e. the 95 per cent BCa confidence intervals do not overlap).

Considering the impact of changing the order of payment questions upon per annum responses, in those subsamples not given the prior budget question, asking for per visit WTP before the per annum question (cell $NB2_a$) lowered the latter to just 60.7 per cent of stated annual WTP when not preceded by a per visit question (cell $NB1_a$). For those subsamples which were given a prior budget question, this disparity increased so that annual WTP preceded by a per visit question (cell $B2_a$) was just 50.2 per cent of the annual WTP otherwise (cell $B1_a$). Again, the BCa confidence intervals indicate that only one of these differences (the latter) is significant, suggesting in this case that the prior per visit question substantially reduced the subsequent stated per annum WTP.

Consideration of the diagonals in Table 3.9 shows that where the apparently negative effect of including a prior per visit WTP question is combined with the

Table 3.10. *Mean WTP (fee) per visit and 95 per cent confidence intervals for each subsample (including payment principle refusals as zeros)*

	Payment ordering scenario	
Budget question	1 (tax then fee) (£)	2 (fee then tax) (£)
NB (not asked)	0.45 (0.35–0.57) [0.35–0.55]	0.20 (0.12–0.32) [0.11–0.29]
B (asked)	0.78 (0.57–1.09) [0.53–1.03]	0.46 (0.33–0.66) [0.30–0.62]

Note: Figures in round brackets are 95% C.I.s calculated by the BCa percentile method, as discussed previously, while figures in square brackets are conventional 95% C.I.s.

positive impact of a prior budget question (cell $B2_a$), then the resultant per annum WTP statement is not significantly different from that elicited in the absence of both preceding questions (cell $NB1_a$). However, comparison of stated per annum WTP when preceded solely by the apparently negative effect of a prior per visit question (cell $NB2_a$) with annual WTP preceded solely by the positive impact of a prior budget question (cell $B1_a$) shows a highly significant difference in WTP responses.

Comparison of the BCa and standard (normal) confidence intervals is also interesting. The distributional assumption underlying the latter does not prevent negative WTP values and the presence of significant numbers of zeros (payment principle refusals), alongside a distribution of non-zero responses containing some relatively high values, results in unreliable confidence intervals. These problems are corrected for in the BCa approach by using empirically derived estimates of bias and skewness which are calculated for each subsample. Upper and lower percentile points are then calculated accordingly. Here we can see that reliance upon conventional (normal) confidence intervals would overemphasise the significance of differences between subsamples.

WTP per visit (fee) responses
Table 3.10 presents mean WTP per visit (via fees) for each subsample and 95 per cent confidence intervals (as previously described). In the subsequent discussion, subsample notation is similar to that used above, with the subscript v indicating per visit (fee) responses.

Considering Table 3.10 we can see that the design effects detected in the per annum experiments have been repeated in the per visit studies. Again the inclusion of a prior question regarding recreation budgets seems to lead to increases in subsequent per visit WTP responses which are significant in both cases. Table 3.10 also shows that the prefixing of per visit WTP questions by per annum questions apparently increases per visit WTP bids. However, examination of the BCa confidence intervals indicates that only one of these two differences is statistically significant.

Consideration of the diagonals in Table 3.10 again tells a consistent story regarding the interplay of budget and ordering effects. Where these tend to shift responses in the same direction (i.e. comparing influences which are both negative in cell $NB2_v$ with influences which are both positive in cell $B1_v$), confidence intervals indicate highly significant differences, but where they work in opposition (comparing cell $NB1_v$ with cell $B2_v$), equality cannot be rejected. Finally, as before, reliance upon normal confidence intervals would generally lead us to overestimate the significance of these results.

Validation

Validation of survey results was carried out in accordance with the criteria set by Mitchell and Carson (1989). A central notion here is the concept of construct validity which is in turn composed of convergent and theoretical validation. In practice, convergent validity testing has generally been achieved by comparing benefits with those of other studies, while theoretical validity has been examined through the estimation of bid functions and analysis of their consistency with theoretical expectations.

Two types of convergent validity test were undertaken. In the first, results from the NB subgroups of this study were compared with the other estimates of UK woodland recreation value discussed earlier in this chapter (there were no studies comparable with the B format subgroups). Tests showed that the results obtained in the present study strongly conformed to expectations from prior research (details are given in Bateman and Langford, 1997a). A second test compared results from the NB subgroups with those from a selection of studies in a similar format of different resources (e.g. wetlands, reservoirs, etc.). It was found that results across these studies were logically related to both substitute availability and the change in provision presented in the contingent market and that the findings of the present study were consistent with these expectations (details are given in Bateman and Langford, 1997b).

Theoretical validation of our results was carried out via statistical investigation of the bid functions underlying WTP responses. A semi-log (dependent) functional form provided the best fit for the per annum data:

$$\ln\text{WTPtax} = 1.20 + 1.50\ \text{BUDGET} - 0.633\ \text{ORDER}$$
$$\phantom{\ln\text{WTPtax} =} (10.6) \quad (11.17) \qquad\qquad (4.76)$$
$$\phantom{\ln\text{WTPtax} =} + 0.390\ \text{GREEN} + 1.08\ \text{NONCAR} + 0.574\ \text{SUPERB} \qquad (3.4)$$
$$\phantom{\ln\text{WTPtax} =} (1.66) \qquad\qquad (3.35) \qquad\qquad (2.88)$$

where:

lnWTPtax = natural logarithm of WTP per annum (tax vehicle)

BUDGET = 1 if respondent had been asked to state annual recreational budget prior to WTP questions; = 0 otherwise

ORDER = 1 if respondent faced a prior per visit WTP question (ordering scenario 2); = 0 otherwise

GREEN = 1 if respondent was a member of at least one of various countryside/wildlife organisations; = 0 otherwise

NONCAR = 1 if the respondent did not travel to the site by car; = 0 otherwise

SUPERB = 1 if the respondent rated scenery at the site on the top of a four-point scale; = 0 otherwise.

Figures in brackets are *t*-statistics.

Equation (3.4) fits the data well (adjusted $R^2 = 33.7\%$), easily satisfying the criteria for theoretical validity discussed previously. The model again indicates the significant influence of budget constraint and question ordering on per annum responses. This finding is repeated in the per visit bid function shown in Equation (3.5), which again satisfies the Mitchell and Carson (1989) criteria regarding the degree of explanation (adjusted $R^2 = 26.4\%$) although the strength of the constant in this model recalls our earlier comments regarding the influence of social norms upon entrance fee WTP responses. Here a linear form fitted the data best, reflecting the clumping of bids around two round-figure amounts (50p and £1).

$$\text{WTPfee} = 0.618 + 0.167\ \text{BUDGET} - 0.167\ \text{ORDER}$$
$$\phantom{\text{WTPfee} =} (8.12) \quad (2.48) \qquad\qquad (1.94)$$
$$\phantom{\text{WTPfee} =} - 0.299\ \text{GREEN} + 0.397\ \text{CAMP} \qquad\qquad (3.5)$$
$$\phantom{\text{WTPfee} =} (3.05) \qquad\qquad (3.16)$$

where:

WTPfee = WTP per visit (entrance fee vehicle)

CAMP = 1 if the respondent often camps in the area; = 0 otherwise

Other variables as defined above.

Figures in brackets are *t*-statistics.

In general the above findings are unremarkable with one exception: the dramatic change in the influence of the explanatory variable GREEN which is positively related to per annum bids (although only significant at the 10 per cent level), but negatively associated with per visit bids (significant at the 1 per cent level). We consider this and other findings below.

Discussion

Budget constraint effects

In both our per visit and per annum responses the inclusion of a prior budget constraint question resulted in a very substantial increase in subsequent stated WTP. Three of the four comparisons which make up this analysis indicated that this difference was statistically significant, a result of some importance for CV research.

The direction of impact is also interesting. Most commentators (Mitchell and Carson, 1989; Willis and Garrod, 1993) discuss cases in which, *a priori*, we would expect that respondents' consideration of annual expenditure upon recreation and consequent budget constraints would lead to a reduction in stated WTP compared to statements made without such consideration. However, here we observed a strong opposite effect whereby respondents who were asked to calculate their present annual expenditure stated significantly higher WTP sums than those not asked the prior budget question.

Why has this effect occurred? It seems to us that two interpretations are possible, one generally supportive of CV and the other critical. The former argues that respondents forced to overtly consider their annual recreational budget find that, on average, this accounts for a significant portion of their total annual expenditure, perhaps more than they realised without such consideration. Certainly, stated annual recreational budgets were not insignificant. The mean budget (£227.30) was considerably affected by the skewed nature of this distribution. Nevertheless, the median value of £120 shows that most respondents had considerable annual recreation budgets. Following this argument then, after considering the apparent importance of recreation in their preference sets, such respondents gave higher WTP sums than would otherwise have been stated. If we accept such a line of reasoning then a supplementary question arises as to which WTP measure (with, or without, the prior budget question) is correct. The argument would seem to suggest that answers formulated following the consideration of available budgets will be less susceptible to mental accounting problems and therefore preferable.

A more critical interpretation of our findings, however, argues that the calculation of the annual budget (which is relatively high compared to WTP) acts as an anchor for subsequent WTP statements. Kahneman *et al.* (1982) suggest that such an effect is most likely to occur where individuals are inexperienced and face considerable uncertainty in forming their response. Here, then, our use of an open-ended WTP elicitation approach may have exacerbated such an effect, as individuals do not have as much experience of setting prices as reacting to them.

Clearly such findings give us pause for thought regarding the degree to which WTP responses may be manipulated by small and apparently defensible changes in questionnaire design. The responsiveness of stated WTP to the inclusion of the budget question is remarkable and a matter of significant concern for CV studies.

Ordering effects

Irrespective of whether or not a budget constraint question was asked, stated WTP per annum amounts were higher when given as an individual's first WTP response than when given after a response to the per visit WTP question (although this effect is only significant in one treatment). A first point to note regarding such ordering effects is that, as indicated in our literature review, these results are not necessarily inconsistent with economic theory. Indeed the work of Carson *et al.* (1992, 1998) and Randall and Hoehn (1992) would lead to such an expectation. However, there are further (although not necessarily contradictory) explanations of these results. A somewhat simplistic interpretation of such findings might be that such respondents were taking prior per visit payments and extrapolating them to produce a per annum sum.[31] However, this would imply that per annum responses made prior to per visit bids were in error.

An alternative explanation of the apparent ordering effect is suggested by our observation that membership of 'green' groups was positively correlated with WTP per annum but negatively related to WTP per visit. We suggest that this apparent disparity arises from a change, induced by the switch in payment vehicle, in the perceived nature of the good under evaluation. When presented with a non-preceded WTP per annum question (ordering scenario 1), respondents recognise a typical payment mechanism for funding public goods in the UK. Individuals understand the redistributive nature of most UK taxes and that such a payment would preserve the common-property, public-good, nature of recreation within Forestry Commission woodlands. Here, then, payments ensure provision for both the payee and other members of society, both types of provision being likely to be valued by the respondent. However, respondents facing ordering scenario 2 are initially presented with a WTP per visit (entrance fee) question. Such payments only ensure access for the payee and imply the exclusion of non-payers. The payment vehicle thus describes a private, rather than a public, good. This perception is liable to be retained when, subsequently, respondents are presented with the per annum WTP question. We

[31] Factors such as discounting, uncertainty and risk mean that we would not expect a simple relationship between per visit and per annum WTP.

can therefore view the apparent ordering effect in per annum responses as arising out of a category shift in perceptions, induced by the payment vehicle, regarding the nature of the good under evaluation. The observed relationship of responses conforms to the perceived loss of services between ordering scenarios 1 (recreation seen as a public good) and 2 (recreation seen as a private good).

If the difference in WTP statements is derived purely from the additional value aspects which respondents feel they obtain from woodland as a public good (bequest, altruism, etc.) rather than as a private good, then, while complicating the matter, this may be viewed as simply reflecting preferences. However, a number of commentators have argued that the evaluation of the same asset as either a public or private good may alter the underlying motivations upon which individual preferences lie. Schkade and Payne (1994) and Blamey (1998) note that evaluations of public goods appear in part to reflect norms regarding civic duty and fairness. Furthermore, Brennan and Buchanan (1984) argue that such valuations may also be influenced by a self-image or expressive value, derived from contributions towards goods which benefit not just the individual but also others in society.

In support of such an argument it is important to emphasise that the study was conducted midway through a high-profile, year-long public debate concerning (and generally opposing) proposals by the then UK government to privatise the Forestry Commission estate, a resource which provides the largest area of open-access recreational land in the UK. Countryside groups and their members were vociferous in their opposition to privatisation, as evidenced in the remarkable swing from positive to negative correlations with WTP as payment vehicles switch from those of a public to a private good. If normative and expressive values do underpin these differences, then, as Sugden (1999b) argues, CV estimates must be considered as being context-specific rather than as absolute valuations of the assets concerned.

A contrary and more critical explanation of the observed ordering effect follows Kahneman *et al.* (1982) in arguing that relatively small prior per visit WTP responses have here downwardly anchored subsequent per annum bids. In the context of our particular experiment, with one WTP response directly preceding another, such an effect is similar to the widely observed phenomenon of starting point bias (Boyle *et al.*, 1985). However, the remarkable and highly significant reversal in WTP correlation signs for members of green groups described above, makes us feel that the public/private goods argument cannot be ignored here. This does not preclude the possibility that the observed ordering effect has been heightened by anchoring/starting point bias, with consequent questions being raised regarding the validity of such results.

Each of the theoretical expectation, public/private goods and anchoring arguments can also be applied as explanations of the observed ordering effects in per visit WTP responses. Here the direction of causation is reversed in that the introduction of a prior per annum WTP question raises per visit WTP (although again only one of these effects is statistically significant). This could be following theoretical expectations, perhaps enhanced by the per annum approach inducing respondents to think of this as being a public as opposed to a private good. Alternatively it may be that the relatively high prior per annum response upwardly anchors subsequent per visit responses, or a mixture of both.

Conclusions

The analysis applied a split-sample approach to the investigation of budget constraint, temporal and ordering effects in CV studies. In three out of four tests significant budget constraint effects were detected. Interpretation of such results is not straightforward as they may be viewed either as the expected consequence of respondents revising bids in the light of further reflection, or as evidence of an anchoring bias. While both explanations may have some validity their implications for future studies are in direct conflict. If budget constraint questions induce respondents to consider more fully their personal circumstances, then, following the recommendations of Arrow *et al.* (1993), some variant of these questions should be included prior to WTP questions. Conversely, if the responses to budget constraint questions anchor subsequent WTP bids, then this suggests that they should be avoided.

Two of the four tests of ordering effects indicated that significant differences were observed. Again, at least two explanations of these results can be proposed. Following Carson *et al.* (1992, 1998), economic theory allows for divergence between measures of the same good elicited at different points in a valuation sequence. Such differences are likely to be exacerbated if the sequence itself induces differing subsamples to view the resource under evaluation as either a public or a private good. Following such an explanation, the divergence in valuations can be seen either as reflecting the differing attributes of such goods, or as arising from a consequent change in the motivations underlying the preferences expressed. However, as with our budget constraint experiment, these divergences can also be interpreted as evidence of prior responses anchoring subsequent bids.

In conclusion, these findings can be viewed either as demonstrating the susceptibility of CV results to design effects or as quantifying the limits of such effects. For the purposes of our subsequent work we adopt the latter position, stressing that the valuation of environmental preferences remains more of an art than a science, but that such values, if treated with due caution, can improve decision-making substantially when compared with standard approaches in which such preferences are implicitly ignored.

The Thetford 2 TC study: a GIS-based investigation of measurement and estimation effects[32]

The analysis of revealed visitation behaviour derived from the TC data gathered in the Thetford 2 survey involved the first application of geographical information system (GIS) techniques to be presented in this volume. The GIS was used to provide estimates of travel time and distance from outset locations to the site. The spatial analytic capabilities of the GIS were then used to perform a sensitivity analysis of common measurement assumptions in TC studies. As we shall see in Chapter 4, the GIS was also used to manipulate TC data so as to generate a transferable arrivals function, capable of estimating the number of visitors both to this surveyed site and to other unsurveyed sites in our wider study area of Wales.

The Thetford 2 TC study was also used to conduct a full sensitivity analysis across a range of unit-value assumptions regarding travel expenditure and time cost and to assess how effects vary between differing estimation procedures, namely ordinary least squares (OLS) and maximum likelihood (ML) techniques. Survey details are as for the Thetford 2 CV study (the questionnaire was designed to facilitate both CV and TC analysis), although here we stress the importance of questions concerning the recreational trip. Respondents were asked to state:

  (i) home address, and trip origin if different to this (e.g. if on holiday away from home)
 (ii) how they travelled to the site
(iii) the perceived travel time and cost
 (iv) the number of other sites visited during the day's trip
  (v) the proportions of the whole day's enjoyment attributable to time spent travelling, time spent at the survey site and time spent at other sites.

Applying GIS to the TC method

One of the most obvious advantages of using GIS techniques in TC studies is to standardise and improve the accuracy in the derivation of travel distance and duration variables. Given that these are the basic elements underpinning estimates of individuals' travel expenditure, travel time and hence travel cost, the potential benefits are clearly considerable. This section describes the procedure by which the GIS was used to calculate travel times and distances.

Using the data collected from the visitor survey, the 1km National Grid reference of trip origin was located by consulting the Ordnance Survey's *Gazetteer of Great Britain* (Ordnance Survey, 1987). Digital road network details were extracted from the Bartholomew 1:250,000-scale database for the UK. This source provides information on road classes, distinguishing fifteen separate categories from minor, single-track country lanes to motorways. Computing constraints made

---

[32] Further details of this study are given in Bateman (1996) and Bateman *et al.* (1996a)

Table 3.11. *Average road speed estimates*

Road type	DoT estimates		Adjusted speeds	
	Rural (1) (m.p.h.)	Urban (2) (m.p.h.)	Rural (3) (m.p.h.)	Urban (4) (m.p.h.)
Motorway	70	50	63	35
A-road primary, dual carriageway	60	40	54	28
A-road other, dual carriageway	55	35	50	25
A-road primary, single carriageway	50	35	45	25
A-road other, single carriageway	40	25	32	18
B-road, dual carriageway	40	25	36	18
B-road, single carriageway	30	17	24	12
Minor road	20	15	14	11

Source: Columns (1) and (2) from Department of Transport (1992, 1993).

it impractical to assemble a detailed road network for the entire area covering origins of Thetford visitors (this ranged from near Newcastle upon Tyne in the north to Hampshire in the south). We therefore defined a study area to include the counties of Norfolk, Suffolk and Cambridgeshire, together with adjoining districts in Lincolnshire and Essex. This encompassed over 92 per cent of the visitor origins.

Typical speeds can be assigned to the different classes of road defined in the Bartholomew's database so enabling travel times to be calculated for discrete sections of road. From these, travel times can be calculated for routes across the whole network. Data on average travel speeds for differing categories of road were obtained from a variety of sources. This exercise revealed both the paucity of such data and some significant differences in estimates. An initial investigation was undertaken using road speeds given in Department of Transport (DoT) sources as detailed in columns (1) and (2) of Table 3.11.

Travel times from each road segment in the network were calculated as:

$$\text{travel time} = \frac{\text{length of road segment (in miles)}}{\text{speed (miles per hour)}} \tag{3.6}$$

Minimum travel time can be calculated by specifying the time from Equation (3.6) as the impedance associated with a particular road segment in the digital network. An algorithm is then used to identify the route between the trip origin and forest site which minimises the cumulative impedance, thereby also deriving the minimum travel time (see Lupien *et al.*, 1987). Utilising the DoT road speeds in Table 3.11, a series of travel times were calculated for a variety of routes between a sample of towns and villages in the area. These were then compared with those generated using the alternative road speeds given in Gatrell and Naumann

(1992) and the Automobile Association's Autoroute route planning software package. Further calibration was achieved by calculation of travel times for a number of routes well known to the authors and their colleagues. These assessments consistently pointed to the conclusion that the DoT road speeds given in Table 3.11 were overestimates of those realistically attainable in the study area. Such a finding reflects the fact that these official road speed estimates are based on limited information regarding the impact of road junctions and other sources of traffic congestion. Although it was feasible to consult Ordnance Survey maps regarding the topology of motorway junctions it was not practicable to conduct a systematic assessment of all junctions (or other traffic constraints) throughout the road network. Accordingly, a sensitivity analysis was undertaken to obtain appropriate adjustment factors by comparing calculated travel times with those regarded as more realistic.[33] Best-fit adjusted road speeds are presented in columns (3) and (4) of Table 3.11.

The calculation of individuals' travel times and distances using the GIS involved three steps. First, the survey site was identified on the road network and an algorithm in the GIS software (Arc/Info) was used to calculate the minimum sum impedance[34] between the destination and each unique segment of road. This produces the minimum cumulative time (in minutes) that it takes to reach the start-point and end-point of each road segment. These times are then stored in an output table (Environmental Systems Research Institute, 1994).

The second step involved finding the nearest point on the road network for each individual visit origin. Travel times from this point to the site were then extracted using both the prepared output table and interpolation between the two end-points of each road segment. Finally, the distance travelled by each visitor along these minimum impedance routes was calculated using further GIS facilities (*ibid.*).

As a test of the validity of these GIS-defined measures, respondents' estimated travel times and distances were compared with their GIS equivalents.[35] Travel time distributions were found to be very similar (a two-sample *t*-test for difference gave a *t*-statistic of 0.09 for which $p = 0.88$). A similar result was obtained regarding travel distances. However, the values highlighted some potential advantages of the GIS approach. These are illustrated in Figure 3.1 which graphs the ratio of stated to GIS-calculated distance against the absolute value of the latter.

Examining Figure 3.1 shows that, on average, the distance measures coincide reasonably well. Most observations have a ratio value of about 1 (i.e. stated =

---

[33] Further details are given in Bateman *et al.* (1999c).

[34] The algorithm used works recursively through the entire road network, keeping information about the minimum impedance route found so far, until all possible route permutations are exhausted.

[35] A similar analysis is reported by Liston-Heyes (1999).

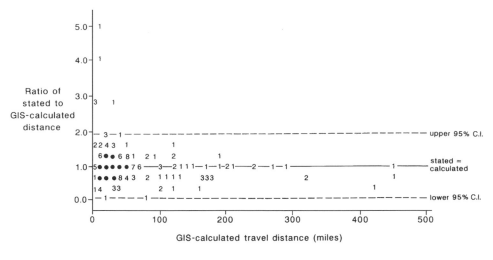

Figure 3.1. Graph of the ratio of stated to GIS-calculated distance against calculated distance. (*Source:* Adapted from Bateman *et al.*, 1996b.)

GIS-calculated values) and there are approximately as many observations below 1 as above. However, given that the GIS distance is based on a minimum impedance algorithm (minimum possible travel time), those respondent estimates below the unity line are likely to be subject to some form of error, a situation which we suspect is due to respondents rounding their stated travel time estimates, e.g. a true travel time of twelve minutes is reported as being ten minutes. Support for such an argument comes from noting that, with a few exceptions (discussed below), a similar distribution of upward rounding errors can be seen lying above the unity line, e.g. a true travel time of eight minutes being reported as ten minutes.

Such results indicate that GIS measures are, for the majority of visitors, good estimates of true travel distance and duration. However, Figure 3.1 shows that for a small minority such a conclusion does not hold. Six respondents (i.e. about 2 per cent of the sample) lie above the upper 95 per cent confidence interval around the unity line. Cross-checking against responses from these parties shows them to be 'meanderers' (see Chapter 2), whose main objective is enjoyment of the journey rather than time spent on site. The relatively low importance of the on-site recreational experience to such respondents will be reflected in their responses to question (v) above which are used as utility weights on travel costs in the TC model. Such a procedure ensures that we only use that portion of travel costs which is due to the on-site recreational experience in calculating the benefit values of that site. Coincidentally, this same procedure drastically reduces the influence of any error due to the use of GIS-based measures for such meanderers. Given this, and the advantages of such measures with respect to rounding errors, we consider that GIS-calculated travel distance and duration provide a good basis for TC studies, an assumption which we test subsequently in this study.

Sensitivity analysis 1: unit-value assumptions and estimation techniques

In Chapter 2 we discussed the various definitions of travel expenditure and time cost which underpin travel costs. Here we test various combinations of each, defining travel expenditure as marginal (petrol only) or total running costs (8p and 23p per mile respectively)[36] and time costs at the following wage rates: 100 per cent (assuming that leisure time is valued at the full wage rate); 43 per cent (the DoT appraisal rate); 0 per cent (assuming that there is no opportunity cost of non-work time); and a best-fit rate (that rate which maximises the model's fit to the data).[37] These combinations defined a series of alternative travel cost (expenditure plus time) variables which were then used as the basis of a number of models to predict visits to the site at Thetford Forest. Other explanatory variables were derived from survey data and are discussed subsequently.

A further issue which our theoretical appraisal highlighted was the impact of varying the estimation procedure employed. In particular, it was noted that the use of ordinary least squares (OLS) techniques failed to allow for the truncation of non-positive visits (i.e. it does not take into account the fact that any on-site survey respondents cannot make less than one visit to the site). This issue can be addressed by the use of maximum likelihood (ML) methods where the underlying likelihood function can be defined to allow for this truncation (for details regarding the present study, see Bateman *et al.*, 1996b). For comparative purposes both OLS and ML estimation methods were applied to the various unit-value permutations described above. Goodness-of-fit measures were given by R^2 statistics for OLS regressions and log likelihood values for ML analyses.

Results

Tests across a variety of functional forms indicated that in all cases the natural log of the number of visits made by a party to the site (lnVISIT) gave the best definition of the dependent variable. To enhance comparability across models a consistent set of explanatory variables was used in all sensitivity analysis models as follows:[38]

---

[36] Automobile Association estimates given in Benson and Willis (1992).

[37] Further permutations, including the use of measures based on respondents' perceived travel costs, are presented in Bateman (1996) and Bateman *et al.* (1996a).

[38] Other variables considered but rejected from the comparative models include: party size; age<25; age>65; membership of any environmental organisation; membership of separate organisations; other main activity dummies.

TC = travel cost (travel expenditure + travel time); various
permutations as discussed previously

HSIZE = household size

HOLS = 1 if respondent was on holiday at time of interview; = 0
otherwise

WORK = 1 if respondent was working at time of interview; = 0
otherwise

LIVE = 1 if respondent lives near site; = 0 otherwise

RATING = respondent's rating of scenery at the site (from 1 = poor to
4 = superb)

NT = 1 if respondent was a member of the National Trust; = 0
otherwise

TAX = 1 if respondent was a taxpayer; = 0 otherwise

MDOG = 1 if respondent's main reason for visit was dog walking; = 0
otherwise

Table 3.12 presents the travel cost coefficient (full functions given in Bateman, 1996) and three consumer surplus (CS) values from ML-estimated models for the various definitions of travel cost considered in the sensitivity analysis.

Given the strong correlations among the various definitions of travel cost, and that the set of other predictors remains constant across models, goodness-of-fit statistics were similar for all the models detailed in Table 3.12 (see details in Bateman, 1996). However, the marginal cost (8p per mile) travel expenditure model using a best-fit (2.5 per cent) travel time assumption provided an overall optimal fit to the data and is therefore our preferred model from the ML analyses (shown in italics in Table 3.12). This is an interesting result as it suggests that time costs, although highly significant in determining trips (see Chapter 4), can be substantially overstated in absolute terms, resulting in large overestimates of consumer surplus (e.g. benefit estimates are nearly 2.5 times higher if the DoT wage rate is used rather than our best-fit rate). A similar degree of benefit overestimation occurs where the poorer-fitting full travel expenditure assumption is employed.

Comparison of benefit estimates from our preferred model with those obtained from the other studies considered in this chapter strongly reinforces the findings of our review of previous research, in that the values obtained from our TC studies are consistently above those derived from CV analyses, the magnitude of this difference being similar across studies. Reasons for this disparity are discussed in the conclusions to this chapter.

In the TC method as shown in Chapter 2, welfare estimates are obtained by integration under the demand curve which is in turn derived from the trip generation

Table 3.12. *Sensitivity analysis: ML models (best-fitting model shown in italics)*

Travel expenditure cost	Travel time cost (wage rate)	Travel cost coefficient (*t*-statistic)	CS per household per annum (£)[1]	CS per household per visit (£)[1,2]	CS per person per visit (£)[1,3]
Marginal (8p/mile)	Zero (0%)	−0.084758 (−3.32)	140.39 (127.55)	3.62 (3.29)	1.21 (1.10)
Marginal (8p/mile)	DoT (43%)	−0.031808 (−2.92)	374.10 (339.87)	9.65 (8.77)	3.22 (2.92)
Marginal (8p/mile)	Full (100%)	−0.016002 (−2.72)	743.61 (675.57)	19.18 (17.42)	6.39 (5.81)
Marginal (8p/mile)	*Best fit (2.5%)*	*−0.077656 (−3.24)*	*153.23 (139.21)*	*3.95 (3.59)*	*1.32 (1.20)*
Full (23p/mile)	Zero (0%)	−0.031207 (−3.32)	381.31 (346.42)	9.83 (8.93)	3.28 (2.98)
Full (23p/mile)	DoT (43%)	−0.020856 (−3.02)	570.56 (518.36)	14.71 (13.36)	4.90 (4.45)
Full (23p/mile)	Full (100%)	−0.013251 (−3.00)	898.02 (815.85)	23.16 (21.04)	7.72 (7.01)
Full (23p/mile)	Best fit (6%)	−0.029540 (−3.32)	402.83 (365.97)	10.39 (9.44)	3.46 (3.15)

Notes: [1] values in each cell are at 1993 prices; lower values (in brackets) are at 1990 prices (for comparison with subsequent chapters). Deflator from Central Statistical Office (1993a).

[2] On average, households visited Thetford Forest nearly fifteen times per annum.

[3] Calculated using median party composition figures of three persons (two of whom were >16 years). Mean party size was considerably skewed by a few large parties and was not thought to provide an appropriate measure. Note that this assumption treats adults and children equally.

function. This function itself also provides a degree of theoretical validation of the study through inspection of the various relationships found to be statistically significant predictors of visits. Equation (3.7) details the trip generation function for our best-fitting ML model.

$$
\begin{aligned}
\ln \text{VISIT} = {} & -0.4853 - 0.0776\ \text{TC} + 0.0718\ \text{HSIZE} - 1.4728\ \text{HOLS} \\
& (-0.819)\quad (-3.235)\qquad (1.326)\qquad\qquad (-2.762) \\
& + 1.7408\ \text{WORK} + 2.2770\ \text{LIVE} + 0.5050\ \text{RATING} - 0.4629\ \text{NT} \\
& \quad (3.840)\qquad\qquad (5.771)\qquad (3.198)\qquad\qquad (-1.915) \\
& + 0.4416\ \text{TAX} + 0.6066\ \text{MDOG} \\
& \quad (1.863)\qquad\quad (2.461)
\end{aligned}
$$

(3.7)

Log likelihood value $= -454.59$ Sigma $= 1.18\,(16.79)$

Variables as previously defined.   Figures in brackets are *t*-statistics.

The model given in Equation (3.7) has expected signs and significance on all explanatory variables (of our standard set of predictors only HSIZE proved to be statistically insignificant). The travel cost variable is highly significant, easily passing a 1 per cent test, and indicating that visits are inversely related to the sum of journey and time costs. More visits are made by those who live or work near the site, who rate the scenery highly, use the location for dog walking (these respondents made a relatively large number of visits) and were taxpayers. Those making less frequent visits included respondents who were on holiday at the time of the survey (most of whom did not live locally) and those who were members of the National Trust, a factor which may either be linked to a wider recreational opportunity set or to an interesting inverse link with income (which we explore in Chapter 4).

Given the findings of our ML analyses, only zero and 43 per cent wage rate time costs were used in the OLS sensitivity analysis, the results of which are presented in Table 3.13. These results confirm our prior ML findings that models using marginal journey costs (8p/mile) and very low (here zero) time costs fit the data best. However, in other respects our OLS-based models do not compare favourably with their ML counterparts. Although comparison of overall goodness-of-fit statistics (log likelihood values versus R^2) is problematic, explanatory variable *t*-values in directly comparable models were generally higher in ML than OLS models, and invariably so with regard to the travel cost variable. Perhaps more importantly from a practical point of view, these results fail both convergent validity (Mitchell and Carson, 1989) and plausibility tests, in that the benefit estimates derived are over five times larger than those obtained from our ML models (which were themselves in line with results elsewhere in the literature). Given this, we can conclude that the theoretical problems inherent in the application of OLS techniques to individual TC valuations

Table 3.13. *Sensitivity analysis: OLS models (best-fitting model shown in italics)*

Travel expenditure cost	Travel time cost (wage rate)	Travel cost coefficient (*t*-statistic)	CS per household per annum (£)[1]	CS per household per visit (£)[1,2]	CS per person per visit (£)[1,3]
Marginal (8p/mile)	*Zero (0%)*	*−0.046776*	*313.19*	*21.38*	*7.13*
		(−2.93)	*(284.53)*	*(19.42)*	*(6.47)*
Marginal (8p/mile)	DoT (43%)	−0.011519	1271.82	86.81	28.94
		(−2.12)	(1155.45)	(78.87)	(26.29)
Full (23p/mile)	Zero (0%)	−0.016801	871.97	59.52	19.84
		(−2.90)	(792.19)	(54.07)	(18.02)
Full (23p/mile)	DoT (43%)	−0.008904	1645.33	112.13	37.38
		(−2.51)	(1494.78)	(101.87)	(33.96)

Notes: [1] values in each cell are at 1993 prices, lower values (in brackets) are at 1990 prices (for comparison with subsequent chapters). Deflator from Central Statistical Office (1993a).
[2] On average households visited Thetford Forest nearly fifteen times per annum.
[3] Calculated using median party composition figures of three persons (two of whom were >16 years). Mean party size was considerably skewed by a few large parties and was not thought to provide an appropriate measure. Note that this assumption treats adults and children equally.

are matched by empirical problems, and that consequently results obtained from such analyses should not be used for decision-making purposes.

Sensitivity analysis 2: measurement issues[39]

In Chapter 2 we noted that certain common simplifying assumptions regarding the measurement of travel time and distance might have the potential to produce biased estimates of consumer surplus. In particular we highlighted the use of centroid rather than actual outset origins and various simplifying assumptions regarding journey routing, notably the use of straight-line distance or constant travel speeds. The use of a GIS allows us to investigate the potential impact of these measurement assumptions by permitting the analyst the following types of flexibility:

(i)   Relatively precise journey origins (accurate, in this study, to 1 km) may be specified;
(ii) Alternatively, centroid journey origins may be defined using a variety of administrative areas;
(iii) Travel distance and travel time may be calculated either using straight lines or by reference to a digital road network. Where the latter approach is used, information on road quality and corresponding speeds can also be incorporated to provide more accurate measures of travel distance and time.

In order to investigate the centroid issue, three types of outset origin were specified: (i) the 1 km resolution outset location used previously; (ii) the geographical centroid defined by UK district boundaries; and (iii) the geographical centroid defined by UK county boundaries.[40] In order to ensure sufficient variation at the county level, the road network had to be extended to cover the entire sample of survey respondents. This was achieved by defining a simpler skeleton digital road network beyond the previously defined area, concentrating upon the main roads. This simplification was considered reasonable given that visitors travelling from a considerable distance were unlikely to make much use of minor roads until they were near to the site.

For each origin at the three resolutions the travel distance and duration measures underpinning travel costs were calculated first by using the minimum impedance algorithm in conjunction with the digital road network (i.e. routing visitors along the least-cost path as described previously) and secondly by using straight-line distances.

The various travel cost measures obtained from all these permutations were then entered into a series of trip generation functions. Statistical tests again indicated

---

[39] Further details of this analysis are given in Bateman *et al.* (1999a).
[40] UK districts and counties roughly correspond to the smallest and largest US counties used as centroids in the TC-based study by Loomis *et al.* (1995).

Applied Environmental Economics

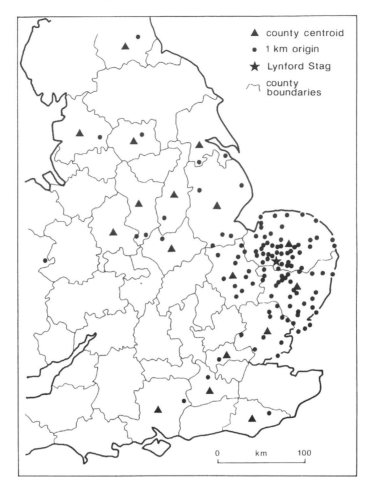

Figure 3.2. Comparison of 1 km grid reference with county centroid trip origins. (*Source:* Bateman *et al.*, 1999a.)

that a semi-log (dependent) functional form provided the best fit to the data. Given our previous findings, ML estimation techniques were employed throughout.

Results

Figure 3.2 illustrates some of the graphical output which can be produced by a GIS and demonstrates the impact of adopting large catchment areas. Here the 1 km outset origins derived from visitors' responses are compared to the county centroids. Inspection of those counties in the vicinity of the site clearly shows that the majority of visitors set out from origins which are closer to the site than the centroids for their corresponding areas. This is likely to be the case irrespective of the size or location of the area. However, the relative error caused by this effect is much greater for areas close to the site than for more distant ones. This

Table 3.14. *Sensitivity analysis: effects of varying outset origin on
TC benefit estimates*

Outset origin	Source of distance and duration measures	CS per household per annum (£)	CS per household per visit (£)	CS per person per visit (£)
1 km grid reference	Digital road network	173.25	4.47	1.49
	Straight line	141.97	3.66	1.22
District centroid	Digital road network	206.40	5.32	1.78
	Straight line	173.71	4.48	1.49
County centroid	Digital road network	364.73	9.40	3.14
	Straight line	338.29	8.72	2.91

systematic bias will result in an overestimate of consumer surplus as discussed previously.

Full results from our analysis are presented in Table 3.14. Here, following the findings of our previous sensitivity analysis, marginal travel expenditure (8p/mile) and best-fit travel time costs (2.5 per cent of wage rate) are used throughout to define travel costs.

Examining Table 3.14 reveals that using straight-line as opposed to road-based measures of travel cost consistently produces lower estimates of consumer surplus. This is as expected and reflects the underestimate of true travel cost produced by straight-line approximations. The resultant underestimation ranges up to 20 per cent; however, this is small compared to the error induced by using large-area centroids as opposed to more accurate estimates of outset origin. While the increase induced by moving from 1 km origins to district centroids is similar to that of changing from road network to straight-line measures, a very substantial impact occurs where we move from 1 km to county centroid origins with benefit estimates more than doubling.

These findings lead us to conclude that the benefit estimates produced by studies adopting large-area centroid origins and/or straight-line-based measures of travel cost should be treated with caution. By contrast, the GIS-based measures derived from the higher resolution origins utilised in the present study seem to offer a substantial improvement in the robustness of benefit estimates.

Thetford 2 TC study: conclusions

Perhaps the primary objective of the Thetford 2 TC study was to show how GIS techniques can enhance the application and validity of the method. These techniques were applied to the fundamental tasks of calculating the travel distance and duration data and have been shown to have a number of advantages over more conventional

Table 3.15. *Valuing recreational visits to woodland: a synthesis of studies*

Study	Method	£ per person per visit[1]	£ per party per visit[2]		
			Mean party size (3.05)	Upper 95% C.I. party size (3.27)	Lower 95% C.I. party size (2.85)
Cross-study analysis (OE WTP use value)	CV	0.60	1.82	1.95	1.69
Wantage (OE WTP/visit study)	CV	0.82	2.50	2.68	2.33
Thetford 2 (ML model)	ITC	1.20	3.59	3.85	3.35

Notes: [1] Figures are best-estimate means (1990 prices). Bateman (1996) also reports 95% C.I.s and alternative estimates based on WTP per annum studies.
[2] The sensitivity analysis on party size treats adults and children equally as party members. Note that the per person per visit value used is kept constant within each row.

approaches. The advantages are perhaps best demonstrated in our second sensitivity analysis which uses the flexibility of GIS to indicate how a number of common measurement assumptions can lead to substantial biases within benefit estimates and, more importantly, how they can be avoided.

The study has also revisited a number of areas of controversy in the existing literature by conducting a sensitivity analysis across a number of common unit-value assumptions and estimation techniques. This analysis quantified the magnitude of potential welfare measure variance as well as yielding some defensible values for use in our subsequent research.

Summary and conclusions

This chapter has presented a considerable number of results regarding the valuation of woodland recreation benefits. From our review of the existing literature we identified a number of CV analyses which provided the basis for a cross-study meta-analysis of values. This work showed that WTP responses were logically linked to the values individuals were asked to assess and to the elicitation method employed. From the various values which can be derived from our cross-study model we emphasise the estimate of use value derived using an OE elicitation method, the latter being conducive to the estimation of the lower-bound values we have emphasised throughout. This result is reproduced in the top row of Table 3.15 which summarises the more robust valuations presented here.

The remaining rows of Table 3.15 summarise selected results from our own valuation work. Reviewing the various research objectives we set ourselves in

Chapter 2 with respect to the CV method, we have seen through the Thetford 1 study the substantial variation in WTP values reported by woodland users as opposed to non-users of woodland recreation, while the Wantage study has contrasted these with the WTA compensation levels demanded by farmers for providing woodland recreation opportunities on their land. Taken together, the three CV studies presented in this chapter also provide evidence of the considerable variation in values induced by choice of elicitation method and payment vehicle. While these effects are, arguably, consistent with theoretical expectations, of greater concern are the substantial impacts induced by adding budget constraint questions and testing question ordering in the Thetford 2 CV study. While we would not contend that these studies are beyond criticism, such findings suggest that values should be treated with some caution and that the conservative approach advocated by H.M. Treasury may be justified.

Turning to consider the objectives for our TC studies set out at the end of Chapter 2, in the Thetford 2 study we have used GIS techniques to investigate the impact of different strategies for measuring travel time and travel distance upon resultant consumer surplus estimates. The GIS has permitted a substantial improvement in defining the journey outset location, modelling journey routing and conducting sensitivity analyses on consumer surplus estimates. We have also examined the impact of various statistical modelling procedures and functional forms upon those estimates. Again we have seen that benefit estimates are highly sensitive to a range of methodological issues, reinforcing the need to exercise care when incorporating benefit estimates in CBAs.

Given these concerns we have omitted the Thetford 1 studies from Table 3.15 as these were principally methodological tests and the values produced have to be treated with considerable caution. We have fewer reservations regarding the validity of CV estimates obtained from the Wantage study. However, as the benefit transfer methods employed in the following chapter require per visit values we do not make any further use of the WTP per annum results obtained from this or the Thetford 2 CV study. The per visit estimates obtained from the latter study are also difficult to apply to a wider context as they are strongly influenced by the various designs used in each sample (and the one readily comparable estimate is included within our cross-study meta-analysis). However, the value obtained from our preferred model in the Thetford 2 ITC study does appear to have reasonable claims to validity and forms the final row of Table 3.15.

Examination of the various values presented in Table 3.15 indicates that they conform well to prior theoretical and empirical expectations in that per party per visit values obtained from our CV studies are similar to, but somewhat smaller than, our TC estimates. Such a finding conforms to the large-sample cross-study comparison of TC and CV studies reported by Carson *et al.* (1996) as well as satisfying a plausibility test.

Given that conservative measures have been emphasised throughout, we use the lower of the two CV values shown (i.e. £1.82 per party per visit) for our subsequent benefit transfer work, both because it gives a more defensible estimate of recreation values and because it is based on a large number of studies. This claim cannot be made for our ITC value. However, the study underpinning this particular value appears robust and has considerable advantages over others in the literature. Given this outcome we also use this value as an upper-bound contrast with the cross-study CV measure within the benefit transfer work discussed in the following chapter.

Finally, although all of the values discussed above have been adjusted in real terms to our 1990 study period, is there any evidence that these values may have changed over time up to the present day? This question is considered in a recent re-examination and extension of our meta-analysis work presented in Bateman *et al.* (2001d). Here, we combine the various CV and TC estimates of woodland per person per visit recreational values into one meta-model. This study utilises multilevel modelling techniques (Goldstein, 1995) to control for intra-unit correlation (IUC) between value estimates produced by each study author and within each forest (i.e. the possibility that estimates produced by a given author are more similar than those produced by taking a random sample from all estimates). The study finds no significant evidence of IUC effects either within authors or within forests. Furthermore, conclusions regarding valuation estimates remain broadly the same as reported here and so are not repeated. However, the expansion of estimates permitted by combining results from all CV and TC studies permitted investigation of whether, controlling for all other significant factors, any time trend in the real value of woodland recreation could be observed. Findings suggest that a small increase in real values was statistically significant across the time series (of seventeen years) considered. While we consider a number of possible reasons for this result we cannot reject the hypothesis that this reflects an underlying real increase in the perceived recreational value of woodland over time. This result is reminiscent of that postulated by Krutilla and Fisher (1975) in their discussion of the value of natural environments over time. Certainly, there seems little reason to suppose that recreation values will decline in real terms over time; rather they should be stable or increase. In Chapter 9 we consider the implications of such trends for our cost-benefit results.

4

Recreation: predicting visits

Introduction

In this chapter we utilise a geographical information system (GIS) to model the predicted number of visitors to a particular woodland site and test the efficiency of the resultant *arrivals function* in estimating visits to other sites. This is achieved through a zonal model which estimates visitor arrival rates from areas around a given site, and which is then applied to other sites through the definition of similar zones around them. Findings from our studies of the value of open-access woodland recreation (discussed in Chapter 3) are then applied to our predicted visits surface to obtain valuations of potential demand.[1]

Estimating an arrivals function

Previous studies

We are concerned with estimating overall visit rates which are applicable across populations, rather than being specific to individuals. By definition, conventional ITC valuation studies refer only to site visitors and say little about non-visitors. As a consequence they are unsuited to determining the absolute number of people who will visit a site. Therefore, our visitor arrivals model has to be composed of variables that have relevance across the population and can be readily transferred between sites.

  To date there has been relatively little research regarding the level and determinants of visits to woodland in the UK. Furthermore, of those few studies which have examined this issue, most have looked at national recreational demand (Willis and Benson, 1989; Whiteman, 1991) rather than that at any particular forest site.

This chapter draws in part upon material presented in Bateman *et al*. (1999c) and we are grateful to the Regional Studies Association for permission to use this material.
[1] The GIS procedures employed here are presented in a non-technical descriptive manner. Further details of the commands used are presented in Bateman (1996).

One notable exception is provided by the work of Colenutt and Sidaway (1973) who model the demand for day-trip visits to the Forest of Dean. Here a combined on-site and household (postal) survey was used to collect information regarding trip origins and the factors determining visits. Analysis of these data revealed that by far the most important factor determining arrivals was travel time, to the effective exclusion of other explanatory variables.

The Colenutt and Sidaway result is important because it suggests that an arrivals function may be estimated relating travel time to the probability of a visit taking place. The analytical power provided by a GIS makes it possible to apply such a function to detailed population data, such as those provided in the UK Census, in order to predict arrivals at any existing or hypothetical site.[2] Obviously, in practice, the validity of taking an arrivals function estimated at one site and applying it to another needs to be carefully assessed in terms of the accuracy of the predictions made. Such a test is carried out and presented subsequently.

Recreation demand: the Thetford Forest study

The objective of this study was to estimate an arrivals function for a given forest which could then be applied across our Welsh study area. The base data for our initial investigation were obtained as part of the Thetford 2 study described in Chapter 3. Here individual journey distance and duration measures, adjusted for the availability and quality of the road network, were calculated for use within the ITC valuation study discussed previously. However, such individual-level variables were inappropriate for use within our arrivals function where travel times were required for all points across the study area rather than just those which were the outset origins of surveyed visitors. We therefore needed to convert our travel time road network data into complete coverage travel time zones which would have relevance to visitors and non-visitors alike. To obtain this continuity of coverage the vector (line) data derived for each individual segment of the road network had to be rasterised.

Rasterisation is a process of converting vector features (here roads) to cells on a regular grid, in this case of 500 m × 500 m squares,[3] covering the extended East Anglian area from which visitors originated. In this study the travel time values assigned to points along roads were reassigned to the grid cells which contained those points. A 'majority filter' was run recursively across the entire study area to smoothly fill in the gaps between roads, providing values for all grid cells and

---

[2] Kliskey (2000) also uses a GIS-based approach to generate models of recreation potential, reporting an empirical analysis of recreational snowmobiling in British Columbia.

[3] This produced a total of 161,195 cells for our entire study area, of which 58,364 were directly filled through the rasterisation process (i.e. they contained roads), the remainder being assigned values through the process described in the text.

Travel time (minutes)
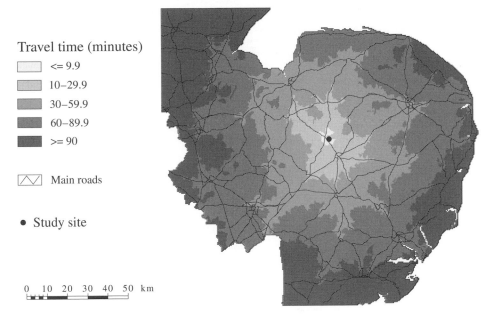

Figure 4.1. Travel time zones for the Thetford Forest study.

producing a continuous travel time surface centred upon the site and fanning out to fill the entire study area. The majority filter worked by means of a 'moving window' (usually eight by eight cells in extent),[4] where the centremost empty cell was assigned the value held by the majority of already assigned cells in the specified window. This approach worked well for the vast majority of cells. However, a few gaps remained in areas very remote from any roads where the filter window did not contain any cells filled directly by the rasterisation process. These grid cells were given the values of their nearest neighbours.[5] For further discussion of these procedures see Bateman *et al.* (1995b, 1999c) and Brainard *et al.* (1997).

Once all grid cells had been assigned a value they were grouped into convenient categories. Inspection of the calculated travel times showed that the extended road network encompassed values up to 120 minutes. Within this range, thirteen time zones were defined. Given the concentration of visit origins around the site, the innermost zones (between 0 and 30 minutes) were tightly defined at five-minute intervals, after which ten- and eventually fifteen-minute bands were used (between 30 and 60 minutes and 60 and 120 minutes, respectively). Figure 4.1 illustrates

---

[4] At the edge of the study area the window could feasibly reduce to as few as four cells (only filled cells are incorporated into the filter). The possibility of an edge distortion does exist but, given the very large number of cells used in the entire Thetford dataset, any such distortion would be extremely minor.

[5] Bateman *et al.* (1995b) undertook an analysis of vector and raster road speeds for this study. This shows that, within the Welsh study area considered subsequently, vector travel times were somewhat shorter than raster equivalents. Following this analysis, raster values were multiplied by a value of roughly 1.2 to ensure parity with the more accurate vector values.

Table 4.1. *Observed and predicted visitor rates*

Time zone[1] (1)	Actual visits[2] (2)	Zonal pop'n[3] (3)	Observed visit rate[4] (4)	Predicted visit rate[5] (5)	Predicted visits[6] (6)
5	13	954	0.0136268	0.0103972	9.9
10	31	21,596	0.0014355	0.0027285	58.9
15	8	13,326	0.0006003	0.0012476	16.6
20	10	14,377	0.0006956	0.0007160	10.3
25	26	26,811	0.0009698	0.0004655	12.5
30	38	58,416	0.0006505	0.0003274	19.1
40	46	191,009	0.0002408	0.0001879	35.9
50	65	405,831	0.0001602	0.0001222	49.6
60	17	375,134	0.0000453	0.0000859	32.2
75	48	776,817	0.0000618	0.0000559	43.4
90	15	562,508	0.0000267	0.0000393	22.1
105	7	253,762	0.0000276	0.0000292	7.4
120	—	—	—	0.0000225	—
150	—	—	—	0.0000147	—
180	—	—	—	0.0000103	—
210	—	—	—	0.0000077	—
240	—	—	—	0.0000059	—
300	—	—	—	0.0000038	—
360	—	—	—	0.0000027	—
500	—	—	—	0.0000014	—

Notes: [1] Upper limit of travel time zone measured in minutes of vehicle travel.
[2] Number of party visits recorded during survey (no repeat visits in sample).
[3] Number of households within each travel time zone as recorded in the 1991 Census.
[4] Column (2) divided by column (3).
[5] Visit rate predicted from the best-fitting arrival function (discussed subsequently).
[6] Predicted visit rate multiplied by zonal population (number of visiting parties).

resultant travel time zones, although for clarity of reproduction these have been amalgamated to five categories.

Once travel time zones were defined the relevant zone for each survey respondent was identified by matching the outset origin of each of the surveyed visitors to the travel time surface. Results from this exercise are presented in the first two columns of Table 4.1. Here column (1) shows the upper limit of each travel time zone (in minutes of vehicle travel to the site) and column (2) records the number of party visits to the site from each zone during the period of the survey[6] (other columns are discussed subsequently). Of the total sample of 351 parties, 324 (92.8 per cent)

[6] The possibility of repeat visits during the survey period was recognised. This was tested for and proved not to be a feature of the survey sample.

originated from time zones encompassed by our GIS road network. This provided a sufficient sample both to estimate an arrivals function and to extrapolate it beyond the limits of our road network.

The desired arrivals function would predict visits as a function of travel time. However, to achieve this it was necessary to account for varying population densities across our time zones (i.e. we needed to calculate a visit rate in terms of party visits per capita). Accordingly a population grid surface was interpolated which coincided in geographic extent with the travel time surface. Totals for persons usually resident in Enumeration Districts (EDs; the finest level of detail available) were extracted from 1991 Census[7] data using the SASPAC software (London Research Centre, 1992) and grid references for ED centroids were obtained from files held at Manchester Computing Centre.[8] Further discussion of the population surface concept is provided in Bracken and Martin (1995) and Martin (1996b).

Allocation of residential populations to the 500 m × 500 m grid cells composing the travel time zones was achieved through a volume-preserving algorithm, using a form of the SBUILD program described by Martin (1990). A mask image was used to prevent allocations outside the study area and initial input to the software consisted of 6,675 centroids with a population of 2,723,971. The surface produced by SBUILD (after cell totals were rounded to the nearest integer) contained a total population of 2,724,133 suggesting that the program produces accurate population estimates, at least at the aggregate level. Detailed inspection indicates that the characteristics of urban areas are well represented in the population surface and the only criticism which might be made is that some areas classed as 'unpopulated' undoubtedly contain isolated properties. This type of deficiency is, however, virtually inevitable given reliance upon data for areal aggregates such as Enumeration Districts and in the context of this research is not thought to represent a significant problem.

Population totals for our defined travel time zones were straightforward to calculate within the Grid module of Arc/Info. By allocating each of the surveyed parties to a travel time zone, summing to derive a total, and dividing by the resident population, a zonal visit rate was calculated. Results from this exercise are shown in Table 4.1. Here column (3) records the zonal population derived as discussed above. Column (4) divides visits from each zone, in column (2), by zonal population to give our observed visit rate. This represents the dependent variable in our arrivals function. The contents of columns (5) and (6) are described subsequently.

---

[7] Crown Copyright, ESRC/JISC purchase.

[8] A check on the accuracy of grid references was then conducted by calculating mean centres and standard distances for the EDs within each ward. This process revealed a few gross errors in grid references, which were corrected.

Table 4.1 indicates the expected, strongly negative, relationship between travel time and visit rate.[9] An examination of this relationship revealed that a double-log model provided a good fit to the data.[10] Equation (4.1) summarises the resulting arrivals function.

$$\ln VR = -1.46 - 1.93 \ln TZ \qquad (4.1)$$
$$(-2.41) \quad (-11.39)$$

where:

VR = observed visit rate (number of party visits from zone i divided by
     zonal population)
TZ = travel time zone (minutes)
R^2 (adj.) = 92.1%. Figures in brackets are t-statistics.

Investigations into potential omitted variables and correlation of residuals failed to reveal any significant problems with Equation (4.1). Given the strength of this relationship we felt confident in extrapolating our arrivals function to more distant travel time zones. Columns (4) and (5) of Table 4.1 list observed and predicted visitor rates, while columns (2) and (6) report actual and predicted visitor numbers. The arrivals function predicted 317.8 party visits from the first twelve travel time zones during the sampling period. This compares with an actual figure of 324, an error of less than 2 per cent.

Our arrivals function refers to those visitors interviewed during the sampling period. One of the main reasons for conducting our survey at Thetford rather than at a Welsh site was that it is one of the very few forests for which accurate daily and weekly visitor records are available (weekly data being held for several years). This information enabled us to allow for those visitors to Thetford who were not interviewed during our sampling period and also to establish that a very stable relationship exists between annual and survey period visits (Bateman, 1996, gives full details of this analysis).[11] This allowed us to extrapolate our sample-period arrivals function to an annual basis. Comparison of predicted with actual annual visits showed a discrepancy of just over 1 per cent.

---

[9] Note that observations from the furthest time zone (120 minutes) were omitted from our analysis (full details of which are given in Bateman, 1996) as this zone was not completely encompassed by the road network (see Figure 4.1).

[10] The small number of observations means that we should exercise some caution here. The double-log form narrowly outperformed a semi-log (dependent) model, while other forms fitted the data poorly. This is similar to the findings of Colenutt and Sidaway (1973) who report results for both forms although it is not made clear which is superior.

[11] This analysis reveals a consistent pattern of visits over the year, in which arrivals were well predicted by seasonal factors, extreme weather events and national holidays.

Applying the arrivals function: predicting arrivals in Wales

Before considering the detail of this analysis it is worthwhile to remind ourselves of its place within the overall study. The objective of the research presented in this section is to yield a map of predicted arrivals to actual or potential woodland sites for a regular grid across our Welsh study area which can then be monetised using the values derived in Chapter 3. This money value map will provide the first element in the analysis of woodland benefits. Maps of the timber and carbon storage value of woodland, derived in Chapters 6 and 7, can then be readily added to this to yield our estimate of the total benefits of woodland. These results can then be compared to the map of agricultural values derived in Chapter 8 to allow us to conduct a spatial CBA of the net benefits of conversion of land from agriculture to woodland in Chapter 9.

Our first concern in the present analysis was to test the validity of our arrivals function against the actual number of visits made at a sample of Welsh woodland sites. A study area boundary was defined and coincident road network and population surfaces constructed in a manner similar to the Thetford analysis. In order to allow for distant travellers to potential woodland sites along the Welsh border, the study area was defined so as to reach deep into England.[12] Appropriate county boundaries were obtained from the Bartholomew database. Road data were extracted, clipped and corrected as described in Chapter 3. B-roads and minor roads outside Wales were deleted, except where their omission created significant gaps in road topology. Roads that were just outside the defined study area were also included (notably the M6 motorway outside Coventry) if their absence seemed likely to have a significant impact on calculations of population accessibility. The resulting road network is illustrated in Figure 4.2.

Roads were again rasterised onto a 500 m × 500 m regular grid. The value assigned to each cell was the class of the road segment (as recorded in the Bartholomew database) with the greatest cumulative length running through the grid square. As a consequence, a long section of road that just clipped the edge of a cell took precedence over a short segment of road that actually had the greatest length within the grid square. This was a feature of the rasterising algorithm and could not be readily circumvented. Urban boundaries were rasterised and overlaid onto the road network to allow separation of urban from rural roads.

Population data and centroids for Enumeration Districts were again obtained from Manchester Computing Centre. The study area encompassed 30,311 Enumeration Districts with a total resident population of 13,821,562. Once centroid grid

---

[12] The study area comprised the following counties and areas: Avon, Cheshire, Clwyd, Dyfed, Gloucester, Greater Manchester, Gwent, Gwynedd, Hereford & Worcester, Merseyside, Mid Glamorgan, Powys, Shropshire, South Glamorgan, Staffordshire, West Glamorgan, West Midlands and Anglesey & Holyhead. Minor islands off the coast of Britain were removed.

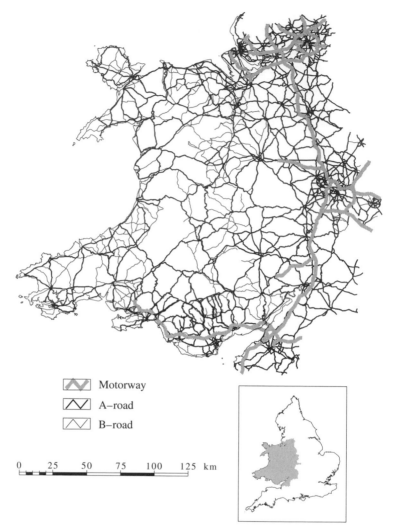

Figure 4.2. Digital road network for Wales and the English Midlands. For cartographic reasons English B-roads and all minor roads are omitted from the map.

references had been checked, the SBUILD program was again used to generate a population surface at 500 m × 500 m grid cell resolution. The program again performed well, yielding a total population estimate of 13,821,361 people. Figure 4.3 illustrates the resulting surface.

With the Welsh travel time zone algorithm and the relevant population surface defined, an actual versus predicted test of our arrivals function was possible. At the time of this analysis the Forestry Commission only held visitor data for five sites in Wales. Furthermore, in conversation with officials it became apparent that two of these were closed for unusually long periods during the year while a third contained several special attractions not normally found at forest sites which raised

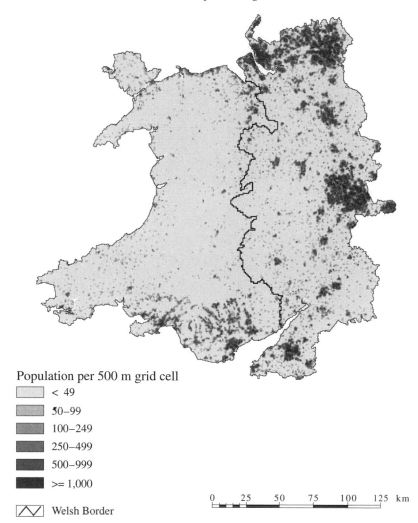

Population per 500 m grid cell
  | < 49
  | 50–99
  | 100–249
  | 250–499
  | 500–999
  | >= 1,000

0   25   50   75   100   125 km

| Welsh Border

Figure 4.3. Population density surface for Wales and the English Midlands. (*Source of population data:* 1991 Census, Crown Copyright, ESRC/JISC purchase. The population density values were calculated using the SBUILD software with 1991 Census Enumeration District centroids.)

visitor numbers above those normally expected for such a location.[13] This sample size and associated complications meant that the desired standard of testing was not feasible (a problem which was not adequately addressed until additional sites subsequently became available and an extended test across more than thirty sites was carried out as described subsequently in this chapter). However, it was decided to undertake a simple comparison of predicted and actual arrivals at each of the five Welsh sites available. For each of these sites, arrivals were predicted by (i) using the

---

[13] These include a museum, catering facilities and a variety of organised recreational activities.

rastering algorithm to define zones and travel times; (ii) interrogating the SBUILD population surface to obtain an estimate of the population in each zone and; (iii) applying this information through the arrivals function given in Equation (4.1) in conjunction with the sample period/annual visitor conversion factor calculated during the Thetford survey. Equation (4.2) simply relates actual to predicted visits per annum.[14]

$$\text{ACTUAL} = 0.903 \text{ PREDICTED} \tag{4.2}$$

$$(4.420)$$

where:

> ACTUAL = actual arrivals at site (party visits per annum)
> PREDICTED = predicted arrivals at site (party visits per annum)
> R^2 (adj.) = 83.0%. Figures in brackets are t-statistics.

Equation (4.2) indicates that, despite the limitations of this analysis, the arrivals function performs as expected with the slope coefficient for PREDICTED not being significantly different from 1. Given this result and the lack of data for further testing we concluded that the arrivals function did provide at least a defensible predictor of annual arrivals at a typical woodland site (i.e. one with similar basic facilities to that found at Thetford).

We were therefore able to make a case for applying the arrivals function to a regular grid of points across the study area and so predict expected annual recreational visits to actual and hypothetical woodland sites across Wales.[15] An important practical issue, however, is the appropriate grid size for such an analysis. Even with the use of a raster structure and other efforts to shorten processing, determination of travel time zones for a representative grid covering the whole of Wales represented a significant computational exercise. Using available computing facilities each site took between fifteen and thirty minutes to process (depending on workload). Assuming the former time, calculation of a 1 km grid surface for the entire area of Wales (some 20,500 cells) would take over 200 days of continuous processing; clearly a coarser sampling scheme was required.

The issue of grid size was investigated by defining two transects across Wales. The first of these ran due east from the coast near Aberystwyth to the English border and was composed of thirteen sites, each separated by 2.5 km, and another five sites at 5 km spacing. The second transect ran from a similar origin due south to a point just outside Swansea and was composed of sites all at 5 km intervals. Travel

---

[14] Analysis confirmed that any constant was not significantly different from zero.
[15] Such estimates do not take into account the substitution effects which would arise in any specific area if a number of woodlands were planted in that locality. The object of the current exercise is to identify those areas where the establishment of a wood would be beneficial. The impact of supply-side changes is considered subsequently.

+ = 5 km grid square centroids

```
0     25    50    75   100   125  km
```

Figure 4.4. 5 km grid points used to generate the predicted woodland visitors surface.

time zones and zonal populations were defined for all of these sites and predicted visits estimated using the arrivals function. Inspection of these predictions showed that both the 2.5 km and 5 km resolution sites were sensitive to changes in local population density and the quality of surrounding road infrastructure (details in Bateman *et al.*, 1995b). The detail afforded by the 5 km grid system indicated that such a resolution was adequate in reflecting the major contrasts in predicted visitor numbers engendered by population density and road availability/quality. Clearly a 2.5 km grid would give greater information regarding rates of change. However, given the very considerable processing demands of such a grid, and the acceptability of results from the 5 km resolution sites, such an approach seemed unnecessary. Accordingly travel time zones were calculated for a 5 km grid for the whole of Wales. The base map of grid points used to generate subsequent visitor potential surfaces is illustrated in Figure 4.4.

Regardless of the chosen resolution, certain sampling problems are difficult to alleviate. Inconsistencies arise from the interaction of the road network with the sampling pattern. Cell values depend upon how far a sampling point falls from any kind of road. Two areas equally far from population and with comparable road infrastructure might have different estimated travel times (and therefore predicted visit numbers) if in one of the areas the sampling point falls right on a road and in the other the sampling point is far from any road. There is no straightforward way around this arbitrariness. However, the findings for the two transects (and subsequently the entire area of Wales) were reassuringly sensible and predictable, suggesting that these inconsistencies had not had any significant impact.

Travel times were calculated for each of the 5 km grid sites as follows. A window was defined around each site and the site rasterised. An allocation process, using a cost impedance grid based on road characteristics (see Brainard *et al.*, 1997), was run to find the shortest path linking the site and each other cell in the raster surface. The impedance necessary to reach each of these locations was assigned to corresponding cells in an output grid. This provided, in minutes of travel, a time-surface output which was then classified into time zones. Information on total residents for each of these areas was subsequently extracted from the rasterised population surface and recorded in a separate file. This process was then iterated across all sample sites in the 5 km grid.

Once time zones and zonal populations had been calculated for all grid points, woodland recreation demand (in terms of total party visits per annum) was predicted using the arrivals function. Figure 4.5 illustrates the resulting predicted woodland visitors surface.

Figure 4.5 strongly reflects the influence of population distribution upon the prediction of recreational woodland visits. In southern Wales the influence of cities such as Swansea and Cardiff and the densely populated 'valleys' area results in relatively high visitor predictions. Similarly, in the north-east, the influence of nearby English cities such as Manchester and Liverpool is very clear. Conversely, in mid Wales and western coastal areas, the sparse population results in very low visitor arrival estimates. Population impacts tend to be compounded by the distribution of higher quality transport infrastructure. This inflates the already high arrival numbers generated by the proximity of large centres of population. However, infrastructure effects are perhaps best demonstrated in areas of relatively low population density such as coastal, mid and north Wales. Figure 4.6 shows this area in detail, superimposing the relevant major road network. Here we can see that the presence of a major road creates a heightened potential visitor corridor as it facilitates visits by individuals from relatively distant travel time zones.

Mapping predicted recreation values

In Chapter 3 we derived various estimates for the unit value of a party visit to a recreational woodland. In particular we emphasised a lower-bound value of £1.82 per

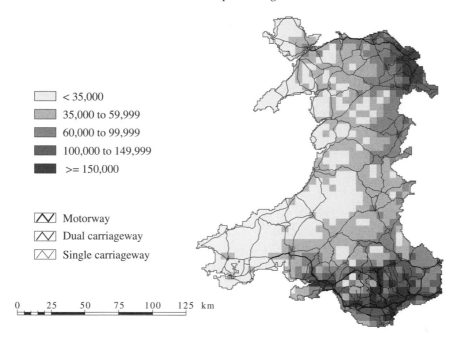

Figure 4.5. Woodland recreation demand in Wales: predicted annual total party visits per site. (*Source:* Bateman *et al.*, 1999c.)

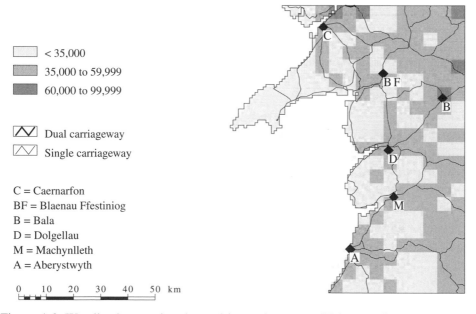

Figure 4.6. Woodland recreation demand in north-western Wales: predicted annual total party visits per site. (*Source:* Bateman *et al.*, 1999c.)

Applied Environmental Economics

a. CV meta-analysis   b. ITC

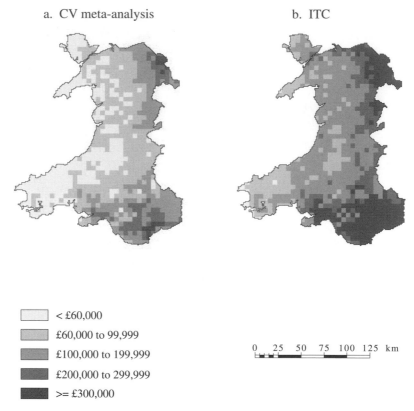

☐ < £60,000

▨ £60,000 to 99,999

▦ £100,000 to 199,999

▩ £200,000 to 299,999

■ >= £300,000

0   25   50   75   100   125   km

Figure 4.7. Predicted value of total annual woodland recreation demand per site using two valuation estimates: (a) lower-bound values based on cross-study analysis of CV values; (b) upper-bound values based on ITC study.

party per visit derived from our cross-study analysis of CV results and an upper-bound estimate of £3.59 per party per visit obtained from our ITC analysis. GIS capabilities were used to apply these values to our estimates of the number of annual party visits to a given (real or hypothetical) woodland to yield predictions of the total annual recreational value of sites. Figure 4.7 illustrates the maps of recreational value produced by this exercise.

The distribution of values within each of the maps shown in Figure 4.7 mirrors that of the base demand map (Figure 4.5). However, the fact that our upper-bound valuation is nearly twice that of our lower-bound estimate is well illustrated here. The degree to which this variability constitutes a cause for concern is uncertain. If we are confident of these bounds then, in a cost-benefit context, if the lower-bound value is sufficient to justify a switch from other land uses into woodland, further precision may be unnecessary. Similarly, if even upper-bound values are not large enough to justify such conversion, then again these estimates are sufficient for decision analysis. Only if the cost-benefit balance lies within these bounds is further precision required. Given this, then, at least as an exercise in methodological development, use of these estimates seems justified.

Extensions

The work described above details the extent of our research to date on the case study area of Wales and is used as the basis of the cost-benefit analysis presented in Chapter 9 of this volume. It also represents our only attempt to date to generate maps of arrivals and recreation values for large areas, embracing both existing and potential recreation sites. However, our recent and ongoing research concerning other areas of Britain extends our methodology for modelling visits and values. In this section we briefly review this work to provide the reader with a flavour of the directions in which this research is developing.

In work described in Lovett *et al.* (1997), Bateman *et al.* (1998) and Brainard *et al.* (1999) we examine how both the number of arrivals and the value of those visits to woodland sites alters according to a range of attribute characteristics. These include:

(i) travel costs, described by the accessibility of the site to the potential visiting population (i.e. taking into account the spatial distribution of the whole of the British population in relation to the study site)
(ii) the socio-economic and demographic characteristics of that potential visiting population (allowing for the possibility that, say, richer households or those with more children may visit such sites more often)
(iii) the availability of substitute woodlands described by an inverse weighted distance to all other British woodlands from all possible visitor outset origins
(iv) site quality characteristics (for example, presence and size of a car park, length of woodland walks, etc.).

These models represent a substantial extension to those described previously, both because of the additional explanatory variable considered and because they permit the estimation of site-specific coefficients, yielding estimates of consumer surplus for each individual site. This allows for the possibility that the value of the recreational experience varies between sites.

The first stage of this analysis involved calculation of a variety of variables describing items (i) to (iv) above for Thetford Forest. These variables were obtained from a variety of sources. Travel distances and times were calculated and population distribution obtained using the GIS as described previously. Data on the

Table 4.2. *Official recreational visit numbers, predictions of arrivals and consumer surplus estimates for twenty-seven English woodlands*

Site name	Official estimate of visits (per annum)	Predicted visits (per annum)	Per party consumer surplus (£ per visit)	Site consumer surplus (£ per annum)
Dunwich	18,980	15,957**	1.56	24,828
Two Mile Bottom	22,636	22,678***	2.72	61,676
Kielder Castle	24,243	56,747*	3.57	202,767
Forest Drive	31,641	26,200**	3.57	93,616
Warksburn	3,794	5,351*	7.42	39,706
Bogle Crag	14,924	47,475	5.38	255,408
Grizedale	85,181	81,015***	3.48	281,824
Noble Knott	7,543	35,407	3.51	124,149
Whinlatter	55,797	60,838***	3.36	204,571
Blackwater	39,338	37,518***	5.19	147,813
Bolderwood	22,963	28,503***	4.86	182,318
Moors Valley	165,552	157,561***	4.14	652,149
Bucknell	21,360	45,526	1.63	74,117
Salcey	77,650	75,644***	2.23	168,735
Wakerley	51,490	42,354***	2.06	87,456
Dalby	130,151	77,804*	3.31	257,260
Chopwell	42,298	54,251*	6.36	344,846
Hamsterley	76,796	71,770**	3.50	251,462
Simonside	12,430	32,526	2.94	95,462
Blidworth Bottom	54,547	41,844***	3.15	131,776
Blidworth Lane	52,754	45,103***	3.16	142,394
Blidworth Tower	37,596	45,288***	2.91	131,660
Chambers Farm	23,605	22,808***	1.92	43,836
Goyt, The Street	84,279	73,400**	2.63	193,058
Normans Hill	30,936	35,975***	2.66	95,748
Thieves Wood	72,276	45,617*	2.66	121,474
Sherwood Centre	38,919	42,325**	1.78	75,430

Notes: * = predictions within 50% of official estimates;
** = predictions within 25% of official estimates.

socio-economic and demographic characteristics of the population were obtained from the UK Census and this information was spatially assigned using the GIS. Distances from each possible outset origin on a regular grid across Britain to each potential woodland recreation substitute site[16] were calculated and an inverse weighting scheme applied (with weights being empirically derived by analysis of the outset origin of visitors to Thetford in relation to substitute availability from those origins) to give prominence to those nearer to each potential outset origin. Finally, site quality characteristics were obtained from the Forestry Commission.

These data were then used to estimate a model to predict visits (and values) for Thetford Forest. This was then transferred to predict arrivals and recreation values at twenty-seven English woodlands[17] for which official estimates of visits were available (although the Forestry Commission freely admitted that these estimates were somewhat approximate). Results from the transfer exercise are detailed in Table 4.2, contrasting official estimates with predictions derived from our transfer function from which estimates of per party and per annum consumer surplus are obtained and detailed.

Considering Table 4.2, our extended transferable model provides estimates which are highly correlated with those of the Forestry Commission ($p < 0.001$).[18] Given the lack of a gold standard for determining the accuracy of either set of estimates, this seems an adequate basis for future research and arguably provides an acceptable planning tool. Certainly this was the opinion of the Forestry Commission which recently asked the authors, together with their colleague Andy Jones (also at the University of East Anglia), to apply this methodology to a larger dataset of nearly 11,000 interviews conducted at forty sites across Britain. When completed, this analysis will be combined with a second, recently finished study (again with Andy Jones) commissioned by British Waterways, examining over 5,000 interviews conducted at fifty-three inland waterway sites across Britain. These studies further extend the methodology set out above by incorporating wider sets of socio-economic, site quality and substitute availability variables (for example, non-woodland substitutes such as waterways, beaches, built heritage and urban attractions are considered). At the time of writing, results from these studies were being prepared for publication. However, in both cases similar messages were clearly given by the data, which are of particular relevance to the work described in this volume. While

[16] Potential substitute sites were taken from a variety of sources including satellite imagery, the Institute of Terrestrial Ecology land use map and a joint Countryside Commission and Forestry Commission large-sample household survey of outdoor recreation.

[17] Brainard *et al.* (1999) consider a further six subsites, that is sites within a larger forest with multiple sites. However, our transfer model was unreliable for such applications, i.e. it only predicts for visitors to a distinct forest rather than for areas within a given forest.

[18] A regression test relating official estimates to our transfer predictions showed a coefficient which was not significantly different from 1 with a constant which was not significantly different from zero.

issues such as the socio-economic characteristics of potential visiting populations, the availability of substitutes and site characteristics are all significant predictors of visits and values, all of these variables are dwarfed by the significance of travel costs. It seems that the business world mantra of 'location, location, location' being the vital determinant of demand applies equally well to the demand for open-access recreational public goods. Indeed omission of all other explanatory variables yields relatively small estimation errors. Given the strength of this result we feel that the analysis presented in preceding sections remains a valid input to the CBA conducted in Chapter 9 of this volume.

Limitations of the predicted recreation values

We now return to our analysis of the case study area of Wales. While we feel that the recreation value maps illustrate the methodological potential of applying GIS techniques in this context, it is important to conclude this chapter with a brief discussion of a number of potential limitations and further issues which would have to be addressed before the full decision-making potential of this approach could be realised.

The supply side

Our analysis only considers the demand side of the woodland recreation 'market'. The recreation value maps indicate the recreation demand for a typical woodland established at any of the 5 km grid intersections of the base map (Figure 4.4). They do not tell us about the supply side of this market. There are two major ways in which the supply side interacts with demand to determine actual visits. First, the existing distribution of woodland will already have soaked up some of our predicted demand. Second, as new forests are planted and (with some time lag) recreational services become available, so demand becomes satisfied. If supply exceeds demand in any one area such that non-congested recreation sites already exist, then the demand for new sites will be lower than that predicted in Figure 4.7 which ignores the distribution of existing sites.

To a substantial degree these concerns are incorporated within the extension work described earlier through the addition of substitute availability variables. However, this work also shows that it is travel time and cost which remain by far the strongest determinant of visits and values. Therefore, while there is clearly scope for using this research to refine our visit prediction maps, the same research suggests that the results summarised in Figures 4.5 to 4.7 remain valid approximations of underlying relationships and are acceptable as an element within our subsequent CBA assessment.

Applicability of the Thetford Forest period to annual conversion factor

As part of our arrivals function calculations we had to convert from the survey period to an annual basis. One concern here is whether the conversion factor used is valid for other sites or unique to Thetford Forest. In order to test this fully we would ideally need data regarding the annual distribution of visits both at Thetford and at any site to which we wish to extrapolate. Unfortunately, as described in relation to Table 4.2, official estimates are still only rough approximations and robust values are currently unavailable for our Welsh study area. Gillam (pers. comm.)[19] suggests that seasonality patterns are likely to be roughly similar across England and Wales and only differ in very remote areas such as the north of Scotland where seasonal peaks are likely to be relatively more pronounced. On the basis of this information, and in the absence of any contrary evidence, we feel that we have adopted a defensible approach to this issue.

Comparability of recreation in Thetford Forest with that in Wales

The major demographic and infrastructure differences which separate Wales from our East Anglian survey site are explicitly accounted for in our arrivals function which allows for both population density and road network quality. Two remaining issues are pertinent here. First, does our survey site provide similar recreational services to those of our visitor potential map? By definition, the answer here is yes, because we are looking at the creation of similar service sites where the major recreational attraction is open-access walking and its associated activities. However, in the absence of data concerning site quality and facilities this approach will not be appropriate for predicting arrivals to non-standard real or hypothetical sites. Second, does the psychological perception of woodland recreation differ between East Anglia and Wales? In considering this we must separate it from the supply-side problem commented upon above. Once such a distinction is made we see no reason to suspect any inconsistency here (although it cannot be ruled out), an assertion reinforced by the earlier work of Colenutt and Sidaway (1973) in the Forest of Dean (on the Welsh border) which reports similar visitation patterns to those observed in our own analyses.

Conclusions

The analysis presented in this chapter has used a variety of GIS techniques to model visits to a specific woodland and then apply the resultant arrivals function to

---

[19] Simon Gillam (Chief Statistician, Forestry Commission) noted that the Thetford Forest estimates were believed to be among the most reliable available and therefore provided a reasonable basis for this analysis.

produce estimates of visitation to similar woodlands across our Welsh study area. The estimates have then been converted into money values using the valuation studies presented previously. Results conform well to prior expectations showing predicted demand to be linked to population distribution and site accessibility.

A number of problems have been identified in the course of this analysis. Both the per visit values and visit number estimates were not sensitive to certain site characteristics. However, the extensions described above provide a methodology for addressing these problems and the results of this recent work suggest that the errors created by such omissions are acceptably small, travel costs being the overriding determinant of visits and values.

Given this we can defend our analysis both on methodological and empirical grounds. Furthermore, the adoption of a sensitivity analysis approach, using upper- and lower-bound valuation assumptions to create an envelope of recreational values, represents a substantial improvement over the common omission of such values from land use planning. In subsequent chapters we augment these with further forest values before making a comparison of aggregate values with those from conventional agriculture in the Welsh study area.

5

Timber valuation

Introduction

In this chapter we assess both the social and private value of timber production. This is the major market-priced output of woodland. Furthermore, while recent policy statements from both the National Assembly for Wales (1999, 2001a; Forestry Commission (FC), 2001a,b) and UK government departments (Department for the Environment, Transport and the Regions (DETR), 2000) emphasise the need to adopt a holistic approach to managing woodlands, explicitly recognising their multipurpose nature, timber production remains, nevertheless, a key element of such a strategy, playing an important role in rural economies (FC, 1998).[1]

The economic and policy imperative to include timber production within any cost-benefit analysis of land use change involving forestry is therefore clear. However, the estimated value of this production depends crucially upon the real price of timber. Because plantation returns are long delayed, any (even small) change in real prices will have a major impact upon net present value (NPV) sums.[2] In order to assess this, the chapter opens with a brief history of commercial forestry in the UK designed to acquaint the reader with the recent, major and trend-breaking increase in domestic timber supply. In the subsequent section both the supply and demand sides of the UK market are modelled so that a balanced view on future prices can be derived. These conclusions are reinforced by time-series analyses of price movements.

---

[1] Note that, while this document explicitly refers to English woodlands, the recent Cabinet Office report to the Prime Minister (Cabinet Office, 2000) makes it clear that this is the first of three strategy documents.

[2] NPV is the sum of discounted net benefits (benefits minus costs) over the lifetime of a project (here a plantation). For further discussion, see Price (1987b); also, see Reed and Haight (1996) who introduce stochastic elements. In practice, felling and management decisions may be highly complex. This was recognised even in the classic optimal rotation model proposed by Faustmann (1849) (see Chang, 1998; Deegen, 2000). However, this decision becomes even more complex when forest-owners are motivated by objectives other than profit maximisation (see, for example, the discussion of owner's amenity benefits by Tahvonen, 1999; or of recreational hunting by Akabua et al., 2000).

Whilst timber value is clearly important, private planting decisions are often determined by the availability of shorter-term grants rather than long-delayed felling benefits, so we devote a section to reviewing the various subsidy schemes available. The next section brings together the preceding discussions regarding prices and grants and information on plantation costs and tree growth to produce the base rotation[3] models upon which our timber valuations are calculated.

The long time horizons inherent in woodland investments bring us to the vexed question of discounting. We discuss the principle of discounting and provide a brief review of the literature regarding the 'correct' discount rate with respect to both social cost-benefit analysis and private investment appraisal. We conclude that as no single, clearly correct discount rate can be identified, a sensitivity analysis approach is required.

The subsequent section provides investment appraisal results from the viewpoint of a private individual (the farmer) and this is then extended to provide a limited social cost-benefit analysis of the timber product of a plantation (i.e. ignoring those externalities dealt with elsewhere in this research). In both cases, NPV and annuity equivalent (defined subsequently) results are reported, the former being the usual fare of the forest economist while the latter are comparable with competing agricultural outputs.

Assessment of all possible woodland tree species was not feasible given both time constraints and a lack of data concerning less popular species. Furthermore, preliminary analysis indicated that costs and benefits of different conifers would be reasonably similar,[4] the same being (broadly) true of broadleaves. Therefore, two 'indicator' species were selected for analysis: Sitka spruce (conifer), and beech (broadleaf).

Historical background

Pre-1945

In terms of land use, British forestry has always been the poor cousin of agriculture. Although the prehistoric 'natural' condition of the land was primarily as forest, the influence of man has consistently been to clear-fell and convert land to agricultural use. Even by the time of the Domesday Book only 15 per cent of England remained under trees.[5] This deforestation trend continued for most of the last millennium with particularly heavy losses occurring in the sixteenth and seventeenth centuries when adoption of advanced husbandry techniques and subsequent enclosure of common land allowed agriculture to confine forestry to marginal areas and private

---

[3] A rotation is the full lifespan of a plantation from planting to felling.

[4] This is of course a relative statement. Differences do exist and are important at the micro level. However, the magnitudes of costs and benefits are similar enough for this to be a defensible assumption in this study.

[5] Pers. comm. Colin Price, Department of Agricultural and Forest Sciences, University of Wales, Bangor.

parklands, the latter often being operated on a non-commercial basis for private amenity values (Rackham, 1976). By 1900 only 4 per cent of England, 5 per cent of Wales[6] and 2 per cent of Scotland and Ireland was under forestry, these being by far the lowest levels in Europe (Rackham, 1976; National Assembly for Wales, 2001a).

At the start of the twentieth century the UK was almost completely dependent upon imports for its timber supply. This strategic weakness was exposed by the German naval blockade of Britain during the First World War. With timber a major input to the UK's vital coal industry it was felt that the creation of a strategic domestic timber supply was essential to the future security of the country and, in 1919, the Forestry Commission was established. Although strategic security of supply was the FC's initial objective this was quickly supplemented by further aims such as the commercial production of timber, the stimulation of employment in areas of rural depopulation and the provision of public benefits such as open-access recreation and wildlife habitats.[7]

Public sector forestry in the UK has from the outset followed an erratic course. A strong initial political will to establish a secure national timber supply ensured that the 1920s were a period of major afforestation, reversing the trend (if not the effects) of the previous millennia. However, as memories of wartime shortages receded and world timber prices slumped, the 1930s saw planting figures fall well behind the 30,000 ha annual target envisaged at the creation of the FC. This slump was offset to some extent by the Commission's own promotion of forestry as a response to rural depopulation trends and a government initiative 'to create a settled force of woodsmen and their families whose livelihood would be enhanced from their own tenanted smallholdings' (Philip, 1976). Nevertheless, the 1930s still saw an overall contraction of new planting.

Post-1945

Figure 5.1 illustrates total, FC and private sector annual planting from 1945 to 2000, providing a starting point for our discussions of the development of both public and private woodland during this period.

Public sector forestry

The end of the Second World War marked the start of the most sustained period of UK forestry expansion in recorded history (see Figure 5.1). Initially, national

[6] An overview of the history of Welsh forestry from prehistoric times to the present is given in National Assembly for Wales (2001a).

[7] In recent years the FC has also defended its existence as a source of import savings and reduction in agricultural subsidy. Pearce (1991) shows the import substitution argument to be invalid.

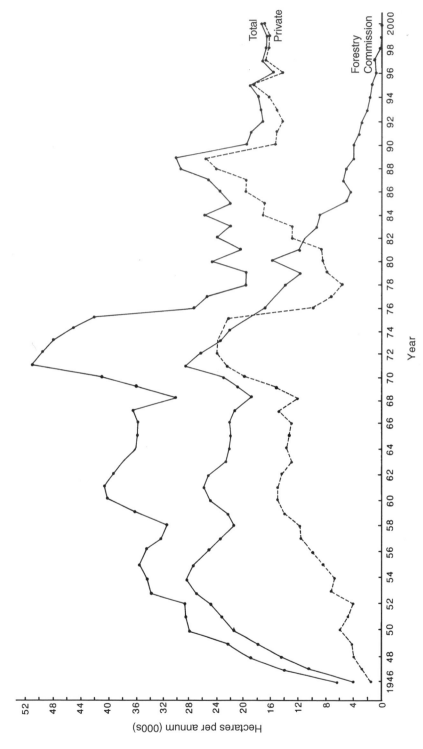

Figure 5.1. Forestry Commission, private sector and total annual forestry planting, Great Britain 1946–2000. (*Source:* Forestry Commission, (1979, 1985b, 1988a, 1989, 1990, 1993, 1994a, 1997, 2001c.)

security concerns and high prices again dominated policy objectives. The post-war adoption of a planned approach to the economy, firm prices and the expansion of the world timber trade ensured that FC planting accelerated to a peak of over 28,000 ha per annum in the decade following the war. The period from the mid 1950s to the early 1970s was characterised by fairly stable public sector planting of about 24,000 ha annually. This was helped by a government decision to allow the FC to operate at a favourably low rate of return compared to other state investments. A discount rate of only 3 per cent[8] was required of the Commission compared to rates of between 5 per cent and 10 per cent for other state-owned enterprises.[9]

The year 1971 marked a significant peak for the FC with plantings exceeding 28,000 ha for the first time since the early 1950s. However, that year also marked a turning point beginning a downward trend in FC planting which has continued for three decades to the present day. The 1970s were a difficult period for the UK economy with the oil crisis and domestic economic problems (in particular relatively high inflation and poor trade balances) leading to heavily depressed growth rates. This put pressure on all areas of public finance, to which the FC was not immune. Contractions in FC employment (Thompson, 1990) accompanied reductions in planting and by 1979 annual planting had dropped to 11,800 ha, i.e. about 40 per cent of the 1971 level.

The election in 1979 of a Conservative government, pledged to the reduction of the public sector in favour of private enterprise, meant that the decline in new planting seen in the 1970s has been extended throughout the 1980s and up to the present day, a trend which was unaffected by the election of a Labour government in 1997. New planting in Wales ceased in 1993, followed by England in 1996 and Scotland in 2000, this latter year being the first since the Second World War in which the FC had not undertaken any new planting.

Arguably, a more serious threat to the absolute scale of FC operations is the disposal of its estate into private ownership, a trend which, as Table 5.1 shows, can be traced back to the early 1980s when an extensive programme of land sales was implemented.[10] Prior to this, the overall size of the estate had grown every year since its creation to stand at 1,264,000 ha in 1981 but this has declined in every year since to stand at 1,052,900 ha in 2000, a reduction of 16.7 per cent.

---

[8] Even lower rates of return were required from plantings carried out in Northern Ireland. From 1989 the FC was set a target rate of return of 6 per cent but, as this is virtually unattainable without explicit valuation of non-market benefits, the Treasury initially allowed new investment decisions to be taken at a 3 per cent rate with the resultant shortfall being written off as Forestry Subsidy (H.M. Treasury, 1991: Annex G). Felling decisions remain at a 5 per cent discount rate to retain compatibility with existing FC appraisal systems.

[9] From 1989 this has been set at 8 per cent for commercial public sector enterprises, with a discretionary rate of 6 per cent applied to projects with returns accruing to the public sector. This latter rate applies to forestry management decisions, with the exception of Forestry Enterprise which is permitted to use a 3 per cent discount rate as an explicit subsidy (Pearce and Ulph, 1998).

[10] See statement by the then Secretary of State reproduced in Appendix V of FC (1985a).

Table 5.1. *Forestry Commission holdings: Great Britain 1978–2000 ('000 ha)*

Year-end	FC plantation		Awaiting planting etc.[1]	Total forest	Total FC estate[2]	Annual change in total FC estate[3]
1978	862.5		83.4	945.9	1,253.2	—
1979	868.2		84.0	952.2	1,256.3	3.1
1980	884.0		78.4	962.4	1,263.4	7.1
1981	895.7		70.2	965.9	1,264.0	0.6
1982	905.5		59.4	954.9	1,258.7	(5.3)
1983	908.7		54.0	962.7	1,250.9	(7.8)
1984	901.7		47.6	949.3	1,209.2	(41.7)
1985	900.5		34.3	934.8	1,181.0	(28.2)
1986	897.5		30.2	927.7	1,165.5	(15.5)
1987	899.7		23.4	926.4	1,156.4	(9.1)
1988	898.5		20.6	919.1	1,149.4	(7.0)
1989	898.2		17.2	915.4	1,144.2	(5.2)
	Productive land	Other woodland[4]				
1990	863.5	34.3	11.2	909.0	1,139.5	(4.7)
1991	858.5	34.5	9.8	902.8	1,133.1	(6.4)
1992	855.3	34.8	5.6	895.8	1,127.5	(5.6)
1993	845.4	37.1	5.1	887.6	1,115.4	(12.1)
1994	826.6	44.0	3.2	873.8	1,099.5	(15.9)
1995	815.6	45.4	2.0	862.9	1,089.8	(9.8)
1996	804.6	46.7	0.8	852.0	1,080.0	(9.8)
1997	795.4	48.3	0.4	844.1	1,073.0	(7.0)
1998	784.7	49.7	0.7	835.0	1,061.8	(11.2)
1999	779.5	50.7	0.6	830.8	1,057.3	(4.5)
2000	774.2	51.1	0.6	825.9	1,052.9	(4.4)

Notes: [1] Between 1979 and 1984 this figure was disaggregated into 'land awaiting planting' and 'scrubland, etc.' with the latter being about 10 per cent of the former during that period.
[2] Total forest + other non-woodland (nursery land + agricultural land + unplantable + forestry workers' holdings).
[3] Numbers in brackets indicate reductions in the FC estate.
[4] Recreational land, etc.
Source: Forestry Commission (1979, 1985b, 1989, 1990, 1993, 1994a, 1996, 1997, 2001c).

Despite numerous ministerial pronouncements on safeguarding public access to land sold by the FC, in almost all cases privatisation has led to the exclusion of the public (Goodwin, 1995).[11] This is particularly serious given that it has been in areas of high population where the proportion of FC woodlands privatised has been

---

[11] In the period from October 1991 to November 1995, of 35,233 ha privatised only 506 ha (1.4 per cent) had freedom of access guaranteed (Goodwin, 1995).

highest (Lean, 1996).[12] Despite recent claims that the present government has 'put a stop to large-scale sales of forest land by the Forestry Commission' (Cabinet Office, 2000: p. 90), disposals have continued under the present Labour administration although arguably at a lower rate than under the previous Conservative government. Given the poor record of ensuring access to private woodlands, this does appear to run contrary to official policy initiatives to promote rural recreation and access as set out in the recent Rural White Paper (DETR, 2000) and suggests a potential failure of 'joined-up government' in this area. However, this trend of loss of open-access land in terms of a reduced FC estate is slightly ameliorated by the increased area of 'other woodland' within the estate, the majority of which is used for recreational purposes. Nevertheless, these gains are more than offset (at least in quantitative terms) by the scale of disposals, suggesting that this remains a cause for concern.

Given this background, recent policy documents promoting the growth of multipurpose woodlands (FC, 1998) can perhaps best be interpreted as indicating continued support for private sector expansion (discussed subsequently) and a reorientation of public sector forestry away from conifer monocultures and towards mixed and broadleaved woodland. This seems most clearly to be the case in our case study area of Wales. In its most substantial woodland policy document since devolution in 1999, the National Assembly for Wales (2001a: p. 45) recently stated that:

> Since substantial areas of coniferous forest will be harvested during the next 30 years, there will be an opportunity to reshape these woodlands to deliver wider benefits to society. The National Assembly's estate can play a leading role in this process since it is made up of over 80% coniferous species, compared to only half in private woodlands.

The same document continues by providing an insight into the National Assembly's definition of the multipurpose woodland they seek to promote over their chosen policy horizon of fifty years: '... multi-purpose woodlands managed for recreation, landscape and wildlife as well as for timber production ... absorbing carbon dioxide and so helping ameliorate climate change' (p. 45).

Such a definition fits well with the cost-benefit analysis conducted in this volume, and this suggests that the results reported in subsequent chapters may have particular resonance within the current policy environment both across Britain and, particularly, within our study area of Wales.

Finally, while expansion of the FC has *de facto* halted, other publicly funded forests are in process of being established, most notably the National Forest currently being developed under the auspices of the Countryside Commission in central England. First proposed in 1987 and defined as a series of woodlands comprising

---

[12] For example, between 1981 and 1996, 91 per cent of FC woodlands in West Yorkshire were privatised; 72 per cent in Durham; 67 per cent in Kent; 53 per cent in Humberside and 43 per cent in Essex (Lean, 1996). However, one countervailing trend has been the growth of charity-funded woodlands (although these are not always open-access) such as those operated by the Woodland Trust (Smith, 1996).

some 30 million trees planted over an area of about 200 square miles (516 km^2), the National Forest is intended to bring economic and quality-of-life benefits to a relatively depressed area (Countryside Commission, 1987, 1993; Cloke *et al.*, 1996). However, examination of the National Assembly for Wales' (2001a) *Strategy for Trees and Woodlands* shows that there are no explicit plans to develop similar projects either within or near to our study area of Wales.

Private sector forestry

From the outset, direct government intervention through the agency of a state forestry service has been complemented by the stimulation of a private forestry sector through the provision of tax relief and other incentives to private individuals who invest in timber production.[13]

Despite these incentives, inexperience meant that initial private sector involvement was very restrained. However, from the late 1950s a proliferation of firms specialising in facilitating private forestry investments considerably eased the practical problems of such investment. These companies located land, arranged purchases, planting and felling, and took care of the tax liability and refunding formalities, thus allowing those for whom tax relief was an attractive proposition to become forest-owners without ever having to visit a plantation or see a tree.

In this way, post-war planting of private woodlands expanded at a steady rate from 1945 to the early 1970s (see Figure 5.1). However, as with the FC, the 1970s were a period of relative decline for the private forestry sector. As the OPEC oil-shock sent the world economy into recession, so the UK's forest-owning elite no longer had the excess taxable income to divert into forest tax-havens. However, these were just the people who benefited from the private sector boom of the 1980s and by 1989 the planting of private woodlands was at its highest ever level. In the search for cheap afforestable land[14] many sites of great ecological value were destroyed (Royal Society for the Protection of Birds, 1987). This factor, and a national outcry against such tax avoidance,[15] caused the government to act and withdraw such tax relief with effect from late 1989 (UK Parliament, 1988).

The removal of tax relief had an immediate impact upon private sector planting, which almost halved from 1989 to 1990. The reason it did not fall further was primarily the existence of a system of planting and maintenance subsidies (discussed subsequently) designed to appeal to land-owners and, to a lesser extent, farmers, rather than to those in search of tax havens. These appear to have generated a

---

[13] Details of these tax relief schemes are given in Bateman (1992).

[14] Unlike most other planting costs, land purchase was not tax-deductible. This led investors to plant on cheap, but often highly unsuitable, wetland areas, destroying valuable natural habitats to produce very poor but highly tax-deductible plantations (Royal Society for the Protection of Birds, 1987).

[15] Culminating in a disparaging *Observer* front-page magazine feature on the hundred largest forest-owners in Britain (Lean and Rosie, 1988). See also *The Times* (1988) and Bloom (1988).

reasonably steady expansion in British private woodlands of just over 15,000 ha per annum throughout the period 1990–2000.[16] However, unlike Forestry Commission operations, much private woodland development falls outside the scope of policy influence, making objectives such as the promotion of multipurpose woodland more difficult to achieve (Selman, 1997).

Historical background: summary

In forestry terms the UK has only recently expanded its domestic supply. Although this grew rapidly in the post-war period, new planting by the FC is now at a total standstill, superseded by private planting at a relatively constant (if, in national terms, low) rate. However, current government policy argues that a holistic assessment of the multipurpose nature of woodland suggests a strong case for further expansion (FC, 1998; DETR, 2000). Certainly, compared to its continental neighbours, the UK lags behind in terms of its forest resource. After eighty years of expansion, less than 11 per cent of the land area of Great Britain is under woodland while about 77 per cent is under agriculture.[17] This compares with EU averages of 25 per cent and 60 per cent respectively.[18] However, this disparity of itself does not constitute a valid case for continued expansion of UK domestic timber supplies. In order to assess this we need first to consider long-term market conditions, and it is to this issue that we now turn.

The UK timber market and long-term prices

Softwoods

The UK's consumption of wood products far outstrips its domestic production, the resultant shortfall being met through timber imports. Indeed, wood products are consistently within the top five import items by value. Much of the empirical work presented in this volume concerns the early 1990s, a period when the UK consumed roughly 45 million m³ of wood products annually,[19] at a cost of £6.3 billion, of which approximately 83 per cent was softwood products (Forestry Industry Committee of Great Britain (FICGB), 1992; FC, 2001c). The past decade has seen an overall modest increase in demand to about 47 million m³ in 1999 at an import cost of about £6.7 billion (United Nations Development Programme (UNDP) *et al.*, 2000; FC, 2001c). With both global and domestic demand for lumber forecast to increase by 20–40 per cent by 2010 (Brown, 1999; Matthews and Hammond, 1999) and

---

[16] Of this about two-thirds was concentrated in Scotland.
[17] Authors' calculations based upon FICGB (1992), UNDP *et al.* (2000) and FC (2001c).   [18] *Ibid.*
[19] Measured in wood raw material equivalent (WRME).

potentially double from present levels by the middle of the twenty-first century (FICGB, 1992; Watson *et al.*, 1998), some commentators have forecast increases in future real prices for timber.[20]

With respect to softwood prices, we see two major flaws in this argument. First, the present level of UK production represents only the early stages of an ongoing substantial expansion of domestic supply engendered by the sustained high levels of planting in the inter-war years and the period from the late 1940s to the 1970s. This is set to continue, with production reaching an estimated peak of nearly 20 million m^3 by the early 2020s and then tailing off (as a result of the curtailing of Forestry Commission expansion since the 1970s) to a plateau of about 12 million m^3 by the 2050s. Second, and more importantly, this expansion of domestic supply has been echoed by an increase in the availability of softwood import supplies (UNDP *et al.*, 2000).[21] World coniferous roundwood production rose from 1,096 million m^3 in 1971 to a peak of 1,307 million m^3 in 1986, slipping back only slightly to a level of 1,295 million m^3 in 1991 (Whiteman, 1995)[22] since when the area of softwood felled in most developed countries has generally been exceeded by the area replanted (UNDP *et al.*, 2000). When combined with arguments regarding ongoing technical change,[23] these factors seem to suggest that real prices for softwood are unlikely to increase in the foreseeable future. Indeed, heavy felling by some Baltic nations during the late 1990s resulted in a fall in UK real timber prices for softwoods over the course of the decade (Forest Enterprise, 2001).

A number of commentators have examined the issue of whether real timber prices have changed significantly over time, the majority concluding in favour of constant real prices (Doran, 1979; Price and Dale, 1982; Pearce and Markandya, undated; Bateman and Mellor, 1990; Bateman, 1996; UNDP *et al.*, 2000). In an in-depth analysis, Whiteman (1995) undertook a time-series analysis of real soft-wood prices from 1870 to 1989. His best-fitting time-series model for this period indicated stable real prices (excluding shocks) prior to the Second World War, a shift to a higher level during the war and a continuation at a higher, but again constant (excluding shocks), level after the war. Whiteman's best estimate was therefore for a constant real softwood price for the foreseeable future. Our own analysis of a shorter time-series from the Second World War up to the early 1990s also supports an assumption of constant real prices, with a single shock to the system during the commodity price boom of the 1970s (Bateman and Mellor, 1990).

---

[20] This argument is reinforced by concerns regarding acid-rain damage to forests (Ewers *et al.*, 1986; Bergen *et al.*, 1992; Pearce, 1993; FC, 1994b). However, estimates indicate that this is unlikely to have any significant impact upon timber supply and consequent prices (Bateman, 1996).

[21] This trend is exemplified by the case of Sweden where, since the 1930s, timber growth has consistently outstripped cutting (Wibe, 1992).

[22] These measurements are in underbark volumes.

[23] Two forms of technical change can be identified: (i) improved plantation husbandry; (ii) increased availability of timber substitutes (particularly in the construction industry; see Leigh and Randell, 1981).

Table 5.2. *High forest by general species: Forestry Commission and private woodland in Great Britain 1947–2000 ('000 ha)*

Forest type	1947	1965	1980	1994	2000
Mainly coniferous high forest	397	922	1,317	1,516	1,584
Mainly broadleaved high forest	380	352	564	615	837
Total	777	1,274	1,881	2,131	2,421

Source: Figures for 1947, 1965 and 1980 are from the occasional Census of Woodlands (FC, 1987; reproduced in Pearce, 1993). Figures for 1994 are from FC (1994a) and include some extrapolation from the 1980 Census. Figures for 2000 are from FC (2001c).

Extending this analysis to the present day (by incorporating data up to March 2001 from Forestry Enterprise, 2001) suggests that the slump in real prices observed in the late 1990s is not statistically significant over this longer period (although of course it would eventually become so if it were sustained for a sufficiently long time).

In conclusion, the consensus view fails to support the hypothesis of future increasing real prices for UK softwoods and we therefore adopt an assumption of constant real prices in the subsequent analysis (although we do note the possibility of unforeseen shocks challenging such an assumption).

Hardwoods

While global reserves of coniferous forest have been reasonably stable or have even grown over the past two decades, the post-war era has seen some decline in temperate hardwoods and a dramatic fall in tropical hardwoods. Considering first the British case, the twentieth century saw a continuation of a centuries-old decline in the area of ancient broadleaf woodlands. In England and Wales this stood at just 142,000 ha in 1933 yet had more than halved by the mid 1980s (Nature Conservancy Council (NCC), 1984). The bulk of this loss arose from conversions to mainly conifer plantations, with the remaining losses generally attributable to agricultural encroachment (NCC, 1984; Council for the Protection of Rural England (CPRE), 1992). However, the planting of new broadleaved woodlands has meant that, since the 1960s, the overall area of broadleaved high forest has consistently risen, as shown in Table 5.2.

While newly planted broadleaved woodland does not have the ecological value of ancient woodland, it does represent an encouraging trend. However, as in the case of softwoods, the UK is far from self-sufficient in hardwoods. The present level of UK domestic hardwood (round and sawn) consumption is about 2 million m^3 per annum. This exceeds domestic production, which fell over the past decade from 1.2 million m^3 in 1991 to 0.8 million m^3 in 1999 as a result of low planting and high felling early in the century (FICGB, 1992; FC, 2001c). While this represents a much higher self-sufficiency rate than for softwoods, and production is forecast to rise to 1 million m^3 per annum in 2001 and remain at that level for at least twenty years (FC, 2001c), nevertheless the UK is highly import-dependent and consequently subject to fluctuations in the world market.

Global stocks of hardwoods have fallen dramatically in the post-war period, primarily as a result of deforestation in the developing, tropical countries of the world in which such trees are predominant. The causes of this deforestation are complex and interlinked and include increasing consumption pressures from both the developed and the developing world (Whiteman, 1995; Global Environment Facility, 1998; World Bank, 1999),[24] population and poverty pressures in the developing world (World Resources Institute, 1994; United Nations Population Division (UNPD), 1998), sustained growth in demand for fuel-wood, to the point where it is currently estimated that half of all global wood consumption is as fuel (UNDP *et al.*, 2000), and forest burning for agricultural expansion and other reasons (Myers, 1990; Elvidge *et al.*, 1999; World Commission on Forests and Sustainable Development, 1999).

The total loss of global forests to date is uncertain but may be as high as 50 per cent (Bryant *et al.*, 1997). What is more certain is that annual net hardwood extraction rates rose from about 0.8 per cent at the end of the 1970s (Doran, 1979) to 1.8 per cent a decade later (Myers, 1990) but have fallen back slightly over the course of the 1990s (Food and Agriculture Organization (FAO), 1997; UNDP *et al.*, 2000). Current losses are the subject of considerable controversy but probably exceed 130,000 km^2 annually (FAO, 1997; Matthews *et al.*, 2000; Tucker and Townsend, 2000; UNDP *et al.*, 2000), a rate which means that by 2010 only Brazil and the Democratic Republic of Congo will have any significant remaining areas of rainforest and both of these will be under unsustainable long-term pressure. Given that the rainforests represent the richest global environment for biodiversity (Davis *et al.*, 1994; Olson and Dinerstein, 1998), the potential exists for species extinction on a scale unprecedented in human history (MacNeill, 1990; Pearce and Warford, 1993; World Resources Institute, 1994; Oldfield *et al.*, 1998; UNDP *et al.*, 2000).

Setting aside the terrible ecological consequences of this destruction, the unsustainable nature of current global hardwood extraction has been seen by some as likely to lead to increases in associated real prices. Indeed, published estimates of such increases can be found, ranging from a credible 0.5 per cent to what we regard

---

[24] While the majority of population growth is in the developing world, a citizen of the developed world consumes up to ten times the ecosystem goods and services of a citizen in the developing world (Global Environment Facility, 1998).

as an unfeasibly high 4 per cent annually.[25] However, this is balanced by opposing views such as that of Whiteman (1995), who argues that while consumption may increase, 'it should be possible to improve forest management to meet these demands, which would then keep timber prices relatively stable'. Certainly the rate of growth in British hardwood planting detailed above should mean that, providing there is not an unforeseen sharp rise in domestic demand, the current rate of UK self-sufficiency may improve, giving something of a domestic buffer against future reductions in global supplies.

This is an area of uncertainty, disagreement and relatively little in-depth research. While we feel that there is a considerably stronger case for real price increases in hardwoods than softwoods, any such rise is likely to be some way off. Furthermore, as our wider study examines the potential for conversions out of existing agricultural land use and into forestry we prefer to adopt conservative assumptions with regard to changes in the future value of both land uses. Adopting any positive rate of real price increase for hardwoods would translate into substantial increases in projected timber values. Instead we prefer to adopt the zero real price rise assumption of Whiteman (1995) and accept that any transpiring price increases will improve the potential for land use conversion to forestry. Such an assumption also allows us readily to revise our calculations in the light of subsequent improved information.

We now turn our attention away from prices towards the other major source of timber-based revenues: grants and subsidies.

Grants

Given the long-delayed nature of forestry returns, government incentives have always played a major role in UK private sector planting decisions. The earliest incentives coincided with the establishment of the Forestry Commission when, in 1919, a scrub clearance and ground preparation grant was introduced. A second planting grant scheme, introduced in 1927, established an enduring trend for broadleaves to be given preferential subsidy rates over conifers, reflecting an early recognition of non-strategic/production objectives within forestry policy.

Following the Second World War a variety of Forestry Commission administered schemes were introduced. Examination of these reveals a gradual movement in forestry policy objectives from simply maximising timber production to initiatives giving equal emphasis to timber, environmental and recreational goals (Johnson and Nicholls, 1991; Bateman, 1996; Winter, 1996; MacFarlane, 2000; DETR, 2000; FC, 1998, 2001b). However, until the late 1980s the overriding force behind the expansion of private sector forestry was tax concessions. The scrapping of most

---

[25] Estimates are from Johnston *et al.* (1967), Doran (1979), Burnham (1985) and Hart (1987).

of these concessions in the 1988 Budget (Lynch, 1989) thrust the role of grants centre-stage as the main means of state support for forestry in the UK, a role which has persisted to the present day.

The majority of woodland grants are administered by the Forestry Commission although other funding bodies are also important and both are considered below. The review presented in this section focuses primarily upon the rates of grant in operation during the period of the early 1990s for which our empirical model operates. However, in comparison with the major changes introduced at the end of the 1980s, the basic structure of this grant aid has varied relatively little over the past decade although grant amounts have generally increased (Winter, 1996; MacFarlane, 2000). A number of recent policy initiatives have stressed plans for expanding forestry both in Britain as a whole (FC, 1998; DETR, 2000) and in our case study area of Wales (National Assembly for Wales, 1999, 2001a; FC, 2001a,b). However, these documents have not put forward policies for an overhaul of the grant-aiding system but rather suggest that levels of aid may be increased in the future (although no specific announcements have been made to date). Therefore, the structure of the model presented here for the early 1990s remains valid today and for the foreseeable future although rates of grant are already dated as they are continually under review.

Forestry Commission administered grants

Throughout the 1980s the FC emphasised its reorientation away from the simple pursuit of timber output and towards wider objectives (FC, 1985c). Such policy was embodied in the introduction, in 1988, of the Woodland Grant Scheme (FC, 1988b) which, alongside the stimulation of timber production and rural employment, explicitly set out to enhance landscape, create wildlife habitat, provide longer-term recreation and sporting facilities and encourage the conservation and regeneration of existing woodlands. Rates of support under the Woodland Grant Scheme (WGS) were revised in 1990 as listed in Table 5.3.

Payments under the WGS were made in three instalments: 70 per cent at planting, 20 per cent after five years and 10 per cent after a further five years (subject to satisfactory establishment). In addition to this a Better Land Supplement (BLS) was payable for planting on arable/improved grassland cultivated (including ploughing) within the previous ten years. BLS was £400/ha for conifers or £600/ha for broadleaves, all payable at planting.

Further enhancement of this package was provided in 1992 by the introduction of the Woodland Management Grant (WMG). This provided an annual addition to the WGS, payable after the first ten years of establishment in return for the setting down and execution of five-yearly management plans designed to

Table 5.3. *Woodland Grant Scheme payments (£/ha)*

Area planted	Conifers	Broadleaves
0.25–0.9 ha	1,005	1,575
1.0–2.9 ha	880	1,375
3.0–9.9 ha	795	1,175
10 ha+	615	975

Source: Johnson and Nicholls (1991).

Table 5.4. *Woodland Management Grants*

Type of WMG	Period of eligibility (age of wood in years)	Rate of grant (£/ha per annum)
Standard: conifer[1]	11–20	10
Standard: broadleaf[1]	11–40	25
Special[1,2]	11 onwards	35
Supplement for small woods[3]		
Standard: conifer	11–20	5
Standard: broadleaf	11–40	10
Special[4]	11 onwards	10

Notes: [1] All these grants are also payable as *additions* where the owner is a farmer under the Farm Woodland Scheme, as compensation for agricultural output forgone (but not for establishment costs).
[2] Higher rates are available for woodlands of special environmental value (nature conservation, landscape or public recreation). The owner will be expected to maintain the wood's character. These grants are available for any forest older than ten years. However, they may be extended to younger or even proposed forest if the Forestry Commission is satisfied that there is demand for such a provision.
[3] Available as additions for all woodlands of less than 10 ha (of correct age).
[4] Available for any woodland (over ten years) of less than 10 ha where the woodland is of special environmental value.
Source: Johnson and Nicholls (1991).

increase the environmental value of the woodlands concerned. Table 5.4 details WMG payments.

The year 1991 also saw the FC introduce the Community Woodland Supplement (CWS), a further addition to the WGS (and WMG) designed to promote recreational woodlands 'within 5 miles of the edge of a town or city and in an area where the opportunities for woodland recreation are limited' (FC, 1991). In implementation this has been interpreted very broadly so that relatively small communities of just a few thousand people are considered sufficient to justify payment of CWS. At its introduction the scheme consisted of a single payment of £950/ha payable at planting. All woodlands qualifying for CWS were allowed WGS and WMG, the latter being paid at the enhanced 'special' rate.

In addition to the above, from 1992 the FC offered a single £100 flat rate payment for each new woodland (irrespective of size) conditional on the drawing up of a management plan (FC, 1991).[26]

Other grant schemes

In 1988 the then Ministry of Agriculture, Fisheries and Food (MAFF) introduced the Farm Woodland Scheme (FWS) to provide annual income support to farmers who establish woodlands on what was previously agricultural land (MAFF, 1987a).[27] The scheme had almost identical objectives to the FC's WGS (and was payable concurrently) with the additional goal of reducing surplus agricultural production. As a consequence, higher rates of FWS were payable on better quality land. Although these rates did not distinguish between conifer and broadleaf woodlands, the period of annual support was longer for the latter.

Poor uptake of the FWS led to its replacement in 1992 by the Farm Woodland Premium Scheme (FWPS) (MAFF, 1992a,b,c). Here farms first applied to the FC for planting grants under the WGS (including BLS, WMG, CWS and the single new woodland payments where appropriate). If approved the farm could then apply to MAFF for FWPS payments as shown in Table 5.5.

For woodlands with less than 50 per cent broadleaves the FWPS is payable in each of the first ten years after planting, a period which is extended to fifteen years for mainly broadleaved woodlands.[28] However, grant repayments with interest are stipulated if land is returned to agriculture within twenty years for the former or thirty years for the latter (MAFF, 1992b).[29]

With respect to our Welsh study area, the creation of the Cambrian Mountains and Lleyn Peninsula Environmentally Sensitive Areas (ESAs) in 1986 and 1987, respectively, seemed to offer the possibility of further grants for broadleaved woodland.[30]

---

[26] In addition to this the FC also provides certain other grant payments for general and coppice management, open spaces and grey squirrel control. Details are given in Johnson and Nicholls (1991).

[27] The FWS also pays planting grants but, since its revision in 1992, these have been identical to those offered under the WGS. Farmers may not collect both FWS and WGS planting grants.

[28] This is considerably more front-loaded than the original FWS which provided lower annual sums but over a longer period.

[29] Farms may also convert land into forestry under the Common Agricultural Policy (CAP) set-aside scheme. Set-aside woodland is not eligible for either FWPS or WGS BLS payments. Standard WGS payments may be received concurrently with set-aside in high productivity areas but as this does not apply for most of our study area we do not pursue this particular permutation any further.

[30] Further grants towards the costs of promoting landscape or countryside conservation are occasionally paid by the Countryside Commission and Nature Conservancy Council while the Agricultural Development Advisory Service (ADAS) can provide certain technical support. However, the occasional nature of such support means that it is not considered further in this study.

Table 5.5. *Payments under the Farm Woodland Premium Scheme*[1]
(£/ha per annum)

Present use	Lowlands	Disadvantaged Area	Severely Disadvantaged Area
Arable/improved grassland	250	190	130
Unimproved	n/a	60	60

Notes: n/a = not available.
[1] The following FWPS restrictions apply: (i) not more than 50 per cent of farm eligible; (ii) not more than 40 ha of unimproved land per farm; (iii) eligibility for arable/improved grassland restricted to land under such usage within the previous three years; (iv) the FWPS as a whole is cash rather than area limited. Further details are given in MAFF (1992b).
Source: MAFF (1992b).

The Welsh Office (1989a) stressed the importance of such features within the Cambrian Mountains ESA while in a subsequent leaflet (Welsh Office, 1989b) payments of £45/ha per annum became available for management of such woodlands. These are clearly specified as additions to existing planting and management grants. However, subsequent publications regarding the Lleyn Peninsula ESA offered lower rates of grant (£15/ha per annum) restricted to existing broadleaf woodland alone (Welsh Office, 1992a,b). Conversations with both ESA authorities in the late 1990s indicated that those anomalies still persisted.

A policy and planning drive away from purely timber-orientated, monoculture conifer plantations was signalled in 1988 when EC Directive 85/337 was implemented via Environmental Assessment (Afforestation) Regulations which made applicants for FC assistance submit an environmental assessment of the proposed forest.[31] In the same year the Department of the Environment, Transport and the Regions (DETR), the ultimate national planning authority, indicated that planning permission for such large conifer plantations would not normally be granted for sites in England. As noted previously, this policy has since been reinforced in policy documents applying to both England (Forestry Commission, 1998) and, more recently, our study area of Wales, with the National Assembly for Wales explicitly promoting the concept of diverse, multipurpose woodland as opposed to conifer monocultures (National Assembly for Wales, 2001a).

---

[31] In practice such assessments became routine requirements for plantations of over 100 ha affecting National Nature Reserves, National Parks, Sites of Special Scientific Interest, etc.

While the policy environment appears to be favourable to further woodland expansions, the planning system may place a brake on this, particularly in the case of farm woodlands. Lloyd *et al.* (1995) report study findings suggesting that some farmers believe that conversions to woodland may be irreversible,[32] a similar result being reported by Crabtree *et al.* (1998). Indeed, our own informal contacts with the Forestry Commission indicated that felling licences would only be granted on condition that affected areas would be replanted.[33] While future policy may change, this means in effect that once farmers place land under trees they may well become legally bound to maintain an equal area of woodland on the farm in perpetuity. This irreversibility of land use may well slow the expansion of farm woodlands and we consider the potential inertia of farmers in reacting to purely financial pressures in the cost-benefit analysis presented at the end of this volume.

Grants: conclusions

Farmers considering diverting land into forestry are eligible for a variety of grants and subsidies. These vary considerably according to which scheme they register under and according to locational factors. In order to allow for this the timber valuation model developed subsequently allows flexibility across the full gamut of grant/subsidy opportunities existing in the early 1990s. Results for these various permutations were identified using the following coding system:

$$S = \text{subsidy rate is (as follows)}$$
$$I = \text{rate for planting on improved grassland or arable land}$$
$$U = \text{rate for planting on unimproved land}$$
$$nda = \text{rate for planting in a non-disadvantaged area}$$
$$da = \text{rate for planting in a disadvantaged area}$$
$$sda = \text{rate for planting in a severely disadvantaged area}$$
$$+CW = \text{rate for planting, given Community Woodland supplement}$$
$$-CW = \text{rate for planting, not given Community Woodland supplement}$$

In the following section we incorporate these subsidies within the wider costs and revenues arising from plantation management.

Plantation costs and revenues

Choice of species

Ideally one would wish to analyse all those species which are likely to be used in a conversion from agriculture to forestry. The feasibility of such an analysis

---

[32] See also Williams *et al.* (1994) which gives further details regarding this study.
[33] This may also adversely affect land prices.

was investigated with the FC's Forestry Investment Appraisal Programme (FIAP). However, while this is an excellent tool for the management of given stands, it was not amenable to the type of modification required to answer the questions posed by this research. Consequently it was decided that two representative species, one conifer and one broadleaf, would be chosen for study.

Among the eight major species of conifer grown commercially in the UK,[34] the Sitka spruce stands out as by far the most dominant, constituting 28 per cent of total forest area, more than double that of any other species (FICGB, 1992). Sitka spruce is capable of producing an average annual yield in excess of 24 m^3/ha over an optimal rotation, with typical UK productivity averaging 12–16 m^3/ha. The rapid growth rate means that optimal felling ages can be very short, from sixty years on poor ground to as little as forty-five years on good sites.[35] The choice of Sitka spruce as a representative conifer therefore reflects a logical and often observed timber-productivity decision. However, this species is not thought to be optimal in terms of recreation value.

Interestingly there is little empirical evidence regarding a connection between tree species and recreation value. In one of the few valuation studies to consider this, Hanley and Ruffell (1992) failed to identify a significant relationship. This may mean that all woodland recreation valuation studies are observing values for outdoor, rather than specifically woodland, activities. However, if we temporarily lurch from the empirical to the anecdotal, it is the authors' firm belief that walkers *do* recognise and appreciate the difference between the claustrophobic atmosphere produced by a species like Sitka spruce (with its dense entanglement of lower branches, tightly packed together to maximise timber yield, set in a bed of stultifying acid pine needles) and, say, the much more airy and open feel of a Scots pine woodland. An even clearer difference is evident when we then consider the gorgeous spaciousness, beautiful trunks and foliage, and verdant undergrowth of an oak or beech woodland.

To allow for this difference we decided to extend our appraisal to consider a representative hardwood. Here the choice was more difficult as the oak is the most abundant broadleaf species but is relatively slow-growing and less productive than the beech, which we selected for study as a more viable hardwood alternative.[36]

---

[34] In descending order of total forest area, major conifers are: Sitka spruce (28%); Scots pine (13%); lodgepole pine (7%); Japanese larch (6%); Norway spruce (6%); Corsican pine (2%); Douglas fir (2%); European larch (2%). Major hardwoods are: oak (9%); ash (4%); beech (4%); birch (4%). The remaining area consists of a range of species (FICGB, 1992).

[35] As discussed subsequently, optimal felling age is a function in part of discount rate rather than just of growing conditions.

[36] There are some ecological arguments in favour of the oak over the beech as the latter creates less understorey and has a less penetrable canopy. However, data availability favoured the beech, which is, despite these drawbacks, ecologically strongly preferable to the Sitka spruce.

Sitka spruce costs and revenues

Costs

Irrespective of species, the majority of plantation costs occur at the start of the rotation (planting, etc.) and at felling. Here we make the common FC assumption that all cutting costs (both thinnings – the extraction of undersized trees at set points during the rotation so as to maximise long-run plantation yield – and felling) are either carried out by contractors or incur contractor-level implicit costs upon the plantation operator. This allows us to use the standing timber price–size curve discussed subsequently.

Estimates for these and other costs (maintenance, fertiliser, fencing, etc.) were obtained from the FC and are detailed in Bateman (1996). Costs may vary somewhat depending upon infrastructure, distance to sawmills, local variation in input supply prices (including labour), intensity of planting, etc. Typical values for such parameters were incorporated within the data supplied by the FC.[37]

Revenues

Four factors are key to the determination of timber revenues:

  (i) the rate of growth
 (ii) the price per m^3
(iii) the discount rate (the rate at which forest managers or policy-makers progressively reduce the present-day value of revenues that will be received further and further into the future)
(iv) available grants and subsidies.

We will address each of these factors in turn.

Growth rate is typically defined using the yield class (YC) measure, which is the maximum average annual increment in volume which a stand of trees can deliver. So, for example, a stand for which this value is 12 m^3/ha per annum is referred to as being YC12.

Since its inception in 1919 the Forestry Commission has collected data quantifying the characteristics of plantations growing in differing yield classes. These 'yield models' have been collated across varying species and management regimes (Edwards and Christie, 1981) and show how, for each yield class, tree volume increases over time. The yield models provide the basic data on tree growth used in our subsequent analysis.

---

[37] Note that costs were representative rather than being varied spatially. This is a potential weakness in the analysis, and other commentators such as Thompson *et al.* (1997) have used spatially sensitive costs. However, the latter study considers an area (British Columbia) forty-five times larger than Wales and uses just three cost-level zones. In effect, therefore, our own study performs well in comparison and we do feel it is reasonable to point out that, while revenues vary very substantially across Wales (as shown in Chapter 6), costs are less variable.

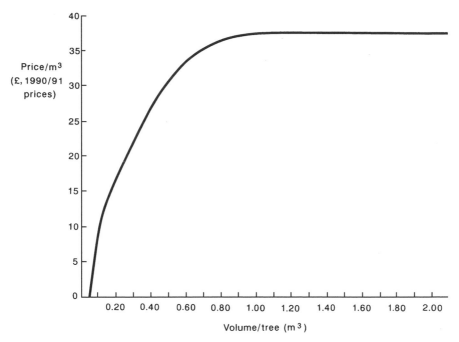

Figure 5.2. Price–size curve for conifers in England and Wales. (*Source:* Drawn from data given in Whiteman, 1990.)

From the perspective of the timber producer, price is far from constant and is instead a function of the mean volume per tree. Simply put, when trees are thin they are of limited use and so their price/m^3 is low. As trees increase in volume so their usefulness, and therefore price/m^3, rises. This continues (at a diminishing rate) to the point where a tree's girth is such that it can be used for sawn wood, telegraph poles and myriad other products. After this point the price/m^3 remains fairly constant and the value of a stand increases only as much as volume does.

Estimation of this 'price–size curve' has been the subject of repeated statistical investigation by the FC (Mitlin, 1987; Whiteman, 1990; Sinclair and Whiteman, 1992). In this study we adopted the findings of Whiteman (1990), primarily because this research uses the same base year as our wider study, but also because this analysis recognises that prices are higher in England and Wales than in Scotland and produces separate models which provide a substantially better fit to the data ($R^2 = 87.5\%$) than the unified analysis for the whole of Britain reported by Sinclair and Whiteman subsequently ($R^2 = 74.7\%$). Figure 5.2 illustrates the price–size curve used in our analysis.

As a stand of trees grows, so thinner trees (known appropriately as thinnings) are removed to help the remainder flourish. The thinning process typically starts about twenty years after planting and then occurs at regular intervals of, say, five years up to felling. The value of thinnings can be calculated via the price–size curve, although for obvious reasons this value is substantially less than that of the main crop. By relating the price–size curve to the timber volume information contained in the yield model we can calculate the timber revenue generated each year from planting to felling and compare this with per annum costs to obtain a value for annual timber net benefit.

The optimal felling age therefore emerges as a key factor in determining the overall value of a stand. As already mentioned this will vary according to the yield class concerned, for, as the FC yield models show (Edwards and Christie, 1981), the faster a tree grows the sooner it reaches its age of maximum annual average product. Therefore, as yield class increases, optimal felling age falls. Early felling is encouraged by the practice of discounting, which we now consider.

Discounting is the process by which revenues and costs occurring in the future are converted into present-day values. By this process, different projects that have returns occurring at different times can be compared on a common footing and investment decisions made. The general result is that costs and benefits arising in the future are not valued as highly as those which occur in the present day. This is for a variety of reasons including a simple preference for earlier rewards ('positive time preference') and the fact that money invested in a project, such as forestry, is no longer available for investment elsewhere, say in a bank, and so there is a lost opportunity, in terms of the interest forgone, which increases over time (the 'opportunity cost of capital'). The further into the future that costs and benefits occur, the more they are discounted. By looking at how this effect increases into the future we can observe the underlying 'discount rate' that is being employed.

The factors determining discount rates are complex and while we return to consider some of these in Chapter 7 we do not attempt to provide a full account of their determinants in this volume.[38] However, what is pertinent here is that changing the discount rate can dramatically alter the present value of a given investment. This is particularly true for forestry where (with the exception of felling expenditures) the bulk of costs occur early in a rotation while felling revenues can be long delayed. This impact can be demonstrated by examining the discount factor (DF) implied by each discount rate. The DF shows the proportion (from 1 to 0) by which future costs or benefits should be multiplied to obtain their equivalent present-day value. Figure 5.3 illustrates the DF for four discount rates (each of which has some relevance for our analysis and which we discuss subsequently) as time progresses from the present (year 0) into the future. As can be seen, for any discount rate, the further into the future that a cost or benefit occurs, the lower is the DF and consequently the

---

[38] Introductions are given in Pearce (1986), Hanley and Spash (1993) and Perman *et al.* (1999). Other useful sources include Lind (1982a) and Markandya and Pearce (1994).

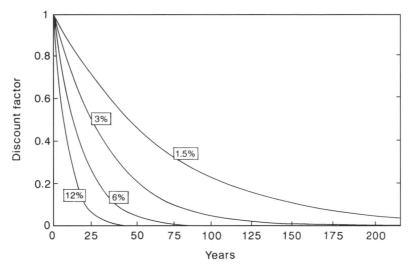

Figure 5.3. Discount factor curves.

lower is the present value of that cost or benefit. Furthermore, we can also see that changes in the discount rate imply very substantial alterations in the speed at which the DF declines. For example, for net benefits (benefits minus costs) occurring fifty years from planting we can see that at a 1.5 per cent discount rate we have DF = 0.5 (i.e. the present-day value is about half the net benefit received in year 50) whereas with a 12 per cent discount rate, DF is virtually zero (i.e. the present value of net benefits received fifty years hence is almost nil).

We discuss the choice of discount rate subsequently, but for now the important message is that discounting can very substantially affect the present-day value of long-term investments like forestry, and the higher the discount rate the lower that present-day value. As stated previously, this increases the impact of YC upon felling date. Just as a higher growth rate results in an earlier optimal felling date, so does a higher discount rate. Discounting makes it in the interest of forest managers to obtain timber-felling revenues earlier rather than later, to the extent that they trade off gains in timber volume against the discounting-induced reduction in the value of that delayed timber volume.

The impact of varying yield class and discount rate upon optimal felling age was calculated using the FIAP software mentioned previously. FIAP operates by maximising the net present value of a stand subject to several user-determined parameters. Results from this analysis are given in Table 5.6 which shows the extent to which felling age declines as both yield class and discount rate increase.

Application of the FIAP software indicated that it was insufficiently flexible to conduct our required analyses concerning variation of grant levels. Therefore, yield

Table 5.6. *Optimal felling age for various discount rates: Sitka spruce, YC6–24*

Discount rate (%)	Yield class									
	6	8	10	12	14	16	18	20	22	24
2	80	78	74	70	69	68	66	66	66	65
3	73	72	69	63	60	58	57	57	56	56
4	68	67	64	58	54	51	50	50	49	48
5	64	62	60	56	52	49	46	44	44	44
6	60	58	56	54	50	47	43	42	41	40
8	54	53	51	50	47	44	42	40	37	35
10	50	48	47	46	44	42	40	38	36	34
12	47	44	43	42	41	40	38	36	34	33

Notes: Optimal felling age (in years from planting) maximises NPV given the relevant discount rate (r) and yield class combination. The above figures treat the planting year as year 0. The table was calculated using FIAP running at the Forestry Commission headquarters at Edinburgh (except for the row for $r = 3\%$ which was interpolated). The authors are obliged to Jane Sinclair and Roger Oakes at Edinburgh for assistance.

The table uses the following FIAP settings: spacing $= 2.00 \times 2.00$; thinning $=$ line, MTT; delay on first thinning $=$ none; stocking $= 85\%$; successor crop NPV $= 0$; price–size curve $=$ GB conifer 1992; thinning price differential (£ 1992/93) $= 0.30/m^3$; charge per m^3 (£ 1992/93) $= 3.68/m^3$.

models for YC6–24 Sitka spruce (from the tables given in Edwards and Christie, 1981) were transferred into a database for use in association with a statistical package (Minitab, 1994) allowing the authors to write macros for repetitive data analysis. In this manner, desired grant scenarios (discussed subsequently) could be specified and their net present values (NPV) calculated.[39] This model allows us to convert yield class estimates into NPV equivalents taking into account any desired grant scenario. Our yield class predictions and their estimated values are given in Chapter 6.

Beech costs and revenues

Costs

Information on hardwood planting costs is far less readily available than for conifers. Data were collected both from interviews with managers of broadleaf woodlands[40] and from certain published sources (Lewis, pers. comm., 1988; Hart, 1987 and pers. comm., 1990). However, the distributions of revenues and costs are similar to

---

[39] Examples of the year-by-year revenue and cost streams derived from such models are detailed in Bateman (1996).

[40] Notably Fred Lewis, Kerswell, Exminster and Cyril Hart, Chenies, Dean.

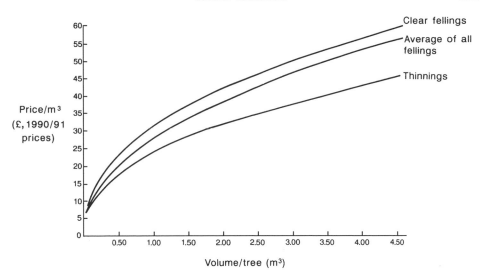

Figure 5.4. Price–size curves for beech in Great Britain. (*Source:* Drawn from data given in Whiteman *et al.*, 1991.)

those for conifers, with high costs at planting and felling, mainly maintenance and thinning costs at other times, and revenues at felling and to a minor degree from thinnings (details are given in Bateman, 1996).

Revenues

The factors affecting broadleaf timber revenues are the same as those relevant to conifers, with price varying positively with tree volume. In their study of price–size curves for broadleaves, Whiteman *et al.* (1991) show that, because thinnings have relatively high extraction costs per m^3, standing prices for thinnings are on average 24 per cent below the price per m^3 paid for clear fell timber. Consequently, two price–size curves are estimated (with a third, average curve being reported for ease of generalised account rather than for individual plantation assessment). As hardwood timber values vary considerably among species, price–size curves are estimated for individual species (unlike the generalised conifer relationship), with those for beech being illustrated in Figure 5.4.

With timber volume and the price–size curve defined, we can calculate annual timber revenues, subtract costs per annum and derive the net timber benefit values for each year from planting to felling. As before, the optimal felling age declines as the yield class and discount rate increase. This relationship was analysed as described previously, results being given in Table 5.7.

Finally, hardwood yield class models and associated revenue and cost streams were linked via spreadsheet to a statistical analysis package to allow them to be integrated with available grants and subsidies. Net present values for any user-defined

Table 5.7. *Optimal felling age for various discount rates:*
beech, YC4–10

Discount rate (%)	Yield class			
	4	6	8	10
2	125	120	119	118
3	105	99	95	93
4	91	85	80	78
5	81	75	71	69
6	75	69	65	62
8	65	59	56	53
10	58	52	48	47
12	53	47	43	42

Notes: Optimal felling age (in years from planting) maximises NPV given the relevant discount rate (r) and yield class combination. The above figures treat the planting year as year 0. The table was calculated using FIAP running at the Forestry Commission headquarters at Edinburgh (except for the row for $r = 3\%$ which was interpolated). The authors are obliged to Jane Sinclair and Roger Oakes at Edinburgh for assistance.

The table uses the following FIAP settings: spacing = 1.20 × 1.20; thinning = broadleaved, intermediate thin; delay on first thinning = none; stocking = 85%; successor crop NPV = 0; price–size curve = broadleaves for 1989/90 T.R.; thinning price differential (£ 1992/93) = 0.30/m³; charge per m³ (£ 1992/93) = 3.68/m³.

yield class/discount rate/subsidy scenario could then be derived as detailed previously for the conifer models.

Discount rates

Any investment in forestry essentially trades off initial costs against delayed benefits. This is conventionally achieved by calculating the NPV of the investment via a discount rate (r) which is influenced by positive time preference, the opportunity cost of capital and other factors discussed subsequently. Now, this research sets out to examine two perspectives on whether agricultural land should be converted to forestry: that of the farmer; and that of society. However, there is good reason to suppose that these two will have differing discount rates.[41] Put at its simplest, if we consider time preference, farmers are mortal while society is, at very least, much

[41] For further discussion on the divergence of social from private discount rates see Baumol (1968), Goodin (1982), Sen (1982), Sagoff (1988), Pearce and Turner (1990), Markandya and Pearce (1994) and Pearce and Ulph (1998).

longer lived (we hope!). Therefore, society is likely to place relatively more weight on delayed returns than is an individual farmer. Accordingly we might expect society to have a lower rate of positive time preference. A similar result is obtained when we consider discounting based on the opportunity cost of capital. For a risk-averse society this should imply a relatively low social discount rate dictated by the rate of return on riskless investments (government bonds, etc.). However, for the private individual the opportunity cost of capital should be relatively high on account of the rates of return available from alternative investments.[42] Both arguments suggest that private (agricultural) discount rates might be higher than social discount rates.

In this section we examine evidence regarding agricultural and social real rates of discount. However, before turning to this we need to address one further complication, the comparability of agricultural and forestry investments. Farmers commonly make decisions on an annual cycle whereas the time horizon of a forester is usually a full rotation of a stand, which typically varies from a minimum of four decades for conifers to over a century for hardwoods. Comparison of annual gross margin with rotation NPV is therefore problematic. Two approaches exist. First, agricultural margins can be assessed and discounted over at least a rotation length. Second, woodland NPV can be converted to an annual equivalent, i.e. the constant annual return (or 'annuity') which, over the length of a rotation, would be valued equally with the standard NPV sum. After discussion with relevant experts[43] it was decided that the former option lacked credibility as farmers (who are the relevant decision-makers) are used to annual rather than rotational decision-making. Therefore, the calculated NPVs for all our yield models (using the relevant agricultural or social discount rate) were converted to annuity equivalents.[44]

Farmers' discount rates

Literature review

A priori we would expect that the relatively lower rates of return exhibited by the agricultural sector (compared to the industrial and commercial sectors) would result in somewhat lower real discount rates than those implied by the government's 8 per cent average rate of return required of public sector agencies selling commercially or the 6 per cent rate used for pure public good activities (H.M. Treasury, 1991; Pearce and Ulph, 1998).[45] However, little explicit work has been published

---

[42] This may be a less strong argument if re-investment is restricted to the agricultural sector where rates of return are historically low.

[43] Notably Colin Price and Rob Willis, University of Wales, Bangor.

[44] The conversion process and related formulae are discussed in Bateman (1996).

[45] The 8 per cent estimate is 'based on average returns on assets achieved in the private sector for activities with low cyclical year by year variability' (H.M. Treasury, 1991). In 2002 H. M. Treasury published consultations signalling a reduction of the pure public sector discount rate from 6 to 3.5 per cent.

in this area, with most commentators examining real rates of return or agricultural interest rates rather than discount rates *per se*.

The early work in this latter area is predominantly American, dating back to Melichar (1979) who proposed that real rates of return were determined by expected rents and actual and expected inflation rates. Feldstein (1980) modified this theory by suggesting that such a mechanism may ultimately be driven by inflation acting upon land prices, while Tanzi (1980) extended this by proposing a further link to the business cycle. However, in an empirical test of these theories, Alston (1986) failed to find a long-run link between inflation and land prices, and Burt (1986) rejected such complex models in favour of a simple long-run equilibrium land price approach which yields an estimate of the real rate of return of 4 per cent per annum.

Turning to the UK, similar results are reported by Cooper (1992) who uses a real interest rate approach, based on the work of Brase and La Due (1989), to estimate a mean value of 4.5 per cent for UK agriculture for the period 1964–90. While agricultural interest rates are highly variable,[46] such a result seems to be roughly echoed by lending practice during our study period. In correspondence with the authors, the National Westminster Agricultural Office (a major source of farm finance) quoted an average real agricultural interest rate of 4 per cent over base rates.[47]

A lower interest rate, averaging 2.44 per cent above base rate, is reported by Cunningham (1990) in a study of MAFF surveys, while MAFF itself employed an agricultural interest rate risk premium of 2.78 per cent above base rate during our study period.[48] However, there are several problems with extrapolating from interest rates to discount rates. First, if base rates change frequently, lags in the adjustment system may confound the analyst. Second, interest rates vary significantly across farms, projects and time.[49] Third, the link between interest rates and discount rates may be weak in that the former relate to returns on new investments rather than on total assets (which are likely to be lower).

In addressing this latter point, Harrison and Tranter (1989) analysed the period 1978/79 to 1986/87, reporting a mean real rate of return on all assets of 2.56 per cent.[50] Positive time preference would suggest that the real discount rate might be somewhat higher than this. Such an argument would support the findings

---

[46] Annual averages range from −13.01 per cent (1976) to +10.08 per cent (1990) in Cooper (1992).

[47] Pers. comm. Sue Train, National Westminster Agricultural Office (NWAO), and letters from Brian Montgomery, Senior Executive, NWAO, July 1993. However, this correspondence highlighted the variation in rates across farms and projects. For example, a range of real rates of 0–5 per cent was given for differing projects and times by Charles Morgan of Chris Grote Farms, Norfolk.

[48] Pers. comm. Douglas Cooper, MAFF, 1993.

[49] This point was made in correspondence with NWAO (see above) and Paul Hill (Wye College) who both stated that while interest rates were roughly 2 per cent above base rates for good risks, they could be much higher for risky investments.

[50] Sample extends across Great Britain. Rates are quite consistent, only ranging from 1.87 per cent to 3.90 per cent.

of Lloyd (1993) who uses a capital asset pricing model of agricultural land prices in England and Wales for the period 1946–89 to empirically derive a long-run real discount rate of 3.6 per cent.

These latter studies provide what we feel is the best evidence on agricultural real discount rates. However, none of these studies is specific to our Welsh study area and so our own rate of return analysis was undertaken.

Empirical work

Two studies of agricultural rates of return in Wales were undertaken: a short time-series analysis of the period 1987–92; and a cross-sectional study of the 1989/90 base year. In both cases data were provided by the Welsh division of the Farm Business Survey (FBS, 1988, 1989, 1990, 1991, 1992) which defines the nominal return as farm income expressed as a percentage of tenants' capital.[51]

Rates of return in Wales, 1987–92

Table 5.8 presents nominal rate of return (RoR_n) statistics for various categories of farm identified during FBS surveys for the years 1987/88 to 1991/92. These categories are further subdivided by farm size.

Statistical analysis was undertaken for all farm categories except pig, poultry and cropping farms as these are minor activities in Wales and were not separately classified after 1989. This showed that specialist or mainly dairy farms achieved significantly higher RoR_n than did other farms. Subsequent analysis also isolated a quadratic relationship with size, measured in British stocking units (BSU), showing that RoR_n rose with size but at a diminishing marginal rate. RoR_n also fluctuated annually although only one year (1988/89) was found to be significantly different from all others. A variety of further variables taken from the FBS database (see discussion in Chapter 8) were also tested and found to be insignificant in predicting RoR_n.

A model was constructed and tested across a variety of functional forms. Our best-fitting model is reported as Equation (5.1). Tests for interactions, multicollinearity, autocorrelation and heteroscedasticity failed to isolate any significant problems with this model.

$$RoR_n = -18.62 + 7.68\,DAIRY + 9.57\,HIYEAR + 1.13\,BSU_t - 0.0105\,BSU_t^2$$
$$(-9.06) \quad (6.32) \qquad (6.53) \qquad (8.38) \qquad (-6.33)$$
$$(5.1)$$

---

[51] The Farm Business Survey (FBS) was an arm of MAFF (operating in Wales under the auspices of the Welsh Office) which conducted annual surveys of a representative sample of farms throughout the country. The sample size averaged 734 farms per annum over our 1987–92 study period; however, many farms are retained in the sample for about three years. The number of distinct farms in the time series is 2,867.

Table 5.8. *Agricultural nominal rate of return (RoR) on tenants' capital: Wales 1987/88–1991/92*

Farm type and size (BSU)	1987/88			1988/89			1989/90			1990/91			1991/92			1987–92		
	n	mean size (BSU)	RoR (%)	n	mean size (BSU)	RoR (%)	n	mean size (BSU)	RoR (%)	n	mean size (BSU)	RoR (%)	n	mean size (BSU)	RoR (%)	n	mean size (BSU)	RoR (%)
Specialist dairy																		
Up to 15.9	30	11.87	10.04	28	11.85	13.89	20	11.37	4.84	17	10.42	−0.13	30	10.15	−6.25	125	11.29	5.96
16–23.9	26	19.57	10.21	18	19.32	13.02	14	19.98	14.29	20	19.27	4.27	26	19.48	9.27	104	19.52	10.64
24–39.9	35	30.82	13.76	38	31.23	26.52	34	30.95	17.81	28	31.63	13.30	35	31.13	15.24	170	31.15	17.44
40 and over	27	67.13	25.10	31	69.03	36.06	36	67.10	27.37	31	63.21	19.69	27	60.70	20.65	152	65.22	25.32
All sizes	118	31.83	18.11	115	32.33	27.77	104	34.21	21.16	96	36.82	15.56	118	34.54	16.25	551	33.85	20.01
Mainly dairy																		
Up to 23.9	14	14.14	6.65	14	14.14	4.78	25	15.38	0.01	15	16.31	−1.12	14	14.15	−2.99	82	15.02	1.06
24–39.9	15	31.45	13.41	13	31.79	18.32	9	31.91	13.72	11	34.61	13.60	15	34.52	13.68	63	32.61	14.72
40 and over	18	56.08	15.55	18	54.48	19.36	15	59.89	16.08	16	73.32	10.05	18	72.21	13.70	85	62.63	15.15
All sizes	47	35.73	13.83	45	36.37	17.31	49	37.96	13.24	42	37.12	8.11	47	41.20	11.67	230	37.59	12.81
Hill sheep																		
Up to 15.9	24	10.13	−3.84	24	10.55	1.34	25	10.03	−18.04	21	9.69	−16.54	22	11.36	−3.15	116	10.33	−8.11
16 and over	27	32.57	13.96	27	31.67	20.06	24	33.68	6.14	32	31.14	−1.04	32	34.28	11.14	142	32.65	9.78
All sizes	51	22.01	10.14	51	21.73	15.99	49	21.62	0.54	53	22.40	−3.84	54	25.20	8.76	258	22.62	6.26
Hill cattle & sheep																		
Up to 15.9	39	10.30	3.91	35	10.64	9.49	34	10.87	−8.81	25	11.52	−11.80	39	10.44	−5.86	172	10.75	−1.94
16–23.9	29	19.07	5.58	32	19.52	12.21	36	18.87	−2.55	23	19.65	−4.06	29	19.99	4.70	149	19.40	2.66
24–39.9	26	30.14	12.87	28	30.33	17.70	29	29.82	5.72	25	31.37	2.57	26	31.41	8.29	134	30.61	9.23
40 and over	14	57.77	20.84	15	57.36	20.12	18	70.36	7.22	20	76.13	−3.53	14	74.04	6.70	81	68.13	9.29
All sizes	108	23.59	12.11	110	23.82	15.85	117	26.13	2.38	93	28.88	−2.85	108	32.12	5.37	536	26.79	6.43
Upland cattle & sheep																		
Up to 15.9	16	9.33	−3.66	16	8.65	3.53	16	9.29	−7.42	19	8.29	−17.65	19	7.56	−15.09	86	8.58	−8.64
16 and over	20	26.21	4.64	20	27.43	7.52	18	23.29	−2.07	23	25.66	−3.53	25	30.43	2.14	106	26.82	1.68
All sizes	36	18.71	2.71	36	19.08	6.60	34	16.70	−3.57	42	17.80	−6.57	44	20.55	−0.81	192	18.65	−0.51
Lowland cattle & sheep																		
All sizes	13	12.64	−1.50	13	12.68	1.38	17	18.14	−5.05	26	22.84	−1.59	31	17.90	−0.06	100	18.11	−1.38

Pig & poultry

Cropping farms

Summary statistics[1]

	(1)			(2)			(3)			(4)			(5)			1987–92		
	n	size	rate[5]	n	size	rate	n	size	rate	n	size	rate	n	size	rate	n	size	rate
Pig & poultry — All sizes	6	29.77	3.96	6	22.64	12.94		*	*		*	*		*	*	12	26.20	8.45
Cropping farms — All sizes	11	44.84	10.96	11	42.89	1.54		*	*		*	*		*	*	22	43.87	6.25
Total no. of farms	390			390			370			394			353			1,897		
Mean		28.07	9.54		27.81	14.06		28.45			29.91	0.61		30.16	5.40		29.23	7.07
Trimmed mean		27.11	9.43		26.75	13.61		27.26			28.61	0.57		29.04	5.67		28.37	6.95
Standard deviation		15.92	7.40		15.93	8.99		17.85			19.40	10.03		18.98	8.94		17.05	8.45
S.E. mean		3.32	1.54		3.32	1.87		3.90			4.23	2.19		4.14	1.95		3.56	1.76
Minimum		9.33	−3.84		8.65	1.34		9.29			8.29	−17.65		7.56	−15.09		8.58	−8.64
Lower quartile		14.14	3.96		14.14	6.60		16.04			17.06	−3.95		16.02	−1.90		18.11	1.06
Upper quartile		32.57	13.83		32.33	19.36		33.94			35.72	9.08		34.53	12.68		33.85	12.81
Maximum		67.13	25.10		69.03	36.06		70.36			76.13	19.69		74.04	20.65		68.13	25.32

Notes: [1] The summary statistics are calculated by omitting the 'All sizes' category means (except where this is the only entry for the category).
[2] The 1987–92 mean rate of return is weighted by annual numbers of farms as is the average BSU size.
[3] * = not available.
[4] n = number of farms in sample.
[5] rate = nominal rate of net return on tenants' capital, calculated as follows:

$$MII = Output - Inputs$$

$$\text{and} \quad RoR = (MII/TC) * 100$$

where:
(i) Output = All returns from an enterprise, plus the market value of any of its products transferred out to another enterprise, plus the market value of any production from the enterprise given to workers or consumed on the farm. In the case of livestock enterprises, the value of purchased livestock and the market value of livestock transferred in from another enterprise are deducted. All totals are adjusted for changes in valuation.

(ii) Inputs = Feeds (purchased concentrates, home-grown concentrates, purchased bulk) + tack and stock keep + veterinary and medicines + other livestock costs + fertilisers + seeds (purchased and home-grown) + other crop costs + labour (farmer and spouse, paid, unpaid, casual) + machinery (contract, repairs, fuels, depreciation) + general farming costs + other land expenses + rent/rental value + rates. (Note that as a nominal farmer/spouse labour cost is included, we are calculating net rather than gross returns.)

(iii) MII = Management and Investment Income; the MII represents the reward for the farmer's (and spouse's) management and interest on the tenants' capital employed on the farm.

(iv) TC = tenants' capital: the value of livestock, machinery, crops (including cultivations) and stores. In the Farm Business Survey tables, tenants' capital is expressed as the average of the opening and closing valuations for these items.

Sources: Data taken from FBS (1988, 1989, 1990, 1991, 1992).

where:

$$\begin{aligned}
\text{RoR}_n &= \text{nominal net rate of return on tenants' capital (per cent)} \\
\text{DAIRY} &= \text{1 for dairy farms (FBS specialist or mainly dairy categories);} \\
&\qquad \text{0 otherwise} \\
\text{HIYEAR} &= \text{1 for 1988/89; 0 otherwise} \\
\text{BSU}_t &= \text{average size of farm type in year } t \\
\text{BSU}_t^2 &= \text{BSU}_t * \text{BSU}_t
\end{aligned}$$

$R^2 = 77.9\%$; R^2 (adj.) $= 76.7\%$; $F = 66.10$; $p < 0.001$; figures in brackets are t-statistics.

Average RoR_n for dairy and non-dairy farms (denoted RoR_n^D and RoR_n^{ND} respectively) over the study period can now be evaluated by substituting each group's mean values for explanatory variables into Equation (5.1).[52] For dairy farms this gives $\text{RoR}_n^D = 12.68$ per cent, while for non-dairy farms this gives $\text{RoR}_n^{ND} = 1.62$ per cent. This large difference between dairy and non-dairy farms is highly significant and indicates the very considerable positive impact which CAP milk quotas have had upon dairy farm incomes and the parlous state of the non-dairy, agricultural sector within our study area. We return to this theme in Chapter 8.

Conversion to real rates of return (RoR_r) was achieved using retail price indices published by the Central Statistical Office (1993b).[53] These show an average inflation rate for the period 1987–92 of 5.81 per cent implying $\text{RoR}_r^D = 6.86$ per cent and $\text{RoR}_r^{ND} = -4.18$ per cent.

Rates of return in Wales, 1989/90

We were particularly interested in RoR_n during our study base year of 1989/90 and for the sample of farms that formed the basis of our analysis of agricultural values (presented in Chapter 8). The finding presented above suggests that this year may be typical of a longer time period. Furthermore, the representative sample of 240 farms provided by FBS for our agricultural analysis included grid reference locations which allowed us to consider a wider range of explanatory variables than previously. These included data covering the environmental attributes of the farm (soil type, altitude, etc.) obtained from the LandIS database discussed in Chapter 6. However, while many such variables were significant predictors of RoR_n they proved to be collinear with the DAIRY and BSU variables considered previously,

---

[52] The assumption of normality implicit in the use of means is relaxed in further testing reported in Bateman (1996) and is shown not to have a significant impact upon findings.

[53] Use of the RPI rather than some farm price index reflects the fact that, ultimately, investment funds could be moved out of the agricultural sector.

and these latter variables provided a superior degree of explanation. Following tests of functional form, our best-fitting model for these 240 farms was:

$$\text{RoR}_n = -39.37 + 12.12 \, \text{DAIRY} + 13.21 \ln \text{BSU} \qquad (5.2)$$
$$\quad\quad (-9.66) \quad\ (6.50) \qquad\qquad (9.51)$$

where:

$$\text{RoR}_n = \text{nominal rate of return, } 1989/90$$
$$\ln \text{BSU} = \text{natural log of farm size in BSU}$$
$$\text{DAIRY} = 1 \text{ if dairy farm; } 0 \text{ if non-dairy farm}[54]$$
$$R^2 = 43.3\%; \ R^2 \text{ (adj.)} = 42.8\%; \ n = 240; \text{ figures in brackets are } t\text{-statistics.}$$

Substituting variable means into Equation (5.2) allows us to calculate the RoR_n for dairy and non-dairy farms, $\text{RoR}_n^D = 15.27$ per cent and $\text{RoR}_n^{ND} = -2.70$ per cent respectively. Adjusting for inflation (which averaged over 9 per cent in 1989/90) implies $\text{RoR}_r^D = 5.81$ per cent and $\text{RoR}_r^{ND} = -12.2$ per cent. These results reiterate our previous conclusion regarding the gulf between dairy and non-dairy farms in Wales. Indeed, here we see the latter group making negative nominal and real rates of return, a situation which is clearly unsustainable in the long run and has been evident in disastrously low income levels in the Welsh non-dairy sector during the 1990s (see Chapter 8).

Farm discount rates: summary

While data are scarce, available information suggests that discount rates for agriculture will be low relative to those in other sectors of the economy. Our survey suggests that estimates of general rates as low as 3 per cent in real terms are quite defensible. However, our analysis of rates of return highlights the great variability which exists in the performance of different sections of the agricultural community and in particular, with reference to Wales, the disparity between dairy and non-dairy farms. As Table 5.8 indicates, during our study period the elite of dairy farms consistently recorded nominal (and sometimes real) rates of return in double figures, while, as subsequent analyses have shown, Welsh non-dairy farms regularly showed negative real rates of return. These latter rates were clearly unsustainable and the exodus from Welsh hill-farming throughout the years of our study period has continued up to the present day.

The link between rates of return and discount rates is not simple, involving as it does consideration of time preference. This may raise discount rates above rates

---

[54] 'Non-dairy' is defined as less than 20 per cent of farm output being milk (n (non-dairy) = 126 of which 124 had zero milk revenue, 1 had 3 per cent milk revenue and 1 had 7 per cent milk revenue (the next farm had 24 per cent milk revenue)).

of return, although studies such as Lloyd (1993) suggest that this will not be by a particularly large amount. In the case of dairy farms, rates of 12 per cent and 6 per cent were selected to provide, respectively, an upper-bound and majority best estimate of real discount rates for Welsh dairy farms during our study period. A 6 per cent rate is also the government's specified discount rate (H.M. Treasury, 1991) for 'returns accruing to the public sector from projects in the public sector' (Pearce and Ulph, 1998: p. 268), a rate which has applied from 1989 to the present. For non-dairy farms, rates were clearly significantly lower, with negative rates of return being the reality for many farms in the sector. However, given the unsustainability of negative rates, we felt that a real discount rate sensitivity range from 1.5 per cent to 3 per cent would both embrace the majority of such farms and provide results which were of more relevance to those non-dairy Welsh farms which have survived the traumas of the 1990s.

Social discount rates

We can now formalise and extend our analysis of the factors influencing discount rates as per Equation (5.3) which draws upon the notation of Pearce and Ulph (1998):

$$r = \delta + \mu g \qquad (5.3)$$

where:

r = discount rate
δ = rate of time preference (the rate at which utility is discounted)
μ = elasticity of the marginal utility of consumption schedule
g = expected growth rate of average consumption per capita

Economic commentators have long acknowledged that the values of the variables identified in Equation (5.3) which are appropriate to decisions affecting just the individual investor may differ from those values appropriate to decisions affecting the whole of society. The official UK social rate is derived from empirical data averaged over a wide variety of sectors giving values of about 2 for each of the elements of the basic discount rate formula detailed in Equation (5.3), i.e. $r = \delta + \mu g = 2 + (2 * 2) = 6$ per cent. However, a wide variety of views exists regarding the value of each of these elements.

Perhaps most controversial is the value of δ, the pure rate of time preference in the social discount rate (r_s). If society is immortal (or aspires to be) then, as very many eminent commentators have pointed out, δ should be very low or zero (Ramsey, 1928; Pigou, 1932; Solow, 1974b, 1992; Broome, 1992; Cline, 1992a,

1993; Fankhauser, 1993, 1995; Price, 1993; Arrow *et al.*, 1996; Pearce and Ulph, 1998). Such arguments have been reinforced by the debate surrounding sustainable development. This has centred upon notions of Rawlsian equity (Rawls, 1972) wherein, to be truly equitable, decisions regarding the use of resources (be they involving man-made, human or natural capital)[55] should be made behind a 'veil of ignorance' with respect to their temporal impact. Such a view is fundamental to the often quoted Brundtland Commission definition of sustainable development as 'development that meets the needs of the present without compromising the ability of future generations to meet their own needs' (World Commission on Environment and Development, 1987). Price (1993) sees this as only interpretable as an abandonment of discounting for global-level social decision-making.

A more 'conventional' view is given by Fankhauser (1993) who sees the requirements of sustainable development as implying that $\delta = 0$, but not necessarily that $r_s = 0$. Pearce and Ulph (1998) review an extensive literature on social δ, reporting a range from 0–1.7 per cent but favouring (for empirical reasons) a relatively high best estimate of $\delta = 1.4$ per cent.

Turning to consider the elasticity of the marginal utility of consumption (μ), Price (1993) reports a wide spread of private sector rates, generally ranging from 0.5 (Squire and van der Tak, 1975) to 3 (Little and Mirlees, 1974).[56] Stern (1977) finds many values in the region of 2.[57] However, we would expect the social preference value of μ to be somewhat lower than that found in the market. This is borne out by Pearce and Ulph (1998) who report a best estimate of social μ of 0.8 with a range of 0.7–1.5.

The social value of g (the expected rate of growth of average consumption per capita) is typically taken as being the real rate of growth of national income. Following such an approach, Lind (1982b, 1982c) argues for a maximum rate of $g = 2$ per cent.[58] However, the sustainable development debate has highlighted the problem that accounting measures such as GDP often ignore changes (frequently losses) in the natural and other non-market capital base of the economy (Repetto *et al.*, 1989).[59] Taking account of these, Pearce and Ulph (1998) suggest a best estimate for g in the UK of 1.3 per cent with a range of 1.3–2.2 per cent.

Taking best estimates from Pearce and Ulph (1998) gives a central estimate of r_s for the UK of about 2.4 per cent (= 1.4 + (0.8 * 1.3)). While this may seem

---

[55] For an introduction to the role of capital types in notions of sustainability, see Turner and Pearce (1993) or Pearce and Barbier (2000). While radical from a neoclassical perspective, more extreme (but very interesting) views are given in the work of Herman Daly (Daly, 1977; Daly and Cobb, 1990; Daly, 1995).

[56] μ is negative but we report modulus values following the convention of Pearce and Ulph (1995).

[57] Stern (1977) reports one extreme value of $\mu = 10$.

[58] Turner *et al.* (1994) point out that real growth in GDP in less developed countries is often much lower or even negative.

[59] Repetto puts forward an adjusted, sustainable national income measure. See also Pearce *et al.* (1989), Pearce and Warford (1993) and Pearce (1993).

low with respect to the Treasury's rate,[60] it is higher than that put forward by certain other commentators, particularly with respect to the discounting of global warming damages (perhaps the most potent challenge to intergenerational equity in the history of man). While not stating any particular rate, Arrow *et al.* (1996) make explicit reference to the range of 0–2 per cent used by Cline (1992a) in his economic analysis of long-run climate change models. Similarly, in his evaluation of the social costs of greenhouse gas emissions, Fankhauser (1993) uses a central (mode) estimate of $r_s = 0.5$ per cent with a range of 0–3 per cent (the upper end being mainly for comparison with other studies).

A further complication arises from the issue of multiple discount rates: the notion that social preferences may diverge radically between projects to the extent that a single discount rate is something of an oversimplification. As Arrow *et al.* (1996) and many earlier commentators have pointed out, the key factor here is substitutability, i.e. the extent to which development benefits (often in terms of man-made capital, K_m) can be traded off against costs (generally in terms of natural capital, K_n). Assuming that sustainability is socially desirable and that both sets of capital can be measured in some comparable numeraire (presumably money), then perfect substitutability would mean that any project would simply have to pass a standard Hicks–Kaldor hypothetical compensation test to be sanctioned.[61] In the literature of sustainable development this has been termed the 'very weak sustainability' rule (Turner and Pearce, 1993), which states that, provided total net benefits (total capital) are non-declining, a project may be sanctioned. This perfect substitutability assumption may be more acceptable for some K_m/K_n swaps (e.g. Sitka spruce plantations into paper, thence into money and so back to new plantations) than for others (e.g. the destruction of SSSIs to make way for motorways[62]), i.e. some K_n destruction is irreversible.

Pearce and Turner (1990) define a continuum of capital types from money (the purest form of K_m), through various types of K_n (trees, land, etc.) to 'critical natural capital' (K_n^c),[63] the last being those services of the planet vital to life support (climate and atmosphere control, ozone layer, etc.). As we move away from money along this continuum, the potential for substitution, rather than staying constant, falls until it reaches zero with K_n^c.

Such a view causes problems for cost-benefit analysis if we feel that the accumulation of K_m does not adequately compensate for the loss of K_n. This is the view of the 'weak sustainability' rule (Turner and Pearce, 1993) which argues that stocks of K_n^c should be inviolate, while K_n should be subject to some safe minimum standard

---

[60] Pearce and Ulph (1998) suggest that for policy purposes the Treasury should use a range of 2–4 per cent.
[61] See almost any cost-benefit text, for example Pearce (1986).
[62] As in the case of the M3 Twyford Down extension in southern England.
[63] The term is borrowed from Pearce and Turner (1990).

(SMS) below which use should be prohibited.[64] A further interpretation, the 'strong sustainability' rule, in effect argues that such an SMS has already been breached and that any further use of K_n should be offset by actual physical compensation in terms of shadow projects restoring, transplanting or recreating levels of any K_n used in future projects.[65]

The divergence between best estimates of r_s given by Pearce and Ulph (2.4 per cent) and Fankhauser (0.5 per cent) or Arrow *et al.* (implicitly 0–2 per cent) can therefore be viewed as comparing a general rate of K_m/K_n substitutability with that of a non-substitutable good: global climate. The implication of such an analysis is that, because of the various rates of substitutability and irreversibility inherent in the differing capital bases of each project, society will have different discount rates for different projects. Furthermore, we could extend this line of reasoning to the individual costs and benefits of a single project so that, in our forestry case study, UK timber (for which losses are reasonably reversible) might attract a higher r_s than recreation benefits (which arguably belong to a more depleted set of K_n), which in turn is more discounted than carbon storage (which contributes to the K_n^c stock of global climate services). Following this argument we examine the impact of using differing discount rates in our forestry case study.

In practice, the variance of r_s within a project is clearly a decision-making nightmare and opens up the potential for discount rate 'management' abuses. Indeed, the avoidance of abuse may be the most cogent argument for adopting a single rate policy. Henderson and Bateman (1995) report numerous examples from around the world of both inter- and intraproject multiple discount rates.[66] However, these appeared to be almost exclusively motivated by policy objectives rather than empirical evidence regarding underlying preferences. Unfortunately, the manipulation of discount rates to give policy-favoured projects a spurious sheen of financial respectability is widespread if invalid.

The desirability of a single rate is therefore clear. The Pearce and Ulph (1998) results (central estimate $r_s = 2.4$ per cent; range $= 2$–4 per cent) are useful here but we have to recognise that probably the recreation benefits, and almost certainly the carbon sequestration benefits, of woodland would attract a lower than average rate of public pure time preference. Accordingly, we have chosen a sensitivity analysis

---

[64] Under weak sustainability, further use of K_n up to the SMS must still be compensated for by re-investment (savings) of the appropriate level of K_m proceeds from each project (Turner and Pearce, 1993).

[65] Under strong sustainability an individual project must compensate K_n both in terms of K_m savings and by appropriate contributions to an offset physical compensation, shadow project fund. Such physical compensation must be actual rather than hypothetical (rejecting the Hicks–Kaldor rule). A still stronger view (very strong sustainability) states that each project must have its own actual physical K_n compensation shadow project (see Turner and Pearce, 1993).

[66] Henderson and Bateman (1995) examine theoretical and empirical arguments in favour of hyperbolic discount rates. Bateman (1996) reassesses all of the analyses presented in this volume using a hyperbolic discount rate and shows that this further increases the potential for transfers from agriculture to multipurpose woodland.

for r_s which includes one rate (1.5 per cent) below the Pearce and Ulph range[67] and another at the centre of that range (3 per cent). For comparative purposes we have also employed the Treasury's 6 per cent public sector discount rate throughout, although we echo the sentiments of Pearce and Ulph that this seems 'very difficult to justify'.

Discount rates: conclusions

Given the major impact which variations in the discount rate will have upon long-delayed forestry returns, we feel that our discussion highlights the need to adopt a sensitivity analysis approach. We feel that real social discount rates of 1.5 per cent and 3 per cent are well justified as a reasonable range here. The Treasury's 6 per cent rate is also included for comparative purposes. Turning to consider farmers' real private discount rates, the 1.5 per cent and 3 per cent rates are useful for assessing decisions in the Welsh non-dairy agricultural sector.[68] Conversely, rates of 6 per cent and 12 per cent roughly describe reasonable limits to apply to dairy farms in Wales.[69]

The private value of timber production

The discussions in this chapter show that the private value of a productive plantation is determined by a variety of factors including species, plantation costs, timber yield, timber price (where both the price–size curve and assumptions regarding future real prices are important), grants and subsidies, and the discount rate. All these factors were brought together by integrating data from the FC yield models (Edwards and Christie, 1981) for Sitka spruce (YC6–24) and beech (YC4–10) within a series of spreadsheets. This allowed easy manipulation of all assumptions (e.g. grant schemes, discount rates, optimal felling age,[70] etc.) to produce a full range of private NPV and annuity equivalent values. Results from this exercise are reported in full in Bateman (1996) which details a variety of permutations, ranging across all species, yield class, discount rate and subsidy scheme scenarios. Results are also calculated for a single, optimal rotation of trees and for a scenario of perpetual replanting after each felling. As this produces a plethora of permutations, we reproduce results for just one scenario here. Figure 5.5 graphs

---

[67] This also reflects the lower-range estimates of Fankhauser (1993) and Arrow *et al.* (1996).

[68] We recognise that a number of these farms may not be attaining rates of return of even 1.5 per cent. However, such farms are unlikely to keep operating in the long term. The 3 per cent rate also provides an assessment under conditions similar to those likely to apply if discount rates are cut as recently proposed by H. M. Treasury.

[69] Discussion of results obtained using hyperbolic discount rates is given in Bateman (1996).

[70] Set as per Tables 5.6 (for conifers) and 5.7 (for broadleaves).

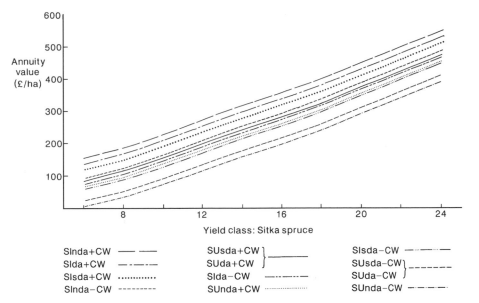

Figure 5.5. Farmers' private timber values for Sitka spruce (annualised equivalents of a perpetual series of optimal rotations: $r = 3\%$). Various yield classes and subsidy types.

annuity equivalents for the full range of Sitka spruce yield classes and all feasible grant scheme registrations (using the abbreviations developed at the end of the earlier section on grants (p. 128) assuming that a system of perpetual replanting is used and a 3 per cent discount rate is applied. Figure 5.6 repeats the analysis for beech.

For both Sitka spruce and beech we see that, as expected, annual equivalent values rise with yield class (just as they fall with discount rate; see subsequent results). As subsidy schemes are not linked to timber productivity the difference between scheme payments is constant across yield classes. Comparison between Sitka spruce and beech is interesting as it shows that, holding yield class constant (i.e. YC 6, 8 or 10), returns from broadleaves are higher than for conifers. This is due to higher prices and subsidy levels for broadleaves and occurs despite the lower felling age of conifers. However, because conifers are capable of much higher yield classes than broadleaves on almost any given site and, more importantly, because such high-yield plantations have much lower felling ages (thus avoiding the severe discounting that occurs with long-rotation broadleaves), they provide much higher annual equivalents than broadleaves.

An overview of discounting impacts is given in Table 5.9 (full details for all yield class/species combinations are presented in Bateman, 1996). Here annualised

Table 5.9. *Farmers' private timber values for high-output Sitka spruce and beech across various discount rates (annualised equivalents of a perpetual series of optimal rotations)*

Discount rate (%)	Farmers' private value (annualised equivalent, £/ha)	
	Sitka spruce (YC24)	Beech (YC10)
1.5	496.30	103.54
3	388.46	80.68
6	219.36	31.21
12	19.45	9.59

Note: Subsidy option for all cases is SUnda−CW = subsidy for previously unimproved grassland, not in a disadvantaged area and without Community Woodland Supplement.

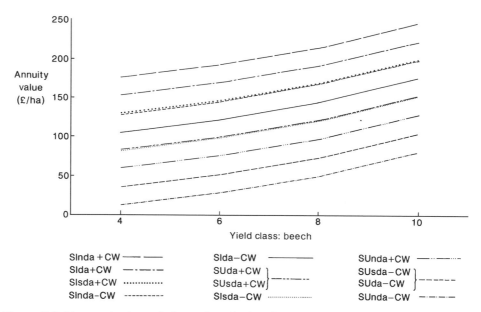

Figure 5.6. Farmers' private timber values for beech (annualised equivalents of a perpetual series of optimal rotations: $r = 3\%$). Various yield classes and subsidy types.

equivalents for highest output Sitka spruce (YC24) and beech (YC10) under one subsidy permutation are given for all the discount rates considered.

In subsequent chapters we examine how forest timber values compare with agricultural returns under a variety of scenarios. However, we now turn to consider the other, non-market, benefits of woodlands.

The social value of woodlands

In moving from the private to the social value of timber production a number of issues need to be addressed. The basic plantation costs and timber (thinnings and maincrop) benefits can defensibly be used in an unaltered form as, unlike the prices of agricultural produce, UK timber prices are not the subject of intervention or otherwise controlled. However, we do have to subtract all grants and subsidies, as these are simply transfer payments, to obtain our baseline social value for timber net benefits (see Bateman, 1996, for further details).

As discussed in our opening chapter, the social value of a woodland is more than just the value of timber therein. In earlier work (Bateman, 1992) we identified and discussed a detailed set of environmental and non-environmental non-market costs and benefits which may arise from afforestation. Here we summarise that discussion by briefly considering the major non-market items which may need to be examined when moving from a private to a social assessment of woodland.

Non-environmental non-market social costs and benefits

Here we discuss four major issues: national security; economic security; import substitution; and employment.

National security
While national security formed the impetus for the creation of the Forestry Commission just after the First World War, and was an important spur to planting after the Second World War, the prospect of the UK being blockaded from receiving timber supplies for any extended period seems rather unlikely. We therefore conclude that there are no significant national security benefits to be derived from the expansion of a domestic supply capability.

Economic security
While not of strategic importance, uninterrupted security of supply does bring avoided-cost benefits. In a study of this issue, Pearce (1991) states that 'an evaluation of the chances of embargoes and other supply interruptions suggests that a small increment in prices of 0.2 to 0.8 per cent to reflect the shadow value of economic security would be justified'. Accordingly, timber benefits were increased by 0.5 per cent in our social evaluation models.[71]

---

[71] Note that this is an across-the-board single increase, not a compounding of an annual real price increase. Consequently the net effect is very small.

Import substitution

As mentioned earlier in this chapter, timber is one of the UK's major import items. In 1999 the UK imported over 21 million m^3 of wood and panels and over 25 million m^3 of pulp and paper (FC, 2001c). Despite this dependence on imports, the basic theory of comparative advantage has long shown that this does not necessarily imply that the UK should strive to change this situation (see, for example, Söderstern, 1980). This theory shows that a given amount of resources should only be invested into reducing timber imports if those same resources cannot be invested more productively in some other manner. Repeated studies of precisely this issue have consistently shown that this is not the case (H.M. Treasury, 1972; Bowers, 1985; National Audit Office (NAO), 1986; Pearce, 1991) and so the import-saving argument is rejected.

Employment

It has been argued that creating jobs in forestry is a good way to stem the ongoing trend of rural depopulation and combat the psychological and other economic costs of rural unemployment. However, numerous studies have suggested that forestry is a relatively expensive and inefficient method of providing rural employment, particularly when compared to agriculture (H.M. Treasury, 1972; Laxton and Whitby, 1986; NAO, 1986; Evans, 1987; Johnson and Price, 1987). Forestry expansion could therefore be seen as creating shadow costs.

Such conclusions were tentatively disputed by studies in the early 1990s which argued that, as Forestry Commission employment was falling and productivity rising, an economic benefit of rural employment might occur over the course of the decade (Thompson, 1990; FICGB, 1992). However, in the event, the steady increase in private woodlands meant that employment in British forestry (excluding primary processing) rose from about 17,000 in the mid 1980s to over 27,000 a decade later (FC, 1985b, 1997). The low-employment/high-productivity argument may be due for a revival in coming years as employment levels have recently fallen to just over 18,000 (FC, 2001c) and it is interesting to note that rural employment has again moved to centre stage as a policy argument for increased forestry (FC, 1998). Our view is that a more likely promoter of the economic case for forestry employment benefits is the parlous state of UK agriculture (discussed in Chapter 8). However, in the absence of a specific and contemporary study these are mere speculations and a cautious approach is to assume that the case for the employment benefits of forestry is unproven.

In conclusion the only clearly valid non-environmental, non-market social benefit we can isolate is a small benefit due to increased economic security of supply and we adjust social values marginally (as indicated above) to reflect this.

Environmental non-market social costs and benefits

Woodlands create a number of social benefits and costs of which we discuss the following major issues: recreation; carbon storage; acidification impacts; landscape amenity; biodiversity effects; and other non-use (bequest and existence) values.

Recreation use and option value

Recreation use value is the major focus of our valuation research as discussed in Chapters 2–4. Because of the potentially significant problems of declining marginal utility,[72] we have decided not to incorporate such benefits within the plantation value models presented in this chapter. Instead these models deal primarily with timber values to which recreation benefits are added in subsequent chapters.[73] One potential deficiency in our research is that travel cost estimates of recreation value ignore option values. These are in theory addressed through our contingent valuation studies; however, we recognise that option value is not a principal aim of these studies.

Carbon sequestration

As with recreation, we deal with carbon sequestration separately (in chapter 7). This is not because of diminishing marginal utility, for (as explained in later chapters) the likely levels of sequestration will not have a significant impact upon the global CO_2 budget, but rather because of the complexities of this issue which we feel deserve separate attention.

Acidification

Forests are cited as both the victims and perpetrators of acidification damage. Although research into the impact of acidic deposition upon trees is abundant (European Commission and the United Nations Economic Commission for Europe, 1994; Marques *et al.*, 2001; Takahashi *et al.*, 2001), relatively little ongoing work concerns the contribution, if any, which trees make to acidic impacts upon soil and watercourses (Hornung and Adamson, 1991). Indeed, some dispute what they term 'the myth of soil acidification', asserting that 'Within its lifetime, a spruce cannot significantly acidify the soil below it' (Baldwin, 1996: p. 1). The Forestry Commission suggests that forests tend to act as a catalytic fixing medium for industrially emitted atmospheric acid (Innes, 1987); others argue that this is only part of the story and that conifers, in particular, directly contribute to a lowering

---

[72] As the area of woodland expands we would expect the increase in recreation opportunities to result in an observable decline in per hectare recreation values. Given supply and demand conditions we would not expect this to be a problem for timber production.

[73] As discussed elsewhere, this implicitly assumes that the monetary evaluations of woodland recreation are surpluses to the amenity value of the present agricultural landscape.

of pH levels (see Harriman and Morrison, 1982; Batterbee, 1984; Edwards *et al.*, 1990;[74] Nisbet, 1990; Grieve, 2001). We take the position that whether or not forests actually generate the acids concerned, they are significantly linked to increased acidification of soils and aquifers in non-buffered areas and therefore do generate costs. Our research in this area has not progressed beyond the stage of a literature survey, although this has shown that the acidification problem is eminently amenable to GIS analysis, which we intend to conduct in future research.[75]

Landscape amenity

The remit of this study excludes the landscape amenity values of forestry. Although the contingent valuation method has been applied to general landscape valuation (see, for example, Willis and Garrod, 1993), these studies have not looked specifically at the impact of woodland. However, a number of hedonic pricing studies have demonstrated that forests do generate significant amenity values, as reflected in property prices (Garrod and Willis, 1992a,b,c; Powe *et al.*, 1997; Peterson and Boyle, forthcoming). Taken together, these studies indicate that while broadleaves generate landscape amenity benefits, certain conifers, including Sitka spruce, can result in amenity losses. Such results therefore constitute a caveat to our own findings. However, our recent research shows that GIS techniques are particularly appropriate to the estimation of landscape values via the hedonic pricing method (Lake *et al.*, 1998, 2000a,b; Bateman *et al.*, 2001a). The GIS allows the definition of 'viewsheds' quantifying what can and cannot be seen from any given location. Derived variables have been shown to be powerful predictors of amenity values (*ibid.*) and we intend to apply such an approach to valuing woodland landscape in future research.

Biodiversity impacts

Work, in collaboration with ecological scientists, is currently ongoing in an attempt to incorporate biodiversity impacts into our model of woodland values. Early findings indicated that afforestation of agricultural areas by conifers such as Sitka spruce is liable to change the balance of bird species to the detriment of some of the most endangered birds in Wales (Bateman *et al.*, 1997c). More recently we combined GIS techniques with data provided by the British Trust for Ornithology to generate algorithms for selecting priority areas for conservation in Wales (Woodhouse *et al.*, 2000).[76] In ongoing extensions to this work we are linking these findings with land use change data to model the relationships between agriculture, forestry

---

[74] This collection of papers focuses exclusively upon acidification in Wales.
[75] Such research would also allow consideration of related issues such as the impact of afforestation upon hydroelectric potential (see Barrow *et al.*, 1986).
[76] See also the GIS-based approaches of Swetnam *et al.* (1998) and Cowling and Heijnis (2001).

and species diversity. This research should provide a mechanism for investigating the biodiversity consequences of policy decisions and consequent land use change in a manner which will link to the CBA assessments presented in this volume.

While there exist substantial (and possibly insurmountable) practical, economic and philosophical problems in the valuation of biodiversity impacts (Garrod and Willis, 1994; Kahn, 1995; Carson, 1998; Shogren *et al.*, 1999), it seems likely that afforestation with non-native species such as Sitka spruce would induce a loss of unknown and potentially substantial magnitude which should be set against the values reported in subsequent chapters. The biodiversity impacts of planting beech woodland are generally (although not exclusively) considered to be positive and should similarly be set against the other values presented subsequently.

Other non-use values

Biodiversity values may arguably provide a proxy for wider existence values (although this is debatable). However, other non-use issues such as bequest values do not feature explicitly in our study (although potentially they may influence our contingent valuation findings) and this provides a further caveat to the accuracy of our results.

Non-market social costs and benefits: summary

We are left with having to acknowledge a number of deficiencies in the extent of our study. While we feel that our analysis is relatively sophisticated and useful in a policy-making context, it remains far from perfect. Nevertheless, those items which we feel to be of major significance (recreation and carbon sequestration) are dealt with outside our rotation model in other chapters. Of the remaining social costs and benefits, economic security arguments seem to justify a minor upward revision of social benefit values which is quantified and incorporated within the rotation values model. Of the remaining issues, acidification, biodiversity and non-use values remain insufficiently addressed but the subject of ongoing research. If we accept that this must remain a partial analysis until that work is complete, we would defend the present study both as a significant improvement on existing CBA assessments of forestry values and, more importantly, as demonstrating an improved methodology for conducting such studies.

Annual equivalent social timber values

Given the above caveats, we can now calculate social net benefit timber values for our plantation models. These include timber values and the value of economic security of supply but exclude recreation and carbon sequestration values which

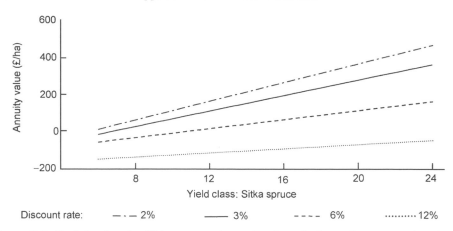

Figure 5.7. Social value for Sitka spruce (annualised equivalent of a perpetual series of optimal rotations). Various yield classes and discount rates.

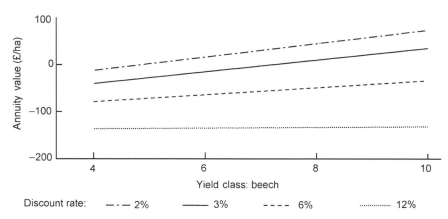

Figure 5.8. Social value for beech (annualised equivalent of a perpetual series of optimal rotations). Various yield classes and discount rates.

are dealt with subsequently. As there is no subsidy dimension to these calculations (remember that we have removed all transfer payments) we can illustrate results across all yield classes and discount rates on a single graph as shown in Figure 5.7 for conifers, and Figure 5.8 for broadleaves.

Comparison of Figures 5.7 and 5.8 shows relationships similar to those observed in the private sector evaluations. Again we see (on this restricted range of value types) that conifers are able to outperform broadleaves (interestingly values for broadleaves are negative for most low yield class/high discount rate combinations, illustrating the impact of discounting on the long rotation periods of such trees). Given that we have excluded recreation and non-user values, such a result is not unexpected.

Conclusions

We have constructed rotation models which, across the full range of yields for our two representative tree species, take into account plantation costs and benefits, real prices, grants and subsidies. We have also considered the difference between private and social perspectives both in terms of differential discount rates and with regard to the differing range of values which the two assessments should appraise. In subsequent chapters the private and social values derived from this analysis are aggregated with our estimates of recreation and carbon sequestration values to provide our overall assessment of the values generated by farm forestry. These values are then compared with those for existing agricultural activities so as to estimate likely conversion rates under a variety of scenarios.

6

Modelling and mapping timber yield and its value

Introduction

In this chapter we present various models of timber production for the two species under consideration: Sitka spruce and beech. In the next section we present a brief review of previous studies. These have exclusively been based upon relatively small-scale surveys of tree growth; furthermore, they have also generally been confined to comparatively small areas and often to one topographic region, e.g. upland areas. Our study differs from these previous models in that it employs a GIS to utilise large-scale existing databases covering a very large and diverse study area: the whole of Wales. The subsequent section presents details regarding the various datasets used in this study and discusses how these data were transformed for the purposes of subsequent regression analysis. Subsequently, results from our models of Sitka spruce and beech growth rates are presented, while the following section presents and analyses GIS-created map images of predicted yield class. The final section applies the findings of the previous chapter to produce monetised equivalents of these results.

Literature review and methodological overview

Literature review

It is clear that tree growth rates depend upon a variety of species, environmental and silvicultural factors. Early work in this field relied on simple rules of thumb based upon relatively little supporting data (Busby, 1974) or analyses of single factors. Reviews across this literature provide a number of clues regarding the specification of a yield class model. An early focus of interest was the impact of elevation upon productivity (Malcolm, 1970; Mayhead, 1973; Blyth, 1974). Subsequent papers considered the various routes by which elevation affected YC including windiness (Grace, 1977), slope and aspect (Tranquillini, 1979). Other

158

work examined the impact of factors such as soil type, soil moisture transport and droughtiness (Page, 1970; Blyth and MacLeod, 1981; Jarvis and Mullins, 1987) and crop age (Kilpatrick and Savill, 1981). However, the estimation of statistical models across the full range of likely explanatory variables is a relatively recent innovation. Amongst such investigations we could find no examples concerning the productivity of beech and believe the model presented subsequently to be the first such investigation of this species. However, there has been more attention paid to the other species under analysis, Sitka spruce, which has been separately studied by both Richard Worrell (then of the University of Edinburgh) and Douglas Macmillan (then of Macauley Land Use Research Institute, MLURI).[1]

While there had been a number of earlier considerations of factors affecting the growth of Sitka spruce (Malcolm, 1970; Malcolm and Studholme, 1972; Mayhead, 1973; Blyth, 1974; Busby, 1974; Gale and Anderson, 1984), the work of Worrell (1987a,b) and Worrell and Malcolm (1990a,b) is notable as being the first to adopt a multiple regression approach across a wide range of explanatory variables. These were: elevation (including separate dummy variables for hilltop and valley bottom sites); windiness; temperature; aspect (measured as sine and cosine); and a full range of soil dummy variables. However, while they provide vital pointers for our own modelling exercise, Worrell's results are not transferable to our Welsh case study. This is partly due to the upland Scottish location of Worrell's experiment but primarily as a result of the focus of his study. Worrell was mainly interested in detecting the influence of elevation upon yield class in upland areas.[2] To this end he selected eighteen principal sample sites,[3] all of which had relatively steep slopes, and took measurements along a vertical transect at each site. By locating samples at sites ranging from 50 m to 600 m above sea level a very strong, central tendency relationship with elevation could be established. However, such a model is only applicable to similar, steeply sloping sites (strictly speaking, only the subset of those found within Scotland), and is not readily generalisable to the plethora of environmental conditions found in an area the size of Wales.

A similar, though less extreme, consideration prevents us applying the findings of Macmillan (1991). Here again the study is geographically confined, this time to lowland Scotland, although the 121 sites used are not selected to emphasise the influence of any particular explanatory variable and are therefore somewhat more generalisable within lowland areas. However, while in many cases this would be adequate, with respect to our study area the topographic variability of Wales means that a model based purely upon lowland data is insufficient for our needs.

---

[1] We are grateful to both Richard Worrell and Douglas Macmillan for extensive discussions of their work.
[2] An important question given that this is the location of much of the existing stock of Sitka spruce.
[3] The number of individual tree measurements is not reported.

Nevertheless, the Macmillan paper is interesting both because it uses multiple regression with a prior principal components analysis (PCA) of explanatory variables (reporting a final degree of explanation of $R^2 = 36.8$ per cent) and because the data collected have been more recently re-analysed using GIS techniques (Elston *et al.*, 1997) to produce a somewhat improved model ($R^2 = 43.9$ per cent)[4], a result which underlines the potential advantages of applying GIS methods within this field.[5]

A short note regarding model fit is justified here. As discussed in the previous chapter yield class (YC) is the average annual growth rate of a plantation assessed over an optimal rotation. YC is therefore given in $m^3/ha/yr$. However, YC values are rounded to the nearest even number so that while we have stands with YC 6 or 8 we do not have sites with YC 7. While this does not invalidate statistical analysis, as YC is the dependent variable, this approach to measurement does induce variance into the dataset and therefore makes high degrees of explanation difficult to attain. As such the absolute value of fit statistics such as R^2 should be treated with some caution and instead we should consider, where possible, relative degrees of fit compared to those attained in other studies.

Overview of modelling approach

These prior studies provide very useful indications regarding the likely explanatory variables which should be considered in our analysis. The differences in modelling approach are also of interest and we consequently decided to investigate both a PCA and standard multiple regression methodology. However, subsequent analysis showed that PCA models were narrowly outperformed by those obtained using standard regression techniques. Given their relatively straightforward interpretation, here standard regression models are reported in preference to those obtained using PCA, results from the latter being given in Bateman and Lovett (1998) and Bateman (1996).

While our approach to modelling is similar, in other key respects the methods of Worrell and Macmillan were not appropriate to the specific types of question asked in our research. Our central aim was to identify areas over the entire surface of Wales which might be suitable for conversion out of agriculture and into forestry. This necessitated the development of a methodology which was capable of producing estimates for both upland and lowland areas and which had the capability of extrapolating such findings across the entire surface area of the country. To this end

---

[4] Although not specified in this or the Macmillan paper, this appears to be an unadjusted R^2 statistic.

[5] Earlier discussions of the potential for applying GIS to forestry research and management are given in Aspinall (1991), Davidson (1991) and Blakeway-Smith *et al.* (1993).

we adopted a GIS-based approach to modelling.[6] This takes our base YC data from the Forestry Commission (FC) Sub-Compartment Database (SCDB) which holds information on each discrete stand (sub-compartment) in the FC's estate (described in detail subsequently).[7] As this covers both upland and lowland sites, results from such a model are more generalisable than those described previously. Use of the SCDB has the added bonus of massively increasing our sample size relative to previous studies. However, rather than relate YC to the environmental variables reported in the SCDB, for reasons discussed below we extract these from a separate source, the Soil Survey and Land Research Centre's Land Information System (LandIS) database (described subsequently).[8]

Data and data manipulation

This research relies upon a range of data sources. Aside from the SCDB and LandIS, further environmental and topographic data were obtained from a variety of sources. In this section we describe all these data and how they were manipulated prior to consideration within the subsequent statistical investigation of tree growth. It is important to remember that, while the SCDB holds detailed data regarding individual plantation sites, it does not extend to the large part of Wales which is unplanted. Therefore the environmental variables given in the SCDB are, for our purposes, unsuitable predictors of YC as complete land surface coverages for these variables are not available and therefore cannot be used for extrapolation of estimates to presently unplanted areas. The complete land area coverages of variables held in LandIS and the other data described subsequently are therefore needed to allow for this extrapolation of regression results.

The FC Sub-Compartment Database (SCDB)

The SCDB is the Forestry Commission's central forest inventory containing details for all stands in the estate. As such it provides an invaluable source of high-quality data, listing many thousands of sub-compartments for a variety of species across both upland and lowland Wales. The FC kindly provided SCDB data collected in the period 1972 to 1993 for a wide range of species among which were just over 6,000 Sitka spruce and over 700 beech records (the disparity reflecting the dominance

[6] For other examples of GIS applied to agricultural or forest planning, see Gemmell (1995), Moxey (1996), Corbett and Carter (1997), Hill and Aspinall (2000) and the ESRI website (e.g. at www.esri.com/industries/forestry/index.html).

[7] We are greatly obliged to Adrian Whiteman, Chris Quine and the Forestry Commission for use of the SCDB.

[8] We are greatly obliged to Arthur Thomasson, Ian Bradley and the Soil Survey and Land Research Centre (Cranfield) for use of LandIS.

of conifers over broadleaves in our Welsh study area).[9] Some of the information given in the SCDB concerned internal FC administration and was not of interest to our investigation and so the final list of variables extracted for this study was as shown in Table 6.1. This also indicates how certain of these data were manipulated to produce further (often binary dummy) variables. In doing this, one-way analyses of variance on the dependent variable (YC) were used to identify likely significant divisions in the data.

The SCDB also contains a variety of environmental variables specific to sub-compartments such as soil type, altitude, terrain type and windblow hazard class. Normally these would be ideal for modelling purposes. However, as the SCDB only holds such data for plantation sites rather than as uninterrupted national coverages, findings based upon such data would not form a suitable basis for extrapolation to other, currently unforested areas. This is somewhat unfortunate as these site-specific data are almost certainly more accurate than those obtainable from more general databases such as LandIS. This means that the regression models produced using LandIS are unlikely to fit the YC data as well as those using the site factor information given in the SCDB. However, for the purposes of this research, the advantage of being able to extrapolate out across the entire surface of Wales and consider currently unplanted areas easily outweighs such costs (which we subsequently argue, on the basis of our results, are likely to be small).

The SSLRC Land Information System (LandIS)

Background

The first systematic attempt to analyse and record British soil information was the 'County Series' of maps initiated by the Board of Agriculture in the late eighteenth and early nineteenth centuries. Until comparatively recently this remained the standard and unsurpassed source of soil data. During the 1940s the Soil Survey of England and Wales (SSEW) began a detailed mapping initiative. However, by the late 1970s, only one-fifth of the country had been covered. In 1979 the SSEW, which in the late 1980s became the Soil Survey and Land Research Centre (SSLRC), commenced a five-year project to produce a soil map of the whole of England and Wales and to describe soil distribution and related land quality in appropriate detail.

The data collected in this exercise were digitised, spatially referenced, and subsequently expanded to include climate and other environmental information (Bradley and Knox, 1995). The resulting Land Information System (LandIS) database was initially commissioned by the Ministry of Agriculture, Fisheries and Food, with the

---

[9] The FC was, as always, most willing to allow access to its data, for which we are most grateful.

stated aim of 'providing a systematic inventory capable of being used or interpreted for a wide range of purposes including agricultural advisory work, but also for the many facets of *land use planning and national resource use*' (Rudeforth *et al.*, 1984, emphasis added). However, while the system has been used in a variety of ways, particularly in relation to modelling agricultural pollution (see examples in Hallett *et al.*, 1996 and the SSLRC website[10]), the present research represents one of the first attempts to use LandIS for its originally intended purpose: national land use planning.

The data

Definitions, derivations and accuracy of the data extracted from LandIS are presented in Bateman (1996) and are summarised in Table 6.2. Further details of LandIS and the data therein are given in Jones and Thomasson (1985) and Hallett *et al.* (1996), with discussion of Welsh conditions given by Rudeforth *et al.* (1984). LandIS data are supplied at a 5 km resolution.

An immediate problem with applying the LandIS data to modelling yield classes arose from the plethora of differing soil codes contained in the database. These are taken from the Soil Survey of England and Wales (1983) which lists many hundreds of separate soil types, a large number of which were present in our Welsh dataset. This level of detail far exceeds that used in previous yield class studies such as Worrell (1987b) who uses seven soil type dummies derived from information given in the SCDB, which in turn relies on the standard FC classification of soils. The large number of soil codes given in LandIS was a problem both because of its implication for degrees of freedom in our intended regression analysis and because any such results would be of little practical use to the forester familiar with an alternative and simpler system. Furthermore, consultations with an expert in the field of soil science and forestry suggested that, for our purposes, many of the SSLRC soil codes could be merged with no effective loss of information and a substantial increase in clarity.[11] Details of the final categorisation are given in the bottom row of Table 6.2.

Other data

Topex and wind hazard

Data referenced to a 1 km grid on both the topographical shelter of a site (topex) and wind hazard were supplied by the Forestry Commission.[12] Topex is usually

---

[10] See www.silsoe.cranfield.ac.uk/sslrc/services/dataproducts/landis.htm.

[11] Dr Bill Corbett of the School of Environmental Sciences, University of East Anglia, and formerly of the Soil Survey of England and Wales, kindly advised on the merging of soil codes to produce a simple eight-category system which groups together similar soils.

[12] Our thanks go to Chris Quine at Roslin, the Forestry Commission's northern research station.

Table 6.1. *Variables obtained from the SCDB*[1]

Variable name[2]	Values	Notes and recodings (in italics)
Grid reference	Easting, Northing	100 m resolution O.S. grid references
Land use/crop type	PHF = plantation high forest	
	PWB = uncleared windblown area	*Uncleared* = 1 if PWB; = 0 otherwise
	PRP = research plantation	*Research* = 1 if PRP; = 0 otherwise
Storey	1 = single storey	*Single* = 1 if single storey; = 0 otherwise
	2 = lower storey	
	3 = upper storey	
Species	SS = Sitka spruce	Used to identify target species
	BE = beech	
	other	
Planting year	Discrete variable	*Plantyr*: year in which stand was planted
Survey year	Discrete variable	*Survyr*: year in which stand was surveyed
Yield class	Even number	*YC*: tree growth rate: average m^3/ha/year over an optimal rotation (the dependent variable)
Productive forest area	Hectares	*Area*: stocked area of the sub-compartment
Unproductive forest area	Hectares	*Unprod*: the area within the sub-compartment which has a permanent effect upon the crop, e.g. rocky outcrops, etc.
Rotation	1 = 1st rotation on formerly non-forest land	*1stRot* = 1 for 1st rotation; = 0 otherwise
	2, 3 etc. = 2nd, 3rd rotation, etc.	*2ndRot* = 1 for 2nd or subsequent rotation; = 0 otherwise
	9 = historical woodland sites	*Historic* = 1 if historic site; = 0 otherwise
	S = ancient, semi-natural woodland	*Semi-nat* = 1 if ancient/semi-natural woodland; = 0 otherwise
Mixture	P = single species crop	*MixCrop* = 1 if mixed species crop; = 0 otherwise
	M = mixed species crop	
Legal status	P = purchased by FC	*Purchased* = 1 if purchased; = 0 otherwise
	L = leased	*Leased* = 1 if leased; = 0 otherwise
	E = extra land, managed by FC outside its legal boundary	*Extra* = 1 if extra; = 0 otherwise

Table 6.1. *(cont.)*

Variable name[2]	Values	Notes and recodings (in italics)
Landscape	1 = National Park	*NatPark* = 1 if National Park; = 0 otherwise
	2 = AONB/National Scenic Area	*AONB/NSA* = 1 if AONB/National Scenic Area; = 0 otherwise
	3 = ESA (where not included in 1 or 2 above)	*OthESA* = 1 if ESA area not included in above; = 0 otherwise
Forest Park	1 = Forest Park	*FPark* = 1 if forest park; = 0 otherwise
Conservation	1 = SSSI (Site of Special Scientific Interest)	*SSSI* = 1 if SSSI; = 0 otherwise
	2 = NNR (National Nature Reserve)	*NNR* = 1 if NNR; = 0 otherwise
	3 = Non-FC Nature Reserve	*NonFCNR* = 1 if non-FC nature reserve; = 0 otherwise
FC conservation	1 = Forest Nature Reserve	*FCNR* = 1 if Forest Nature Reserve; = 0 otherwise
	2 = Other FC conservation	*FCcons* = 1 if other FC; = 0 otherwise
Ancient monument/Woodland	S = scheduled ancient monument	*Ancient* = 1 if S, U or W; = 0 otherwise
		Monument = 1 if S or U; = 0 otherwise
	U = unscheduled ancient monument	
	W = ancient woodland	
		Further recodes from above:
		NpAonbSa = 1 if any of *NatPark* or *AONB/NSA*; = 0 otherwise
		Cons = 1 if any of *NNR*, *NonFCNR*, *FCNR*, *FCcons*; = 0 otherwise
		Reserve = 1 if any of *Cons*, *AONB/NSA*, *OthESA*; = 0 otherwise
		Park = 1 if any of *NatPark*, *FPark*, *SSSI*; = 0 otherwise

Notes: [1] Except where shown otherwise.
[2] Variables are listed in the order in which they appear in the database.

determined as the sum of the angle of inclination for the eight major compass points of a site (Hart, 1991). Thus, a low angle sum (low topex value) represents a high degree of exposure. The resultant GIS data coverage was labelled *Topex1km*.

Table 6.2. *Variables obtained from LandIS*

Variable name	Label	Definition
Accumulated temperature	*Acctemp*	Average annual accumulated temperature (in °C) above 0°C
Accumulated rainfall	*Rainfall*	Average annual accumulated rainfall (in mm)
Available water	*Avwatgra*	Amount of soil water available for a grass crop after allowing for gravity-induced drainage
	Avwatcer	As for *Avwatgra* but adjusted for a cereal crop
	Avwatpot	As for *Avwatgra* but adjusted for potatoes
	Avwatsb	As for *Avwatgra* but adjusted for sugar beet
Moisture deficit	*Mdefgra*	The difference between rainfall and the potential evapotranspiration of a grass crop
	Mdefcer	As for *Mdefgra* but adjusted for a cereal crop
	Mdefsbpt	As for *Mdefgra* but adjusted for a sugar beet/potatoes crop
Field capacity	*Fcapdays*	Average annual number of days where the soil experiences a zero moisture deficit
Return to field capacity	*Retmed*	Median measure from a distribution of the number of days between the date on which a soil returns to field capacity and 31 December of that year
	Retwet	The upper quartile of the above distribution (measure of return to field capacity in wet years)
	Retdry	The lower quartile of the above distribution (measure of return to field capacity in dry years)
End of field capacity	*Endmed*	Median measure from a distribution of the number of days between the 31 December and the subsequent date on which field capacity ends
	Endwet	The upper quartile of the above distribution (measure of the end of field capacity in wet years)
	Enddry	The lower quartile of the above distribution (measure of the end of field capacity in dry years)
Workability	*Workabil*	A categorical scale indicating the suitability of the land for heavy machinery work in spring and autumn
Spring machinery working days	*SprMWD*	The average number of days between 1 January and 30 April where land can be worked by machinery without soil damage
Autumn machinery working days	*AutMWD*	The average number of days between 1 September and 31 December when land can be worked by machinery without soil damage
Soil type	*Soil*X	SSLRC soil type classification code: *Soil1* = lowland lithomorphic; *Soil2* = brown earths; *Soil3* = podzols; *Soil4* = surface water gley; *Soil5* = stagnogley (perched watertable); *Soil6* = ground water gley; *Soil7* = peats; *Soil8* = upland lithomorphic; *Soil23* = areas with *Soil2* or *Soil3*

Blakeway-Smith *et al.* (1994) define wind hazard on the basis of four factors: wind zone, elevation, topex and soil type.[13] The resultant continuous variable (*Wind1km^2*) is inversely linked with tree productivity and growth rates.

Elevation and associated variables

The work of Worrell and Malcolm (1990a) shows that elevation and its associated characteristics are key predictors of yield class. However, such a variable is not included in the LandIS database and the SCDB only gives heights for existing plantation sites. Clearly for extrapolation purposes this is inadequate and so an alternative source of data was required. At the time the research was undertaken access to the Ordnance Survey digital elevation models (DEMs) was impractically expensive for UK university researchers (although a more recent access agreement has altered this situation). Therefore a DEM was created from three other sources: the Bartholomew 1:250,000 digital contour database for the UK, summit points from Bartholomew's paper maps and the spot heights of plantations from the SCDB. The accuracy of the derived DEM was tested by omitting various data points from the calculation, using the DEM to estimate heights from those points and comparing actual with predicted values. These tests (detailed in Bateman, 1996) showed that the DEM performed well and so was re-estimated using all available data and incorporated into our yield class estimation model. The elevation data were also used to generate two further GIS surface variables: slope angle (*Dsl2*) and aspect angle (*Wsaspgr2*). Data on all these variables were produced at a 500 m × 500 m cell resolution.

Creating GIS surfaces for explanatory variables

Prior to the regression analysis two fundamental issues had to be addressed regarding the definition of a common extent and resolution for the environmental variables as these parameters differed across the various data sources used. Data were supplied at a wide array of resolutions ranging from the (nominal) 100 m accuracy of the SCDB to the 5 km tiles of the LandIS variables. While the technical operation of interpolating from a coarse to a finer resolution is relatively straightforward within a GIS (Berry, 1993), it needs to be recognised that the precision achieved may be rather higher than the underlying accuracy of the data (Goodchild, 1993), so deciding upon a common unit size was a matter for some deliberation. Standardisation upon the smallest unit (100 m) did not seem a sensible choice. For instance, the 100 m reference used in the SCDB is, the FC admit, spuriously

---

[13] Blakeway-Smith *et al.* (1994) also discuss a funnelling variable which tends to have higher values in valley bottoms. Zobeck *et al.* (2000) show how GIS techniques can also be adapted to the prediction of wind erosion of soils, which may in turn impinge upon yields.

precise. On the other hand, aggregation up to the 5 km scale of the coarsest data was thought likely to result in a loss of much relevant detail (e.g. for topographic features). As a compromise, a 1 km grid was settled upon and all the data were converted to this resolution.

The spatial extent of Wales was defined by converting a vector outline of the Welsh coast and border with England (from the Bartholomew 1:250,000 scale database) to a raster grid representation consisting of 1 km^2 cells. This resulted in a layer within the GIS containing 20,563 land cells and values of the variables in the LandIS and non-SCDB datasets described above were then estimated for each grid cell.[14] For characteristics such as topex or elevation this was done by aggregation and averaging, whereas with the LandIS variables each 1 km grid square was given the value of the 5 km cell it fell within. With all data now at a common resolution and extent we now had the necessary complete surfaces of potential predictor variables for use in our regression model and from which extrapolation across all areas, whether currently planted or not, would be possible.

A final task concerned the extraction of values for all environmental variables for each yield class observation in the SCDB. This was achieved by using point-in-polygon operations within the GIS to identify the 1 km grid cell corresponding to each sub-compartment grid reference.

Yield models for Sitka spruce and beech

Sitka spruce

Our regression analyses followed the approach set out by Lewis-Beck (1980) and Achen (1982). An initial objective concerned the identification of an appropriate functional form for our models. Tests indicated that a linear model performed marginally better than other standard forms and, given that such a form is both easily interpretable and typical of other studies, this seemed a sensible choice.[15]

A variety of stepwise regression analyses were undertaken yielding models composed of raw variables, PCA factors and a combination of these. Resultant models are reported in full in Bateman (1996) and Bateman and Lovett (1997, 1998). For reasons of brevity, here we only report the best-fitting regression models for Sitka spruce and beech. These models used raw variables rather than PCA factors as predictors of YC. Furthermore, a number of observations are omitted from these models, mainly those for which the measurement of YC was taken relatively soon

---

[14] This exercise revealed some relatively minor missing observations in the LandIS database. Measurements for these cells were proxied using interpolation and related techniques. For details see Bateman and Lovett (1997).

[15] Semi-log (dependent and independent), double-log and quadratic forms were also tested and cross-product terms investigated.

Model 6.1. *Best-fitting regression model predicting Sitka spruce YC*

Predictor	Coeff.	S.d.	*t*-ratio	*p*
Constant	16.7097	0.3487	47.92	<0.001
Rainfall	−0.00167	0.00011	−15.65	<0.001
Wselvgr2	−0.00878	0.00039	−22.31	<0.001
Topex1km	0.02426	0.00759	3.20	0.001
Soil23	0.80489	0.08046	10.00	<0.001
Soil1	−4.8827	0.9660	−5.05	<0.001
Area	0.00395	0.00038	10.43	<0.001
Plantyr	0.04989	0.00484	10.31	<0.001
1stRot	−1.9280	0.1093	−17.64	<0.001
MixCrop	−0.30832	0.07670	−4.02	<0.001
Park	0.94769	0.09385	10.10	<0.001
Ancient	0.9266	0.3089	3.00	0.003
Uncleared	2.6411	0.2276	11.61	<0.001
Unprod	−0.08543	0.00814	−10.49	<0.001
Reserve	−0.43395	0.09452	−4.59	<0.001
Semi-nat	−5.1415	0.7644	−6.73	<0.001

$n = 4{,}307$ $R^2 = 43.0\%$ $R^2(\text{adj.}) = 42.8\%$

after planting (full details in Bateman and Lovett, 1998).[16] Assessment of YC for young trees is inherently more difficult than for more mature stands and tests indicated that omitting those stands measured at a particularly young age improved model fit, suggesting that such a procedure reduced random measurement error and yielded more reliable results (results for models without any observations omitted are given in Bateman and Lovett, 1998, and are similar in coefficients to those reported here). This procedure left a sample of 4,307 Sitka spruce sub-compartments, for which our best-fitting model is reported as Model 6.1.

The first point to note about Model 6.1 is that the use of the SCDB permitted a very substantial increase in sample size, which, at over 4,300, compared very favourably to the few hundred observations typically used in many YC studies. This is in part responsible for the comparatively high degree of explanation provided by the model, which exceeds all conventional studies and is comparable with the GIS-based study of Elston *et al.* (1997) cited previously.

Inspection of the model revealed a number of highly significant predictors of YC. With respect to the environmental characteristics of sites we can see that YC fell with increasing rainfall (*Rainfall*)[17] and elevation (*Wselvgr2*) and increased as

[16] The idea of omitting plantations which were measured relatively soon after planting was suggested by Chris Quine and Adrian Whiteman of the Forestry Commission and Douglas Macmillan of the Macauley Land Use Research Institute, to whom we are grateful.

[17] This result underscores the fact that Wales is a high rainfall area. Waterlogging rather than drought is the main water-related problem in the area.

topographical shelter improved (*Topex1km*). Because of its categorical nature, soil type is considered as a series of dummy variables, two of which proved statistically significant. YC was significantly elevated by planting on brown earth or podzol soils (*Soil23*, which is a simple combination of *Soil2* and *Soil3*) and significantly depressed by planting on lowland lithomorphs (*Soil1*). Both results conformed to prior expectations.

The model also highlighted the importance of silvicultural factors. The positive relationship with the size of the plantation (*Area*) is interesting and, to our knowledge, has not previously been formally identified. This would seem to indicate that trees growing as part of a large plantation are more likely to thrive than those in small areas. This might be because large stands provide advantages in terms of the ease of adopting species-specific management regimes, or because such stands tend to condition their environment to their own advantage (for example, by reducing competition from both flora and fauna). Conversely, this latter factor may be one of the pressures militating against smaller stands. A strong and positive influence of the time variable (*Plantyr*) is also identified. This is usually explained as reflecting improvements in silvicultural methods such as the introduction of ploughing, fertiliser applications or enhancement of the genetic stock.

Two further silvicultural factors were identified. Trees planted on ground which has not been previously used for afforestation (*1stRot*) perform worse than those planted in successive rotations. This may be because second rotation trees have, on average, been planted more recently than those in the first rotation (although a relatively low correlation with *Plantyr* indicated that this may not be all of the story) or because second rotation trees inherit a nutrient-enriched and/or pH-modified soil base from their forebears. Trees also seem to perform less well when grown in a mixed species plantation (*MixCrop*) than in monoculture, a finding which suggests that there may be a timber productivity benefit associated with the amenity cost of the latter.

Next, a number of site factors arising from the interaction of environmental characteristics and management practice appear important. YC was significantly higher in parkland areas (*Park*), a result which may reflect more careful silvicultural management. The higher YC associated with planting in areas which were previously ancient woodland (*Ancient*) seems to be the corollary of the impact of *1stRot*. A further and rather interesting boost to growth is implied by the variable *Uncleared* which identifies trees growing in areas that have been previously affected by windblow but have not yet been cleared. It seems that the surviving trees actually profit from windblow in that their immediate neighbours (and competitors) are removed, thus boosting their access to sunlight and nutrients. However, while growth rate may benefit from such events, the ensuing lack of cover raises the probability that the survivors will subsequently fall victim to windblow themselves.

Table 6.3. *Comparing actual with predicted YC for Sitka spruce*
(cell contents are counts)

Actual YC	Predicted YC									All
	4	6	8	10	12	14	16	18	20	
4	0	0	1	0	0	0	0	0	0	1
6	0	0	7	63	0	0	0	0	0	70
8	1	3	12	161	220	0	0	0	0	397
10	0	0	9	169	395	141	0	0	0	714
12	0	0	4	176	516	285	63	0	0	1,044
14	0	0	0	90	415	276	124	33	1	939
16	0	0	0	0	201	313	179	33	1	727
18	0	0	0	0	0	152	144	45	3	344
20	0	0	0	0	0	0	41	26	3	70
22	0	0	0	0	0	0	0	1	0	1
All	1	3	33	659	1,747	1,167	551	138	8	4,307

Predicted YC compared to actual YC	Percentage of total sample
Prediction is two classes too high	12.8
Prediction is one class too high	23.4
Predicted YC equals actual YC	27.9
Prediction is one class too low	25.2
Prediction is two classes too low	11.4

Finally, three negative environmental/management factors were identified. Plantations with higher amounts of unproductive land (*Unprod*) not surprisingly perform worse than otherwise similar sites. Sub-compartments which fall within the boundaries of conservation areas (*Reserve*) also exhibit relatively lower YC, as do areas which are allowed to remain as semi-natural habitat (*Semi-nat*). These results may reflect the application of less intensive silvicultural techniques in such areas.

In order to examine its predictive capabilities, Model 6.1 was assessed by rounding the predictions to the nearest point on the YC scale and then comparing them with actual YC for the 4,307 observations used in the model. Results of this analysis are presented in Table 6.3 which shows that 76.5 per cent of YC predictions are within one division of actual YC.

Beech

Compared to the situation for Sitka spruce, the SCDB contains only a small number of beech compartments within our study area. These observations were analysed in a similar manner to before (for full details see Bateman and Lovett, 1997, 2000a), and this analysis identified a much higher proportion of stands being assessed

Model 6.2. *Optimal model for beech*

Predictor	Coeff.	S.d.	t-ratio	p
Constant	−4.428	1.923	−2.30	0.022
Wselvgr2	−0.00386	0.00091	−4.22	<0.001
Plantyr	0.07995	0.01279	6.25	<0.001
AONB/NSA	0.4751	0.2710	1.75	0.081
OthESA	−1.4812	0.4969	−2.98	0.003
$n = 205$		$R^2 = 35.7\%$	R^2(adj.) $= 34.4\%$	

at relatively young ages. Details of models using all observations are given in Bateman (1996) and Bateman and Lovett (1997), with related analysis being given in Bateman and Lovett (2000a). However, here we report results for only the subset of 205 sites unaffected by the early measurement problem. The best-fitting model for these sites is reported as Model 6.2.

Examining Model 6.2 we can see that, as for our Sitka spruce results, the yield class of beech declines with increasing elevation (*Wselvgr2*) and rises as we consider more recently planted sub-compartments (*Plantyr*). However, the smaller sample size of just over 200 observations fails to reveal many of the previously noted relationships, with just two management regime variables proving significant (and one of these only at $\alpha = 10$ per cent). Nevertheless, the overall degree of explanation is reasonably satisfactory as is the predictive power of the model, as indicated in the actual versus predicted test summarised in Table 6.4.

As a side analysis, regression models for both species under investigation were re-estimated after inclusion of variables representing the aspect of each sub-compartment. In both cases, aspect variables proved to have only a weak impact on yield class;[18] however, the nature of this effect is interesting and is illustrated in Figure 6.1 which compares the results with those of Worrell and Malcom (1990b) in their study of Sitka spruce in the uplands of northern Britain.

Inspection of Figure 6.1 tells a clear and coherent story. In the upland areas of northern Britain the intensity of the prevailing westerly wind causes aspect to be a major factor determining tree growth such that trees in relatively sheltered, east-facing ($\theta = 90°$) sites perform significantly better than those facing west ($\theta = 270°$). The radiative energy advantage of south-facing slopes is completely negated by the impact of the prevailing wind. In our Welsh study of Sitka spruce we consider both upland and lowland sites. Here both the magnitude and statistical significance of the impact of aspect is reduced. Furthermore, the reduction in the power of the prevailing wind (occurring because we are considering sites at lower altitude as well as the less arduous conditions of Wales relative to northern Britain) means that

---

[18] At best only significant at $\alpha = 10$ per cent. Full details are reported in Bateman and Lovett (1997, 1998).

Table 6.4. *Comparing actual with predicted YC for beech*
(cell contents are counts)

Actual YC	Predicted YC			
	4	6	8	All
2	0	1	0	1
4	9	29	2	40
6	7	66	20	93
8	0	29	37	66
10	0	0	5	5
All	16	125	64	205

Predicted YC compared to actual YC	Percentage of total sample
Prediction is two classes too high	1.5
Prediction is one class too high	23.9
Predicted YC equals actual YC	54.6
Prediction is one class too low	20.0
Prediction is two classes too low	0.0

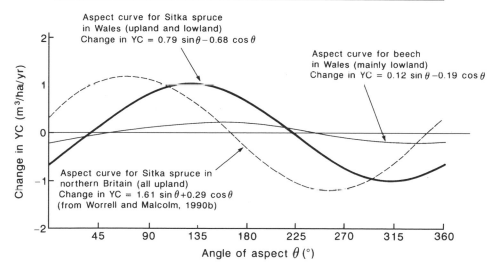

Figure 6.1. Aspect effects for Sitka spruce and beech in differing locations.

the solar energy advantage of southerly sites can now be detected, as our aspect effect is now maximised at south-east (rather than east) facing sites. This trend is continued when we consider our beech sub-compartments. Here, most sites are at lower elevations such that the absolute magnitude (and statistical significance) of the aspect effect is markedly reduced. Furthermore, the reduction in the impact of the prevailing westerly wind means that the solar energy advantage of being south-facing is further boosted such that we find that the aspect curve for beech sites now peaks for sites facing south-south-east.

Mapping yield class

We have now estimated yield class (YC) models for both of the tree species considered. In this section these models are used to generate GIS-based maps of YC which are presented and analysed below.

Producing predicted yield class maps within a GIS

To generate a YC map (or, more specifically, a raster image) the GIS requires data on predictor variables for all the grid cells in the area for which we wish to estimate yield, in this case the 20,563 1 km squares representing the entire land area of Wales. If we take our model (6.1) of Sitka spruce yield as an example, we can see that this is predicted by a constant and a number of explanatory variables. The constant is in essence a data layer in its own right which has identical values (here 16.709) for all land grid cells. The first explanatory variable in this model is the predictor *Rainfall* for which we have estimates from the LandIS database. We can therefore begin to build up our predicted YC map by employing the GIS software to calculate a new raster map which contains the values from multiplying the values in the *Rainfall* grid by the relevant coefficient (−0.00167).

The above procedure was repeated for all predictor variables. However, some variables were related to management (e.g. *Area*), policy (e.g. *Reserve*) or when the site was planted (e.g. *Plantyr*). These are not specifically spatial variables so they were treated by holding them at certain fixed values (i.e. as for the constant) and varying some of them in a sensitivity analysis. The variables *MixCrop*, *Ancient*, *Unprod*, *Reserve*, *Park*, *Uncleared* and *Semi-nat* are all dummies for infrequently occurring, unusual sites and were consequently held at zero (their modal value) for all analyses. Similarly the variable *Area* was held at its median value of 33 ha. Given the very low value of the coefficient on this variable and its relatively small range (see the descriptive statistics given in Bateman, 1996), sensitivity analysis did not seem justified here. However, this was not the case for the variables *Plantyr* and *1stRot* and full sensitivity analyses were conducted for these.

Once the data coverage for each predictor variable has been multiplied by its estimated coefficient all the resulting maps can be overlaid and their values summed to obtain the final prediction of YC in each area. The same methodology was then employed to generate a YC map from our beech model.

Timber yield maps for Sitka spruce

In producing YC maps based on our Sitka spruce model we considered the impact of changing the *Plantyr* variable from 0 (being the base year in which the Forestry Commission started to plant Sitka spruce) to 75 (being the present day, i.e. Sitka spruce planting commenced about 75 years ago) thereby arguably reflecting technological progress over that period. For both of these analyses we initially held *1stRot* = 1, i.e. we examined first-rotation trees at both of these time periods. However, many present-day Sitka spruce plantations are now in their second rotation. Therefore, we also tested the effect of letting *1stRot* = 0 (i.e. second rotation) when *Plantyr* = 75.

Raster maps were produced using the procedure outlined in the previous section. Plate 1a illustrates the predicted YC image created from our Sitka spruce model with *Plantyr* = 75 (present day) and *1stRot* = 0 (replanting on a previously planted site).

Inspection of Plate 1a clearly shows the very strong influence which environmental characteristics have upon our predictions of YC. The influences of lower altitude, better soil and lower rainfall combine to produce high YC. The pattern of lower YC produced by higher elevations is particularly noticeable, with the mountain ranges of Snowdonia, the mid Cambrians and the Brecon Beacons clearly evident. Less extreme upland areas such as the Preseli Mountains produce YC values which lie between these extremes. Also rather noticeable are the adverse effects of the rain-shadow lying to the east of the Cambrians which results in large areas of relatively depressed YC values stretching in some cases up to the English border. The negative impact of sandy and estuarine soils upon growth can also be seen in the small but significantly depressed areas of low yield at places such as the tip of the Gower Peninsula and nearby Pembrey, the southernmost part of Anglesey and the Llandudno peninsula.[19]

Plate 1a assumes *1stRot* = 0 (i.e. predictions for plantations which are not in their first rotation) and *Plantyr* = 75 (i.e. predictions for trees planted in the mid 1990s). To provide a contrast with these assumptions, maps of predicted YC for Sitka spruce with *Plantyr* = 0 (i.e. trees planted at the start of Forestry Commission operations in 1920) and *1stRot* = 1 (i.e. sites with trees in their first rotation) were also produced. Following the predictions of Model 6.1 both of these latter scenarios give lower YC predictions than those illustrated in Plate 1a, although the pattern of YC variation remains similar. These differences are quantified in Table 6.5 which presents the frequency distributions of predictions from these three scenarios. As can be seen, differences are substantial, with these two alternatives producing appreciably lower YC predictions in each case.

While our YC maps seem highly plausible (and we would defend them as such for the majority of Wales), Table 6.5 and Plate 1a do indicate a weakness in our models in their ability to estimate YC for extreme environmental conditions such as, for example, mountain tops. Our best-fitting model for Sitka spruce fails to

---

[19] Interestingly both Pembrey and Newborough (Anglesey) are the sites of large forests, underlining the point that forests are often confined to the most marginal land.

Table 6.5. *Predicted Sitka spruce YC under three scenarios*

YC	*Plantyr* = 75; *1stRot* = 0		*Plantyr* = 75; *1stRot* = 1		*Plantyr* = 0; *1stRot* = 1	
	Freq.	%	Freq.	%	Freq.	%
2	—	—	—	—	10	0.049
4	—	—	1	0.005	46	0.224
6	1	0.005	15	0.073	367	1.785
8	16	0.079	54	0.263	2,255	10.966
10	56	0.272	504	2.451	4,691	22.813
12	554	2.694	2,524	12.274	8,747	42.538
14	2,609	12.688	5,106	24.831	4,447	21.626
16	5,209	25.332	9,287	45.164	—	—
18	9,416	45.791	3,072	14.939	—	—
20	2,702	13.140	—	—	—	—
Mean	17.05		15.12		11.38	

Notes: The column headings define the values of the variables *Plantyr* and *1stRot* used in each map, where: *Plantyr* = year in which stand was planted (0 = 1920; 75 = 1995); *1stRot* = 1 if stand is the first planted in that sub-compartment, = 0 otherwise (i.e. sub-compartment is in second or subsequent rotation).

The frequency columns refer to the number of 1 km grid squares. Each map consists of 20,563 such squares.

predict any sites of less than YC6. However, clearly if trees were planted at or near mountain peaks they might well not survive or would at best produce only very low YC. Similarly our model does not predict any cells to have YC in excess of 20, yet our dataset indicated a few cases of YC being as high as 24. We therefore appear to be overestimating YC at the lower extreme and under estimating at the upper end of the range.

Two factors seem pertinent in explaining this. First, we are predicting average YC over 1 km grid squares. This will tend to remove extremes and therefore gives some support to our findings. Second, as there is relatively little planting at the extremes of altitude, low YC observations are under-represented in the FC's sub-compartment database resulting in a lesser ability of statistical models based on such data to estimate accurately for such locations.[20] However, while these are problems, the actual versus predicted YC comparison reported in Table 6.3 suggests that the degree of over- and underestimation at the tails is not too serious.

[20] A third possibility, discussed in Bateman (1996), is a resolution issue. Our DEM estimates elevations based upon surrounding points and therefore may not fully capture the upper extremes of altitude. Any underestimation of elevation at the tops of mountains may result in overestimation of YC at those points.

Table 6.6. *Predicted beech YC under two scenarios*

	Plantyr = 162; *1stRot* = 1		*Plantyr* = 144; *1stRot* = 1	
YC	Freq.	%	Freq.	%
3	—	—	1	0.005
4	—	—	84	0.409
5	17	0.083	1,970	9.580
6	421	2.047	10,437	50.756
7	7,003	34.056	8,071	39.250
8	12,925	62.856	—	—
9	197	0.958	—	—
Mean	7.69		6.25	

Note: The frequency columns refer to the number of 1 km grid squares. Each map consists of 20,563 such squares.

Timber yield maps for beech

As with Sitka spruce, we attempted to produce maps of predicted beech YC considering the impact of changing the *Plantyr* and *1stRot* variables. In the case of the *Plantyr* variable, unlike our Sitka spruce analysis there was no distinct year in which beech planting commenced. Thus, although we have a date at which *Plantyr* = 0, this corresponds simply to the oldest record in the dataset (some 162 years ago) rather than to some actual initial planting date. Accordingly it was decided to adopt a somewhat different strategy here and our sensitivity analysis examined two values: *Plantyr* = 144 (which equalled both the mean and median planting date of the early 1970s); and *Plantyr* = 162 (mid 1990s). The dataset showed that most beech sub-compartments were in their first rotation and so this sensitivity analysis was not performed, *1stRot* being held at a value of 1 for all beech images.

We therefore produced two YC maps for beech and Plate 1b illustrates the version holding *Plantyr* = 162 (and *1stRot* = 1). Both maps show a similar pattern of YC distribution to that of Sitka spruce; however, the range of these distributions is far narrower than for the latter as is shown in Table 6.6. As before, *ceteris paribus*, increasing *Plantyr* leads to a rise in predicted YC.

Producing timber yield value maps

In Chapter 5 we developed models for estimating timber values which were sensitive to a variety of factors including the following:

(i) species: Sitka spruce or beech
(ii) a full range of yield class levels
(iii) a full range of subsidy and grant schemes

  (iv) single, optimal-length rotation or perpetual replanting
   (v) a range of discount rates
  (vi) private or social values
 (vii) NPV and annuity sums.[21]

Note that, at this point in our analysis, we have not included the woodland recreation values discussed previously or the carbon storage values estimated in the following chapter. Therefore, the 'social' values referred to above and in the remainder of this chapter are only those directly associated with the production of timber. Essentially these take the private values received by farmers or other forest operators and remove grant and subsidy transfer payments and add in the timber-related shadow values (such as the value of ensuring supply continuity) discussed in Chapter 5.

These models produce timber value/YC curves for each combination or 'scenario' of the above factors such as those illustrated for a variety of subsidy schemes in Figures 5.5 and 5.6. As those diagrams showed, for any given subsidy scheme, timber value is approximately linearly related to YC. This result provides a ready method for converting our maps of timber YC to maps of timber value.

For each species and all combinations of factors (iii) to (vi) above, a linear equation linking predicted timber value to YC was estimated (details for all combinations are given in Bateman, 1996). In all cases a simple straight-line model provided an excellent fit.[22] As an example, the function predicting farmers' private annuity value, calculated at a 3 per cent discount rate, for perpetually replanted Sitka spruce receiving grants at non-disadvantaged area rates is:[23]

$$\mathrm{ANN}_3^{SS} = \begin{matrix} -136.32 \\ (-17.88) \end{matrix} + \begin{matrix} 21.32 \ \mathrm{YC} \\ (44.90) \end{matrix} \tag{6.1}$$

where:

ANN_3^{SS} = farmers' private annuity value per hectare of perpetually replanted Sitka spruce timber production, calculated using a 3 per cent discount rate

  YC = yield class

$R^2(\mathrm{adj.})$ = 99.6%. Figures in brackets are t-statistics.

With the resultant suite of regression equations having been estimated, the GIS was used to convert our YC maps to their timber value equivalents. For each scenario this was achieved by selecting the appropriate YC map and conversion regression equation. The GIS was then used first to multiply predicted YC across the timber

---

[21] The relation of NPV and annuity sums was discussed in Chapter 5. Annuity values are likely to be of more interest to the farmer than NPVs.

[22] Lowest $R^2(\mathrm{adj.})$ = 97.2 per cent.

[23] So, for this example, predicted ANN_3^{SS} for YC20 Sitka spruce = £290/ha (see the lower curve in Figure 5.4).

yield map by its coefficient in the conversion equation, and second to subtract the constant given in the same equation. The resultant map contains predicted timber values for the desired scenario.

Using this procedure NPV and annuity value maps were created for a variety of scenarios. Figure 6.2 illustrates the social (i.e. removing grants and subsidies) NPV map for perpetually replanted Sitka spruce timber production calculated using a 3 per cent discount rate (remembering that non-timber values such as recreation and carbon sequestration have yet to be added to this value). The distribution of values reflects that of the YC image (Plate 1a) upon which it is based and so comments remain as before.

The number of permutations of the factors considered in this analysis precludes full reporting here (details are given in Bateman, 1996). However, Tables 6.7 and 6.8 report social NPV and annuity equivalents for Sitka spruce timber values across three discount rates, while Tables 6.9 and 6.10 repeat this analysis for beech. For any given discount rate, the distribution of values is given in terms of (i) the number of 1 km grid squares in our study area falling in each value category and (ii) that frequency count expressed as a percentage of the 20,563 1 km squares which constitute Wales.

Considering Tables 6.7 to 6.10 we can see that, for both species, the choice of discount rate has a substantial impact upon values, with higher rates yielding lower NPV and annuity sums. This effect is somewhat more pronounced in the case of Sitka spruce, a result which reflects its short rotation length relative to beech. With a long rotation length (such as that for beech) discount factors are already relatively low at felling irrespective of the chosen discount rate. In such cases, variation in that rate has less impact upon NPV and annuity values than for short rotation species where, with low discount rates, discount factors are still reasonably high at felling. This effect also explains why discounted Sitka spruce values are higher than those for beech despite the latter attracting higher nominal values at felling. In the absence of other monetised benefits, these results clearly illustrate why market-led assessments of forestry projects argue in favour of planting conifers rather than broadleaves.

Conclusions

We have estimated yield class models for Sitka spruce and beech based in part upon variables drawn from GIS databases covering the whole of Wales. This has allowed us to use those models to produce predicted yield maps for both species for the entire Principality. We have then used these maps in conjunction with the timber value model derived in Chapter 5 to produce NPV and annuity equivalent maps. In general we are reasonably happy with this analysis. However, we should mention at

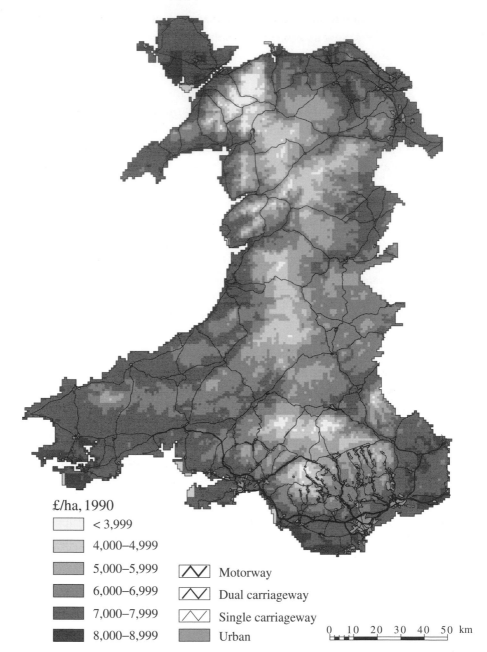

Figure 6.2. Predicted timber social NPV sums for perpetually replanted Sitka spruce: 3% discount rate.

Table 6.7. *NPV sums for perpetually replanted Sitka spruce timber across various discount rates*

| | Discount rate, r (%) | | | | | |
| | 1 | | 3 | | 6 | |
NPV (£/ha, 1990)	Freq.	%	Freq.	%	Freq.	%
−500– −1	—	—	—	—	1	0.005
0–499	—	—	—	—	31	0.151
500–999	—	—	1	0.005	187	0.909
1,000–1,499	—	—	2	0.010	2,232	10.854
1,500–1,999	—	—	8	0.039	5,786	28.138
2,000–2,499	—	—	20	0.097	11,208	54.506
2,500–2,999	—	—	24	0.117	1,118	5.437
3,000–3,499	1	0.005	48	0.233	—	—
3,500–3,999	—	—	163	0.793	—	—
4,000–4,499	4	0.019	514	2.500	—	—
4,500–4,999	5	0.024	1,019	4.956	—	—
5,000–5,499	10	0.048	1,307	6.356	—	—
5,500–5,999	11	0.053	1,757	8.544	—	—
6,000–6,499	8	0.039	2,556	12.430	—	—
6,500–6,999	17	0.083	3,380	16.437	—	—
7,000–7,499	23	0.112	4,055	19.720	—	—
7,500–7,999	62	0.302	4,534	22.049	—	—
8,000–8,499	80	0.389	1,173	5.704	—	—
8,500–8,999	207	1.007	2	0.010	—	—
9,000–9,499	352	1.712	—	—	—	—
9,500–9,999	525	2.553	—	—	—	—
10,000–10,499	649	3.156	—	—	—	—
10,500–10,999	739	3.594	—	—	—	—
11,000–11,499	826	4.017	—	—	—	—
11,500–11,999	1,112	5.408	—	—	—	—
12,000–12,499	1,194	5.807	—	—	—	—
12,500–12,999	1,595	7.757	—	—	—	—
13,000–13,499	1,820	8.851	—	—	—	—
13,500–13,999	2,162	10.514	—	—	—	—
14,000–14,499	2,225	10.820	—	—	—	—
14,500–14,999	2,605	12.668	—	—	—	—
15,000–15,499	2,600	12.644	—	—	—	—
15,500–15,999	1,561	7.591	—	—	—	—
16,000–16,499	168	0.817	—	—	—	—
16,500–16,999	2	0.010	—	—	—	—
mean (£)	13,362		6,707		2,023	
s.d.	1,938		1,189		438	

Table 6.8. *Annuity values for perpetually replanted Sitka spruce timber across various discount rates*

| Annuity(£/ha, 1990) | Discount rate, r (%) | | | | | |
| | 1 | | 3 | | 6 | |
	Freq.	%	Freq.	%	Freq.	%
−25−−1	—	—	—	—	1	0.005
0–24	—	—	—	—	21	0.102
25–49	—	—	3	0.015	53	0.258
50–74	1	0.005	16	0.079	479	2.329
75–99	2	0.010	22	0.107	2,183	10.616
100–124	15	0.073	60	0.292	4,068	19.783
125–149	18	0.088	263	1.279	7,318	35.588
150–174	34	0.165	993	4.829	6,434	31.289
175–199	115	0.559	1,682	8.180	6	0.029
200–224	411	2.000	2,413	11.735	—	—
225–249	1,044	5.077	3,962	19.268	—	—
250–274	1,460	7.100	5,175	25.167	—	—
275–299	1,994	9.697	5,626	27.360	—	—
300–324	3,010	14.638	348	1.692	—	—
325–349	4,172	20.289	—	—	—	—
350–374	4,837	23.523	—	—	—	—
375–399	3,380	16.437	—	—	—	—
400–424	70	0.340	—	—	—	—
mean (£)	329		246		133	
s.d.	54		48		30	

Table 6.9. *NPV sums for perpetually replanted beech timber across various discount rates*

| NPV(£/ha, 1990) | Discount rate, r (%) | | | | | |
| | 1 | | 3 | | 6 | |
	Freq.	%	Freq.	%	Freq.	%
500–999	—	—	—	—	20,563	100.000
1,000–1,499	—	—	10	0.049	—	—
1,500–1,999	—	—	1,281	6.229	—	—
2,000–2,499	10	0.049	14,524	70.626	—	—
2,500–2,999	97	0.472	4,748	23.088	—	—
3,000–3,999	5,410	26.307	—	—	—	—
4,000–4,999	15,046	73.165	—	—	—	—
mean (£)	4,251		2,327		942	
s.d.	495		331		317	

Table 6.10. *Annuity values for perpetually replanted beech timber across various discount rates*

| Annuity(£/ha, 1990) | Discount rate, r (%) | | | | | |
| | 1 | | 3 | | 6 | |
	Freq.	%	Freq.	%	Freq.	%
40–49	20	0.097	20	0.097	37	0.180
50–59	179	0.870	327	1.590	16,203	78.797
60–69	1,798	8.744	4,756	23.129	4,323	21.023
70–79	6,253	30.409	10,841	52.721	—	—
80–89	8,960	43.573	4,619	22.463	—	—
90–99	3,353	16.306	—	—	—	—
100–149	—	—	—	—	—	—
150–199	—	—	—	—	—	—
200–249	—	—	—	—	—	—
250–310	—	—	—	—	—	—
mean (£)	81		74		58	
s.d.	13		12		12	

least one point of caution regarding the methodology developed in this study. The YC regressions fit the data quite well by the standards of models reported in the literature. Furthermore, the equations linking YC to NPV and annuity equivalents also fit well. If this were not the case the possibility exists that errors in the first of these models might be further propagated by those in the second. This is a point to be wary of in any wider application of such a methodology.

Accepting that such a possible problem does not seem to be present here, the timber value maps produced permit a common unit comparison with the recreation value maps produced previously. Given that woodland recreation frequently takes place in productive woodlands it seems reasonable to assume that these values may be additive.

We now turn our attention to the last forest value we shall consider in our analysis: carbon sequestration.

7

Modelling and valuing carbon sequestration in trees, timber products and forest soils

Introduction

The global process of industrialisation which has grown so rapidly over the past two centuries has, in more recent years, led to detectable increases in the concentration of insulating greenhouse gases (GHGs). These have in turn resulted in increases in global temperatures, and these are expected to continue rising with GHG emissions for the foreseeable future (Houghton *et al.*, 1992; Wigley and Raper, 1992; IPCC, 1996a, 2001a, 2001b; Zecca and Brusa, 1997). The most recent report of the Intergovernmental Panel on Climate Change (IPCC) summarises the findings of contemporary research as showing:

that the globally averaged surface temperatures have increased by 0.6 ± 0.2 °C over the 20th Century; and that, for the range of scenarios developed in the IPCC *Special Report on Emission Scenarios* (SRES), the globally averaged surface air temperature is projected by models to warm 1.4 to 5.8 °C by 2100 relative to 1990, and globally averaged sea level is projected by models to rise 0.09 to 0.88 m by 2100. (IPCC, 2001b: p. 3)

The consequences of such climatic change are uncertain but potentially highly adverse (Warr and Smith, 1993; Parry, 1993, 2000). The IPCC concludes that:

Projected climate changes during the 21st Century have the potential to lead to future large-scale and possibly irreversible changes in Earth systems resulting in impacts at continental and global scales.... Depending on the rate of ice loss, the rate and magnitude of sea-level rise could greatly exceed the capacity of human and natural systems to adapt without substantial impacts. (IPCC, 2001b: p. 6)

Growing concern regarding climate change has raised interest in the potential for using forestry as a way of reducing atmospheric concentrations of carbon dioxide (Sedjo, 1989; Myers, 1990; Nordhaus, 1991a; Galinski and Kuppers, 1994),

---

This chapter extends the analysis presented in Bateman and Lovett (2000b).

the gas which in absolute terms provides the largest contribution to global insulation. Two issues of scale should be emphasised here. First, given the scale of global fossil fuel use, carbon sequestration in forests can only be a stopgap measure, providing temporary relief in advance of necessary reductions in emissions.[1] Second, stocks of carbon and the potential for future sequestration in temperate woodlands are relatively small compared to those of tropical forests, while both are dwarfed by the storage and sequestration potential of the world's oceans (IPCC, 2000; Matthews *et al.*, 2000; UNDP *et al.*, 2000).[2] Accepting these caveats does not diminish the value of carbon sequestration (irrespective of the biome concerned), while issues of practicality and cost highlight the fact that forest ecosystems may be considerably more amenable to initiatives to change policy than are the ocean depths.

Carbon sequestration benefits therefore constitute a separate category of forest value (Dore *et al.*, 2001). Such benefits have been recognised both by economists and policy-makers internationally (IPCC, 2001b). In our study area of Wales the National Assembly's recent *Draft Document on the Future of Agriculture* (National Assembly for Wales, 2001b) explicitly recognises the need to commission research concerning ways in which both forestry and farming can contribute to cutting emissions and promoting carbon sequestration.

This chapter attempts to quantify the impact upon carbon storage of afforesting an area of previously unplanted land.[3] However, assessment of this benefit is not straightforward. An initial and daunting problem concerns the valuation of sequestered carbon. This has been a subject of heated debate within the economics literature. A number of articles have been heavily criticised for failing to grasp the complexity of the climatic processes which underlie global warming. We reviewed the literature in some detail in Bateman (1996) and defend our use of the valuation work of Sam Fankhauser as being both more sophisticated and based upon significantly more realistic climate change models than preceding work. A brief review of the debate is presented at the start of the next section.

Our review of literature also considered the physical processes of carbon sequestration in trees and forest soils, carbon storage within timber products, and eventual liberation back to the atmosphere, for carbon storage within trees is only a transitory process and total storage can only grow while the volume of timber increases. Nevertheless, the potential for expanding forest areas (heightened in the

---

[1] As Nowak (1993) emphasises, planting 10 million trees per annum for the next fifty years will sequester less than 1 per cent of US emissions during that period.

[2] Global carbon stocks in the vegetation and soils of tropical forests are estimated at 212 GtC (gigatonnes of carbon) and 216 GtC respectively. By comparison those for temperate forests are 59 GtC and 100 GtC. These compare to estimates for all biomes of 466 GtC in vegetation and 2,011 GtC in soils, the majority of this storage being in seas and oceans (IPCC, 2000).

[3] We do not appraise the current storage of carbon in the study area. For estimates of the latter, see Cannell and Dewar (1995).

EU by surpluses of agricultural land) means that forests do provide a vital breathing space before policy and technological change can address the root cause of global warming.

The following section presents a brief overview of our research methodology. This is then applied to the modelling of carbon sequestration in both Sitka spruce and beech trees, while the next section considers subsequent liberation of carbon from the products and felling waste of both species. The impacts of afforestation upon soil carbon levels are then considered. Results from these analyses are presented, including the monetary value maps necessary to make results compatible with the findings of previous chapters.

Literature review[4]

This section opens by considering the ongoing debate concerning the valuation of carbon emissions and their storage. It then moves to consider three aspects of carbon sequestration by means of afforestation: the storage of carbon in trees; its post-felling liberation; and the impact of afforestation upon soil carbon flux.

The shadow price of carbon emissions

While a number of studies have examined the costs of fixing carbon via afforestation, relatively few have attempted to quantify its benefits. For our purposes the most interesting of these are those adopting a damage-avoided approach to valuation. If accurate, estimates produced by such methods are shadow prices which may be directly incorporated within the cost-benefit framework which underpins our wider study.

The pioneering work on the shadow price of CO_2 emissions is that of Nordhaus (1991b,c). Using a very simple model and assuming a 3 per cent discount rate he calculates social costs of $7.3/tonne of carbon (tC) emitted. This estimate has provoked a number of critical responses (Ayres and Walter, 1991;[5] Daily *et al.*, 1991; Cline, 1992a; Grubb, 1992; Price, 1997b). Typical of these, Cline (1992a) highlights the simple linear structure of the underlying model, implying

---

[4] For a review of land use and climate change issues and policy, see the essays in Adger *et al.* (1997) and Sedjo *et al.* (1997). Other economic and physical analyses from around the world of the impacts of forests upon carbon storage are given in Maclaren and Wakelin (1991), Kauppi *et al.* (1992), Makundi *et al.* (1992), Kurz *et al.* (1992, 1994), Kolchugina and Vinson (1993), Turner *et al.* (1993, 1995), Backlund *et al.* (1995), Maclaren *et al.* (1995), Bureau of Transport and Communications Economics (1996a,b), Maclaren (1996a,b), Mauldin and Platinga (1998), Motha and Heyhoe (1998) and IPCC (2001a,b).

[5] It is somewhat ironic that Ayres and Walter criticise the Nordhaus (1991b,c) estimates as too low given that in an earlier paper they assess emissions damage costs at $5–10/ton CO_2 ($18–37/tC) (Walter and Ayres, 1990). In their subsequent critique of Nordhaus they apply different assumptions to his model to produce a damage estimate of $30–35/tC (Ayres and Walter, 1991). However, given the problems of the simple linear Nordhaus model, such estimates must be treated with caution.

both a constant level of CO_2 emissions[6] and a constant shadow price through time.

In subsequent work Nordhaus (1992a,b) addresses many of these criticisms. His Dynamic Integrated Climate Economy (DICE) model uses optimal economic growth analysis in combination with a climate model which feeds climate changes back into the economy as damages. The resulting carbon shadow prices are similar to his earlier estimates ($5.3/tC in 1995 rising to $10/tC in 2025). However, Nordhaus' results have again been criticised by Cline (1992b) who suggests that the parameter values used result in an underestimation of true costs.

A similar model, utilising a more detailed economy component, is used by Peck and Teisberg (1992a,b). Their Carbon Emission Trajectory Assessment (CETA) model produces estimates of the shadow price of carbon ranging from $10/tC in 1990 to $22/tC in 2030. Given that the CETA model is structurally similar to DICE, the main reason explaining differences in the shadow price estimates produced appears to be discrepancies in assumptions regarding carbon damages.

Important contributions to the shadow pricing debate are provided by the papers of Fankhauser (1993, 1994a,b, 1995). These introduce a fully stochastic, greenhouse damages model, explicitly recognising the highly non-linear and uncertain aspects of the climate process. Uncertainty is incorporated by modelling all key parameters as random variables.[7] The model consists of modules examining: future emissions; atmospheric concentration; radiative forcing; temperature rise; annual damage; costs of sea-level rise protection; and discounting.

The issue of discounting is, arguably, the central problem in the appraisal of global warming response, and this is a focal point for much research (Howarth, 1996; Azar, 1998; Hasselmann, 1999; Pollock, 1999; Revesz, 1999; Hammitt and Harvey, 2000). Fankhauser (1994b) tackles the discounting problem in a direct, although still debatable, manner. Considering the literature on the subject, he sets the pure rate of time preference (ρ) as a random variable with upper and lower bounds of 0 and 3 per cent respectively and with a best guess (modal) value of 0.5 per cent. Similarly, the income elasticity of utility (ω) is defined as a random variable with upper and lower bounds of 0.5 and 1.5 respectively and a best guess (modal) value of 1. This random variable discounting captures the uncertainty regarding these parameters. Furthermore, if we recall our discussion of discounting in Chapter 5, the low discount rate resulting from such a choice of parameter values seems defensible as a reflection of social preference regarding the assessment of global warming impacts. However, to allow comparability with other studies

---

[6] Annual CO_2 emissions are predicted to rise from 7.4 GtC in 1990 to 9–14 GtC by 2025 (IPCC, 1992). Climate processes are clearly not first-order linear.

[7] Here triangular distributions (using upper/lower bounds and the best-guess estimate) are generally assumed although where upper and lower bounds were unknown a modest range of ±10 per cent around the best guess was used.

Table 7.1. *The social costs of CO_2 emissions ($/tC): comparison across studies*

Study	Measure	1991–2000	2001–2010	2011–2020	2021–2030
Nordhaus (1991a,b)[1]	Best guess (mode)	←———	7.3 (0.3–65.9)		———→
Ayres and Walter (1991)[1]	Best guess (mode)	←———	30–35		———→
Nordhaus (1992a)[1]	Best guess (mode)	5.3	6.8	8.6[2]	10.0
Peck and Teisberg (1992b)[1]	Best guess (mode)	10–12[2]	12–14[2]	14–18[2]	18–22[2] (3.4–57.6)
Fankhauser (1994b)[3]	Expected (mean)	20.3	22.8	25.3	27.8
	5th percentile	6.2	7.4	8.3	9.2
	95th percentile	45.2	52.9	58.4	64.2
	standard dev.	14.3	16.0	17.5	19.0
	skewness	2.5	2.5	2.5	2.4

Notes: Figures in brackets denote confidence intervals.
[1] Discount rate = 3 per cent for all studies except Fankhauser (1994b).
[2] Figures measured from graph as reported in Fankhauser (1994a).
[3] Random variable discounting: $\rho = (0, 0.005, 0.03)$; $\omega = (0.5, 1, 1.5)$.

Fankhauser also conducts a conventional discounting sensitivity analysis using values of $\rho = 0$ and 0.03 with $\omega = 1$ throughout.

The Fankhauser (1994b) model differs therefore from its predecessors in at least three important aspects:

(i) it models climate feedback mechanisms in a more detailed and realistic manner
(ii) it uses expected (means) rather than best guess (modal) values
(iii) it employs a discount rate sensitivity analysis.

Table 7.1 contrasts results from Fankhauser's (1994b) random variable discounting model of CO_2 damage costs with those discussed previously. For the latter, only a best guess (modal) value is reported. In contrast and to emphasise the importance of damage distributions, Fankhauser reports expected (mean) values as well as 5th and 95th percentiles, standard deviation and skewness. Given factors (i) to (iii) above, the discrepancy between Fankhauser's results and those of other studies are to be expected.

The Fankhauser model was adopted as a cornerstone of the report by the Intergovernmental Panel on Climate Change into the socio-economic impacts of the greenhouse effect (IPCC, 1996b).[8] Accordingly, we feel justified in adopting the

---

[8] These figures are slightly above the sum of $20/tonne used by the World Bank in a retrospective appraisal of their previous funding decisions (World Bank, 1996).

above values for use in this study. However, as our analysis extends long beyond the 2021 horizon considered by Fankhauser, we have to make some assumptions regarding carbon sequestration values beyond that point. After reviewing the literature it became apparent that simply extending the trend of Fankhauser's estimates risks error if greenhouse abatement measures are implemented (although the decision, in 2001, of President George W. Bush to withdraw the United States from emission reduction obligations set under the 1997 Kyoto Climate Change Convention means that the future for global abatement policy is very uncertain). Given the lack of any firm evidence it was decided to treat the final (2021) carbon value as an equilibrium level extending throughout the remainder of our analysis. While this is clearly a key assumption we felt that no other course of action was justified given the uncertainty that exists within the literature.[9]

Carbon storage in trees[10]

Much of the woody biomass of a tree is carbon; therefore, growing new trees fixes carbon over the lifetime of those trees. However, the relation between timber yield and carbon storage is not straightforward.

Timber yield models provide information on the merchantable volume (MV) of trees throughout a rotation (Edwards and Christie, 1981). MV only concerns the saleable volume of a tree but may be related to total woody volume (TWV) by allowing for branchwood, roots, etc. (Matthews, 1991; Rasse *et al.*, 2001). The TWV/MV ratio is very high in the early life of a tree but falls rapidly as MV rises with age.[11] TWV is in turn related to the tree's dry weight (DW) via its specific gravity (SG). SG varies substantially across species, being about 0.33 for Sitka spruce and 0.56 for beech (Lavers, 1969; Thompson and Matthews, 1989a). However, the proportion of DW which is carbon is roughly similar for Sitka spruce and beech at about 49 per cent (G. Matthews, 1993).

While timber yield and species affect carbon storage, forestry management also has a major impact. The move from unmanaged woodland to managed plantation results in a significant increase in MV (Bateman and Lovett, 1997). However, profit maximisation results in smaller stems being periodically removed (thinned) so as to promote the growth of a reduced number of larger, high-value trees. This alone causes a substantial reduction in potential carbon storage (Matthews, 1992).

---

[9] It should be noted that the process of discounting very greatly diminishes the impact of this assumption. In effect it is the initial period (for which we have published valuation estimates) which is of paramount importance.

[10] This section draws upon Sedjo *et al.* (1995) and conversations during 1994 and 1995 with Robert Matthews, mensuration officer at the Forestry Commission's Research Station, Alice Holt Lodge, Farnham.

[11] This study uses the TWV/MV relationship given in Matthews (1991). As an example of how this changes with tree age, Matthews reports a ratio value of 3.0 at age 20 for YC12 Sitka spruce, falling to a value of just below 2.0 at age 40 and declining more slowly thereafter to about 1.4 at age 75.

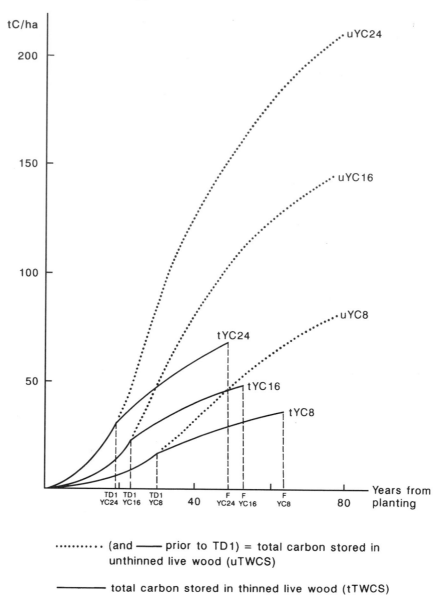

Figure 7.1. Total carbon storage curves for unthinned and thinned Sitka spruce: 5% discount rate.

Furthermore, the practice of discounting leads both to higher-yield stands being felled on a shorter rotation than those in slower growing areas, and to all trees being cut before they attain their maximum carbon carrying capacity.

Figure 7.1 illustrates the impact of these management decisions upon three stands of Sitka spruce growing at yield classes (YC) 8, 16 and 24 (where YC8 denotes a stand producing on average 8 m³/year/ha over an optimal rotation). Here yield class models (Edwards and Christie, 1981) are combined with data on carbon storage in Sitka spruce (Cannell and Cape, 1991; R. Matthews, 1993) to plot out carbon storage curves for both thinned and unthinned (denoted tYC and uYC respectively) stands.[12] Unthinned stands produce a characteristic S-shaped carbon storage curve. Thinned stands follow this curve up to the date of first thinning (TD1), which arrives sooner for faster-growing stands (as does the date of felling; F).[13] After TD1 the tYC curve becomes much more shallow than its uYC counterpart. Furthermore, the relatively early F terminates the former curve considerably before that for unmanaged crops. Therefore, while plantation forests may represent a new carbon sequestration gain over previous land uses (see below), thinned stands sequester less carbon than unthinned crops.[14] Furthermore, as noted by numerous commentators (Thompson *et al.*, 1997; van Kooten and Bulte, 1999; Thornley and Cannell, 2000; Healey *et al.*, 2000), there is clearly a trade-off between managing forests for timber yield and optimising carbon storage.

Carbon liberation from wood products

Once a tree is felled its fixed carbon store begins to be liberated back to the atmosphere as CO_2. This may occur quite quickly if the wood is used as fuel, left to decompose (e.g. small trimmings) or used for short-term purposes. The carbon liberation rates resulting from these various end uses can differ substantially. For example, Thompson and Matthews (1989a) compare conventionally grown YC16 Corsican pine with short rotation coppice (SRC) poplar plantations, noting that the latter fixes significantly more carbon per annum than the former. However, because SRC is generally used as fuel, its long-term average sequestration rate is significantly lower than that of Corsican pine which is typically used for more durable products.[15]

---

[12] Note that a number of studies have considered a possible feedback loop between the greenhouse effect and tree growth whereby higher atmospheric CO_2 concentrations lead to enhanced timber yield (Waggoner, 1983; D'Arrigo *et al.*, 1987; Heath *et al.*, 1995; Murray *et al.*, 1995; Eamus and Jarvis, 1989; Cannell and Cape, 1991; Kellomaki *et al.*, 1997; Bucher-Wallin *et al.*, 2000). However, evidence also exists to indicate that some trees may reduce rates of CO_2 uptake within a CO_2-enriched atmosphere, an effect which may differ between species (Egli, *et al.*, 2001). These factors are still the subject of research and are not incorporated in our model.

[13] Figure 7.1 and underlying calculations use a 5 per cent discount rate to determine TD1 and F. As the discount rate is increased so TD1 and F decrease. For a full sensitivity analysis, see Bateman (1996).

[14] R. Matthews (1993) also considers the carbon emissions associated with felling, etc. However, these are found to be relatively minor, and substantial net carbon storage benefits are found, particularly where wood is subsequently used for biofuel as a substitute for existing high-carbon fuels such as oil or coal.

[15] Marland and Marland (1992) and R. Matthews (1993) highlight an important consequence of such examples: where timber is used as fuel and substitutes for existing high-carbon fossil fuels, a further net benefit will accrue. We have not adopted such an assumption in our analysis because of uncertainties regarding likely substitution rates. In effect we assume that capital commitments to non-timber fuelling systems mean that any conversion rate will be very low.

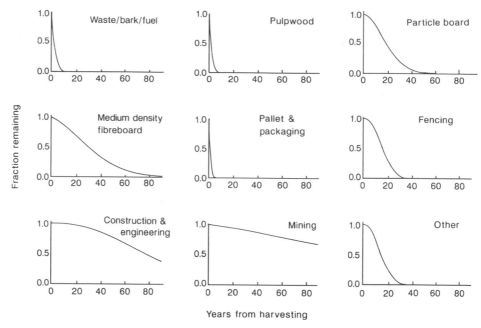

Figure 7.2. Longevity of Sitka spruce timber when put to different uses. (*Source:* Thompson and Matthews, 1989b.)

A rigorous examination of the impact of end use upon carbon fixing is given in Thompson and Matthews (1989a,b). Results are obtained for a variety of species, those for Sitka spruce being graphically summarised in Figure 7.2.

Figure 7.2 makes it clear that end use has a major influence upon plantation average carbon storage levels. Indeed, Matthews (1995) cites this as the major determinant of overall carbon storage, being significantly stronger than factors such as silvicultural management regime.[16] In order to incorporate this effect within a general carbon flux model we also require information regarding the proportion of wood allocated to each end use. Statistics gathered from a variety of sources are summarised in Table 7.2 which provides a breakdown of 1991/92 UK domestic production data divided into softwood and hardwood species.

Carbon flux in soils

Determinants of soil carbon levels

All soils contain a certain natural level of carbon. This generally consists of decaying soil organic matter (SOM) although a small amount (usually less than

---

[16] A further issue, considered by Matthews (1992), is the level of manufacturing emissions associated with differing end uses. These are relatively high for capital-intensive products such as paper and low for sawn wood, etc.

Table 7.2. Softwood and hardwood end uses for UK domestic production 1991/92

Product	Softwood				Hardwood			
	Production ('000 m^3)	% of total	Modal liberation year (from felling)	95% carbon liberation (years from felling)	Production ('000 m^3)	% of total	Modal liberation year (from felling)	95% carbon liberation (years from felling)
Sawn logs	2,925	49.292	70	150	558	49.512	150	300
Board	1,154	19.447	15	40[1]	87	7.720	15	40
Paper	936	15.774	1	5	138	12.245	1	5
Mining	23	0.004	40	200	<1	<0.001	40	200
Fuel[2]	142	2.393	1	5	114	10.115	1	5
Other[2]	142	2.393	15	30	114	10.115	40	80
Bark	612	10.313	1	5	116	10.292	1	5
Total	5,934	100.000	—	—	1,127	100.000	—	—

Notes: [1] Based on this being almost exclusively particleboard as per statistics given in Forestry Commission (1992).
[2] Based on assumption that roughly 50 per cent of 'Other Industrial Wood' (FICGB, 1992) is fuel-wood, as per statistics given in Forestry Commission (1992).

Sources: Carbon liberation dates from Cannell and Cape (1991) and Thompson and Matthews (1989a,b). Production data from FICGB (1992) and Forestry Commission (1992); Adrian Whiteman, pers. comm., 1993.

5 per cent) is held as soil organisms (Jenkinson, 1988). On uncultivated soils a number of natural factors influence soil carbon content. These include soil texture, moisture, temperature and the lignin content of the natural plant cover (Parton *et al.*, 1987). In lowland areas the quantity and type of organic material returned to the soil as dead plant tissue is, in the long run, balanced by the decomposition of SOM and release of CO_2 and water (Jenkinson, 1988). Such soils are therefore in carbon balance. However, soils which are poorly drained and frequently water-logged (typically in upland areas) exhibit very slow decomposition rates.[17] Where organic deposition exceeds decomposition, peat is formed (Askew *et al.*, 1985). Such soils have no predetermined upper limit for SOM levels (although average levels can be calculated) and consequently may have very high carbon contents (Adger *et al.*, 1992).

On cultivated soils a variety of additional factors may influence soil carbon levels, including tillage regime, crop selection, addition of fertiliser and organic matter, irrigation and residue treatments[18] (Parton *et al.*, 1987). The transition from uncultivated to intensive arable land, particularly where bare fallow rotation systems are used, is commonly associated with very significant losses in SOM (Klimowicz and Uziak, 2001). The majority of a soil's carbon is held near the surface and repeated tillage exposes the SOM to the atmosphere, increasing decomposition rates significantly above natural levels (Jenkinson, 1988). Tiessen *et al.* (1982) reports a 35 per cent fall in carbon levels over a seventy-year period as a result of switching grassland into cropping.[19] Jenkinson (1988) reports a similar loss over roughly thirty years for an area of old established grassland switched into various arable crops, the loss being greatest where land was regularly ploughed with no crop cover being sown.

The growth of intensive agriculture world-wide during the twentieth century has led to massive depletions in soil carbon levels.[20] These depletions have provided a major source of global CO_2 emissions (Bridges and Batjes, 1996) which is 'second only to fossil fuel combustion in contributing to historical increases of global carbon dioxide concentrations' (Post *et al.*, 1990).

Afforestation and soil carbon

The potential for forest soils to store carbon is well known (Kaiser *et al.*, 2001; Neff and Asner, 2001; Rasse *et al.*, 2001); indeed, the majority of a forest's stored

---

[17] Harrison *et al.* (1995) report a strong negative relation between soil moisture deficit and carbon content. See also Edwards (1975).

[18] For example, whether or not stubble is burned.

[19] Clay and silt loam soils. Use of leguminous crops reduced losses from 35 per cent to 18 per cent (Tiessen *et al.*, 1982).

[20] Although there is evidence that cultivated soils may outperform forests in consumption of carbon monoxide (King, 2000).

carbon is held in its soils rather than its vegetation (Brown, 1998; UNDP *et al.*, 2000). However, until recently, relatively little work had been done on the long-term effects of afforestation upon soil carbon levels in the UK. An important early exception was provided by the work of Jenkinson (1971, 1988) who examined two areas which had been arable for many years before being abandoned and allowed to revert to woodland for some eighty years. This natural afforestation resulted in very considerable increases in soil carbon.

R. Matthews (1993), in his model of Sitka spruce forest carbon budgets, combines the work of Jenkinson with that of Whitehead *et al.* (1975) and Wilson (1991) in formulating his soil carbon flux predictions.[21] Here soil is assumed to have previously been under intensive cropping resulting in an initial, pre-afforestation, soil carbon content of 30 tC/ha. This is assumed to rise to approximately 70 tC/ha some 200 years after planting and reach a subsequent maximum of 100 tC/ha. Similar results are reported by Sampson (1992) in a study of two US sites which exhibit long-term soil carbon equilibrium increases of about 50 tC/ha arising from afforestation.

In a study using similar soil and management conditions, Dewar and Cannell (1992) report soil carbon storage curves for hardwoods which are similar to those of R. Matthews (1993) suggesting that there is not a particularly significant species effect here. More recent research provides some, although mixed, evidence on whether or not different tree species induce different rates of soil carbon storage (Prïha *et al.*, 2001). Given this uncertainty, we do not differentiate between species in this respect. However, other factors can have very substantial impacts upon soil carbon flux.

The major determinants of soil carbon change under afforestation are soil type and prior usage, from which we can estimate present carbon levels and predict long-term equilibrium levels under afforestation.[22] Adger *et al.* (1992) report equilibrium soil carbon levels for a variety of soils and land uses. This work was combined with information gathered in conversations with Professor David Jenkinson (Rothamsted), Dr Robert Sheil (University of Newcastle upon Tyne) and Professor Steven McGrath (Rothamsted), to whom we are grateful, to produce estimates of the full

---

[21] A further assumption, that clear felling will not reduce soil carbon providing replanting occurs within one year, is also made by R. Matthews (1993) with reference to the work of Edwards and Ross-Todd (1983). However, recent work by Harrison *et al.* (1995) suggests that SOM may decline during the first fifteen years following replanting after which it begins to rise again slowly, taking anything up to sixty years to return to equilibrium. See also Adger and Brown (1994).

[22] The SSLRC LandIS system provides the best source of soil type data for England and Wales. Land cover data may be obtained from the ITE/NERC database. Furthermore, 5 km soil property, nutrient and elements maps are provided in McGrath and Loveland (1992) although the data supporting these maps were not available for this study. Alternative approaches include use of the CORINE land cover database (European Union, 1992) as employed by Cruikshank *et al.* (1995). Milne and Brown (1997) use the ITE land cover data to produce 1 km resolution maps of carbon storage in vegetation and soils for the whole of Great Britain. Our own work examines potential changes rather than current storage levels.

Applied Environmental Economics

Table 7.3. *Post-afforestation changes in equilibrium soil carbon storage levels for various soils previously under grass (tC/ha): upland and lowland sites*[1]

Soil type	Upland sites			Lowland sites		
	Under grass	Under trees	Change	Under grass	Under trees	Change
Peat	1,200	450	(750)	n/a	n/a	n/a
Humic gley	180–400	250–450	50–70	180–350	180–450	0–100
Podzol	200–400	250–450	50	100–200	100–450	0–250
Brown earths	n/a	n/a	n/a	100–120	100–250	0–130
Humic stagno podzol	180–400	250–450	50–70	120–350	120–450	0–100
Stagnogley	170–400	170–450	0–50	100–120	100–450	0–330

Notes: [1] Use prior to afforestation is assumed to be long-established agricultural pasture (dairy, cattle or sheep).
n/a = not applicable; soil type not common at this altitude.
Brackets indicate negative amounts.
Source: See text.

range of changes which could occur through afforestation of various soil types. This analysis was extended to consider both lowland and upland areas which, because of varying rainfall and land use, may exhibit significantly different rates of soil carbon accumulation. Table 7.3 presents results from this analysis.

Inspection of Table 7.3 shows that afforestation is generally synonymous with long-term increases in soil carbon storage levels and that these increases are liable to be somewhat larger in lowland sites because of the prevalence of more intensive prior agricultural land uses.[23] The one clear exception to this trend arises where planting occurs on previously unplanted peat soils. Here the extremely high prior levels of soil carbon are substantially reduced by the planting and tree growth processes (Cannell *et al.*, 1993; Davidson and Grieve, 1995; Harrison *et al.*, 1995).[24] Although UK forests are at present net absorbers of atmospheric carbon,[25] in an analysis of the carbon dynamics of land use in Great Britain during the period 1947–80, Adger *et al.* (1992) calculate that the planting of coniferous trees on peatlands, combined with the widespread substitution elsewhere of old-growth

[23] Feedback links between global warming and changes in forest soil carbon sequestration are investigated by Dalias *et al.* (2001).

[24] Cannell *et al.* (1993) examine the direct carbon flux impact of planting on peatbogs and suggest that there is a threshold depth of disturbance or ploughing of peat above which the net impact of afforestation is increased emission over one rotation, but below which there was net sequestration of carbon (although this study, like our own, ignores the effect upon other greenhouse gases such as methane). Updegraff *et al.* (2001) examine the relationship between changes in temperature and water table and emission of carbon dioxide and methane from peatlands. See also Steinkamp *et al.* (2001).

[25] Cannell and Dewar (1995) estimate current sequestration due to the total UK forest estate at 2.5 million tC per annum. Adger and Subak (1996) provide estimates for agricultural land.

broadleaf forest, with high carbon storage, by new conifer plantations, has resulted in the forestry sector being a net contributor to carbon emissions, a result which reinforces the need to incorporate soil carbon flux within our analysis.

Given the impact of discounting upon our subsequent valuations of carbon flows, the shape of the soil carbon flux function is clearly important. The general consensus is that marginal soil carbon flux is relatively high in the years following initial planting and declines smoothly to reach equilibrium over some extended period (Cannell and Milne, 1995a,b). Robert Shiel (pers. comm., 1994) suggests that roughly 95 per cent of the net change in soil carbon will occur within 200 years of planting. Both R. Matthews (1993) and Dewar and Cannell (1992) illustrate total soil carbon storage curves which have negative exponential shapes. Combining these pieces of information allows us to model both total and marginal soil carbon storage curves.

Methodology

Functional relationships are estimated for our three model elements:

(i)   carbon storage in live wood
(ii) carbon emission from thinnings and wood products
(iii) carbon storage or release (as appropriate) from afforested soils.

Functions for both Sitka spruce and beech were estimated on a per hectare per annum basis.

A number of factors were relevant to selecting the period for the analysis. These were the long time periods involved in these various functions (e.g. rotations of more than 100 years); the overlapping of functions (e.g. the wood product liberation curve from an initial rotation will not have run to zero before the second rotation is felled and a second such curve commences); and the impact of discounting (e.g. low discount rates will produce significant non-zero discount factors far into the future). In the light of these factors, it was decided that the analysis should be extended to cover a 1,000-year time period with replanting assumed to follow within a year of felling throughout this period. This allows the calculation of equilibrium carbon flux effects (although the subsequent process of discounting exponentially favours short-term impacts).

Once functions have been estimated we can readily calculate the per hectare net carbon storage (or emissions) for a selected species in any given year as follows:

(i)   The carbon storage function for live trees of a given species and yield class is taken and run from planting to felling date (F). This function is restarted after each F to simulate replanting;
(ii) Emissions from thinnings and products deriving from prior rotations are summed and subtracted from (i). Note that the emissions functions from any given rotation will

extend beyond the lifespan of the next rotation, i.e., such functions overlap such that in any given year there may be emissions from more than one previous rotation. However, there are no emissions prior to first thinning of the initial rotation;[26]

(iii) The net soil carbon flux function is applied from the date of first planting. Predicted sequestration (or emission) is added (subtracted) from the sum of (i) and (ii) to yield the marginal net annual change in carbon storage.

The above calculations are performed for each year in our 1,000-year analysis. The process is then repeated using the other YCs considered in stage (i) above. Finally the entire calculation is repeated using functions for the other species under consideration.

Valuation of the marginal net annual change in carbon storage is achieved by reference to the relevant unit values for each year given in Fankhauser (1994b) as discussed previously. We thereby derive a stream of marginal carbon storage values for each species, and within each YC, under consideration. These are undiscounted values to which any desired discount rate may be applied to calculate net present value or annuity equivalents as required.

As a final step we use our GIS to apply these various valuations to the maps of predicted YC for the two species under consideration presented in Chapter 6. In so doing we produce maps of live wood carbon storage value. The GIS is also used to relate our soil carbon values to the LandIS soil type data layer and produce a map of soil carbon flux values.[27] By superimposing these maps and adding their values we obtain a joint live wood and soil carbon sequestration value map. Finally, by subtracting the thinnings and wood product emissions levels for the relevant species, we obtain a map of the overall net carbon flux value for a given species for all locations in our case study area. Such a map allows us to readily identify those areas which, if afforested, would yield optimal carbon storage values.[28]

Modelling carbon storage in trees

Carbon storage in Sitka spruce live wood

As discussed previously, carbon sequestration in an unthinned standing crop follows an approximately S-shaped time trend. Figure 7.1 showed that in thinned crops the total carbon storage curve is non-linear, following the unthinned S-shaped growth curve up to TD1 after which a significantly shallower path is followed until the rotation ends at F (as the majority of UK plantations are subject to thinning we shall concentrate upon such stands for the remainder of this analysis). However, as we showed in Chapter 5, within each species both TD1 and F can be shown to

---

[26] Note that we ignore emissions from vehicles and machinery involved in planting and felling.
[27] Skidmore *et al.* (1991) use an expert systems approach to map forest soils from a GIS.
[28] Cieszewski *et al.* (1996) provide an analysis of error propagation within carbon flux assessments.

be functions of yield class and discount rate.[29] Carbon storage modelling therefore needs to reflect this complex interaction of diverse factors.

While a simple approach to this problem would be to use long-term equilibrium storage levels (such as those reported by Dewar and Cannell, 1992), this would ignore the low levels of carbon storage occurring in the early years after initial planting. Given that we wish to discount storage values, this overstatement of early sequestration could result in a substantial upward bias in benefit estimates. A superior approach is suggested by Pearce (1991, 1994) who, in the first major UK study of this issue, adopts a negative exponential total carbon storage function. While clearly better than a simple average, this approach still results in some overstatement of early storage rates as the marginal storage curve implied by the differential of a negative exponential shows annual net storage being highest during the initial planting year and declining thereafter.

To avoid these problems we start the modelling process by explicitly considering the S-shaped curve which is total carbon storage in unthinned live wood (uTWCS). The Bureau of Transport and Communications Economics (BTCE, 1996a) discusses a number of functional forms for modelling this curve; however, for simplicity we adopt the cubic given in Equation (7.1):

$$uTWCS_{i,YC,t} = \beta_{1iYC} + \beta_{2iYC}t + \beta_{3iYC}t^2 + \beta_{4iYC}t^3 \qquad (7.1)$$

where:

$$i = \text{species (for Sitka spruce, } i = SS; \text{ for beech, } i = BE)$$
$$YC = 4, 6, 8, \ldots 26 \text{ (for } i = SS)$$
$$t = \text{years from planting } (t = 0, 1, 2, \ldots F)$$

A priori we would expect $\beta_1 = 0$, $\beta_2 > 0$, $\beta_3 > 0$ and $\beta_4 < 0$.[30] In order to estimate Equation (7.1), data for Sitka spruce YC12 were taken from R. Matthews (1992, 1993).[31] Initial investigations confirmed that an optimal statistical model based on Equation (7.1) gave estimates of β_1 which were not significantly different from zero (as expected) and so this element was dropped from our final model which is reported as Equation (7.2).

$$uTWCS_{SS,12,t} = 0.43727t + 0.10747t^2 - 0.0010267t^3 \qquad (7.2)$$
$$(4.40) \qquad (28.09) \qquad (-29.21)$$

$$R^2 = 99.9\%; n = 81. \text{ Figures in brackets are } t\text{-statistics.}$$

---

[29] Recall that discount rate is held constant in Figure 7.1 such that only the yield-class effect is illustrated.

[30] The β_4 term provides a potential advantage over non-declining functional forms such as the logit, which cannot capture a possible reduction in the volume of a stand if left unmanaged with natural regeneration permitted.

[31] These data are based upon a superior total/merchantable volume function to that used in Matthews (1991) upon which the estimates of Pearce (1991) are based.

Not surprisingly, given the predictability of tree growth patterns, Equation (7.2) fits the data extremely well. All estimated coefficients are very highly significant ($p < 0.001$ in all cases) and have expected signs and magnitudes.

We now need to generalise across yield classes. The work of Cannell and Cape (1991) shows that, within a given species, carbon storage varies linearly across YC. We can therefore derive a species-specific YC adjustment factor, which we denote A_{iYC}, to permit us to adjust from the YC of our baseline data (YC12) to any other Sitka spruce YC. Cannell and Cape (1991) report curves linking timber volume, biomass, carbon storage and stand age for a variety of Sitka spruce YCs. Using this information we can estimate an adjustment factor for Sitka spruce of $A_{SS,YC} = 0.08333$ YC (note that when YC $= 12$ then $A_{SS,12} = 1.0$).[32] A generalised function for $uTWCS_{i,YC}$ for i $=$ SS and any YC can then be derived as in Equation (7.3):

$$uTWCS_{SS,YC,t} = A_{SS,YC} * uTWCS_{SS,12,t} \qquad (7.3)$$

These functions will continue to rise until $t =$ F. However, as noted, F is a complex function of both the discount rate (r) and YC. This relationship was investigated using the YC/discount rate analysis of optimal felling dates reported in Chapter 5. Our resultant best-fit model is shown in Equation (7.4):

$$F_{SS,YC} = 114.43 - 997.3r + 7167r^2 - 2.8657YC + 0.05919YC^2 \quad (7.4)$$
$$\phantom{F_{SS,YC} =} (32.67) \quad (-6.25) \quad (3.62) \quad (-9.21) \quad\quad (5.79)$$

where:

$F_{SS,YC} =$ optimal felling date for a given yield class (YC) of a specified tree species (here Sitka spruce, SS)

$r =$ discount rate (expressed as a decimal)

$R^2 = 96.6\%$; $n = 39$. Figures in brackets are t-statistics.

Equation (7.4) fits the data extremely well for the range of observed F with all parameters significant at $p < 0.001$. It shows, as noted previously, that F declines with both r and YC, although the clear significance of the square terms in Equation (7.4) indicates that this is not a simple, straight-line relationship.

We now consider thinned crops. To do this we first need to estimate TD1. Examination of the yield models given in Edwards and Christie (1981) shows a clear relationship between TD1, F and YC as demonstrated in Table 7.4 for their Sitka spruce yield models.

---

[32] For derivation, see Bateman (1996).

Table 7.4. *Date of first thinning (TD1) for Sitka spruce yield models*
(r = 0.05 throughout)

YC	Optimal felling year (F)[1]	Year of first thinning (TD1)[2]	Ratio (TD1/F)
6	68	33	0.485
8	67	29	0.433
10	64	26	0.406
12	58	24	0.414
14	54	22	0.407
16	51	21	0.412
18	50	20	0.400
20	50	19	0.380
22	49	18	0.367
24	48	18	0.375

Sources: [1] From Chapter 5, this volume.
[2] From Edwards and Christie (1981); models for 2m spaced planting with no delay in thinning.

Inspecting Table 7.4 shows that, as YC rises and F falls, so TD1 declines. One simple method of capturing this relationship is to first model the ratio TD1:F as a function of YC as shown in Equation (7.5):

$$\text{RATIOTD1}_{SS,YC} = 0.48149 - 0.0049061 YC \qquad (7.5)$$
$$(32.21) \quad (-5.27)$$

where:

$$\text{RATIOTD1}_{SS,YC} = \text{ratio of TD1 to F across YC for Sitka spruce}$$
$$R^2 = 77.7\%; n = 10. \text{ Figures in brackets are } t\text{-statistics.}$$

While the small sample size used in Equation (7.5) is not ideal, individual *t*-statistics are highly significant and, as no further data are available, this seems a reasonable approach. TD1 can now be calculated for any given YC by multiplying the corresponding felling date by Equation (7.5) as shown in Equation (7.6):

$$\text{TD1}_{SS,YC} = (0.48149 - 0.0049061 YC) * F_{SS,YC} \qquad (7.6)$$

As shown in Figure 7.1, once thinning commences total tree carbon storage falls progressively below that predicted by our uTWCS function. Using data from R. Matthews (1991, 1992, 1993) we can measure this proportion as the thinning factor (TF) detailed in the final column of Table 7.5.

Statistical investigation showed that $TF_{SS,t}$ (the thinning factor for Sitka spruce in year *t*) could be well predicted by the natural log of the number of years since

Table 7.5. *Thinning factor for Sitka spruce (TF$_{SS,t}$): YC12*

Years after date of first thinning ($t^* = t - TD1$)	Total unthinned tree carbon storage (tC/ha) (uTWCS$_t$)	Total thinned tree carbon storage (tC/ha) (tTWCS$_t$)	Reduction in total potential tree carbon storage arising from thinning (tC/ha)	Thinning factor $\left[TF_{SS,t} = \dfrac{tTWCS_t}{uTWCS_t} \right]$
0	50	50	0	1.00
5	67	55	12	0.83
10	84	61	23	0.73
15	109	71	38	0.65
20	133	82	51	0.62
30	169	95	74	0.56
40	192	107	86	0.56
50	206	116	90	0.56
60	211	120	91	0.56

Source: Based on data in R. Matthews (1991, 1992, 1993).

thinning had commenced in a given plantation (denoted t^* where $t^* = t - TD1$ for all $t \geq TD1$; note that where $t < TD1$ (i.e. before thinning commences) we constrain TF to equal 1). Equation (7.7) details our best-fitting model of TF$_{SS,t}$.

$$TF_{SS,t} = 1.000 - 0.1158 \ln t^* \qquad (7.7)$$
$$(37.90) \quad (-13.41)$$

$R^2 = 96.3\%$; $n = 9$. Figures in brackets are t-statistics.

We are now able to calculate total live wood tree carbon storage for thinned stands of Sitka spruce in any year t (tTWCS$_{SS,YC,t}$):

$$tTWCS_{SS,YC,t} = uTWCS_{SS,YC,t} * TF_{SS,t} \qquad (7.8)$$

The function shown in Equation (7.8) increases in each year from planting until felling after which replanting is assumed to follow within one year and the function returns to zero and restarts its growth path. Given that this model is discontinuous it cannot readily be differentiated. Consequently, marginal carbon storage was calculated by solving equation (7.8) iteratively for each year in our time series and calculating the annual change.[33]

---

[33] Care was taken to ensure that restarting of the growth path following felling was not recorded as a fall in tree carbon storage. All carbon liberation is captured by the function relating to felling waste and timber products.

Carbon storage in beech live wood

The modelling of carbon storage in beech live wood followed the methodology used for Sitka spruce and therefore will be only briefly described. Information regarding sequestration in beech is somewhat sparser than for its widespread coniferous counterpart, so much so that our analysis is based upon the estimates for oak (YC4) given in Dewar and Cannell (1992), adjusted by consulting the YC4 model for beech given in Edwards and Christie (1981). This exercise relies on the findings of G. Matthews (1993), who suggests that, within YC bands, carbon storage for oak and beech will be similar. Using this approach, observations on the S-shaped unthinned carbon storage curve $uTWCS_{BE,4,t}$ were built up for use in the estimated model:

$$uTWCS_{BE,4,t} = 0.2414t + 0.030752t^2 - 0.00014252t^3 \qquad (7.9)$$
$$(2.17) \qquad (13.73) \qquad (-13.24)$$

$R^2 = 99.9\%$; $n = 26$. Figures in brackets are t-statistics.

As with Sitka spruce, the model of total carbon storage in unthinned beech live wood fits the data very well. All parameter estimates are highly significant ($p < 0.05$ for t and $p < 0.000$ for t^2 and t^3) and coefficients have expected signs and magnitudes (the latter differing logically from those of our Sitka spruce model).

An adjustment factor for beech ($A_{BE,YC}$) was calculated as before to allow comparison across YC, the data given in Dewar and Cannell (1992) implying that $A_{BE,YC} = 0.25$ YC (note that when YC = 4, then $A_{BE,4} = 1.0$). A generalised function for $uTWCS_{i,YC}$ for i = BE and any YC can then be derived as:

$$uTWCS_{BE,YC,t} = A_{BE,YC} * uTWCS_{BE,4,t} \qquad (7.10)$$

We can now estimate F for beech as a function of r and YC using the data reported in Chapter 5. Our best-fit model is:

$$F_{BE,YC} = 173.86 - 1901.4r + 8870.8r^2 - 5.387YC + 0.2500YC^2 \quad (7.11)$$
$$(20.78) \quad (-18.07) \quad (11.99) \quad (-2.25) \quad (1.47)$$

$R^2 = 97.8\%$; $n = 32$. Figures in brackets are t-statistics.

Equation (7.11) fits the data very well and reconfirms the relationships noted regarding Sitka spruce. All estimates are significant at $p < 0.05$ or better with the exception of the YC^2 term which has $p = 0.152$. While this is in itself insignificant the term is retained both for comparison with our previous model and because it yields a slight improvement in adjusted model fit.

Table 7.6. *Date of first thinning (TD1) for beech yield models*
(r = 0.05 throughout)

YC	Year of first thinning (TD1)[1]	Optimal felling year (F)[2]	Ratio (TD1/F)
4	35	81	0.432
6	30	75	0.400
8	25	71	0.352
10	25	69	0.362

Sources: [1] From Edwards and Christie (1981); models for 1.2m spaced planting with no delay in thinning.
[2] From Chapter 5, this volume.

The year of first thinning (TD1) is also estimated as before. Table 7.6 presents the data for this analysis. As can be seen, the lack of variation in YC for British beech considerably reduces the number of observations available.

As before we now estimate $RATIOTD1_{BE,YC}$, as shown in Equation (7.12):

$$RATIOTD1_{BE,YC} = 0.47666 - 0.012861YC \qquad (7.12)$$
$$(15.29) \qquad (-3.03)$$

$R^2 = 82.1\%$; $n = 4$. Figures in brackets are *t*-statistics.

The very low number of observations underpinning Equation (7.12) is problematic although it is not clear how further data could readily be generated. Nevertheless, relationships are as expected and this seems acceptable as a methodological exercise. TD1 can now be calculated for any given YC as:

$$TD1_{BE,YC} = (0.47666 - 0.012861YC) * F_{SS,YC} \qquad (7.13)$$

Dewar and Cannell (1992) do not report any information from which a thinning factor (TF_{BE}) might be derived. However, we can obtain an estimate for this by examining the beech yield models of Edwards and Christie (1981). Figure 7.3 illustrates implicit TF_{BE} from data given in the latter.

Inspection of Figure 7.3 shows that $TF_{BE,t}$ is very similar to $TF_{SS,t}$ as detailed in Table 7.5. In both cases TF follows a roughly logarithmic pattern, falling rapidly once thinning commences and becoming fairly stable after about thirty years. We can therefore assume an approximate equality between these relationships and use Equation (7.7) to define $TF_{BE,t}$. Given this, we are now able to calculate total live wood tree carbon storage for thinned stands of beech in any year

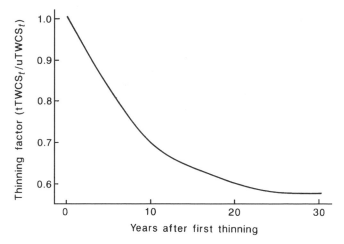

Figure 7.3. Thinning factor for beech. (*Source:* From data given in Edwards and Christie, 1981.)

t ($\text{tTWCS}_{\text{BE,YC},t}$) as:

$$\text{tTWCS}_{\text{BE,YC},t} = \text{uTWCS}_{\text{BE,YC},t} * \text{TF}_{\text{BE},t} \tag{7.14}$$

Modelling carbon liberation from felling waste and timber products

The methodology adopted for modelling carbon liberation from felling waste and timber products was common to both Sitka spruce and beech. Earlier in this chapter it was shown that end use has a major impact upon overall carbon flux. Examining Table 7.2 indicates that, for all but the shortest lifespan products, carbon liberation appears to follow a roughly normal distribution. Short lifetime products (those from which virtually all carbon is liberated within five years of felling) have modal liberation during the year of felling after which liberation rates fall swiftly over time. Assuming an approximately straight-line, downward-sloping liberation distribution for the latter and a normal distribution centred upon the modes listed in Table 7.2 for all other products, we obtain the product-specific carbon liberation schedules illustrated in Figure 7.4 for Sitka spruce and Figure 7.5 for beech. These are expressed as a proportion of the total amount of carbon stored by one hectare of live wood (i.e. excluding soil flux) during the course of a full rotation.

In Figure 7.4, panels (a) to (e) show carbon liberation distributions for Sitka spruce products and waste categorised according to longevity. So, for example, from panel (a) we can see that nearly 10 per cent of the total carbon stored in live wood by a rotation of Sitka spruce is liberated in the year of felling ($t = 0$) via short lifetime (five year maximum) products (e.g. paper and fuel) and waste (including felling waste). Conversely, panel (c) shows that in the same year only

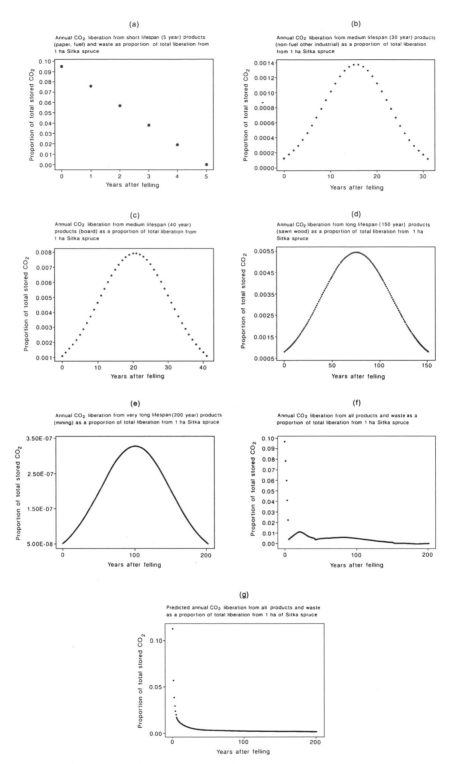

Figure 7.4. Annual carbon liberation distributions for products and waste expressed as a proportion of total carbon sequestration in wood from one rotation of Sitka spruce.

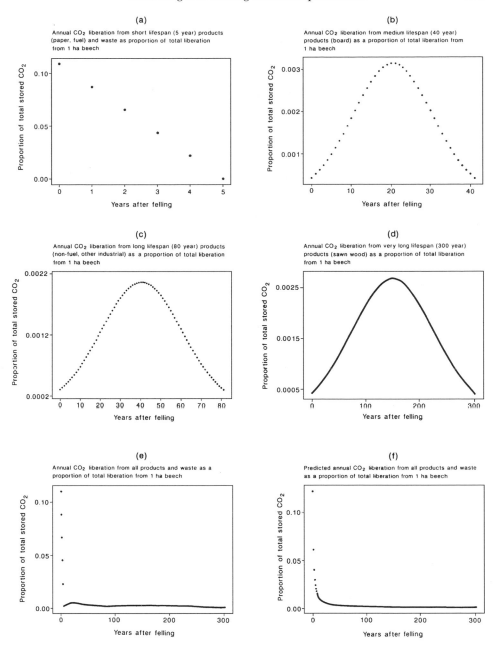

Figure 7.5. Annual carbon liberation distributions for products and waste expressed as a proportion of total carbon sequestration in wood from one rotation of beech.

0.1 per cent of total live wood stored carbon is liberated via medium lifespan (forty year maximum) products (e.g. board). Panel (f) sums all these distributions to produce an overall carbon liberation distribution. This shows that liberation is highest in the felling year and then falls rapidly to some low positive amount which then gradually declines over an extended period. A number of statistical models were fitted to these data, the optimal model being reported in equation (7.15) with predictions being illustrated in panel (g) of Figure 7.4.

$$LIB\%_{SS,t} = 0.0017146 + 0.110363\,ETREND_{SS,t} \qquad (7.15)$$
$$(6.30) \qquad\qquad (36.53)$$

where:

$LIB\%_{SS,t}$ = annual carbon liberation from all products and waste as a proportion of the total carbon stored in live wood by one rotation of Sitka spruce

$ETREND_{SS,t}$ = $1/(1+t')$ where $t' = 0$ at felling (F) and maximum $t' = 200$

$R^2 = 87.0\%$; $n = 201$. Figures in brackets are t-statistics.

The $ETREND_{SS,t}$ variable provides a good fit to the carbon liberation data as illustrated by the similarity between actual and predicted liberation distributions shown in panels (f) and (g), respectively, of Figure 7.4. Equation (7.15) implies that all carbon stored in live wood by a rotation of Sitka spruce will be liberated by $t' = 200$, after which we constrain $LIB\%_{SS,t}$ to equal zero.

Turning to Figure 7.5, panels (a) to (d) detail carbon liberation proportion distributions by product category for beech, while panel (e) illustrates their sum. Again this was modelled using a variety of approaches and functional forms with the best model being:

$$LIB\%_{BE,t} = 0.0007818 + 0.121461\,ETREND_{BE,t} \qquad (7.16)$$
$$(4.01) \qquad\qquad (45.97)$$

where:

$LIB\%_{BE,t}$ = annual carbon liberation from all products and waste as a proportion of the total carbon stored in live wood by one rotation of beech

$ETREND_{BE,t}$ = $1/(1+t')$ where $t' = 0$ at felling and maximum $t' = 300$

$R^2 = 87.6\%$; $n = 301$. Figures in brackets are t-statistics.

Equation (7.16) for beech has the same form and explanatory variable as for Sitka spruce in equation (7.15). A similar high degree of fit is achieved, as illustrated by comparing actual and predicted liberation in panels (e) and (f), respectively, of Figure 7.5. Equation (7.16) implies that all carbon stored by a rotation of beech will be liberated by $t' = 300$ after which we constrain $LIB\%_{BE,t}$ to equal zero.

Modelling carbon storage and loss from soils

Examining Table 7.3 it is tempting to conclude that we should model individual soil category carbon changes, including some element for altitude. Indeed the integrative and analytical capabilities provided by a GIS invite such an approach. However, we are painfully aware of the paucity of data that underpins Table 7.3 and of the numerous complications (such as the implications of replanting) which have yet to be quantified. We therefore adopt a simplified and conservative approach to modelling soil carbon flux along the lines of Dewar and Cannell (1992), Sampson (1992) and R. Matthews (1993), all of whom assume a constant, smooth and marginally diminishing carbon flux path for all soils.

Erring on the conservative side, Table 7.3 supports a net long-term increase in soil carbon equilibrium levels for non-peaty soils at a range of altitudes of about 50 tC/ha. For peat soils a net long-term loss of some 750 tC/ha seems defensible. Following our literature review we know that for both peat and non-peat soils the rate of carbon flux will be highest immediately after felling and decline such that 95 per cent of soil carbon change will have been achieved after about 200 years.

Equation (7.17) calculates the proportion of the total change in soil carbon (PROPTΔSC$_t$) which will have been achieved in any year t, where $t = 0$ at planting. Notice that PROPTΔSC$_t = 1.00$ when $t = 263$ (based on the assumption that 95 per cent of total soil carbon change occurs by $t = 199$) after which it is constrained to equal 1.00 throughout the remainder of the period under analysis.

$$PROPT\Delta SC_t = 0.1793022 \ln TIME1_t \qquad (7.17)$$

where:

$$TIME1_t = t + 1 \text{ and } t = 0 \text{ at planting.}$$

Equation (7.17) implies a diminishing marginal proportion of soil carbon change over the period $0 \leq t \leq 263$ (i.e. annual carbon changes are highest in the year in which the first rotation is planted and decline thereafter). These marginal values can be obtained by simple, one-period differencing. Multiplying these annual proportions by the total change (50 tC/ha for non-peat soils and -750 tC/ha for peat soils) gives the annual soil carbon gains and losses (in tC/ha).

Results

Net carbon storage in live wood, products and waste

Setting aside soil carbon impacts (discussed subsequently), the carbon storage and liberation equations reported above for Sitka spruce and beech were operationalised through a custom-written Fortran program.[34] This program yielded estimates of carbon sequestration value by species for a range of YC and discount rates. For

---

[34] This program is listed, with sample output, in Bateman (1996).

Table 7.7. NPV of net carbon flux (sequestration in live wood and liberation from products and waste) for an optimal rotation of Sitka spruce: various yield classes and discount rates (£, 1990)

Discount rate (%)	YC4	YC6	YC8	YC10	YC12	YC14	YC16	YC18	YC20	YC22	YC24	YC26
1.5	811	1,166	1,491	1,815	2,122	2,415	2,692	3,002	3,308	3,609	3,902	4,228
2	699	1,007	1,290	1,570	1,837	2,089	2,364	2,634	2,897	3,151	3,404	3,652
3	536	774	1,005	1,208	1,415	1,629	1,816	2,015	2,199	2,391	2,567	2,781
5	342	496	643	785	916	1,035	1,160	1,278	1,393	1,503	1,626	1,761
6	284	411	535	653	761	859	963	1,060	1,156	1,253	1,367	1,466

each discount rate/YC combination, three net carbon sequestration values were calculated:

(i) the net present value (NPV) of the initial optimal rotation
(ii) the NPV of a perpetual series of optimal rotations (to $t = 1,000$, assuming replanting after felling), and
(iii) the annuity equivalent of the latter.

Bateman (1996) reports full results of all these analyses for all three measures. For brevity, here we report just the first of these measures for Sitka spruce (Table 7.7) and beech (Table 7.8).

Considering Tables 7.7 and 7.8 we can see that both yield class and discount rate have highly significant impacts upon net carbon sequestration values. The data reported in these tables allow us to estimate, for each tree species, a series of linear regression equations where, for each specified discount rate, the net present value of sequestration is related to yield class.[35] The resultant regression models are reported in Table 7.9.

As can be seen, the models reported in Table 7.9 fit the data well. These models can now be applied to our maps of predicted timber YC, as derived in Chapter 6, to produce maps of the net carbon sequestration value derived from consideration of storage in live wood and emissions from thinnings and wood products (but not soil carbon impacts) for the entire Welsh study area. Discounting effects can be analysed by simply selecting the equation from Table 7.9 which refers to the desired species/discount rate combination. As examples, Figure 7.6 illustrates the resultant NPV map for an optimal first rotation of Sitka spruce using a 3 per cent discount rate,[36] while Figure 7.7 illustrates the respective value for beech.

The images detailed in Figures 7.6 and 7.7 strongly reflect the underlying pattern of timber yield and consequently echo the environmental determinants of such growth rates. Notice that the pattern of net carbon flux values is similar for the two species, reflecting lower growth rates in the upland areas running down the centre of the country and higher yields in bisecting valleys and on superior lowland soils. However, carbon flux NPV sums are consistently higher for Sitka spruce than for beech. This arises because the superior growth rate of Sitka spruce directly fixes more carbon, more quickly, than beech does. As a consequence the former is far less affected by the process of discounting, and resultant NPV levels are higher.

Figures 7.6 and 7.7 are calculated holding the discount rate constant at 3 per cent. Table 7.10 relaxes this restriction and, for both of the species under consideration, compares the NPV of net carbon flux for live wood, waste and products across a

---

[35] Bateman (1996) also reports equations predicting the NPV in perpetuity and the annuity equivalent carbon storage values.

[36] This rate is chosen here to reflect recent debate concerning an appropriate social discount rate (Pearce and Ulph, 1998); see Chapter 5.

Table 7.8. *NPV of net carbon flux (sequestration in live wood and liberation from products and waste) for an optimal rotation of beech: various yield classes and discount rates (£, 1990)*

Discount rate (%)	YC2	YC4	YC6	YC8	YC10	YC12
1.5	886	1,673	2,401	3,059	3,690	4,326
2	706	1,332	1,889	2,421	2,941	3,437
3	466	875	1,246	1,607	1,924	2,262
5	242	454	649	830	1,003	1,178
6	186	349	497	638	775	907

Table 7.9. *NPV of carbon in live wood, waste and products from an optimal rotation of Sitka spruce and beech: linear predictive equations with yield class as the single explanatory variable: various discount rates*

Species	Discount rate (%)	Intercept (*t*-value)	Slope (*t*-value)	R^2 (adj.)
Sitka spruce	1.5	254.32 (14.62)	152.83 (145.11)	99.9
Sitka spruce	3	187.70 (9.90)	100.46 (87.48)	99.9
Sitka spruce	6	106.77 (9.06)	52.71 (73.89)	99.8
Beech	1.5	281.86 (4.68)	341.52 (44.20)	99.7
Beech	3	148.14 (4.92)	178.34 (46.18)	99.8
Beech	6	56.18 (5.54)	71.80 (55.19)	99.8

range of discount rates.[37] The table gives frequency counts and percentages for the number of 1 km cells within each value band.

Analysis of Table 7.10 shows that both the choice of discount rate and the choice of species have substantial impacts upon net carbon storage values. As before we find that the slower timber growth rate of beech results in lower discounted values of carbon sequestration than those for Sitka spruce. However, as expected, this divergence of values between species declines as the discount rate falls.

Extending the analysis to include soil carbon flux

Equation (7.17) defined the total proportion of soil carbon flux (sequestration or liberation) achieved in any year (*t*) for any tree species. This equation was differenced to calculate the marginal proportion change in any year *t*. The actual marginal change in soil carbon was then obtained by multiplying the total change over the full period under analysis (50 tC/ha for non-peaty soils; −750 tC/ha for peaty soils) by the marginal proportion change in each year. This annual soil carbon gain or

---

[37] Annuity equivalents are reported in Bateman (1996).

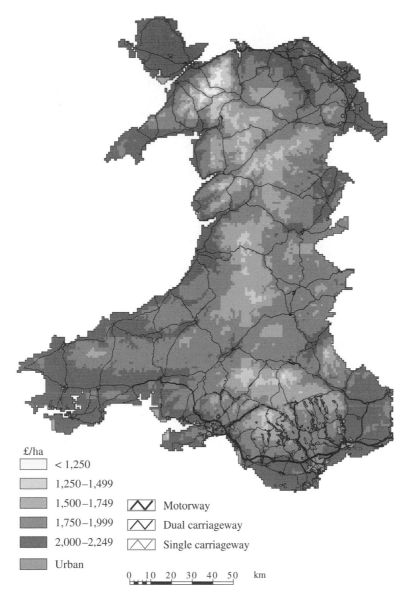

£/ha
- ☐ < 1,250
- ☐ 1,250–1,499
- ☐ 1,500–1,749
- ☐ 1,750–1,999
- ☐ 2,000–2,249
- ☐ Urban

Motorway
Dual carriageway
Single carriageway

0 10 20 30 40 50   km

Figure 7.6. NPV of net carbon storage in live wood, products and waste from an optimal first rotation of Sitka spruce: 3% discount rate.

loss was subsequently valued using the Fankhauser values as discussed previously. These values were then discounted at various rates, and net present value perpetuity sums calculated as shown in Table 7.11.[38]

[38] Given that soil carbon change is a slow process (Milne and Brown, 1997), taking many rotations to complete, calculation of first rotation NPV sums is of less interest here than in our analysis of tree carbon fixing values. Annuity equivalents are reported in Bateman (1996).

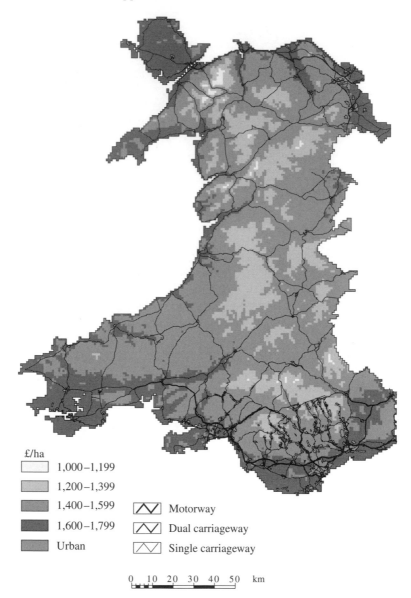

£/ha

□ 1,000–1,199

■ 1,200–1,399

■ 1,400–1,599   ⬒ Motorway

■ 1,600–1,799   ⬒ Dual carriageway

■ Urban   ⬒ Single carriageway

0 10 20 30 40 50   km

Figure 7.7. NPV of net carbon storage in live wood, products and waste from an optimal first rotation of beech: 3% discount rate.

Maps of soil carbon flux values were created by applying the values given in Table 7.11 to a soil map derived from the LandIS database (see the discussion in Chapter 6). Given the lack of detailed information concerning soil flux impacts, the resultant maps (reproduced in Bateman, 1996) contain only two values, representing the presence or absence of peaty soils, the latter being generally confined to extreme upland areas where carbon storage is already low due to depressed tree growth rates.

Table 7.10. *NPV of Sitka spruce and beech carbon flux for live wood, waste and products: various discount rates (r)*

	Sitka spruce						Beech					
	r = 1%		r = 3%		r = 6%		r = 1%		r = 3%		r = 6%	
NPV (£/ha)	Freq.[1]	%	Freq.[1]	%	Freq.[1]	%	Freq.[1]	%	Freq.[1]	%	Freq.[1]	%
250–499	—	—	—	—	1	0.005	—	—	—	—	161	0.783
500–749	—	—	—	—	228	1.109	—	—	—	—	20,402	99.217
750–999	—	—	5	0.024	8,042	39.109	—	—	—	—	—	—
1,000–1,249	—	—	50	0.243	12,292	59.777	—	—	159	0.773	—	—
1,250–1,499	5	0.024	624	3.035	—	—	—	—	7,809	37.976	—	—
1,500–1,749	27	0.131	3,621	17.609	—	—	1	0.005	12,595	61.251	—	—
1,750–1,999	71	0.345	8,648	42.056	—	—	41	0.200	—	—	—	—
2,000–2,249	571	2.777	7,615	37.033	—	—	387	1.882	—	—	—	—
2,250–2,449	2,036	9.901	—	—	—	—	4,057	19.730	—	—	—	—
2,500–2,749	3,561	17.318	—	—	—	—	8,457	41.127	—	—	—	—
2,750–2,999	6,371	30.983	—	—	—	—	7,620	37.057	—	—	—	—
3,000–3,249	7,643	37.169	—	—	—	—	—	—	—	—	—	—
3,250–3,499	278	1.352	—	—	—	—	—	—	—	—	—	—
Mean	2,859.75		1,900.39		1,005.36		2,907.06		1,518.99		608.08	
s.d.	384.82		319.28		266.81		320.42		273.61		236.07	

Note: [1] From a total of 20,563 1 km land cells.

Table 7.11. *NPV perpetuity sums*[1] *for soil carbon
flux: all tree species (£/ha)*

	Discount rate (%)		
Soil type	1.5	3	6
Non-peaty	743	601	476
Peaty	−11,144	−9,018	−7,141

Notes: [1] Calculated for $t = 0$ to 999.

Table 7.12. *Number of 1 km land cells*[1] *at differing levels of NPV for net carbon
flux (live wood, waste, products and soils): Sitka spruce, various discount rates* (r)

Soil type	NPV (£/ha, 1990)	$r = 1\%$	$r = 3\%$	$r = 6\%$
Peaty	−9,500:−9,001	33	—	—
	−9,000:−8,501	438	—	—
	−8,500:−8,001	5	—	—
	−8,000:−7,501	13	117	—
	−7,500:−7,001	—	298	—
	−7,000:−6,501	—	14	—
	−6,500:−6,001	—	—	489
Non-peaty	500:999	—	—	3
	1,000:1,499	—	1	9,650
	1,500:1,999	—	181	10,421
	2,000:2,499	32	7,907	—
	2,500:2,999	538	11,985	—
	3,000:3,499	5,349	—	—
	3,500:3,999	13,933	—	—
	4,000:4,499	222	—	—

Note: [1] From a total of 20,563 1 km land cells.

In order to assess the full impact of tree planting upon carbon flux, the undiscounted marginal soil carbon storage values were added to the undiscounted annual
net carbon flux values for live wood, products and waste calculated previously. The
resultant total annual carbon flux values were then discounted at various rates to
yield the net present value for any desired period. Table 7.12 lists the NPV of total
net carbon storage for Sitka spruce across various discount rates (values for beech
are similar but reflect our comparison in Table 7.10 by being consistently below
those for Sitka spruce; as such they are not reproduced here).

   The most striking feature of Table 7.12 is the highly bipolar distribution of results.
Planting on peat soils causes very large soil carbon losses which overwhelm any

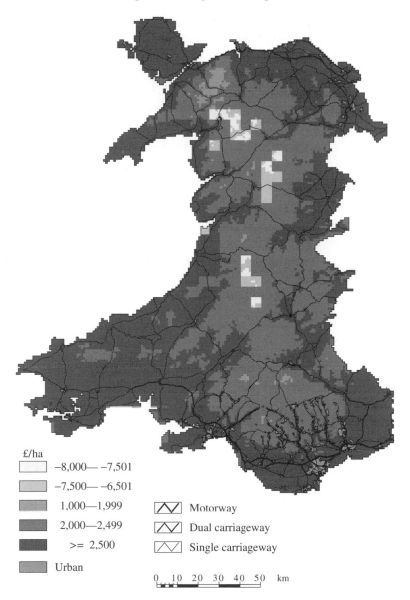

£/ha

☐	−8,000— −7,501
▨	−7,500— −6,501
▨	1,000—1,999
▨	2,000—2,499
▨	>= 2,500
▨	Urban

⟁	Motorway
⟁	Dual carriageway
⟁	Single carriageway

0   10   20   30   40   50   km

Figure 7.8. NPV of net carbon flux (live wood, products, waste and soils), Sitka spruce: 3% discount rate.

values generated by storage in live wood. Elsewhere, however, the value of carbon storage is both positive and substantial. Given the nature of this distribution, mean values and variance measures are somewhat inappropriate; however, the spatial distribution of values is well illustrated in Figure 7.8 which shows the NPV values for net carbon flux generated by Sitka spruce when assessed using a 3 per cent discount rate.

Consideration of Figure 7.8 shows that, with respect to carbon storage values, planting on peat soils is clearly to be avoided, a result which underpins the findings of Adger *et al.* (1992) discussed previously. However, elsewhere such planting is creating substantial public-good benefits which have not commonly figured in CBA appraisals of forestry proposals.

Summary and conclusions

The objective of this chapter was both generally to advance the methodology for modelling carbon sequestration and, specifically, to produce maps of the value of net carbon flux induced by planting trees in locations across Wales. This was achieved by first reviewing the existing literature regarding the value of carbon sequestration or liberation *per se.* Here we concluded that the work of Fankhauser represents the current state of the art and duly adopted his valuations for use later in the chapter. Our second and principal objective was to construct, for both of the tree species under investigation, models of the quantity of carbon sequestered, or liberated, from three sources: the growth of live wood; changes in the carbon content of woodland soils; and carbon liberation from felling waste and timber products. To allow for the long-term nature of these processes, these models were run over a highly extended period. Valuation of the various carbon storage and emission flows was then achieved by reference to unit values reported in the literature. A GIS was used to apply the live wood carbon sequestration and waste/product emission analyses to existing models of predicted tree growth rates for a large study area. Similarly our soil carbon flux model was related to data on soil type distribution. The GIS was then used to overlay results from these various analyses to permit the construction of a net carbon flux valuation map for both of the species under consideration.

Such maps are directly compatible with those estimated in previous chapters for woodland recreation and timber production values. In Chapter 9 we combine all of these maps to derive the total value generated by woodland in a given area. However, before that, in Chapter 8, we examine the value of agricultural output in those areas, which would constitute the major opportunity cost of conversion of land use from farming into woodland.

8

Modelling opportunity cost: agricultural output values

Introduction

Having concluded our assessment of the monetary value of land under forestry we now turn to consider the prime opportunity cost of such a decision, namely the value of the major land use in Wales: agriculture. This chapter presents models of net agricultural income[1] received by farmers (referred to as the 'farm-gate' value) and its social or 'shadow price' equivalent which adjusts for the various subsidies and other transfer payments which characterise UK agriculture.[2] As before, a GIS-based approach is used to generate maps of such values for the entire study area. This permits subsequent comparison of total woodland values with those for agriculture (see Chapter 9).

The following section presents the necessary policy background. This establishes the broad and progressively strengthening economic case for the transfer of at least some land out of conventional agriculture and into alternative land uses and overviews the theoretical and methodological basis of our analysis. An overview of developments since our 1990 study period is also presented, showing that there has been a clear worsening of the economic situation for farmers in our study area, which means that our analysis will provide a conservative estimate of the potential for land use change from farming to forestry.

The following two sections outline the GIS-based methodology employed and discuss the data. For modelling purposes, farms in the sample were clustered into distinct groups as explained in the next section, which also reviews definitions of farm-gate and shadow value of production. Thereafter, the results of the modelling

---

This chapter is an extension of the analysis presented in Bateman *et al*. (1999d)

[1] An alternative approach to valuation might be to examine land prices. However, these have been distorted through subsidised over-use of agricultural land (North, 1990). Furthermore, in debating land purchase as a route towards reducing agricultural output, Colman (1991) argues that, at best, such land purchase schemes will be on a minor scale.

[2] Note that, just as for the case of woodland, certain agricultural externalities are not assessed, for example landscape amenity (see Fleischer and Tsur, 2000).

exercise for both sheep and dairy farming are discussed and the consequent GIS maps are presented. The final section provides a summary and conclusions.

Policy background in the UK

Government intervention within the British agricultural sector can be traced back to at least the Middle Ages (Ernle, 1919) and so it would be wrong to characterise farms as being purely subject to market forces prior to the UK's entry into the EEC in 1973.[3] Nevertheless, the simultaneous entry into the Common Agricultural Policy (CAP) heralded one of the most fundamental changes in the organisation of agriculture in Britain's peacetime history.

The initial CAP support system

The policy principles of the CAP were laid down in 1957 as Article 39 of the foundation document of the EEC, the Treaty of Rome (European Economic Community, 1962). This advocated a basically expansionist ideology enshrined in various potentially conflicting intentions to ensure (i) producer efficiency (ii) market stability (iii) consumer equity, and (iv) a 'fair' standard of living for farmers.[4] In considering the subsequent interpretation and implementation of these aims, commentators have highlighted both the post-war demand for greater food security and the fact that the CAP is a product of the Treaty of Rome and was therefore seen as a cornerstone of the underlying desire, particularly by the Commission of the European Community (CEC), for greater political union among member states (Bowler, 1985; McInerney, 1986; Fennell, 1987; Gilg, 1996).

In practice, a special section of the Community budget, the European Agricultural Guidance and Guarantee Fund (usually known by its French acronym FEOGA), was created to finance the expansion of EEC agriculture. Rather than assistance being paid directly to farmers it was decided that each year the Council of Ministers would set a 'target price' for each commodity, usually significantly above the prevalent world price. This internal EEC target price was principally maintained by imposing an import levy upon non-EEC produce. However, while this was adequate for most goods where the EEC was a net importer, if domestic supply exceeded demand, then the possibility of surpluses depressing internal prices arose. To combat this a system of export subsidies was introduced, payable where internal EEC prices fell below an 'intervention price' level set somewhere below the target price but above world price. Figure 8.1 illustrates the essentials of the support system.

---

[3] Market restrictions and intervention prior to 1973 are discussed in Bowers and Cheshire (1983), Blunden and Curry (1985), Robinson (1990), Smith (1990), Ritson (1991a) and Cobb (1993).
[4] Discussion of these aims is presented in Blunden and Curry (1985), Franklin (1988), Fearne (1991), Ritson (1991b) and Gilg (1996).

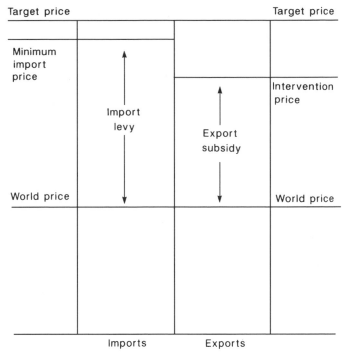

Figure 8.1. Model of a typical CAP price support system. (*Source:* Adapted from Ritson, 1991a.)

A further complexity arose from the internal operation of the CAP prior to monetary union. Support prices were fixed in European Currency Units (ECU) and so had to be translated into actual payments via national currencies. However, fluctuations in exchange rates could lead to substantial and quickly transmitted instability in producer prices. Therefore, for agricultural goods alone, EEC member states were allowed to maintain prior exchange rates (known as 'green' currency) for converting CAP support prices into domestic prices. This system caused differences in realised support prices for the same commodity across countries and if left unchecked would have led to goods moving from low-price to high-price countries prior to their sale into intervention. Consequently, an interim system of border taxes and subsidies (known as Monetary Compensation Amounts, MCA) on intra-EEC trade was also introduced (Fennell, 1987; Ritson, 1991a). The advent of the European Union (EU) Single Market on 1 January 1993 swept away internal borders, making MCAs unworkable. While a strong exchange rate mechanism (ERM) would have reduced many problems, the exit of the UK from the ERM on 16 September 1992 precluded this option and necessitated a compromise solution wherein green currencies effectively 'float', with devaluation in the 'green pound' occurring regularly (Neville and Mordaunt, 1993). This complication persists for the UK following its decision in 1999 not to join the first wave of EU monetary union and fluctuations in the green pound remain a source of problems for UK farmers.

Operation of the CAP in the UK: 1973 to the early 1990s

The UK's entry into the EEC and the CAP in 1973 coincided with the world commodity price boom which was primarily responsible for a substantial increase in agricultural prices, but for which the CAP got much of the blame (Britton, 1990; Hodge, 1990a; Robinson, 1990; Ritson, 1991b). UK food prices rose by 18 per cent in 1974 and 24 per cent the following year (Capstick, 1991). Indeed the retail food price index kept above that of other items for the remainder of the 1970s and the first half of the 1980s (*ibid.*), a trend echoed in the growth of land prices during the period (Harvey, 1991a). During the mid 1970s the price guarantee system and world-wide price buoyancy resulted in increased agricultural stability and incomes (Blunden and Curry, 1985; Hill, 1990; Moyer and Josling, 1990) although this was bought at the cost of welfare losses to consumers and taxpayers (Morris, 1980; Australian Bureau of Agricultural Economics, 1985). However, the natural consequence of increased price subsidies was over-use of land for agricultural purposes (North, 1990), increased food production, and with it higher support costs, which with sluggish growth in domestic demand (Harrison and Tranter, 1989) could only result in higher export subsidies and intervention storage costs (Blunden and Curry, 1985; Buckwell, 1989; Smith, 1990; Cobb, 1993). During the late 1970s and early 1980s the total budget costs of the CAP rose by around 25 per cent per annum (Cobb, 1993) with FEOGA guarantee expenditure increasing from about ECU 2.5 billion in 1970 to nearly ECU 30 billion in 1988 (Moyer and Josling, 1990).

The price pressure of this level of support led to an increased misallocation of resources (Marsh and Swanney, 1980; Tarrant, 1980; Body, 1982; Buckwell *et al.*, 1982; Hill, 1984)[5] and resultant inefficiencies, which meant that as producer subsidy equivalents rose from about 30 per cent to peak at over 60 per cent in 1987, so the net economic loss (sum of producer and consumer welfare effects) of the CAP rose to exceed ECU 9 billion in 1986 (Josling, 1993). Despite widespread criticism, little was done in practical terms to alleviate a rapidly worsening situation. Many commentators both then and since have identified the decision-making framework as the principal cause of this policy response lag, with particular criticism being aimed at the willingness of the Council of Ministers to avoid difficult decisions and put the short-term concerns of their national agricultural constituencies before the long-term need for budgetary prudence (Marsh and Swanney, 1980; Hill, 1984;

---

[5] EEC subsidies and consequent increase in exports and depression of world prices also had major impacts upon non-EEC countries and in particular the less-developed world (Anderson and Tyers, 1991). The economic consequences of this effect are considered subsequently in this chapter.

Bowler, 1985; Fennel, 1987; Hodge, 1990b; Smith, 1990; Fearn, 1991; Josling, 1993; Winters, 1993; Gilg,1996; Billing, 1998). The UK was by no means innocent of such prevarication; for example, the green pound was frequently devalued during this period, thus raising MCA payments to UK farmers (Harris *et al.*, 1983). In essence, then, the CAP exhibited all the signs of a classic intervention failure (Burrell, 1987; Tyers and Anderson, 1987; Rosenblatt *et al.*, 1988; Anderson and Tyers, 1991).

Eventually the EEC was forced to acknowledge that something had to be done about the spiralling CAP budget (CEC, 1985a). While thresholds upon guarantees had been introduced in 1982 (Cobb, 1993), the first substantial response came with the introduction of milk quotas (CEC, 1985b). While the Council of Ministers still provided a brake upon reform (CEC, 1989, 1990), nevertheless gradual reductions in support for milk (European Economic Community, 1987) and cereals were introduced (CEC, 1987) and in real terms prices began to fall throughout the late 1980s (Moyer and Josling, 1990; Hubbard and Ritson, 1991). This coincided with a reduction in non-price support; for example, UK grants dropped from almost £200 million in 1983/84 to about £23 million in 1988/89 with capital allowances being cut in 1986 (Cobb, 1993).

The severity of these real-price decreases meant that by 1990 the food price index had fallen below that of general prices (Capstick, 1991) and agricultural incomes were in decline (Howarth, 1985; Organisation for Economic Cooperation and Development (OECD), 1987; Hill, 1990; Moyer and Josling, 1990). However, continued increases in productivity and falls in demand (Capstick, 1991; CEC, 1992a) meant that the budgetary costs of the CAP were persistently high and the system remained one of intervention failure (Anderson and Tyers, 1991; Josling, 1993). One of the consequences of this situation was that more land was being used for agriculture than was economically efficient, with estimates of surplus agricultural land in the UK ranging from 0.7 million to 5 million hectares (North, 1990; Harvey, 1991b; Potter *et al.*, 1991).

Our study period of 1990 was therefore set within a period when market intervention was unable to reverse long-term agricultural decline, characterised by falling real prices and incomes and over-use of land for farming. We now turn to consider the extent to which these trends have altered or intensified up to the present day.

Operation of the CAP in the UK: the early 1990s to 2001

The early 1990s saw a fusion of concerns regarding the financing of the CAP with long-standing but ongoing concerns regarding the negative environmental impacts of present land use (Nature Conservancy Council, 1977; Shoard, 1980; Body, 1982; Hodge, 1990a,c; MacKenzie, 1990; Whitby, 1991a,b; Turner *et al.*, 1994). These dual pressures of increasing subsidy cost and environmental degradation led many commentators to consider the possibility of reorienting support away from conventional production measures and towards a more holistic agri-environmental system where both food and amenity become recognised and remunerative farm outputs (Baldock and Conder, 1987; Bowers, 1987; Blunden and Curry, 1988; Department of the Environment, 1988; Potter, 1988, 1990; Royal Society for the Protection of Birds, 1988; Hodge, 1990d; Neville-Rolfe, 1990; Cobb, 1993; Colman, 1993).

At the national level a number of UK national policies attempted to address these joint aims including the Alternative Land Use and Rural Economy (ALURE) package (Ministry of Agriculture, Fisheries and Food (MAFF), 1987b) which introduced Environmentally Sensitive Area (ESA) payments, the Premium Scheme (MAFF, 1990), and the Countryside Stewardship Scheme (MAFF, 1992d) which arose from the Government White Paper *Our Common Inheritance* (H.M. Government, 1990). However, while some saw these as a significant reorientation of UK agricultural policy and recognition of the symbiosis of land use and the environment (Blunden and Curry, 1988; Department of the Environment, 1988; Neville-Rolfe, 1990; Colman, 1991, 1993) others criticised the limited funding for such schemes (Robinson, 1990; House of Lords, 1992; National Farmers Union (NFU), 1992). A more fundamental response, at the EU level, to pressures for agri-environmental reform was embodied in the Fifth Action Programme on the Environment (CEC, 1992b), commonly known as the MacSharry Reforms after the then European Commissioner for Agriculture, Ray MacSharry. These proposed a substantial reduction in price support compensated by direct payments to farmers which would be conditional upon placing land into non-productive 'set-aside' with further requirements to reduce negative environmental impacts. Although subsequently watered down, the principle of such reforms was accepted (CEC, 1992c,d; Neville and Mordaunt, 1993).

The MacSharry Reforms have been complemented by a variety of agri-environmental policies (AEPs) including further ESA schemes, Countryside Stewardship, Nitrate Sensitive Areas, Countryside Access, etc. (Evans and Morris, 1997; Hanley *et al.*, 1999; MacFarlane, 2000). However, funding for AEPs has always been relatively modest, with annual spending amounting to about 2.5 per cent of the total of £2,857 million of CAP funds spent in the UK in 1996/97 (Hanley *et al.*, 1999).[6]

The small-scale increases of AEP payments during the 1990s pale in comparison to the substantial falls in real agricultural prices which occurred over the decade. With the exception of a brief period of substantial growth between about 1993 and 1995, the decade was a period of unprecedented decline in farm incomes.

---

[6] Norman *et al.* (1994) provide an early treatise on the application of GIS techniques to target AEPs.

By 1998, total income from farming (TIFF)[7] in the UK fell to £2.51 billion, its lowest level for twenty-five years. After a small rise in 1999, estimates for 2000 showed a further fall to £1.88 billion (DEFRA, 2002). At the farm level, incomes fell across all sectors to levels which were lower than those of our study period at the start of the decade (Countryside Agency, 2001). As the Rural White Paper concluded, 'Farming is going through its most difficult period since before the Second World War. Farm incomes have fallen by around 60% over the past five years. No sector of farming has been unaffected' (Department for the Environment, Transport and the Regions, 2000: p. 89). Similarly a Cabinet Office report to the Prime Minister stated that 'Any assessment of rural areas must begin with the acknowledgement that agriculture, the countryside's most visible and most typical activity, is facing major problems, and that many sectors and people within it are facing real crisis' (Cabinet Office, 2000: p. 4). This was particularly true in Wales where the 1990s proved a desperate time for agriculture, as quantified in Table 8.1.

Table 8.1 shows that all sectors of Welsh farming have experienced sharp declines in agricultural prices and incomes. These have triggered a fall in the number of farms as both farms and herds/flocks increase in size. Declining prices mean that Welsh farmers are now heavily reliant upon subsidies, as recognised in the recent National Assembly for Wales draft policy for the future of agriculture:

Farmers are overwhelmingly reliant on subsidy for this income. Direct CAP subsidies now account for 420% of the net farm income of the average farmer in Wales: this figure would be far higher if indirect support was taken into account. (*National Assembly for Wales, 2001b: section 1.1*)

Welsh farmers have attempted to bolster falling incomes through increasing the number of beef cattle and sheep. In part this has been facilitated by the increase in permanent grassland and reduction in rough grazing noted in Table 8.1. However, this has also been attempted through increases in stocking density, extending a trend which dates from at least the UK's entry into the CAP. Figure 8.2 illustrates this trend, showing the relationship between altitude and stocking intensity for four periods ranging from the early 1970s to the late 1990s. This shows that in each period stocking densities increase with height above sea level, but that densities have consistently increased at all altitudes over the past thirty years.

Wales now has one of the highest sheep stocking densities in the EU (Fuller, 1996) leading to considerable problems of overgrazing and consequent adverse impacts upon biodiversity (Fuller *et al.*, 1995; Dobson, 1997; Woodhouse *et al.*, 2000). In particular, large increases in the number of sheep over successive decades have been blamed for a significant fall in the density and variety of wildlife observed in

---

[7] The preferred and internationally agreed measure of aggregate agricultural income.

Table 8.1. *Change in Welsh agriculture 1990 to 2000*

Measure	1990	2000	Change (%)
Dairy			
Number of dairy cows ('000)	326.8	268.6	−17.8
Number of farms	6,374	4,307	−32.4
Average herd size	51	62	+21.6
Beef			
Number of beef cows ('000)	202.4	223.3	+10.3
Number of farms	11,332	9,326	−17.7
Average herd size	18	24	+33.3
Average market price (per kilo)[1]	£1.04	£0.84	−19.2
Sheep			
Number of sheep & lambs ('000)	10,866.6	11,148.0	+2.6
Number of farms	17,587	15,088	−14.2
Average flock size	618	739	+19.6
Average market price (per kilo)[1]	£1.56	£0.84	−53.8
Incomes			
Dairy index[2]	100	36	−64.0
Cattle and sheep (Less Favoured Areas) index[2]	100	24	−76.0
Cattle and sheep (non Less Favoured Areas) index[2]	100	−6	−106.0
Land use			
Permanent grass ('000 ha)	904	933	+3.2
Rough grazing ('000 ha)	516	442	−14.3
Woodland etc. ('000 ha)[3]	50	58	+16.0

Notes: [1] Pounds (sterling) per kilo liveweight.
[2] Incomes index includes subsidies and holds 1989/90 to 1991/92 = 100.
[3] Includes set-aside land; excludes arable land.
Sources: National Assembly for Wales (2000, 2001c).

Wales (National Assembly for Wales, 2001b). For example, the number of breeding pairs of lapwings in Wales has fallen from about 14,000 in 1970, to 7,500 in 1987 and to just 1,700 in 1998 (*ibid.*).

Examination of Welsh agricultural statistics (National Assembly for Wales, 2000, 2001b,c) shows that our 1990 study period was firmly on a declining trend line extending from the late 1970s to the present. Although the present state of farming is indeed parlous, inspection of trends in farm income shows that, if anything, the increase in real agricultural incomes seen in the period from about 1993 to 1995 was against the general decline seen over the past two decades. Looking into the future we see no signs of any impending change in these trends either in Wales or across the UK in general. The most recent CAP reform proposals, known as Agenda 2000,

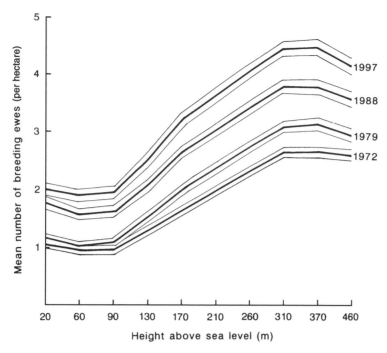

Figure 8.2. Sheep stocking intensity in Wales, 1972 to 1997. (*Source:* Woodhouse, 2002.) The figure shows the mean number (thicker lines; 95% C.I.s shown either side of each line) of breeding ewes per hectare of farmland for 2 km cells in Wales relative to height above sea level.

extend recent policy trends through a continuation of reductions in output-related price support and increased reliance upon area-based measures (Billing, 1998; Hanley *et al.*, 1999; Brouwer and Lowe, 2000a,b; Lowe and Baldock, 2000). Increased measures for agri-environmental support are complemented by further movement away from paying subsidies on a per animal (headage) basis, moves which are specifically designed to discourage excessive stocking in ecologically fragile environments such as the Less Favoured Area designation which embraces most of Wales. Such policies are backed at the UK national level in strategy documents such as the Rural White Paper (Department for the Environment, Transport and the Regions, 2000).

This policy and economic environment means that if Welsh farmers try to compete on price alone they will continue to perform badly. This situation is explicitly recognised by the National Assembly for Wales (2001b), whose agricultural policy recognises farming as a sector in rapid decline which needs to rapidly diversify out of sole reliance upon food production into other activities including, among others, farm woodlands. Although farmers have long been recognised as being resistant to diversification there is recent evidence to suggest that the persistent nature of agricultural decline, compounded by unforeseen and highly damaging shocks such as the BSE crisis and the more recent foot and mouth epidemic, has made farmers more receptive to ideas of diversifying their activities out of traditional food production and into other enterprises. A survey of farmers in England and Wales conducted in 2000 found that 59% of farmers said they would either definitely (26%) or possibly (33%) seek new income from outside their farming businesses (Countryside Agency, 2001). Similarly 48% of farmers said they would either definitely (19%) or possibly (29%) seek to diversify into non-farming use of land, resources or buildings (*ibid.*). This suggests a confluence of economic, policy and psychological factors which together make more viable the type of land use change considered in this study.

Conclusions: the potential for change

This policy review clearly shows the potential for economic gains (both in the sphere of market efficiency and the provision of environmental benefits) from the reform of agricultural policy. In particular there is the possibility of welfare improvements by inducing conversions out of conventional agriculture and into alternative land use such as the woodland option considered in this study. Furthermore, our review of events since our study period shows that declining agricultural values mean that our findings are likely to underestimate the true potential for efficiency gains from such land use change. However, while the possibility of creating positive social net benefits clearly exists, such transfers are unlikely to occur unless we also consider the consequent market value to producers. In subsequent sections we discuss approaches to the modelling of both the shadow and market values of agriculture so that such a comparative analysis can be undertaken.

Developing a GIS-based modelling methodology

Despite the considerable potential of utilising the spatial analytic capabilities of a GIS for modelling in agricultural economics, until recently such systems have only been used to a limited extent (Moxey, 1996). However, whenever there are economic issues with a spatial dimension (e.g. changing patterns of land use, policy measures which are area-sensitive), then the ability to overlay and integrate spatial data (relating, say, to land characteristics) with economic data (which might relate to the farm business), means that a GIS provides the opportunity for much greater realism, comprehensiveness and relevance in modelling. The present analysis adopts such an approach in order to generate estimates of farm-gate and shadow values of agricultural output which could then be used, *inter alia*, to model changing patterns of land use.

Following a review of the literature (Bateman, 1996), it was decided to make an analysis of farm profitability the basis of our modelling methodology. This is a common approach (e.g. Chambers and Pope, 1994) and accords with that adopted by the UK study which most closely resembles the present research, namely the NERC/ESRC Land Use Modelling Programme (NELUP) at the University of Newcastle upon Tyne (O'Callaghan, 1995, 1996).[8] Both the present and NELUP studies use a GIS to integrate the physical environment into an analysis of farm profitability (Moxey and Allanson, 1994; Watson and Wadsworth, 1996; Moxey and White, 1998). However, unlike our own study, the NELUP model did not have access to individual farm-level data (discussed below) but instead depended upon aggregated, parish-level, agricultural census information collected by the Farm Business Survey (Allanson *et al.*, 1992).[9] This is a substantial drawback as it limits the scope for using the capabilities of a GIS to relate the input-output situation of a particular farm to the characteristics of its biophysical environment.

The analytical framework which we present in this chapter was developed iteratively as a result of empirical investigation. An initial single model attempting to relate farm income measures to a variety of input intensity measures (e.g. livestock per hectare), environmental factors (e.g. soil type) and what we refer to as modification variables (e.g. fertiliser per hectare), proved to be overly simplistic for two reasons.[10] First, farm output decisions, and hence incomes, are subject to institutional rules (most noticeably, in the study area, whether or not a given farm holds a milk quota) to the extent that farms cannot be considered a homogeneous group. Second, investigations indicated that, even within a homogeneous subgroup of farms, a single model did not adequately describe a farmer's decision process with regard to how the farm environment influences input and output decision-making and hence income (Bateman and Lovett, 1992).

In order to address the first of these issues, farms were classified into broadly homogeneous groups or sectors (using a cluster analysis described subsequently) within which policy constraints were similar. The second issue was tackled through a two-stage modelling procedure: in stage 1, income values were determined by the array and intensity of inputs utilised; while in stage 2, the inputs employed were dependent on the prevailing biophysical characteristics and possible modifications of those characteristics. Cross-section regression analysis was then used to estimate the parameters of the stage 1 and stage two relationships within each sector. The stage 1 profit–input relationship within each sector was

---

[8] An alternative, linear programming approach is the Land Use Allocation Model described by Jones *et al.* (1995).

[9] Note, however, that a small farm-level study of ten farms has been conducted under the NELUP programme (Oglethorpe and O'Callaghan, 1995).

[10] The single equation approach was also hampered by multicollinearity between input and biophysical variables (Bateman and Lovett, 1992). Our multistage approach to addressing multicollinearity owes much to Smith and Desvousges (1986).

specified as:

$$\pi_{ij} = f_j(I_{1ij}, I_{2ij}, \ldots, I_{pij}, \ldots, I_{kij}) \tag{8.1}$$

where:

π_{ij} is the profit level of the ith farm ($i = 1, \ldots, n$) in the jth sector ($j = 1, \ldots, m$)

I_{pij} is the intensity of use of the pth input ($p = 1, \ldots, k$) on the ith farm in the jth sector

The stage 2 input–biophysical environment relationship for each input in each sector was specified as:

$$I_{pij} = g_{pj}(B_{1ij}, B_{2ij}, \ldots, B_{hij}, \ldots, B_{zij}, M_{1ij}, M_{2ij}, \ldots, M_{rij}, \ldots, M_{vij}) \tag{8.2}$$

where:

B_{hij} is the level of the hth biophysical variable ($h = 1, \ldots, z$) on the ith farm in the jth sector

M_{hij} is the level of the rth biophysical modification variable ($r = 1, \ldots, v$) on the ith farm in the jth sector

The biophysical variables were stored on a grid cell (raster) basis within the GIS for the entire extent of the study area (see the discussion of data below). Therefore, by holding the modification variables at appropriate levels for the farm sector under consideration, we could use the regression parameters of Equation (8.2) to produce maps of predicted levels for all inputs for that sector. Subsequently a map of predicted income for the study area could be derived by applying the regression parameters of Equation (8.1) to the maps of predicted input levels.

The approach taken characterises farm decision-making as a process in which the farmer first considers the institutional rules and constraints within which the farm must operate,[11] then assesses the physical environment of the farm and the extent to which it may be modified (as described in Equation (8.2)), and finally, decides the type and level of inputs to use which in turn determine outputs and farm profitability (as per Equation (8.1)). We recognise and fully acknowledge the fact that, from a sociological perspective, such a model remains naïve. In particular, the writings of the Wageningen school (Röling, 1993, 1994; van der Ploeg, 1993) show that many economic models of farm decision-making omit consideration of factors such as a farmer's mind-set, intrinsic knowledge base, personal and social experience, risk aversion (and its interaction with the former factors), access to and quality of the local community knowledge base, etc. These are important influences which we do not deny and recognise as a limitation of our model.

---

[11] One further fundamental constraint is the difficulty for the farmer of moving from one farm to another. Often the farmer may face insurmountable problems in undertaking such a change.

The data

The models outlined above require individual farm-level data on both biophysical characteristics and the variety of input, output and related variables which define a farm. The Farm Business Survey of Wales (FBSW) provided the necessary farm-level cost and revenue data, while biophysical characteristics were taken from the LandIS database compiled by the Soil Survey and Land Research Centre (SSLRC, Cranfield) and other sources. These data are briefly reviewed below.

During the 1989/90 study period the FBSW interviewed and obtained full accounts data for a representative sample of 571 farms across Wales.[12] Farms were geographically referenced according to the location of the farmhouse and for the purposes of this analysis these points were used to assign each farm to a 1 km grid square. Access to the full FBSW dataset was permitted, although interviews with surveyors, who had visited each of the farms concerned, showed that many of the farms in the dataset were unsuitable for inclusion in the present study because either the farmhouse was not located on the land managed or the farm itself covered a diversity of environments, e.g. both lowland and upland areas affording winter shelter and summer grazing. Retention of such farms within the sample risked confounding the relation between farm performance and biophysical characteristics, which would have negated the fundamental research objective of producing models of the output value of a given area of land under a specified usage.[13] Such mixed environment farms were therefore excluded along with those with large non-agricultural incomes, leaving a final sample of 240 farms. The FBSW dataset is based upon full details of the annual accounts of the sample (which by law have to be surrendered, on demand, to the FBSW). It is consequently a highly detailed and rich dataset. Table 8.2 illustrates this by reproducing the annual record sheet for one particular farm, in this case a typical dairy enterprise (to preserve anonymity the grid reference has been changed, as have farm size details, and all financial particulars have been erased). Individual farm details for each of the items listed in Table 8.2 were made available. As can be seen, the level of information afforded by the data is very considerable.

As discussed in Chapter 6, the SSLRC Land Information System (LandIS) was compiled for the Ministry of Agriculture, Fisheries and Food to facilitate 'land use planning and national resource use' (Rudeforth *et al.*, 1984). It represents the most comprehensive and detailed source of information on the biophysical characteristics of land across England and Wales. LandIS includes long-term averages for a variety of agroclimatic variables at a 5 km grid cell resolution. A summary of the variables

---

[12] This is a routine, annual survey which typically interviews samples of this size. Farms are legally obliged to join the sample when selected.

[13] Note that the exclusion of such farms means that our models are not designed for predicting the incomes of farms which straddle differing environments. However, as made clear here, our objective is to value differing land uses in differing locations, rather than farms *per se*.

Table 8.2. *FBSW annual farm account data: example of a typical farm record*

Farm type: Specialist Dairy   Business size group: 24–39.9 BSU   Farm number: 12345
Location (OS grid ref.): Easting 2170; Northing 3010
Farm area (excluding common grazing):
    actual hectares 69.78
    effective hectares 65.56   Size of business (BSU) : 36.98
                                                Year ending: 31 March 1990

OUTPUTS BY VALUE[1]		INPUTS BY VALUE[2]	
Dairy	• milk	Feed	• purchased concentrates
	• cattle		• home-grown concentrates
	• net milk quota[3]		• purchase bulk feed
	• valuation change	Tack and stock keep	
Other cattle	• cattle	Veterinary & medicines	
	• valuation change	Other livestock costs[4]	
Sheep	• wool	Seeds	• purchased
	• sheep		• home-grown
	• valuation change	Fertilisers	
Pigs	• pigs	Other crop costs[5]	
	• valuation change	Paid labour[6]	• regular
Poultry	• eggs		• casual
	• poultry	Machinery	• contract work
	• valuation change		• repairs
Other livestock	• livestock		• fuels
	• valuation change	General farm costs[7]	
Crops	• main crops	Land expenses	
	• by-products, forage & cults		
Miscellaneous[8]			
FARM OUTPUT		**FARM INPUT**	

FARM SURPLUS = FARM OUTPUT − FARM INPUT

Subsidies & grants	• cattle	Rent & rates	
	• sheep		
	• miscellaneous		
FARM REVENUE = FARM OUTPUT + Subsidies & grants		FARM EXPENSES = FARM INPUT + Rent & rates	

EXCESS OF REVENUE OVER EXPENSES = FARM REVENUE − FARM EXPENSES

Notional outputs	• benefit value	Notional inputs	
	• of farm houses		
		Machinery depreciation	
TOTAL OUTPUT = FARM REVENUE + Notional outputs		TOTAL INPUT = FARM EXPENSES + Notional inputs + Machinery depreciation	

NET FARM INCOME[9] = TOTAL OUTPUT − TOTAL INPUT

INCOME MEASURES	EFFICIENCY MEASURES
Net farm income *less* value of manual labour of farmer & spouse	Milk yield per cow (litres) Milk sales per cow (by value) Lambs reared per ewe (no.)

Table 8.2. (*cont.*)

Investment income	Fat lamb sales per ewe (no.)[10]
plus value of managerial	Return on tenant's capital (%)
input of paid managers	Standard man-day availability[11]
Management & investment income	Standard man-day requirement[11]

TENANT'S CAPITAL	LAND UTILISATION (Hectares)	
Livestock	Tillage	• cereals
Machinery		• roots & fodder
Crops	Grassland	• hay
Stores		• silage
Total tenant's capital		• pasture
	Fallow & land let	
	Rough grazing	• sole
	Woods, roads & buildings	
	Total area	
	Rough grazing	• common
	Bare land and forage hired	

LIVESTOCK	Opening number	Closing value	Average number
Dairy cattle			
Other cattle			
Sheep			
Pigs			
Poultry			
Other livestock			
Total livestock			

Notes:

[1] Outputs include any produce given to workers and consumed or used on the farm. Outputs of livestock are given net of any purchases made. Output includes valuation changes which are detailed in the section headed 'Livestock'. Milk output includes quota transactions and any superlevies paid have been deducted.

[2] Inputs include stock changes as well as purchases made during the year.

[3] Net milk quota comprises quota compensation payments, payments for quota 'leased in' and 'leased out', and superlevy payments where applicable.

[4] Other livestock costs include purchased bedding materials and other costs incurred specifically for livestock enterprises.

[5] Other crop costs include crop protection chemicals and other costs incurred specifically for crop enterprises and forage.

[6] Labour costs include cash wages and salaries, other employer's expenses and the value of perquisites.

[7] General farm costs include electricity, water and telephone charges, licences, insurances, subscriptions, etc.

[8] Miscellaneous output includes contract work, farm cottage rents and profit on resale of purchased agricultural produce.

[9] Amount of which is BLSA also specified in FBSW records (BLSA = breeding livestock stock appreciation, i.e. that part of livestock valuation changes relating to the breeding 'stock on the farm'; details are given in the section headed 'Livestock').

[10] On some farms, fat lamb sales per ewe will include fat lambs from the previous year's lamb crop.

[11] Standard man-day availability is the number of eight-hour 'man-days' used on the farm during the year. Standard man-day requirement is the number of eight-hour 'man-days' conventionally regarded as necessary to maintain the farm's enterprises during the year.

Source: FBSW (1990).

Table 8.3. *Agroclimatic variables obtained from LandIS*

Variable name	Label	Definition
Accumulated temperature	Acctemp	Average annual accumulated temperature above 0°C (in °C)
Accumulated rainfall	Rainfall	Average annual accumulated rainfall (in mm)
Field capacity	Fcapdays	Average annual number of days where the soil experiences a zero moisture deficit (in days)
Return to field capacity	Retmed	Median measure from a distribution of the number of days between the date on which a soil returns to field capacity and 31 Dec. of that year (in days)
	Retwet	The upper quartile of the above distribution; a measure of return to field capacity in wet years (in days)
	Retdry	The lower quartile of the above distribution; a measure of return to field capacity in dry years (in days)
End of field capacity	Endmed	Median measure from a distribution of the number of days between 31 Dec. and the subsequent date on which field capacity ends (in days)
	Endwet	The upper quartile of the above distribution; a measure of the end of field capacity in wet years (in days)
	Enddry	The lower quartile of the above distribution; a measure of the end of field capacity in dry years (in days)
Available water	Avwatgra	Soil water available for a grass crop after allowing for gravity-induced drainage; the difference between water content at field capacity and at permanent wilting point adjusted for grass rooting model (in mm)
	Avwatcer	As Avwatgra but adjusted for a cereal crop (in mm)
	Avwatpot	As Avwatgra but adjusted for potatoes (in mm)
	Avwatsb	As Avwatgra but adjusted for sugarbeet (in mm)
Moisture deficit	Mdefgra	Difference between rainfall and the potential evapotranspiration of a grass crop (in mm)
	Mdefcer	As Mdefgra but adjusted for a cereal crop (in mm)
	Mdefsbpt	As Mdefgra but adjusted for a sugarbeet/potatoes crop (in mm)
Workability	Workabil	A seven-point ordinal scale indicating the suitability of the land for heavy machinery work in spring and autumn (ordinal scale)
Spring machinery working days	SprMWD	Average number of days between 1 Jan. and 30 Apr. when land can be worked by machinery without soil damage (in days)

Table 8.3. (*cont.*)

Variable name	Label	Definition
Autumn machinery working days	AutMWD	The average number of days between 1 Sept. and 31 Dec. when land can be worked by machinery without soil damage (in days)
Lowland relief region[1]	Lowrelif	Lowland topographic relief denoted as regions 4, 5 and 6 in Rudeforth *et al.* (1984) (dummy variable)
Soil type[2]	SoilX	SSLRC soil type classification code (various dummy variables for differing soils – specified in notes to regression models)

Note: All the variables listed are continuous unless specified otherwise. For further information on definitions and measurement, see Jones and Thomasson (1985) or Bateman (1996), except for: [1] from Rudeforth *et al.* (1984: p.19); and [2] from Soil Survey of England and Wales (1983) as recategorised by Bateman (1996) and Bateman and Lovett (1998). Some variables were transformed (e.g. by taking natural logarithms) prior to regression analysis; all such transformations are detailed in notes to regression models.

selected for use in this study is given in Table 8.3 (some of which were also discussed in Chapter 6). Further details regarding the compilation of the agroclimatic database and the geostatistical procedures used to interpolate measurements onto a 5 km resolution grid are given by Jones and Thomasson (1985), Ragg *et al.* (1988), Hallett *et al.* (1996) and at the SSLRC website.[14]

To supplement the characteristics extracted from LandIS, measures of elevation and associated variables were generated from the Bartholomew 1:250,000 digital map database for the UK. Contours and spot heights were processed within the GIS to produce a digital elevation model (DEM) of Wales and estimates of elevation, slope angle and aspect were then calculated at a 500 m resolution and subsequently averaged to provide values for 1 km grid cells across the study area.

Integrating the farm and biophysical variables involved linking databases of varying resolutions. The approach taken was akin to a point-in-polygon method (Burrough and McDonnell, 1998) with the grid reference of each farmhouse being used to select values from the 1 km resolution grids of topographic variables and the 5 km cells of the LandIS agroclimatic measures. Characterisation of the biophysical environment facing each farm business was therefore a little generalised, but thought to be appropriate given the nature of the data sources available and the size of the study area. It also should be emphasised that the geographical matching of farm and environmental variables in this study is considerably more meaningful than in previous research reliant on agricultural census data aggregated to parishes.

[14] See www.silsoe.cranfield.ac.uk/sslrc/services/dataproducts/landis.htm. Harrison *et al.* (1991) provide an early examination of the use of GIS in the analysis of countryside data.

Table 8.4. *Farm cluster characteristics: average income and mean percentage of total revenue from specified activities in each cluster of farms*

Cluster	No. of farms	Average income (£/ha p.a.)	Mean percentage of total annual revenue from each activity					
			Milk	Cattle	Sheep	Other livestock	Crops	Misc.
1	86	83	0.4	29.7	64.4	0.1	3.4	0.5
2	107	509	77.8	11.1	7.1	0.5	2.4	0.3
3	29	47	1.8	63.9	28.3	0.5	1.9	0.6
4	10	223	17.2	27.7	39.5	0.4	0.8	13.5
5	2	1,145	0.0	18.2	7.8	74.6	1.1	0.1
6	6	58	5.1	20.1	14.3	0.9	56.6	1.2
All	240	283	35.9	25.1	31.7	1.0	4.1	0.9

Farm sectors and farm income

Initial investigations revealed some substantial contrasts between different groups of farms, most noticeably in terms of principal activity and resultant income levels (Bateman and Lovett, 1992). Ignoring this issue could have led to the underestimation of standard errors and exaggeration of the degree of explanation of any single model applied across all farms. Rather than adopt *ad hoc* rules for sectoral definition, a two-stage classification process was implemented. Firstly, a principal components analysis (Norusis, 1985) was undertaken using farm-level data concerning the proportion of total revenue derived from each of six groups of output activities. Farms were subsequently grouped on the basis of their scores on the six components using a hierarchical agglomerative technique based on the Ward error sum of squares (ESS) statistic (Ward, 1963). Scrutiny of the output of this analysis (particularly the ESS increments in the agglomeration schedule) suggested that a six-cluster solution was the most appropriate.[15] Table 8.4 lists activity and income-level statistics for each cluster.

It was decided that sample sizes were insufficient to justify further analysis of clusters 3 to 6. This left the two principal agricultural sectors for Wales: farms in cluster 1 specialised in sheep production with substantial production of beef cattle (hereafter referred to as 'sheep farms'); while farms in cluster 2 specialised in dairying (hereafter referred to as 'milk farms'). As a final test of sectoral homogeneity, standard diagnostic tests for outliers were employed (Minitab, 1992). This identified one outlier in cluster 1 and three in cluster 2 and these farms were

---

[15] Note that these are reasonably similar to those defined by the FBSW. However, unlike the latter, they do not further subdivide farms according to their size as this may be (and subsequently proved to be) a significant determinant of per hectare farm income.

omitted to leave a final sample of 85 sheep farms and 104 milk farms. The most striking difference between these two clusters was a wide disparity in income levels with mean net income per hectare on milk farms being nearly six times that on sheep farms.

An issue which proved more complex than expected was the definition of appropriate measures of what the farmer perceives as his/her annual net income (which we term farm-gate income, FGI) and of the shadow value equivalent of this (note that to permit comparability between farms of differing size all values referred to subsequently are adjusted to a per effective hectare basis[16]). An immediately appealing measure in the FBSW dataset is the 'net farm income' (NFI) variable.[17] However, following initial investigation (Bateman and Lovett, 1992) this variable was found to be unsuitable for general modelling requirements because, while its output value minus input value part (denoted 'farm surplus' in FBSW publications) is, as expected, positively correlated with the quality of the biophysical farm environment (the variables $B_{1ij}, B_{2ij}, \ldots, B_{hij}, \ldots, B_{zij}$ in Equation (8.2)), for sheep farms the opposite relationship occurs with respect to the 'subsidies and grants' constituent of NFI.[18] This tends to suppress the link between environmental adversity and overall income level which is a substantial focus of interest in this study.

The definition of the correct measure of farm income is inherently problematic and is itself the subject of research (Sturgess, 1996). Following conversations with Tim Jenkins (FBSW Director, Aberystwyth) it was decided to base statistical investigations of agricultural value upon the farm surplus variable with subsequent adjustments of predicted values to estimate FGI. An appropriate definition was agreed with FBSW:

FGI = farm surplus + (subsidies and grants − rent and rates − depreciation)

(8.3)

To obtain FGI requires an estimate of (.) in Equation (8.3). Actual observations on (.) can be used to define an adjustment variable, ADJFGI, which is the absolute difference (in £/ha) between FGI and farm surplus. This variable was defined for both the sheep and milk sectors (producing variables ADJFGIS and ADJFGIM respectively). ADJFGIS was generally positive and found to vary according to the

---

[16] This adjustment was at the individual farm level using FBSW data on effective farm area (the latter omits land under roads, buildings, etc.). This applies to all regression models and results reported subsequently.

[17] For precise definition of this and subsequent FBSW terms, see FBSW (1990).

[18] This is in itself interesting as it shows that, at least on sheep farms, subsidies and grants do compensate for environmental adversity. Further complexity arises because the unpaid labour element of NFI is positively correlated with such adversity, i.e. farmers attempt to combat poor physical environments by devoting relatively more labour to the farm.

biophysical environment (increasing with environmental adversity); accordingly a simple regression model was used to predict its value.[19] In contrast, a simple flat rate of £95 was found to be adequate for ADJFGIM.

The farm-gate price received by farmers for their produce tells us the financial value (to farmers) of that output but it does not necessarily correspond to the wider social value of that output. In order to move closer to the latter we adjust for the following five factors.

(i) *Market price support*. The Organisation for Economic Co-operation and Development produces annual estimates both of the value of output and the value of market price support disaggregated for all major farm products in each member-nation (OECD, 1992). Using this information, a rate of market price support can be calculated and subtracted from the market price of the goods concerned.

(ii) *Direct subsidies and grants*. OECD (1992) also gives values for the amount of direct subsidies and grants paid to farmers. However, unlike our market price support calculation, such a rate of support cannot be said to be a reasonable approximation of the direct payments received by each farm. Fortunately, the FBSW data supplied for this research details individual farm direct subsidies and grants disaggregated under three headings: cattle, sheep, and miscellaneous. Consequently, individual payments can be directly subtracted from the total output value of each farm.

(iii) *Input subsidies*. Rates of input subsidy for each output heading were calculated from data given in OECD (1992). Ideally we would wish to allocate costs to individual outputs and remove input subsidies from these different cost portions. However, given that the same inputs are used on a variety of outputs, such an allocation of costs was not possible. An alternative approach is to calculate input subsidy values for each output by applying relevant input subsidy rates to the value of each output. These can then be added to total input costs.

(iv) *Levies*. These are in effect negative market price supports and can be treated in the same manner. Whereas adjusting for market price support will lower shadow value (with respect to market price), adjusting for levies (where applicable) will reverse the direction of movement (although the value of levies is invariably far below that of market price support).

(v) *Impacts of the above upon world price levels*. The policy instruments above have had a considerable and depressing impact upon world market prices for agricultural produce which needs to be considered in our shadow pricing exercise (Rosenblatt *et al.*, 1988). Roningen and Dixit (1989) provide estimates of the rates of world price increase of various farm products resulting from a general liberalisation of agricultural policy as implied by adjusting for the above instruments.[20]

[19] See Bateman (1996) and subsequent discussion of Table 8.4.
[20] Taken from Roningen and Dixit (1989: p. 16, table 5). The trade liberalisation adjustment attempts to remove the distortions inherent in actual world prices stemming from policy intervention in the agricultural sectors of the main developed countries in the late 1980s.

The resulting shadow value (SV) is not the full social value of agricultural output as we ignore non-market externalities. However, such a value is more compatible with cost-benefit analysis than are the farm-gate-based FGI values discussed previously. The SV corresponding to farm surplus was calculated by adjusting the recorded financial values of outputs and inputs to estimated world price equivalents for the sample year. Two steps were involved in this calculation. First, output values were adjusted for market price support and co-responsibility levies and input values were adjusted for input subsidies.[21] Second, the adjusted output value for each farm product was multiplied by a trade liberalisation coefficient which attempted to capture the effect of multilateral agricultural trade liberalisation on the world price of that product. For ease of computation a combined shadow value adjustment factor for sheep and milk farms (SVadjs and SVadjm) allowing for all of these elements was calculated. Results from this analysis indicate that the SV of output was around 55 per cent of farm surplus for the milk farms, a figure that rose to about 60 per cent for the sheep farms in our sample.

We have now established definitions whereby we can identify both FGI and SV. Both of these are derived from farm surplus which we now define as π_{ij} in Equation (8.1). One set of Equations (8.1) and (8.2) is estimated for each of the two farm sectors under consideration.

Modelling farm surplus

Regression analysis proceeded in line with the principles described by Lewis-Beck (1980), particular attention being paid to problems of multicollinearity. Referring back to the modelling terminology defined earlier, we first estimated the stage 1 value function (Equation (8.1)) which defines the input–profit relationship. This identified the explanatory input variables which were best able to predict farm surplus and which subsequently formed the dependent variables in the stage 2 equation set (Equation (8.2)) which defined the input–biophysical environment relationship.

The dataset was extensively investigated with a variety of specifications and functional forms being tested. Table 8.5 reports the best-fitting stage 1 model of farm surplus per effective hectare for the sample of sheep farms and milk farms.

Given their cross-sectional nature, both models have a relatively high degree of explanatory power.[22] Examining the model for sheep farms we can see that farm surplus increases with livestock intensity ($live/eh), with the efficiency of that

---

[21] All adjustments made were based on data from OECD (1992); further details are given in Bateman (1996).

[22] There is debate as to what is an acceptable value for adj. R^2 in cross-sectional studies. Hanley (1990) recommends a value of 0.2 while Mitchell and Carson (1989) suggest 0.15. The current study relies primarily on the former, more demanding, rule. Note also that the F ratio is significant in all cases and the null hypothesis of zero coefficient of determination is rejected at 1 per cent significance for all our results.

Table 8.5. *Best-fitting stage 1 models of farm surplus/ha on sheep (cluster 1) and milk (cluster 2) farms*

Farm surplus/ha for sheep farms		Farm surplus/ha for milk farms	
constant	−207.77	constant	4.80
	(−3.35)		(0.05)
lambs/ewe	180.87	$live/eh	0.467
	(4.97)		(7.38)
$live/eh	0.151	gShep%TO	−3, 543.2
	(3.95)		(−5.13)
$f&sLab/h	0.010	genC/h	1.680
	(2.91)		(2.75)
grants%	−210.43	$mlk/cow	0.241
	(−2.15)		(2.67)
		pLab/h	−0.510
			(−2.63)
		catt%FR	−460.6
			(−2.43)
R^2 (adj.)	0.62		0.67
n	85		104

where:
lambs/ewe = no. of lambs reared per ewe per annum (efficiency measure)
$live/eh = value of livestock per effective hectare (input intensity)
$f&sLab/h = notional value of farmer and spouse labour input per hectare (input measure)
grants% = total subsidies and grants (direct payments) expressed as a proportion of total farm revenue (grant dependency measure)
gShep%TO = sheep grants expressed as a proportion of farm total output value (grant dependency measure)
genC/h = general farm costs (electricity, water and telephone charges, licences, insurances, subscriptions, etc.) per hectare (input intensity)
$mlk/cow = the value of milk produced per cow (efficiency measure)
pLab/h = value of paid labour per hectare (efficiency measure)
catt%FR = value of cattle output expressed as a proportion of total farm revenue (enforced diversity measure)
Figures in brackets are *t*-statistics.

livestock (lamb/ewe) and with the amount of labour a farmer and/or spouse devotes to the farm ($f&sLab/h). However, increased revenue dependency upon direct payments (grants%) is synonymous with relatively lower levels of farm surplus.

The stage 1 model for milk farms performs even better than that for sheep farms, achieving a very satisfactory degree of explanation given that this is a cross-sectional analysis. As before we find positive relationships between farm surplus and input intensity ($live/eh, genC/h). Similarly, farm efficiency is a clear determinant of farm surplus, which increases with the value of milk produced per cow ($mlk/cow)[23] and falls as more paid labour is required per hectare (pLab/h). Finally, we have two variables showing that where milk farms have to rely increasingly upon lower margin, non-core activities such as sheep and cattle (gShep%TO, catt%FR) so farm surplus values tend to decline.

The second stage of the modelling process entails the estimation of predictive models for each of the stage 1 explanatory variables for both types of farm. Thus, stage 2 models are concerned with predicting the relationship between biophysical characteristics and agricultural inputs. Table 8.6 presents the results of the stage 2 models for sheep farms.

Given their cross-sectional nature, the models have reasonable explanatory power, with the possible exception of the model for labour inputs. Inspection of the lamb/ewe model shows that the value of this input efficiency measure is lower for soils prone to waterlogging (lnFCdays), but improves where modification leads to better forage availability (Silag%, $crop/h). Consideration of these variables raises a problem regarding how they should be treated when using the model to predict lamb/ewe for the entire study area. We have full coverage for all of the biophysical variables (i.e. a raster layer for lnFCdays can readily be created within the GIS) but the same is not true of the modification variables. A typical approach to such problems is to hold such variables at defensible constant values.[24] An analysis of the distribution of both modification variables showed them to be somewhat skewed and so, for the purposes of prediction, both were held at their median values ($crop/h = 19.50; Silag% = 0.145).

Livestock intensity ($live/eh) is well predicted by the next model, being negatively related to increased susceptibility to waterlogging (lnFCdays) and positively related to improved access to the land (SprMWDSq) and forage availability (Silag%), the latter being treated as before in generating predictions of $live/eh. The third model shows farmer and spouse labour input rising in more waterlogged areas (Endwet) and following a negative quadratic with respect to accessibility (SprMWD, SprMWDSq), suggesting that as accessibility declines so does labour input but at a declining rate indicative of some minimum level below which labour input will not fall. However, the strongest relationship is with farm size, with small farms exhibiting significantly higher levels of farmer and spouse labour input. Again for predictive purposes this variable was held at its median value (<140eh = 1).

The final stage 2 equation for sheep farms predicts the proportion of total farm revenue derived from subsidies and grants (grants%). Here the dependent variable is purely predicted by biophysical variables which provide a good degree of explanation. As discussed previously, sheep farm grants are a function of environmental adversity, in this case modelled by increased waterlogging and slope.

---

[23] This is analogous to the lamb/ewe variable in the stage 1 model for sheep farms.
[24] See, for example, Garrod and Willis (1992a).

Table 8.6. *Best-fitting stage 2 models for sheep farms*

	Dependent variable			
Predictor	lambs/ewe	$live/eh	$f&sLab/h	grants%
Constant	3.510	2,711.9	−791.0	−1.292
	(5.99)	(4.38)	(−0.29)	(−4.94)
lnFCdays	−0.452	−410.0	—	0.272
	(−4.30)	(−3.70)		(5.70)
SprMWD	—	—	−710.0	—
			(−2.41)	
SprMWDSq	—	1.421	78.59	—
		(2.44)	(3.27)	
Endwet	—	—	37.86	—
			(2.60)	
lnSlope	—	—	—	0.032
				(2.93)
Silag%	0.59	1,035.8	—	—
	(3.16)	(6.14)		
$crop/h	0.001	—	—	—
	(2.57)			
<140eh	—	—	2,191.4	—
			(3.56)	
R^2 (adj.)	0.37	0.45	0.25	0.39
n	85	85	85	85

where:
Biophysical variables:
lnFCdays = natural log of the number of days per annum for which soil is at field capacity
SprMWD = number of spring machinery working days
SprMWDSq = square of number of spring machinery working days
Endwet = the end of field capacity period as measured in 'wet' years
lnSlope = natural log of mean farm slope angle
Modification variables:
Silag% = proportion of farm area put to silage
$crop/h = value of crops per hectare
<140eh = dummy for smaller farms (less than 140 effective hectares)
Figures in brackets are *t*-statistics.

Table 8.7 presents the stage 2 models for milk farms. The model for predicting livestock intensity ($live/eh) on milk farms fits the cross-sectional data well.
Livestock intensity declines in areas of higher waterlogging risk (lnEwet) and rises
in areas considered suitable for delicate crops (lnAWpot). There is also a positive
general association with lowland relief areas (Lowrelif). Farmers can also improve the ability of the farm environment to support livestock both directly through
the fertilisers (Fert/h) and indirectly through inputs of concentrates (pConc/h). As

with our sheep models, for predictive purposes data on the biophysical variables (here lnEwet, lnAWpot and Lowrelif) are available for the entire study area. However, as before, we hold the modification variables (here Fert/h and pConc/h) at representative constant values. In the livestock intensity model both modification variables exhibit a slightly skewed distribution and so are held at their median values (pConc/h = 241.2; Fert/h = 88.36).

In the model predicting the proportion of farm total output value derived from direct payments for sheep (gShep%TO), the dependent variable exhibits a quadratic relationship with the waterlogging measure (Enddry), falling at a declining rate as the end of field capacity period increases. This model is relatively weak compared to previous stage 2 models. Nevertheless it does satisfy our theoretical validity criteria (R^2(adj.) > 0.2). However, this is not true of the next model which predicts the general farm costs per hectare input intensity measure (genC/h) and accordingly we have grounds for doubting the validity of using such a model to predict the value of this input in the stage 1 model for milk farms. However, inspection of genC/h showed it to be reasonably normally distributed across farms and so it was decided to hold it at its mean value (85.23) in the stage 1 equation.[25] This is clearly not ideal but it is a recognised and unbiased way of addressing such a problem.

The explanatory power of the best-fitting model for the input efficiency measure $mlk/cow (the value of milk produced per cow) for our milk farm sample is rather better, although a collinearity problem between the two variables AWcerSq and SprMWD (both of which are related to soil moisture) makes their interpretation problematic. Nevertheless, these variables were retained on the grounds that they substantially improved prediction of the dependent variable, which is the prime purpose of the stage 2 models. Other variables are more straightforward to interpret. Soil classes 2 and 3 refer to some of the best (brown earth) soils found in the study area[26] while the variable Lowrelif indicates lowland areas. As expected both are positively related to milk yields as is a higher level of concentrate usage (pConc/h).[27] Interestingly, and in contrast to sheep farms, higher levels of labour input on milk farms seem to be an indicator of inefficiency and consequent lower yields. This seems reasonable and is backed up by the negative sign on paid labour input in the stage 1 milk farm model. It seems that whereas low income levels mean that sheep farmers have no option but to devote additional unpaid labour to their farms, milk farms are generally operating at a much higher level of efficiency where profit maximisation can often be enhanced through cost reductions.

As before, the modification variables are held as constants when the stage 2 models are used for predictive purposes. Here both f&sLab/h and pConc/h were

---

[25] So in the stage 1 model we multiply the coefficient on genC/h by the mean value of the variable, i.e. 1.680 * 85.23 = 144.7.

[26] See Bateman (1996) for further details.   [27] Tests revealed no significant multicollinearity problem.

Applied Environmental Economics

Table 8.7. *Best-fitting stage 2 models for milk farms*

	Dependent variable					
Predictor	$live/eh	gShep%TO	genC/h	$mlk/cow	pLab/h	catt%FR
Constant	468.0 (0.28)	0.1279 (1.93)	44.19 (3.47)	481.0 (4.49)	227.30 (2.65)	0.092 (7.31)
lnEwet	−736.8 (−2.72)	—	—	—	—	—
lnAWpot	804.6 (2.88)	—	—	—	—	—
Lowrelif	140.24 (2.05)	—	—	84.10 (2.29)	—	—
Enddry	—	−0.002 (−2.34)	—	—	—	—
EnddrySq	—	0.00001 (3.06)	—	—	0.032 (3.03)	—
AWgrSq	—	—	0.002 (2.15)	—	—	—
AWcerSq	—	—	—	0.016 (3.27)	—	—
SprMWD	—	—	—	−11.141 (−2.64)	—	—
soil2&3	—	—	—	152.25 (3.86)	—	—
RainSq	—	—	—	—	−0.0003 (−4.10)	—
MdefCerl	—	—	—	—	−4.802 (−4.58)	—
Grazseas	—	—	—	—	1.0426 (3.17)	—
ElevSq	—	—	—	—	−0.0006 (−2.54)	—
lnSlope	—	—	—	—	—	−0.022 (−2.49)
sinAsp	—	—	—	—	—	−0.026 (−2.16)
pConc/h	0.743 (4.79)	—	—	0.336 (4.03)	—	—
Fert/h	2.296 (3.69)	—	—	—	—	—
f&sLab/h	—	—	0.081 (4.39)	−0.376 (−4.43)	−0.147 (−2.96)	—

Table 8.7. *(cont.)*

Predictor	\$live/eh	gShep%TO	genC/h	\$mlk/cow	pLab/h	catt%FR
	Dependent variable					
ehaHay	—	—	—	—	—	0.008 (3.38)
R^2(adj.)	0.44	0.24	0.20	0.29	0.27	0.16
n	104	104	104	104	104	104

where:
Biophysical variables:
lnEwet = natural log of the end of field capacity period as measured in 'wet' years
lnAWpot = natural log of available water, measured for potato crop
Lowrelif = farm in SSLRC relief regions 4, 5 or 6 (lowland)
Enddry = end of field capacity period as measured in 'dry' years
EnddrySq = Enddry * Enddry
AWgrSq = square of water availability for grass crop
AWcerSq = square of water availability for cereals
SprMWD = spring machinery working days
soil2&3 = farm located on soil types 2 (brown earths) and/or 3 (podzols)
RainSq = square of the average rainfall (mm per annum) on farm
MdefCerl = soil moisture deficit for cereals
Grazseas = length of grazing season (days per annum)
ElevSq = square of farm elevation (m) above sea level
lnSlope = natural logarithm of average slope on farm
sinAsp = sine of aspect
Modification variables:
pConc/h = value of purchased concentrates per hectare.
Fert/h = value of fertiliser per hectare
f&sLab/h = notional value of farmer and spouse labour input per hectare
ehaHay = effective hectares of farm put to hay
Figures in brackets are *t*-statistics.

found to have somewhat skewed distributions and so were held at median values of 135.6 and 241.2 respectively.

The next model considers another input efficiency measure, namely the value of paid labour per hectare on milk farms (pLab/h). Analysis of this model shows that the level of paid labour employed on farms is lower in areas of relative environmental adversity (indicated by high values of the RainSq, MdefCerl and ElevSq variables) and higher in areas were the environment is more benign (high values for Grazseas and EnddrySq). It is perhaps not surprising to find that the amount of paid labour on farms is inversely related to the farmer and spouse labour input, suggesting that as a farmer's income increases so he/she substitutes paid labour for personal effort. For predictive purposes f&sLab/h is again held at its median value.

Finally the last stage 2 model is concerned with predicting catt%FR, an indicator of a particular, lower margin, non-core activity on our milk farms. This model fails our criterion of theoretical validity. However, catt%FR was approximately normally distributed and was consequently set to its mean value (0.1107) for predictive purposes within the stage 1 equation for milk farms.[28]

The various stage 1 and stage 2 models provide empirical estimates of the relationship between the biophysical environment, levels of inputs and resultant output values on our sheep and milk farms. These estimates can now be applied to the prediction of FGI and SV for both sectors across the entirety of the study area, thereby yielding vital information concerning the potential for land use change and policy impact within the area.

Mapping market and shadow values for farms

An initial attempt to implement our GIS-based methodology revealed that the range of certain biophysical variables across the whole study area was somewhat greater than that of the sample farms. This was most noticeable for the milk farm sample, which lacked substantial upland observations. In general there was not a problem across the vast majority of the study area, but it was at the extremes, particularly in very mountainous areas, that models were effectively being used to predict outside the range of available data.

In practice, there are two possible solutions to such a problem (Altman and Gardner, 1989): either we can refrain from prediction in such areas or we can truncate each biophysical variable to some level represented in our farm sample data. The latter course of action was preferred as it was felt that having holes in the final map of predicted values would be confusing. Affected cells were set to the upper or lower limit of the farm sample data as appropriate. For our sheep farm models, over 90 per cent of the 20,563 1 km land cells constituting the entire surface of Wales suffered no truncation of any variable, 8 per cent of cells had one variable truncated and less than 2 per cent of cells suffered further truncation. However, for our milk sample these proportions were 74, 10 and just over 15 per cent respectively. The reason for this difference is simple, namely that there are relatively few milk farms in extreme upland areas. Consequently we have to be circumspect about predictions of milk farm values in such locations.

Farm surplus values were now estimated by running the various stage 2 models (using truncated biophysical variable surfaces as appropriate) to predict the input variables for the stage 1 models; from these, farm surplus values were then estimated. Table 8.8 details these values for both sectors, emphasising the highly

---

[28] So in the stage 1 model we multiply the coefficient on catt%FR by the mean value of the variable, i.e. $-460.6 * 0.1107 = -50.99$.

Table 8.8. *Predicted farm surplus values for sheep and milk farms*

Farm surplus (£/ha)[1]	Sheep farms		Milk farms	
	No. of cells	% of all cells[2]	No. of cells	% of all cells[2]
0.00–49.99	2,483	12.1	7	0.1
50.00 99.99	6,346	30.9	37	0.2
100.00–149.99	9,492	46.2	248	1.2
150.00–199.99	1,728	8.4	463	2.3
200.00–249.99	323	1.6	825	4.0
250.00–299.99	191	0.9	261	1.3
300.00–349.99	—	—	274	1.3
350.00–399.99	—	—	317	1.5
400.00–449.99	—	—	307	1.5
450.00–499.99	—	—	500	2.4
500.00–549.99	—	—	1,295	6.3
550.00–599.99	—	—	2,342	11.4
600.00–649.99	—	—	4,845	23.6
650.00–699.99	—	—	5,067	24.6
700.00–749.99	—	—	3,171	15.4
750.00–799.99	—	—	543	2.6
800.00–849.99	—	—	61	0.3

Notes: [1] Categories chosen to facilitate easy comparison with values reported in other chapters.
[2] There are 20,563 1 km land cells in the study area.

significant difference in profitability between the sectors. This difference becomes more extreme if we recall that there are relatively few milk farms in areas of environmental adversity, i.e. those cells at the lower end of the distribution of predicted farm surplus probably refer to very few (if any) real-world milk farms.

By applying the adjustment factors (ADJFGIS and SVadjs for sheep farms and ADJFGIM and SVadjm for milk farms) to the estimates of farm surplus the predicted market and shadow values of output for each sector can be obtained. Considering the sheep farm sector first, Plate 2a shows the resulting GIS-generated map for predicted farm-gate income (FGIs) while Plate 2b illustrates predicted shadow value (SVs). The distribution of predicted values is similar across these maps and conforms strongly to prior expectations. Values are lowest in the Snowdonia, Cambrian and Brecon mountains and increase with movement into lowland areas. Localised variation due to soil quality and related impacts can also be detected. The somewhat blocky nature of parts of these maps is primarily due to these latter effects, as the LandIS variables are at a 5 km resolution whilst the other biophysical measures are recorded on 1 km grid cells. Given this, the overall picture provided by these results seems highly plausible.

Table 8.9. *Predicted farm-gate income and shadow values for sheep and milk farms*

| | Sheep farms | | | | Milk farms | | | |
| | FGIs | | SVs | | FGIm | | SVm | |
Value (£/ha)[1]	No. of cells	% of all cells[2]	No. of cells	% of all cells[2]	No. of cells	% of all cells[2]	No. of cells	% of all cells[2]
−100.00–−50.01	—	—	—	—	3	0.1	—	—
−50.00–−0.01	—	—	—	—	37	0.2	—	—
0.00–49.99	—	—	7,414	36.1	219	1.1	32	0.2
50.00–99.99	—	—	12,389	60.3	418	2.0	364	1.8
100.00–149.99	8,296	40.4	728	3.5	887	4.3	1,184	5.8
150.00–199.99	11,506	56.0	32	0.2	264	1.3	452	2.2
200.00–249.99	527	2.6	—	—	251	1.2	468	2.3
250.00–299.99	234	1.1	—	—	336	1.6	734	3.6
300.00–349.99	—	—	—	—	284	1.4	2,640	12.8
350.00–399.99	—	—	—	—	479	2.3	7,510	36.5
400.00–449.99	—	—	—	—	1,186	5.8	6,566	31.9
450.00–499.99	—	—	—	—	2,231	10.9	613	3.0
500.00–549.99	—	—	—	—	4,582	22.3	—	—
550.00–599.99	—	—	—	—	5,228	25.4	—	—
600.00–649.99	—	—	—	—	3,467	16.9	—	—
650.00–699.99	—	—	—	—	608	3.0	—	—
700.00–749.99	—	—	—	—	83	0.4	—	—

Notes: [1] Categories chosen to facilitate easy comparison with values reported in other chapters.
[2] There are 20,563 1 km land cells.

This analysis was repeated for milk farms and Plate 2c shows the map for predicted farm-gate income (FGIm) while Plate 2d details predicted shadow value (SVm). As both the adjustment factors, ADJFGIM and SVadjm, are constants applied to predicted farm surplus values, these only differ in terms of absolute values. For both we can see strong topographic and soil effects (see, for example, the band of poorer soils extending down the centre of the Pembroke peninsula). As before, the predicted values conform strongly to prior expectations.

Comparing Plates 2a–2d, it is clear that, for each sector, shadow values lie substantially below farm-gate income levels. However, the strongest contrast is between sectors, with milk values very much higher than their sheep equivalents. Table 8.9 illustrates this contrast by summarising frequency distributions for all four variables. This table quantifies the very wide disparities in both farm-gate income and shadow value levels between the sheep and milk sectors. As noted with respect to farm surplus, this disparity becomes even sharper when we recognise that milk farms tend to be concentrated upon better land, i.e. the lower, say, 10 per cent of milk values will, in reality, contain very few actual milk farms.

Summary and conclusions

Any attempt to influence patterns of land use requires an evaluation of the existing usage of that land. This chapter has developed a GIS-based methodology for the estimation of both the market and shadow values of agricultural output for our study area. This methodology permits explicit incorporation of biophysical data within the economic modelling of output values. The capacity to combine diverse spatially referenced data afforded by the use of a GIS allows such modelling to be undertaken at a highly disaggregated level, and yields readily interpretable maps of predicted values as well as more conventional quantitative analyses. These valuation maps are highly compatible not only with those estimated elsewhere in this study but also with the decision-making approaches being developed and employed by agencies such as the Countryside Commission, Forestry Commission and National Assembly for Wales in their land use and planning roles (Countryside Commission and Forestry Commission, 1996; Forestry Commission, 1998).

The application presented in this chapter provides models and mapped estimates of both the market and shadow values of output of the two major farming sectors in the study area: mainly sheep and mainly dairying farms. Results show that, for both sectors, shadow values were considerably below corresponding market values. Furthermore, sheep farm values were substantially lower than those enjoyed by the dairy sector. Both sectors have suffered further losses in real incomes since our study period, implying that our estimated rates of land use conversion are likely to provide lower bounds on the actual potential for efficiency gains from such changes.

The spatial detail of information provided by the resultant GIS-generated maps permits analysts and policy-makers to assess issues such as the likely extent and location of land use response to changes in policy parameters. They also permit ready integration with the maps of woodland recreation, timber and carbon seques-tration value estimated in previous chapters to allow us to evaluate the net benefits of transfers out of agriculture and into woodland, a task to which we now turn.

9

Cost-benefit analysis using GIS

Introduction

In this chapter we assess the net benefits of converting land out of agriculture and into woodland. This appraisal is made from a number of standpoints. We have considered two types of agricultural production (sheep and milk) each assessed in two ways (farm-gate and social[1] values), and two species of tree (conifer, represented by Sitka spruce, and broadleaf, represented by beech). Furthermore, we have assessed a variety of woodland benefits (recreation, timber and carbon sequestration) allowing us to consider a succession of definitions of what, in economic terms, constitutes a woodland. Finally, we have assessed the net benefits of land conversion using a variety of discount rates.

The results presented here consider various permutations of the factors discussed above. In essence our approach starts with the present agricultural values of a specific farm type (say sheep farming) and subtracts various definitions of woodland benefits (say, timber and carbon storage) assessed at a given discount rate (say 6 per cent). Thus a negative outcome would indicate that woodland benefits outstrip those of agriculture, and vice versa for positive sums. These various net benefit value estimates are obtained by using the GIS to overlay the respective value maps and adding or subtracting values as necessary.

A general caveat to our findings concerns the fact that our study data period is the early 1990s rather than the present day. As discussed at some length in Chapter 8, the intervening years have seen a relative decline in the values of agriculture both generally across the UK and in our study area of Wales. This means that our findings will tend to overestimate the value of farming and hence somewhat underestimate the potential for land use conversion into forestry. However, we are

[1] In this chapter we refer to 'social' rather than 'shadow' values as we are attempting to examine a wider range of internal and external benefits and costs than that considered in the analysis of agriculture alone presented in the previous chapter. We recognise that any definition of 'social' value is open to the criticism that the ensuing set of values is incomplete.

not unduly perturbed by this state of affairs for, in any policy assessment, it is also easy to underestimate the forces of inertia, tradition and risk aversion which can induce lag to a decision which seems economically optimal. In short we are much happier with a situation in which our findings are conservative than we would be if intervening forces had moved against land use conversions.

A further caveat to our calculations concerns the extent to which the marginal benefits of woodland are constant or diminishing. The maps of timber value created in Chapter 6 implicitly assume that the expansion of supply generated by any new planting would have no net impact upon the price of timber. Given that the vast majority of the timber consumed in the UK is imported, and that the price is in effect fixed on the world market, this seems a reasonable assumption. Similarly the maps of carbon sequestration value presented in Chapter 7 assume that the extra carbon stored by any new planting would have a negligible effect upon the unit value of carbon storage. Again, given the relatively minuscule proportion of excess atmospheric carbon which would be removed by such afforestation, this seems a very reasonable assumption. However, we cannot extend this line of reasoning to the recreation value maps created in Chapter 4. Here any substantial increase in the supply of recreational sites is liable to impact upon any excess demand[2] such that the value of any further sites is diminished. In effect, as the number of sites increases so substitute availability rises and the marginal recreational value of woodland falls.

To allow for this we have treated woodland benefits in the following manner. In the first of three stages agricultural values are assessed against timber values alone. Results for the farm-gate perspective include the various forest grants and subsidies available to farmers as well as incurred planting and maintenance costs (as in Chapter 6). This analysis is in effect mimicking the actual decision faced by farmers and provides a useful cross-check between our valuation estimates and the real world. In order to provide social value assessments of the agriculture versus timber trade-off we remove subsidies from both sides of the equation, a procedure which shifts the balance in favour of forestry which has a lower level of subsidisation than does conventional agriculture.

The second step adds carbon values to those derived from timber and reassesses the net benefits of conversion from agriculture.[3] Again values are calculated from both farm-gate and social perspectives.

---

[2] The impact of substitutes is considered in Bateman *et al.* (1998) and Brainard *et al.* (1999). However, comparison with the work of Willis and Benson (1989), as reviewed in Chapter 3, suggests that for any given individual woodland our estimates are likely to be reasonable and may even be lower-bound values.

[3] Dore *et al.* (2001) also compare agricultural values with timber and timber plus carbon sequestration values in a study of marginal farming regions in northern Saskatchewan, concluding that the latter exceeds the former in about twenty of the thirty years considered (the exception being the 1970s). However, the study is not spatially disaggregated and estimates total annual values only.

Finally, the third stage of analysis adds in recreational values and recalculates conversion net benefits. However, here we have to recognise the diminishing marginal value of recreation as outlined above. Because of this we cannot have confidence in the overall value sum created by such a calculation. Consequently we can only use this stage to identify those areas which would generate the very highest net benefits from conversion. This in itself is a highly useful result given that, in reality, resource limits mean that only a finite, and probably relatively small, amount of funds will be available to support conversion. Using the methodology outlined here enables the identification of prime sites for such conversion.

From the perspective of the farmer, comparison of agriculture with the timber plus carbon value (and with the timber, carbon and recreation value) does not have any immediate resonance with the actual market situation as neither carbon nor recreation values have any market or subsidy 'price'. However, these calculations do indicate the net benefits which farmers could receive if they were compensated for carbon and recreation values in the same manner in which timber values are realised (i.e. via market prices and subsidies).

All three definitions of woodland values (timber only; timber plus carbon; timber, carbon and recreation) have direct relevance when viewed from the standpoint of society which is interested in both the marketed and non-marketed values of woodland.

Results

Results are categorised first by whether we take a farm-gate or social value perspective. Further disaggregation is by the definition of woodland values discussed above and then by the discount rate, woodland species and farm sector under consideration. We begin by holding the discount rate and woodland species constant and examine results by farm sector. We then vary the tree species and finally change discount rate to present a full sensitivity analysis.

Results for the 6 per cent discount rate

In this section we hold the discount rate at 6 per cent throughout. This is a useful initial level to use for the calculation of social values as it is the current (at the time of writing) government rate for socially beneficial projects both now and in our study period. Our analyses of rates of return (Chapter 5) suggests that it is somewhat higher than that commonly used on sheep farms although it may be representative of rates used on some milk farms. We begin our discussion of results by considering potential conversions to conifer woodland.

Conversion from agriculture to conifer woodland

We begin this section by presenting results for conversion from sheep farms to conifer woodland, subsequently turning our attention to the milk farm sector.

Sheep farms

Table 9.1 reports results from one full run of our cost-benefit model holding the discount rate at 6 per cent and analysing the annual per hectare net benefit value of conversion from sheep farming into conifer woodland. Our analysis uses data recorded for (or interpolated to) a 1 km square basis and the entirety of Wales comprises some 20,563 such squares. Each column presents the distribution of values estimated for these squares.

The table is organised into two blocks each comprising four columns. The first block details farm-gate values (columns (1) to (4)) while the second gives social value equivalents (columns (5) to (8)). For both blocks the columns refer to successively wider definitions of woodland benefits. The first columns of each block (columns (1) and (5)) consider only the timber value while the next (columns (2) and (6)) add in carbon sequestration values. Lastly, two columns in each block add in woodland recreation values. Columns (3) and (7) use a lower-bound recreation value (derived from the contingent valuation (CV) cross-study 'meta-analysis' discussed in Chapter 4), while columns (4) and (8) use an upper-bound value (derived from our individual travel cost method (ITCM) analysis, also presented in Chapter 4).[4]

Column (1) of the farm-gate values block of Table 9.1 indicates the net benefit to farmers of converting from sheep farming to woodland under the present regime of grants and subsidies (defining woodland values as purely grants, subsidies and the net benefits of timber production). Remembering that negative sums show situations where these woodland values outstrip the present sheep values, we can see that, in the vast majority of cases (over 90 per cent of cells) the net benefits to farmers of staying in sheep production exceed those of converting into woodland. This difference is relatively marginal with the net benefit of remaining in agriculture being, in almost all cases, less than £100/ha and with almost 10 per cent of cells showing a small net benefit from conversion.[5] Nevertheless, the clear picture is

---

[4] The CV cross-study meta-analysis and ITCM study derive mean recreation values of £1.82 and £3.59 per party visit respectively. These values are somewhat lower than, although comparable to, those estimated for the study area by Willis and Benson (1989). Site-based values were converted to per hectare equivalents by dividing through by a mean site area of 4,000 hectares (Willis and Benson, 1989; Anna Chylack, Forestry Commission, pers. comm. 1994). The resulting values are within the range quoted by Benson and Willis (1993).

[5] Note that it is at the extremes that the truncation effect discussed in Chapter 8 will apply. These will tend to mask the lowest agricultural values and so conversion could be beneficial in somewhat more than 10 per cent of cases although this effect will be minor (particularly with respect to sheep farms where there is relatively little truncation).

Table 9.1. Distribution of the net benefits of retaining sheep farming in Wales as opposed to conversion to conifer (Sitka spruce) woodland:[1] 6% discount rate

Lower limit (£/ha/yr, 1990)	Upper limit (£/ha/yr, 1990)	Farm-gate values				Social values			
		timber only (1)	timber+ carbon (2)	timber+carbon+ recreation (CVM) (3)	timber+carbon+ recreation (ITCM) (4)	timber only (5)	timber+ carbon (6)	timber+carbon+ recreation (CVM) (7)	timber+carbon+ recreation (ITCM) (8)
−475.00	−450.01								24
−450.00	−425.01								35
−425.00	−400.01								132
−400.00	−375.01								122
−375.00	−350.01				25				274
−350.00	−325.01				99				220
−325.00	−300.01				90				610
−300.00	−275.01				133			117	1,004
−275.00	−250.01				232			213	1,472
−250.00	−225.01			9	285			474	3,153
−225.00	−200.01			153	737		284	1,687	6,478
−200.00	−175.01			266	1,131		7,136	5,121	4,346
−175.00	−150.01			599	1,582		8,292	7,671	1,639
−150.00	−125.01		5	2,097	3,617	7	3,446	3,446	427
−125.00	−100.01		899	5,852	6,153	771	757	1,081	111
−100.00	−75.01		8,286	6,612	3,849	10,540	125	208	21
−75.00	−50.01		6,895	3,005	1,459	7,438	27	40	6
−50.00	−25.01	18	2,840	1,074	467	1,486	6	15	
−25.00	−0.01	1,978	809	272	164	296	1	1	
0.00	24.99	10,811	248	117	46	24			
25.00	49.99	5,929	84	17	5	1			

50.00	74.99	1,287	7						1
75.00	99.99	323	1						
100.00	124.99	188							
125.00	149.99	29							
150.00	174.99								
175.00	199.99								
200.00	224.99								
225.00	249.99								
250.00	274.99								
275.00	299.99			3	29	10			
300.00	324.99			64	146	92			
325.00	349.99			236	263	210	20	4	
350.00	374.99			177	48	164	87	28	11
375.00	399.99			9	3	13	199	142	57
400.00	424.99						160	249	228
425.00	449.99						23	62	181
450.00	474.99							4	12

Notes: [1] Negative sums indicate areas where woodland values exceed agricultural values. Blank cells indicate that no 1 km cells fall into this category. There are 20,563 1 km cells.

that when we consider farmers' perceptions of income, then, under the levels of woodland grant and subsidy operating during our study period, our analysis predicts very little conversion from sheep farming to woodland in the study area. This was indeed the situation on the ground with sources at both MAFF (Fearn, 1990) and the Forestry Commission (Adrian Whiteman, pers. comm., 1994) suggesting that very few Welsh farms had entered forestry schemes at that time.

Does this result provide validation for our estimates? As indicated, the 6 per cent discount rate used here is somewhat higher than the one we would expect sheep farmers to use in their everyday decision-making, yet it produces a result which is consistent with observed behaviour. There are a number of persuasive reasons explaining this result. These centre around the common observation that decision-makers in almost any field (and notably agriculture) demand a premium from risky or unfamiliar investments. Such diversification brings inherent uncertainty for the farmer regarding the levels of labour, capital, skill and entrepreneurship which will be required, as well as uncertainty regarding the ultimate returns from such an enterprise. This is particularly true of forestry which, for the farmer, is both very different from the well-known patterns of sheep production and involves a time scale which is an order of magnitude different from any of the decisions he/she usually encounters.

Cobb (1993) reviews a number of studies of agricultural risk premiums and reports on his own large-sample survey of UK farmers which revealed that they required very substantial increases in gross margin before they would consider conversion into low input extensification options such as that promoted under the Countryside Stewardship Scheme. Cobb feels that this is primarily due to farmers' preferences for familiar activities or agricultural techniques and to apprehension about the unfamiliar.[6] Our own research (see Chapter 3 and Bateman *et al.*, 1996b) found that this is also the case with respect to conversions out of conventional agriculture and into woodland. Here substantial increases in profit rates were required before agreement to convert was forthcoming. As discussed in Chapter 5, Lloyd *et al.* (1995) suggest that one reason for this may be a belief by farmers that conversions to woodland may be irreversible, reducing future opportunities, and may possibly lower land prices. Such perceptions are fostered by the long commitment period of grant schemes and the requirement for replanting as a proviso in the granting of felling orders.

The risk premiums associated with such conversions can be modelled in a number of ways, one of which is to apply a higher discount rate than that normally used for

---

[6] Another interesting possibility explaining negligible conversion rates is explored by Saarinen (1966). In a study of US farmers who would, on purely financial grounds, have been better off giving up a specific type of farming, Saarinen found a consistent overoptimism about future performance, which persisted over long periods. However, he did identify a subset of innovative farmers who were receptive to the possibility of diversification.

standard investments. That is, in effect, what is being done in the farm-gate values reported in Table 9.1 and we can see that our model produces a result which closely resembles what is observed in the real world (as in column (1)). We return to this theme subsequently (see discussion of Table 9.5 below).

Given that we now have support from the real world for the predictions of our model, the 'timber only' farm-gate values (column (1)) also provide useful indications of the responsiveness of sheep farmers to increases in the level of timber grants and subsidies. Our results suggest that even a modest increase in the real level of such subsidies may produce significant increases in the financial viability of conversion. Given that the higher discount rate used here implicitly takes into account farmers' risk aversion, then we might expect this to translate into actual conversions. Some 10,811 cells (over 50 per cent of all cells) show an excess of sheep values over timber woodland values of less than £25/ha/yr. This suggests that while subsidies are currently too low to be effective, substantial conversions may be induced from modest increases in these subsidies.

While the results shown in Table 9.1 are of interest, the GIS-generated maps from which they are derived are more informative (although less easy to summarise). Plate 3a shows the map which underpins our farm-gate valuation of the conversion from sheep farming to woodland under present subsidy levels (column (1)). As can be seen, the majority of areas produce positive differences between sheep farming and timber, i.e. under present circumstances and if we only consider the market-priced benefits of forestry (timber and subsidies), then farm-gate income is generally higher under sheep than woodland. The map shows that this difference is smallest in mainly lowland, valley-floor areas, indicating that it is in these locations that conversions might be most profitable.

The social value equivalent of the above analysis is given in the first column of the second block of Table 9.1 (column (5)). The transfer savings created by a move out of sheep and into the relatively less subsidised production of timber mean that the social net benefits of such conversion are significantly higher than their farm-gate equivalents. This difference is very apparent in Table 9.1 because very nearly 100 per cent of cells record negative values, i.e. even when we only include timber benefits, the social value of woodland generally exceeds that of sheep production. This result is all the more powerful when we recall that the 6 per cent discount rate used here is the same as that used by the UK government for such calculations.

Comparison of columns (1) and (5) is revealing. While a conversion from sheep to woodland is unattractive from the farm-gate perspective, it generates net benefits from society's point of view. The potential clearly exists for a win/win bargain in which society pays some of its subsidy savings back to farmers as compensation for lost income, so that each side benefits. Given that the magnitude of social benefits is similar to that of farm loss, such a compensation scheme would, on these figures, need to be carefully constructed. However, once we widen our definition of woodland benefits the case for compensation becomes much more clear cut.

The second column of each block (columns (2) and (6)) adds in net carbon sequestration values to the benefits of woodland. In the case of the farm-gate values we are in effect modelling the impact of assigning to farmers the net carbon flux value associated with planting trees on their land. In the general case where such planting causes an increase in carbon storage we credit farmers with these values as a hypothetical subsidy. In the more rare case of planting on peat soils, farmers are now debited with a hypothetical charge against the farm account equivalent to the value of carbon liberated.

The impact of this expanded definition of woodland values is highly significant, moving the vast majority of farms (over 95 per cent) to a situation where conversion from sheep farming to woodland creates an increase in farm-gate income (column (2)). However, the large carbon losses associated with planting on peat mean that there are now a small number of farms which would generate strongly negative values from such conversion. This bimodal distribution is echoed in the social value equivalent of this analysis (column (6)). However, here the additional savings of agricultural subsidies substantially improve the net benefits of conversion to woodland.

In effect, then, we only have to expand our definition of the social benefits of woodland to include net subsidy savings, timber production and carbon sequestration to justify very substantial conversion out of Welsh sheep farming and into woodland. This conclusion is further reinforced if we now also consider the recreation benefit values created by making that woodland open-access.[7]

Given our reservations regarding the accuracy of recreational benefit measures, we have used two alternatives here. These are a lower-bound estimate obtained from our cross-study analysis of CV estimates, and an upper-bound measure obtained from our ITCM study. These are used to produce the third and fourth columns of each block. As noted, substitution effects mean that wholesale conversion to woodland would not attain the values shown in these columns. However, the results do indicate that the conversion of just a few select sites (which would not induce major substitution effects) would create woodlands of very high value in some locations. This story is repeated in both blocks, with the social value columns ((7) and (8)) exceeding farm-gate values (columns (3) and (4)) by a significant amount, mainly attributable to subsidy savings.[8]

---

[7] This statement hinges on the assumption, discussed in Chapter 4, that woodland recreational values are measures of surplus over the values created by general agricultural land use.

[8] Subsidy savings constitute the major difference between columns (1) and (5), a difference which is maintained across subsequent pairs of comparable farm-gate and social values.

Precise location of these prime conversion sites is facilitated by inspection of the net benefit value maps underpinning these columns. Plate 3b illustrates the social net benefit of conversion from sheep to woodland with the latter defined as the sum of timber, carbon storage and recreation values (measured using the lower-bound CV estimate), i.e. column (7). From a policy-making perspective this map illustrates the interpretative advantages of the methodology employed. Optimum sites for conversion are easily identified and (remembering that negative sums indicate areas where woodland values exceed those of agriculture) corresponding estimates of the monetary net benefit of such conversion are given.

While Plate 3b is readily interpretable, its message throws a critical light over past policy decisions. As the map clearly shows, the prime sites for conversion are located in lowland areas (with high timber productivity and carbon storage) and near to centres of high population and accessibility (yielding high recreation values).[9] This is particularly noticeable in South Wales where the urban centres of Cardiff and Swansea, augmented by the infrastructure effect of the M4 motorway, result in very high recreational values in addition to the excellent timber yields and consequent carbon sequestration levels engendered by these lowland areas. Conversely, conversion is least justified in upland areas, most noticeably upon peat soils where our analysis shows that retention within agriculture is clearly preferable. This result seems eminently sensible and accords with the sentiment made popular in the 1980s that policy-makers should 'bring forests down the hill' (MacFarlane, 2000). However, as this slogan implies, actual planting decisions have been almost completely at odds with such logic. The recreational needs of the majority lowland urban populace have not been recognised, and forests have in the main been planted in inaccessible upland areas – quite the reverse of the action suggested by Plate 3b. This policy seems to have been led by a desire to reduce the land purchase costs of planting trees, in ignorance of the economic value of such a strategy.

Milk farms

A second set of comparisons is presented in Table 9.2 which maintains the woodland species as conifer and holds the discount rate at 6 per cent but now examines potential conversions out of milk production. To allow further comparison with previous results, Plate 3c shows the net benefit map for the farm-gate value of converting from milk production to conifer woodland when only timber values and subsidies are considered (i.e. the present-day decision facing milk farmers; column

---

[9] There is a fascinating comparison here with the prescriptions of von Thunen's (1826) *Isolierte Staat* and subsequent land use analysis. For example Haggett *et al.* (1977: p. 206) note (without the benefit of specific analysis) that although financially non-viable, 'in highly urbanized areas the demand for "recreational" wooded areas may sometimes lead to its persistence in areas of high accessibility'.

Table 9.2. *Distribution of the net benefits of retaining milk farming in Wales as opposed to conversion to conifer (Sitka spruce) woodland:*[1] *6% discount rate*

Lower limit (£/ha/yr, 1990)	Upper limit (£/ha/yr, 1990)	Farm-gate values				Social values			
		timber only (1)	timber+carbon (2)	timber+carbon+recreation (CVM) (3)	timber+carbon+recreation (ITCM) (4)	timber only (5)	timber+carbon (6)	timber+carbon+recreation (CVM) (7)	timber+carbon+recreation (ITCM) (8)
−275.00	−250.01				13				
−250.00	−225.01		3	24	39				
−225.00	−200.01		29	32	75				3
−200.00	−175.01		35	74	82			4	62
−175.00	−150.01		70	77	128		11	55	122
−150.00	−125.01	21	84	145	173		60	107	160
−125.00	−100.01	29	175	197	191		105	191	270
−100.00	−75.01	65	184	210	221	2	211	289	422
−75.00	−50.01	94	227	250	258	37	308	297	568
−50.00	−25.01	168	266	273	260	103	344	422	682
−25.00	−0.01	203	290	209	208	188	423	413	737
0.00	24.99	293	181	182	210	362	322	473	887
25.00	49.99	355	176	164	215	442	299	763	1,180
50.00	74.99	389	136	149	224	543	377	1,174	2,114
75.00	99.99	166	150	150	351	339	1,080	2,324	3,176
100.00	124.99	160	147	251	542	285	1,775	3,849	3,826
125.00	149.99	163	173	351	530	302	4,272	4,658	3,523
150.00	174.99	163	227	443	702	523	5,446	3,522	1,693
175.00	199.99	143	420	765	1,163	1,401	3,331	1,031	388
200.00	224.99	175	743	1,058	1,700	2,245	1,234	316	151
225.00	249.99	215	1,003	1,649	2,162	4,969	351	131	72
250.00	274.99	277	1,239	2,389	2,572	5,138	86	33	28
275.00	299.99	527	2,359	2,978	2,630	2,636	29	20	10

300.00	324.99	847	3,296	2,976	2,475	808	10	4	9
325.00	349.99	1,089	3,113	2,589	1,898	184	7	14	22
350.00	374.99	1,578	2,616	1,676	796	41	19	30	48
375.00	399.99	2,618	1,734	639	252	15	38	54	86
400.00	424.99	3,224	784	240	183		83	95	78
425.00	449.99	3,025	321	149	55		100	79	37
450.00	474.99	2,389	118	28	21		33	9	17
475.00	499.99	1,380	30	28	27		15	24	26
500.00	524.99	559	27	20	20		25	22	16
525.00	549.99	140	20	15	11		14	22	16
550.00	574.99	75	9	13	12		25	19	21
575.00	599.99	29	11	8	15		17	8	4
600.00	624.99	4	12	18	12		2	4	33
625.00	649.99		16	9	9		35	56	26
650.00	674.99		15	21	14		26	10	19
675.00	699.99		10				23	29	31
700.00	724.99			3	3		27	12	
725.00	749.99		3		4				
750.00	774.99		1	9	37				
775.00	799.99		34	34	6				
800.00	824.99		11	4	14				
825.00	849.99		14	24	13				
850.00	874.99		19	23	25				
875.00	899.99		20	17	12				
900.00	924.99		12						

Notes: [1] Negative sums indicate areas where woodland values exceed agricultural values. Blank cells indicate that no 1 km cells fall into this category. There are 20,563 1 km cells.

(1) of Table 9.2), while Plate 3d indicates the social value of conversion when the broad definition of woodland (timber, carbon storage and recreation, with the latter again measured using our CV cross-study value) is used (column (7)).

The overall pattern of values shown in Table 9.2 is similar to that for sheep farms, with expansion of the definition of woodland benefits increasing the value of the latter. However, the pattern of farm-gate values illustrated in Plate 3c (where woodland benefits are defined as arising just from timber and subsidies) is different to its sheep farm equivalent (Plate 3a). Here we find that the optimal locations for conversion to woodland (shown as negative sums) are clustered in upland rather than lowland areas. This difference in itself is of interest and shows that in contrast to the sheep sector, where it was the superiority of woodland in the lowland areas which was the driving force behind the net benefit of conversions, here it is the fall-off in milk farm values as we approach the most upland areas which allows woodland to become viable – but only at the extremes of topography. This difference is repeated in our social value analysis of the wider definition of woodland values (Plate 3d) where, with the exception of peat soil regions, it is again the upland areas which show more promise of net conversion benefits (in contrast to the sheep farm equivalent illustrated in Plate 3b).

The sheep and milk farm analyses differ not only in their relative pattern but also in the absolute level of conversion values. Even when all possible woodland values are considered, milk values almost always substantially exceed those generated by woodlands. Given that we know there are very few milk farms in the extreme upland areas of Wales this differential is probably even stronger than Table 9.2 indicates. Furthermore, as the discount rate used here is not out of line with (and may even be below) that likely to be used by milk farmers in everyday decision-making, any increase in the discount rate due to risk aversion would only reinforce the result. The social value assessment given here uses the government discount rate and so results are valid as they stand.

In summary, conversions out of milk production and into woodland are generally not justified by this study. We now extend our analysis to consider changes in the species of tree used in conversions.

Conversion from agriculture to broadleaf woodland

Sheep farms

Table 9.3 presents results for conversions from sheep farming to broadleaf woodland, maintaining the discount rate at 6 per cent. It is useful to contrast these results with the sheep to conifer conversion summarised in Table 9.1. In the latter, if we consider only timber values, conversion generally (but not always) fails to generate net benefits when viewed from the farm gate, but almost always creates social gains. However, the case for conversion is less clear in Table 9.3 where the slow growth rates associated with broadleaves mean that delayed timber benefits are heavily discounted; indeed, it is discounting which principally drives the differences between Tables 9.1 and 9.3. Accepting such a discount rate means that in less than half of the cells is conversion from sheep farming to broadleaved woodland justified upon social grounds and in no case do farm-gate values support conversion.

Broadening the definition of woodland benefits to include carbon sequestration does improve the farm-gate case for conversion, although in almost all cases the value of sheep farming marginally outperforms that of woodland. However, social values now generally support conversion except on areas of peat soil.

We now turn to consider recreation values. With respect to conversions to conifers we have up to this point focused attention upon the lower-bound CV measures. However, while evidence of a link between tree species and recreation values is somewhat anecdotal (see Hanley and Ruffell, 1991, 1992), we feel that the use of upper-bound measures has at least some justification with respect to broadleaf woodlands. The use of such measures does significantly improve the apparent viability of land use conversions, with virtually all cells producing net social benefits and most generating farm-gate gains from conversion. However, because we expect strongly declining marginal recreation values for additional woodlands in any given area (i.e. once a given locality has a recreational woodland then the marginal value of an additional woodland is relatively low) then we cannot take the values given in columns (4) and (8) of Table 9.3 at face value. This being so, it is of more interest to use this analysis to identify optimal locations for conversion rather than to look at total values. Plate 3e illustrates the farm-gate value of conversion using our wider definition of woodland benefits (and the upper-bound ITCM value of recreation), i.e. the net benefit map underpinning column (4), while Plate 3f illustrates the social value equivalent of this analysis, i.e. column (8).

It is clear from both Plate 3d and Plate 3f that, when our wider woodland benefits definition is applied, the net benefits of conversion from sheep rearing are highest in areas of high population accessibility (enhancing recreation values) and decrease as we move to more remote locations. The only areas where conversion is never justified are on peat soils where large-scale carbon liberation occurs. This echoes, in particular, the results shown in Plate 3b.

Analysis of the social values illustrated in Plate 3f indicates that the South Wales valleys are an area of particular interest. In the highly populated valleys and around the cities of Cardiff and Swansea there is a clear and very substantial net social benefit from conversion out of sheep farming and into multipurpose broadleaf woodland. This falls rapidly as we move away from such areas and into the sparsely populated upland areas which run down through the centre of Wales or the more inaccessible Pembroke and Lleyn peninsulas which characterise the west coast of

Table 9.3. Distribution of the net benefits of retaining sheep farming in Wales as opposed to conversion to broadleaf (beech) woodland:[1] 6% discount rate

Lower limit (£/ha/yr, 1990)	Upper limit (£/ha/yr, 1990)	Farm-gate values				Social values			
		timber only (1)	timber+ carbon (2)	timber+carbon+ recreation (CVM) (3)	timber+carbon+ recreation (ITCM) (4)	timber only (5)	timber+ carbon (6)	timber+carbon+ recreation (CVM) (7)	timber+carbon+ recreation (ITCM) (8)
−350.00	−325.01								
−325.00	−300.01								25
−300.00	−275.01								54
−275.00	−250.01								151
−250.00	−225.01				25				174
−225.00	−200.01				114				312
−200.00	−175.01				126			14	431
−175.00	−150.01				193			177	923
−150.00	−125.01				294			434	1,159
−125.00	−100.01			25	465			1,259	3,345
−100.00	−75.01			223	993		236	5,089	7,128
−75.00	−50.01			469	1,411		5,775	8,588	5,160
−50.00	−25.01			1,517	3,916	3,166	10,289	3,891	925
−25.00	−0.01		427	5,676	7,000	6,669	3,074	401	190
0.00	24.99	1	6,345	8,991	4,538	8,822	464	140	94
25.00	49.99	3,400	10,816	2,500	608	1,392	232	81	3
50.00	74.99	8,894	1,703	294	172	317	4		
75.00	99.99	6,810	295	211	125	197			
100.00	124.99	872	269	74	17				
125.00	149.99	173	101	91	77				
150.00	174.99		118	3					

Range							
175.00 – 199.99	214						
200.00 – 224.99	159						
225.00 – 249.99	40						
250.00 – 274.99							
275.00 – 299.99							
300.00 – 324.99							
325.00 – 349.99							
350.00 – 374.99					418	165	
375.00 – 399.99					57	305	34
400.00 – 424.99			51		14	19	380
425.00 – 449.99		3	343	174			65
450.00 – 474.99		393	88	282			10
475.00 – 499.99		86	7	33			
500.00 – 524.99		7					

Notes: [1] Negative sums indicate areas where woodland values exceed agricultural values. Blank cells indicate that no 1 km cells fall into this category. There are 20,563 1 km cells.

the country. The map also amply illustrates the ready interpretability of results generated by the methodology developed in this research.

Milk farms

We now briefly consider the viability of transfers from milk farming to broadleaf woodland. Results for this analysis are presented in Table 9.4. As before, while the pattern of results obtained for milk farms is similar to that for sheep farms, the absolute values are very different, with insignificant levels of conversion being justified under either the farm-gate or social value analysis. Given this, we do not discuss these findings further here.

Conversions between milk and sheep farming

In the above analyses we have calculated both farm-gate and social net benefit sums for conversion from sheep farming to woodland and from milk farming to woodland. However, these results also allow us to consider the net benefits of potential conversions between the two farming types (assuming a hypothetical lifting of the market entry restrictions currently imposed by milk quotas) and to ask whether this is more likely than a move into woodland. For simplicity in the following discussion we will refer to the net benefits of conversion to conifer woodland although the analysis could also be repeated for broadleaves, producing roughly similar results.

Considering those farm-gate values which farmers might actually have received during our study period (i.e. ignoring non-timber woodland benefits), then we have shown that in lowland areas sheep farming generally, but only marginally, outperforms woodland, with some conversions being viable where poorer soils predominate (for example, the north-west of Wales as illustrated in Plate 3a). However, the farm-gate value of dairying (Plate 3c) always and very substantially outperforms that of woodland in such lowland areas and consequently exceeds the value of sheep farming by a similar extent. Moving to consider upland areas, the farm-gate value of sheep farming always exceeds that of woodland, this excess being in places over £100/ha. The picture for milk to woodland conversions in upland areas is more mixed. While in areas of less extreme elevation milk values still exceed those of woodland by over £200/ha, in the highest areas the situation changes rapidly as dairy values fall rapidly, and the net benefits of retaining milk production drop below £100/ha. Thus, in the most mountainous areas, conversion to woodland becomes profitable. Therefore, we can see that our model predicts that the farm-gate value of sheep farming exceeds that of both woodland and milk production in these upland areas. Such a prediction is borne out by actual farming practice in these regions (see Chapter 8).

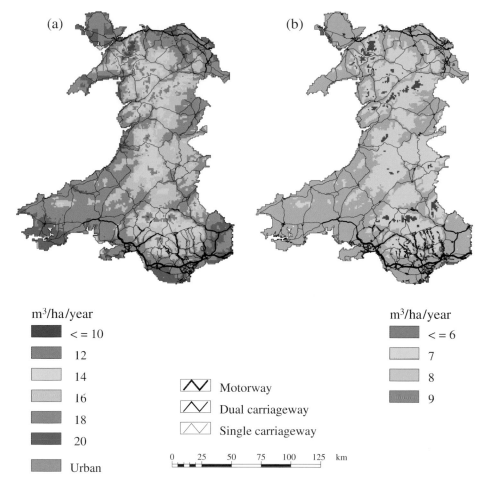

m³/ha/year

■ <= 10
■ 12
■ 14
■ 16
■ 18
■ 20
■ Urban

⊿ Motorway
⊿ Dual carriageway
⊿ Single carriageway

0   25   50   75   100   125   km

m³/ha/year

■ <= 6
■ 7
■ 8
■ 9

Plate 1. Predicted timber yield class (YC): (a) Sitka spruce; (b) beech.

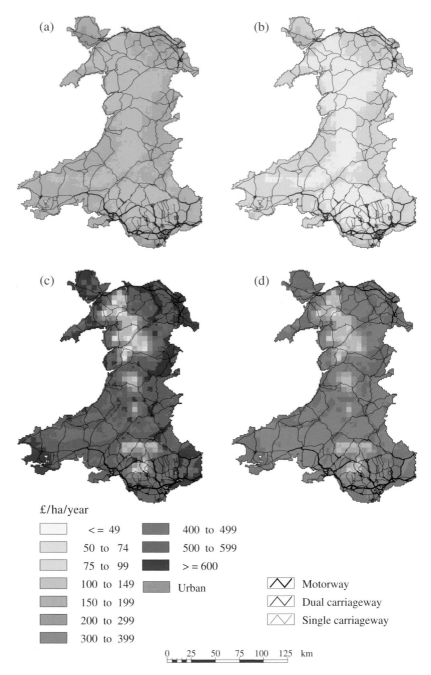

£/ha/year

☐	<= 49	
☐	50 to 74	
☐	75 to 99	
☐	100 to 149	
☐	150 to 199	
☐	200 to 299	
☐	300 to 399	

☐	400 to 499
☐	500 to 599
☐	>= 600
☐	Urban

Motorway
Dual carriageway
Single carriageway

0   25   50   75   100   125   km

Plate 2. (a) Predicted farm-gate income for sheep farms; (b) Predicted shadow value for sheep farms; (c) Predicted farm-gate income for milk farms; (d) Predicted shadow value for milk farms.

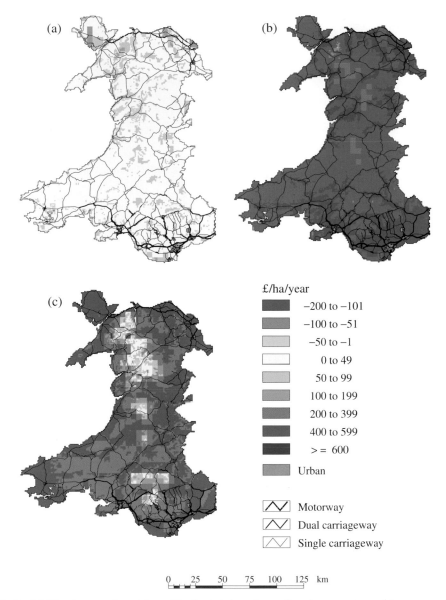

£/ha/year
- −200 to −101
- −100 to −51
- −50 to −1
- 0 to 49
- 50 to 99
- 100 to 199
- 200 to 399
- 400 to 599
- >= 600
- Urban

Motorway
Dual carriageway
Single carriageway

0   25   50   75   100   125   km

Plate 3. (a) The farm-gate net benefit of retaining sheep farming as opposed to conversion to conifer woodland (defined as timber plus grants only, i.e. present situation): 6% discount rate; (b) The social net benefit of retaining sheep farming as opposed to conversion to conifer woodland (defined as timber, carbon storage and recreation, the latter measured using contingent valuation): 6% discount rate; (c) The farm-gate net benefit of retaining milk farming as opposed to conversion to conifer woodland (defined as timber plus grants only, i.e. present situation): 6% discount rate.

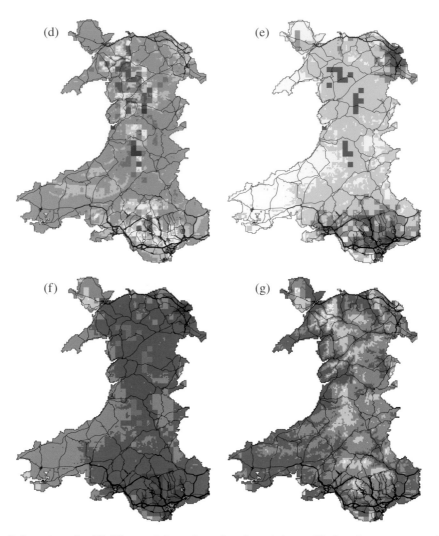

Plate 3 (*continued*). (d) The social net benefit of retaining milk farming as opposed to conversion to conifer woodland (defined as timber, carbon storage and recreation, the latter measured using contingent valuation): 6% discount rate; (e) The farm-gate net benefit value of retaining sheep farming as opposed to conversion to broadleaf woodland (defined as timber, carbon storage and recreation, the latter valued using the ITC measure): 6% discount rate; (f) The social net benefit of retaining sheep farming as opposed to conversion to broadleaf woodland (defined as timber, carbon storage and recreation, the latter valued using the ITC measure): 6% discount rate; (g) The farm-gate net benefit of retaining sheep farming as opposed to conversion to conifer woodland (defined as timber plus grants only, i.e. present situation): 3% discount rate.

Turning to consider social values, it is perhaps most valid to define woodland value using the full range of benefits considered in this study. Using this measure we can see that woodland substantially outperforms sheep farming (Plate 3b) but is itself consistently outperformed by dairying (Plate 3d) in lowland areas. Therefore, in a scenario of full agricultural liberalisation and with farmers being paid for positive externalities we would expect no conversions from dairying but complete conversion from sheep farming, primarily into milk (if all policy restrictions had been lifted) with woodland as a possible second choice.[10] However, such a result ignores the impacts upon milk price of such a supply expansion and given the very strong likelihood of entry restrictions remaining upon the milk market we believe that this does not invalidate analysis of the social benefits of potential conversions from sheep farming to woodland in lowland areas.

In the uplands the social value of woodland exceeds that of sheep farming in all but peat soil regions, with net benefits of conversion generally in the range of £100 to £200 per hectare. For dairy farming the picture is again less clear with about the same area converting as not. In the former, the net benefits of conversion generally range up to about £100/ha with only a few areas exceeding this. Consequently, assuming no entry barriers or requirement for risk premiums, we would expect all sheep farms to convert, with approximately the same number turning to woodland as to milk farming. Given the improbable nature of such assumptions we do not foresee movement from sheep to milk production, so this implies that all conversion would be towards woodland. The one exception throughout is the peat soil regions, where afforestation is never justified on social grounds.

Results for the 6 per cent discount rate: summary

Looking back across the full range of analyses conducted using the 6 per cent discount rate we can see that an economic case can be made for conversion from sheep farming, particularly in lowland areas with high population accessibility, but that under the subsidy schemes available in our study period such conversion was not financially attractive to the farmer. (The intervening years have changed little here, with subsidies still not being available for most of the non-market benefits of woodland.) Considering the choice of species, conifer woodlands generally seem to be a more viable option for conversion than broadleaves. However, in the following chapter we discuss omissions from this analysis (e.g. acidification impacts and biodiversity effects) which are generally favourable to broadleaf trees and militate against certain coniferous species. Given this, it is interesting to note that our analysis of broadleaf values indicates that, using the wider definition of benefits, conversions from sheep farming usually generate net benefits.

---

[10] As noted in Chapters 1 and 5, this is only a partial CBA; we were not able to consider all possible opportunity costs – a characteristic failing of many practical CBA applications.

Table 9.4. *Distribution of the net benefits of retaining milk farming in Wales as opposed to conversion to broadleaf (beech) woodland.*[1] *6% discount rate*

Lower limit (£/ha/yr, 1990)	Upper limit (£/ha/yr, 1990)	Farm-gate values				Social values			
		timber only (1)	timber+ carbon (2)	timber+carbon+ recreation (CVM) (3)	timber+carbon+ recreation (ITCM) (4)	timber only (5)	timber+ carbon (6)	timber+carbon+ recreation (CVM) (7)	timber+carbon+ recreation (ITCM) (8)
−225.00	−200.01				16				
−200.00	−175.01		3	17	20				
−175.00	−150.01		17	15	26				
−150.00	−125.01		14	35	100				25
−125.00	−100.01	11	49	100	118			21	74
−100.00	−75.01	20	81	156	188		31	44	148
−75.00	−50.01	19	187	146	186		61	181	203
−50.00	−25.01	79	136	270	295	11	192	288	371
−25.00	−0.01	174	283	335	326	27	309	440	520
0.00	24.99	158	455	253	179	118	608	415	358
25.00	49.99	293	146	175	117	304	268	224	419
50.00	74.99	489	151	78	129	518	191	254	452
75.00	99.99	346	103	160	149	648	247	255	649
100.00	124.99	154	130	148	178	216	233	418	769
125.00	149.99	100	153	133	203	233	250	628	923
150.00	174.99	148	142	138	249	255	376	889	1,675
175.00	199.99	140	125	156	364	230	838	1,987	2,995
200.00	224.99	150	140	289	404	340	1,638	3,120	3,558
225.00	249.99	157	203	296	458	465	2,934	4,164	3,341
250.00	274.99	128	237	385	601	1,283	4,699	3,956	2,465
275.00	299.99	183	329	702	1,274	1,910	4,236	2,349	959
300.00	324.99	255	758	1,079	1,402	3,843	2,386	342	152
325.00	349.99	239	964	1,350	2,026	4,449	473	96	17

350.00	374.99	446	1,172	2,142	2,353	3,908	103	3	1
375.00	399.99	931	1,947	2,492	2,472	1,471	1	4	25
400.00	424.99	1,011	2,671	2,800	2,238	297	18	33	49
425.00	449.99	1,483	2,903	2,583	2,250	37	32	96	119
450.00	474.99	2,286	2,708	2,157	1,234		131	128	83
475.00	499.99	2,740	2,213	1,257	583		95	18	6
500.00	524.99	2,564	1,231	344	121		7	21	18
525.00	549.99	2,568	424	144	104		17	3	13
550.00	574.99	1,807	216	35	9		11	22	34
575.00	599.99	1,003	80	4	7		25	26	7
600.00	624.99	328	8	11	13		38	24	21
625.00	649.99	116	9	14	24		1		
650.00	674.99	36	21	20	9		2	4	31
675.00	699.99	1	16	8	24		24	41	19
700.00	724.99		24	22	24		24	5	8
725.00	749.99						25	38	56
750.00	774.99						38	26	
775.00	799.99		2	2	4		1		
800.00	824.99		2	24	28				
825.00	849.99		25	18	18				
850.00	874.99		21	6					
875.00	899.99				10				
900.00	924.99		25	25	28				
925.00	949.99		13	25	26				
950.00	974.99		25	14					
975.00	999.99		1						

Notes: [1] Negative sums indicate areas where woodland values exceed agricultural values. Blank cells indicate that no 1 km cells fall into this category. There are 20, 563 1 km cells.

Table 9.5. *Distribution of the net benefits of retaining sheep farming in Wales as opposed to conversion to conifer (Sitka spruce) woodland.[1] 3% discount rate*

Lower limit (£/ha/yr, 1990)	Upper limit (£/ha/yr, 1990)	Farm-gate values				Social values			
		timber only (1)	timber+ carbon (2)	timber+carbon+ recreation (CVM) (3)	timber+carbon+ recreation (ITCM) (4)	timber only (5)	timber+ carbon (6)	timber+carbon+ recreation (CVM) (7)	timber+carbon+ recreation (ITCM) (8)
−575.00	−550.01								29
−550.00	−525.01								128
−525.00	−500.01								73
−500.00	−475.01				9				199
−475.00	−450.01				37				217
−450.00	−425.01				125			61	378
−425.00	−400.01				116			155	803
−400.00	−375.01				169			321	1,170
−375.00	−350.01				234			992	1,823
−350.00	−325.01			93	478		37	2,725	4,216
−325.00	−300.01			200	912		2,963	5,814	5,056
−300.00	−275.01			359	1,233		6,962	4,959	2,954
−275.00	−250.01			1,263	2,170	3	5,092	2,653	1,612
−250.00	−225.01		246	3,435	4,326	839	2,865	1,475	934
−225.00	−200.01		3,998	5,464	4,565	7,486	1,518	601	288
−200.00	−175.01		6,549	5,304	2,721	6,505	412	217	126
−175.00	−150.01	18	4,452	2,455	1,532	3,570	156	58	37
−150.00	−125.01	2,024	2,568	1,487	907	1,689	36	21	21
−125.00	−100.01	7,549	1,499	676	361	352	17	15	8
−100.00	−75.01	5,610	554	238	113	82	13	6	2
−75.00	−50.01	3,032	141	60	36	20	2	1	

−50.00	−25.01	1,671	34	18	20	14	1		16
−25.00	−0.01	526	16	15	8	3	14	18	10
0.00	24.99	98	14	6	1		7	26	70
25.00	49.99	17	2	1	4		51	109	143
50.00	74.99	15	1	10	13		169	199	194
75.00	99.99	3	16	8	10		207	122	51
100.00	124.99		5	29	74		36	13	5
125.00	149.99		53	106	146		5	2	
150.00	174.99		167	196	181				
175.00	199.99		194	124	56				
200.00	224.99		48	13	6				
225.00	249.99		6	3					
250.00	274.99								
275.00	299.99								
300.00	324.99								

Notes: [1] Negative sums indicate areas where woodland values exceed agricultural values. Blank cells indicate that no 1 km cells fall into this category. There are 20,563 1 km cells.

Our analysis of milk farms suggests that, in general, there is not a strong economic case for conversions from this sector to either conifer or broadleaf woodland. One further interesting difference here is the result that if any such conversions were justified these would be in upland (but non-peat) areas. This seems mainly attributable to a rapid fall-off in milk values as we reach the upland extremes of the Welsh environment. However, we again remind ourselves of the relative scarcity of milk farms in such environments.

Having analysed the effects of changing tree species we now consider the effect of changing discount rates. Given our discussions in Chapter 5 and above, any increase in rates seems unrealistic (and will almost inevitably rule out any possibility of conversion), so a reduction seems more interesting.

Results for the 3 per cent discount rate

A 3 per cent discount rate is worth considering for two reasons: first, it more closely approximates what we believe to be the rate used by sheep farmers for everyday decision-making; secondly, it is closer to the social discount rates recently proposed by many commentators and currently being considered by H. M. Treasury. The 3 per cent rate thus has applicability to the sheep farm-gate results and to both the sheep and milk farm social value analyses.

Conversion from agriculture to conifer woodland

Sheep farms

Table 9.5 reports results from the analysis of conversions from sheep to conifer using a 3 per cent discount rate. Considering column (1) we can see that lowering the discount rate to 3 per cent makes conversion from sheep into woodland beneficial for almost all farmers even when we only consider timber values and the availability of grants and subsidies during our study period; Plate 3g presents the corresponding map of values. Given that this scenario represents the available returns to farmers, why does such a rate of conversion not occur? The answer, as before, is most likely to be related to a risk premium. A farmer's risk premium can either be modelled as a higher required discount rate (as discussed earlier in this chapter) or, at existing discount rates, as a requirement that unfamiliar goods, such as those provided by forests, provide a substantially higher income than does conventional production (our discussion of Table 9.2 is relevant here). As before, net savings on subsidies mean that social values of conversion under this scenario (column (5)) are substantially above farm-gate values; indeed, using this analysis, all Welsh sheep farms should be converted to woodland. Given that we are here ignoring all non-timber benefits, this is a powerful result.

For both farm-gate and social value analyses the addition of carbon sequestration values again produces a bimodal distribution, with the majority of cells now more strongly benefiting from conversion to woodland (columns (2) and (5)). The further addition of recreation values reinforces this result.

Milk farms

Table 9.6 repeats the above analysis but now considers conversion from milk farms. Given the discussion presented in Chapter 5, the 3 per cent discount rate is not especially relevant to farm-gate analyses of milk farm conversions. However, that same chapter shows that such a rate is, arguably, relevant to social values (although it is currently being considered by the UK government for such purposes). Examining the social values block we can see that it is only when carbon sequestration values are included that significant conversions are justified. Here about 18 per cent of cells generate net social benefits from conversion, a proportion which rises substantially when lower-bound (most appropriate for conifers) CV-based recreation values are added, although substitution effects mean that this has to be a significant overstatement of conversion viability. Examination of the maps underpinning these results confirmed that it is high population, high accessibility, lowland areas which generate the largest net benefits from conversion.

Conversion from agriculture to broadleaf woodland

Sheep farms

As before we now hold the discount rate constant (at 3 per cent) and consider the impact of conversions to our representative broadleaf tree species, beech. Table 9.7 shows results for sheep farms. Considering first the farm-gate values, the contrast between our 3 per cent discount rate analyses of conversions from sheep to conifers as opposed to broadleaves is very marked. Whereas present timber values and related grants were sufficient to generate net farm-gate benefits from conversion in the former instance (Table 9.5, column (1)), for the latter such conversion fails to pass the cost-benefit test (Table 9.7, column (1)). Given that grants for broadleaf trees exceed those for conifers, this result seems to be due to the longer rotations, and hence delay to felling benefits, typical of broadleaves.

Addition of carbon sequestration benefits makes conversion of just over 10 per cent of cells apparently profitable from a farm-gate perspective (column (2) of Table 9.7). However, the likelihood of farmers requiring a risk premium means that in reality we would not expect conversions to occur until recreation benefits are also paid. Even if, as argued previously, higher rate recreation values can be justified for broadleaf woodlands, then such a premium means that relatively high increases in subsidies would be required to generate attractive levels of farm-gate income.

Table 9.6. *Distribution of the net benefits of retaining milk farming in Wales as opposed to conversion to conifer (Sitka spruce) woodland.*[1] *3% discount rate*

Lower limit (£/ha/yr, 1990)	Upper limit (£/ha/yr, 1990)	Farm-gate values				Social values			
		timber only (1)	timber+carbon (2)	timber+carbon+recreation (CVM) (3)	timber+carbon+recreation (ITCM) (4)	timber only (5)	timber+carbon (6)	timber+carbon+recreation (CVM) (7)	timber+carbon+recreation (ITCM) (8)
−375.00	−350.01				4				
−350.00	−325.01		2	10	38				
−325.00	−300.01		14	37	52				5
−300.00	−275.01		36	50	68		2	12	33
−275.00	−250.01	2	55	68	95		15	23	117
−250.00	−225.01	17	70	91	144		27	83	118
−225.00	−200.01	34	96	176	180		83	134	236
−200.00	−175.01	63	193	192	178	10	142	218	452
−175.00	−150.01	78	185	188	197	36	243	285	464
−150.00	−125.01	132	204	206	230	90	285	286	722
−125.00	−100.01	209	226	258	296	165	325	475	890
−100.00	−75.01	234	278	252	253	311	395	614	1,085
−75.00	−50.01	303	219	182	255	357	398	1,003	1,393
−50.00	−25.01	324	180	179	274	451	513	1,592	2,423
−25.00	−0.01	309	164	175	427	450	1,330	2,975	3,503
0.00	24.99	191	154	260	527	358	2,934	4,134	3,924
25.00	49.99	180	198	408	608	481	4,981	4,419	2,846
50.00	74.99	165	252	498	853	1,129	4,462	2,250	1,029
75.00	99.99	159	502	937	1,388	2,023	2,350	905	426
100.00	124.99	191	881	1,261	1,862	4,699	932	385	271
125.00	149.99	245	1,031	1,835	2,445	5,083	447	241	182
150.00	174.99	416	1,677	2,803	2,572	3,050	246	165	136
175.00	199.99	788	2,922	3,104	2,851	1,167	139	109	78

200.00 224.99	1,030	3,386	3,071	2,253	435	85	45	31
225.00 249.99	1,276	3,123	2,098	1,389	189	29	28	27
250.00 274.99	2,548	2,164	1,218	471	57	26	18	21
275.00 299.99	3,220	1,156	450	243	15	19	23	15
300.00 324.99	3,316	616	198	126	7	19	14	19
325.00 349.99	2,440	246	107	72		24	29	23
350.00 374.99	1,501	104	58	40		16	10	16
375.00 399.99	746	51	29	24		19	22	28
400.00 424.99	254	32	34	31		26	26	19
425.00 449.99	125	29	15	4		22	25	22
450.00 474.99	31	6	4	2		20	15	9
475.00 499.99	22			4		9		
500.00 524.99	13	3	10	22				
525.00 549.99	1	34	45	35				
550.00 574.99		23	6					
575.00 599.99		2	10	13				
600.00 624.99		15	20	25				
625.00 649.99		22	11	12				
650.00 674.99		12	9					
675.00 699.99								

Notes: [1] Negative sums indicate areas where woodland values exceed agricultural values. Blank cells indicate that no 1 km cells fall into this category. There are 20,563 1 km cells.

Table 9.7. *Distribution of the net benefits of retaining sheep farming in Wales as opposed to conversion to broadleaf (beech) woodland:*[1] *3% discount rate*

Lower limit (£/ha/yr, 1990)	Upper limit (£/ha/yr, 1990)	Farm-gate values				Social values			
		timber only (1)	timber+carbon (2)	timber+carbon+recreation (CVM) (3)	timber+carbon+recreation (ITCM) (4)	timber only (5)	timber+carbon (6)	timber+carbon+recreation (CVM) (7)	timber+carbon+recreation (ITCM) (8)
−400.00	−375.01								
−375.00	−350.01								25
−350.00	−325.01								14
−325.00	−300.01								178
−300.00	−275.01								102
−275.00	−250.01				25				308
−250.00	−225.01				61			1	364
−225.00	−200.01				158			102	709
−200.00	−175.01				141			334	1,047
−175.00	−150.01				260			740	1,962
−150.00	−125.01			19	397		24	2,826	5,691
−125.00	−100.01			165	795		2,492	7,718	7,189
−100.00	−75.01			350	1,222		9,828	7,432	2,089
−75.00	−50.01			897	2,181	362	6,691	619	287
−50.00	−25.01		42	3,284	6,196	6,512	740	205	92
−25.00	−0.01		2,967	8,853	6,668	10,498	231	97	17

0.00	24.99		11,859	5,629	1,533	2,565	68		
25.00	49.99	567	4,288	462	182	405			
50.00	74.99	7,413	398	175	156	220			
75.00	99.99	10,549	259	140	11	1			
100.00	124.99	1,336	92	81	88				
125.00	149.99	231	169	19					
150.00	174.99	257					12	194	68
175.00	199.99	135					395	279	331
200.00	224.99	75					82	16	90
225.00	249.99			1	71				
250.00	274.99		16	198	319				
275.00	299.99		378	270	97				
300.00	324.99		95	20	2				

Notes: [1] Negative sums indicate areas where woodland values exceed agricultural values. Blank cells indicate that no 1 km cells fall into this category. There are 20,563 1 km cells.

Table 9.8. *Distribution of the net benefits of retaining milk farming in Wales as opposed to conversion to broadleaf (beech) woodland:*[1] *3% discount rate*

Lower limit (£/ha/yr, 1990)	Upper limit (£/ha/yr, 1990)	Farm-gate values				Social values			
		timber only (1)	timber+carbon (2)	timber+carbon+recreation (CVM) (3)	timber+carbon+recreation (ITCM) (4)	timber only (5)	timber+carbon (6)	timber+carbon+recreation (CVM) (7)	timber+carbon+recreation (ITCM) (8)
−300.00	−275.01								
−275.00	−250.01								
−250.00	−225.01				8				
−225.00	−200.01			11	15				
−200.00	−175.01		11	18	21				
−175.00	−150.01		20	18	61				9
−150.00	−125.01	3	22	63	114			11	44
−125.00	−100.01	20	69	113	136		14	27	106
−100.00	−75.01	11	124	147	179		32	106	158
−75.00	−50.01	55	156	192	217	3	111	203	278
−50.00	−25.01	91	214	266	306	28	235	344	413
−25.00	−0.01	204	273	379	266	64	371	433	460
0.00	24.99	174	395	175	174	216	528	359	471
25.00	49.99	345	143	155	130	362	238	231	436
50.00	74.99	543	118	92	159	710	255	258	488
75.00	99.99	202	121	191	144	357	228	343	809
100.00	124.99	151	159	128	205	213	230	552	822
125.00	149.99	113	146	126	201	253	309	754	1,375
150.00	174.99	153	129	150	349	248	566	1,457	2,428
175.00	199.99	145	148	259	412	292	1,396	2,619	3,388
200.00	224.99	142	205	320	532	401	2,128	4,117	3,564
225.00	249.99	145	236	360	561	926	4,374	4,160	3,295

250.00	274.99	161	325	643	959	1,649	4,986	3,258	1,436
275.00	299.99	209	687	981	1,506	3,204	3,272	954	322
300.00	324.99	270	962	1,262	1,789	4,722	916	130	44
325.00	349.99	355	1,014	1,843	2,212	4,259	156	56	28
350.00	374.99	796	1,601	2,392	2,546	2,189	29	8	20
375.00	399.99	949	2,495	2,847	2,267	377	13	20	27
400.00	424.99	1,214	2,947	2,521	2,360	89	26	25	9
425.00	449.99	2,031	2,786	2,455	1,520	1	25	24	19
450.00	474.99	2,686	2,310	1,576	817		11		3
475.00	499.99	2,836	1,680	543	150		2	4	40
500.00	524.99	2,710	614	117	95		27	43	7
525.00	549.99	2,055	209	91	35		21	3	10
550.00	574.99	1,155	117	13	3		20	52	54
575.00	599.99	399	12	2	1		44	12	
600.00	624.99	175	3	3	3				
625.00	649.99	62	2	24	36				
650.00	674.99	3	26	18	10				
675.00	699.99		20	5	0				
700.00	724.99		0	1	11				
725.00	749.99		20	30	27				
750.00	774.99		18	33	26				
775.00	799.99		26						

Notes: [1] Negative sums indicate areas where woodland values exceed agricultural values.
Blank cells indicate that no 1 km cells fall into this category. There are 20,563 1 km cells.

Turning to consider social values, and remembering that sustainability criteria may justify use of the 3 per cent rate here, we can see that even if we only consider timber benefits a large majority (84 per cent) of cells would pass a cost-benefit test of conversion. Addition of carbon benefits indicates that almost the only cells that would not pass such a test are those located on peat soils. Further addition of recreation benefits merely reinforces this result.

Milk farms

Table 9.8 summarises results for a conversion from milk production to broadleaf woodland under a 3 per cent discount rate. Consideration of the farm-gate values detailed here has to be tempered by the knowledge that a 3 per cent rate is lower than that we would expect milk farmers to use for everyday decision-making (and that a risk-weighted rate would be even higher than this). Even so, Table 9.8 indicates that the long delays associated with broadleaves mean that farm-gate values do not justify anything but the most minor conversions even when all benefits are paid. The situation with social values is very similar, with little conversion out of milk being justified.

Other discount rates

Given the above discussions and comparisons with observed rates of conversion, it seems likely that farmers are attaching significant risk premiums to any decision to convert to woodland, an observation made elsewhere regarding other non-standard production (Cobb, 1993). This can be modelled either as a required surplus of net benefits or as an inflated discount rate. Given this, consideration of further reductions in discount rate does not appear to be justified.[11]

CBA summary and the present situation

CBA summary

Inspecting the analyses presented in this chapter we feel that the link between our value estimates calculated at a 6 per cent discount rate, the wider case for using such a rate and the rates of conversion observed in reality is compelling. Furthermore, the fact that this is also the UK government's current discount rate for socially beneficial projects makes the analyses reported in Tables 9.1 to 9.4 of particular interest.

Considering results for a 6 per cent discount rate and taking conifer woodlands first, we found (Table 9.1) that for sheep farmers the level of grants and subsidies

---

[11] Analyses of lower discount rate scenarios were undertaken. These merely extended the trends observed when we moved from a 6 per cent to a 3 per cent discount rate.

paid during our study period was insufficient to justify conversion, a situation which seems unlikely to have changed up to the present day. However, increasing these transfers in line with the wider definition of external woodland benefits would substantially shift the balance of farm-gate values in favour of conversion. Furthermore, our analysis suggests that relatively modest increases in woodland subsidy could result in significant rates of uptake among Welsh sheep farmers. Interestingly, our analysis of social values shows that these are already strongly in favour of conversion and that the increase in subsidies outlined above could generate very substantial net social benefits. However, turning to consider milk farms, Table 9.2 suggests that neither farm-gate nor social values justify substantial transfers out of this sector and into conifer woodlands.

When we consider potential conversions to broadleaf woodlands, Table 9.3 shows that, relative to conifers (Table 9.1), the longer rotation periods mean that the 6 per cent discount rate militates heavily against conversion from sheep farming, although this is still generally justified if all the non-market benefits of woodland are appraised or we shift from farm-gate to social value assessments. However, Table 9.4 shows that with a 6 per cent discount rate conversions from milk farming to broadleaf woodland are not generally justified.

Shifting to a 3 per cent discount rate considerably increases the benefits of woodland and so strengthens the case for conversion from sheep farming. However, while such a rate may theoretically be justified for the calculation of social net benefits, it is not in line with present government policy and does not seem to reflect sheep farmers' attitudes towards this type of conversion. Furthermore, this switch does not fundamentally alter the position with regard to farm-gate values on milk farms although some positive net social benefits may be derived from conversion if a wide definition of woodland benefits is employed. Such a low discount rate may not be valid for assessment of farm-gate values on milk farms.

Clearly, if conversions are to occur, then both farm-gate and social valuations indicate that these will be most readily derived from the sheep farm sector. In reality, decision-makers are likely to be faced with only limited resources to effect such conversions. In such situations our methodology is particularly suited to the identification of optimal sites for conversion onto which subsidies can be targeted. Plate 3f provides a useful illustration of this capacity, showing how we can target sites according to the net social benefits created by conversion.

Our results also reveal an interesting dichotomy between economic analysis and policy practice. We have shown that highly populated, readily accessible, lowland areas provide the optimal location for conversions out of agriculture and into woodland. Such sites combine high rates of tree growth with high recreational demand. However, it is only in recent years, with the advent of the Community Woodland Scheme and similar schemes, that policy has begun to recognise the strength of this argument.[12] The legacy of virtually all preceding policies has been a concentration of woodlands in upland areas, inaccessible to the majority of the population. Figure 9.1 illustrates the present locations of Forestry Commission conifer woodlands in Wales (superimposed upon an elevation map). Comparison with our maps of optimal conversion areas reveals the disparity between those areas and the actual locations of the current woodland stock. The overall message of our analysis is clear: extended economic analysis of both the internal and external net benefits of conversion shows considerable justification for bringing forestry down the hill.

The present situation

Finally, we can consider the extent to which the findings presented in this chapter need to be modified by events which have occurred since our 1990 study period. First, let us consider the timber, carbon-fixing and recreation values which dominate our analysis of woodland.

The analysis of timber values presented in Chapter 5 considered a variety of studies examining possible trends within real timber prices. Arguments can be put forward in favour of both increases and decreases in real prices. However, the weight of long-term analysis currently suggests that neither viewpoint can be adequately established and that an assumption of constant real prices is less prone to error than either of the alternatives. Such a view is reinforced by recent government policy papers describing an expanding and vibrant forest estate and industry. This target can only be achieved, in the absence of new planting by the Forestry Commission, by maintaining the real value of woodland grants and subsidies, which form a substantial portion of the discounted income received by forest-owners. Similarly, as noted in Chapter 7, the increasingly pessimistic predictions of the IPCC and other experts regarding the apparent acceleration in climate change suggests that carbon sequestration values will be at least non-declining and arguably may increase in real terms over time. Such assumptions seem well founded given the recent US exit from the Kyoto Climate Change Convention on reductions in greenhouse gas emissions.

Considering the real value of open-access woodland recreation, in our conclusions to Chapter 3 we presented results suggesting that such values were non-declining and may even be rising slowly over time. Models of economic development suggest that such results are to be expected as economic growth leads to increasing demand for leisure activities. Although studies of changing work patterns can challenge the assumption that growth necessarily leads to increased voluntary

---

[12] Interestingly it may well be a non-governmental organisation, the Woodland Trust, which plays a significant role in future forest development, funded in part by a grant of over £6 million from the Millennium Fund (Smith, 1996).

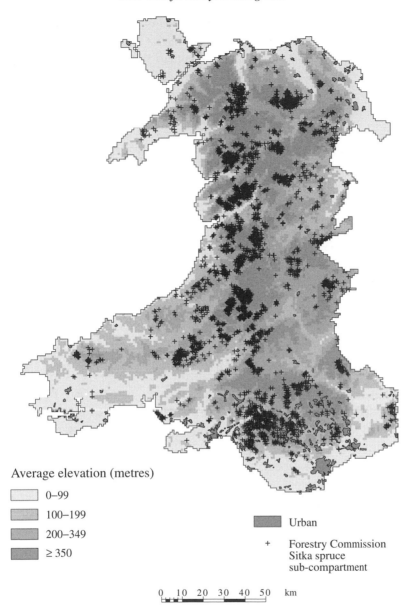

Figure 9.1. Location of Forestry Commission sub-compartments of Sitka spruce in Wales (superimposed upon elevation).

leisure time, increased affluence should raise the unit value of recreation services especially for environmental quality goods such as woodland recreation. Again, assumptions of non-declining values appear justified.

Overall, therefore, our assumptions of constant real values for the timber, carbon sequestration and recreational benefits of woodland seem reasonable and may even turn out to be conservative. Note, however, that from a farm-gate perspective only timber and related subsidies provide direct income streams to the prospective farm forester and therefore the gulf between the market and social value of woodland seems set to persist for the foreseeable future.

Turning to consider the opportunity cost of agriculture, the 1990s have been, with the exception of a few good years just before the middle of the decade, a torrid and depressing period for farming both across the UK and within Wales. Although real agricultural prices have fallen significantly over the 1990s this trend does not represent the full extent of impacts upon farm incomes in Wales. Reductions in real subsidy levels have compounded price falls such that incomes have more than halved in all major sectors over the decade. The magnitude of these losses is so large that the next decade will almost certainly see a continuation of the reduction in farm numbers seen over recent years. Those that survive may well benefit from policy measures intended to address the current problem. However, as recognised by the National Assembly for Wales, a return to general levels of profitability based upon traditional agriculture seems a distant prospect in Wales.

Taking these trends together we can see that from a farm-gate perspective the attractiveness of forestry as an alternative to conventional agriculture does seem to have improved over the course of the 1990s, making our findings appear as conservative estimates of the efficiency gains of conversions. However, this does not mean that this change will be sufficient to induce large-scale change in the near future. For the reasons explained in this chapter, farmers may be risk-averse with respect to changing activities and, while woodland may have improved some-what in its financial viability, this may not be sufficient to overcome the perceived security offered by traditional agriculture (although this seems the security of a familiar poverty). However, what the trends of the 1990s do clearly suggest is that the superiority of multipurpose woodland over certain sectors of Welsh agriculture, when viewed from a social values perspective, is likely to have grown over the course of the decade. This means that the economic CBA case is stronger than ever for restructuring transfer payments to reflect the non-market values of woodland and so facilitate land use conversions out of the most inefficient areas of Welsh farming. Given this, our social value findings can justifiably be described as con-servative estimates of the current value of transferring land out of farming and into multipurpose woodland.

10

Conclusions and future directions

Introduction

This research draws upon a series of interrelated studies designed to provide an improved cost-benefit analysis of a proposed conversion of land use out of conventional agriculture and into woodland. The analysis covers a number of diverse questions and is necessarily complex. Consequently a number of conclusions can be drawn. To simplify this process, we first review the achievements of this research before considering, in the subsequent section, the problems of the study and ongoing work. This is followed by our concluding comments.

Summary of research

As reviewed in the opening chapter of this volume, woodland produces a variety of market-priced and non-market benefits and costs. The first phase of this research was concerned with monetary valuation of one of the principal non-market benefits, woodland recreation. Given the open-access nature of this good, which produces no internal return to the land-owner but is of significant social value, we were forced to rely upon non-market valuation methods. Chapter 2 reviewed these methods, highlighting the theoretical appropriateness of both the contingent valuation (CV) and travel cost (TC) techniques. The chapter also provided a theoretical analysis of the values elicited by these methods.

Chapter 3 opened with an appraisal of UK applications of these methods to the valuation of woodland recreation. This review raised a number of interesting issues; for example, studies failed to identify any significant link between recreational values and tree species. We also highlighted a number of problems with prior studies in terms of their methodology, data analysis and reporting. In an effort to identify values which could be transferred to woodlands in our study area, cross-study analyses of both TC and CV estimates were conducted. These yielded separate and significantly different valuation measures for subsequent consideration.

285

Concerns regarding prior applications were in part the motivation behind our own studies of recreation value, also presented in Chapter 3. Here we investigated a number of study design issues, analysing the impact which differing approaches had upon resultant value estimates. While our initial study was somewhat crude, we feel that subsequent studies provided some idea of the potential impact of design effects upon recreation value estimates. More specifically we found that CV estimates varied significantly with issues such as question ordering, the inclusion or exclusion of questions regarding recreational budgets, choice of willingness to pay format, payment vehicle and respondent type. While much of this variation can be interpreted in line with economic theory, this does raise the complex question of which value is the most appropriate for practical purposes. Our research into the TC method found that its valuations were also subject to variation according to the methodology employed. In particular we assessed the impacts of measurement effects, choice of unit values and estimation technique. Variations in estimates were found to be just as wide, or even wider, for the TC as for the CV approach. However, the chapter also presents the first of a series of GIS-based analyses which dominate the latter part of this volume. Here GIS techniques were used to improve the measurement of key variables underpinning the TC method so as to produce more accurate estimates of recreational values.

Chapter 4 opened by considering the equally important question of how many people will visit a specified woodland site. Data from our field studies were used to estimate a visit demand function which, although theoretically simple, exhibited some methodological sophistication and proved reasonably reliable in predicting visits when assessed against a subsample of sites for which actual arrivals were known. Combining this with the various recreational visit values estimated previously, we obtained a range of woodland recreation benefit values. These varied according to the valuation method used and methodological assumptions employed. From these we identified a preferred upper- and lower-bound estimate of recreation value for use in subsequent analyses.

The next three chapters switched the focus of analysis to consider tree growth and its related benefits. Throughout this we considered two species of tree: a representative conifer (Sitka spruce) and a typical broadleaf (beech). Chapter 5 assessed the costs and benefits of planting these species, producing estimates of net present value and its annuity equivalent. This necessitated a study of the appropriate discount rates for the various decision-makers under consideration (farmers and policy-makers). The chapter also provided market and shadow price assessments to facilitate investigation of the value of woodland both to the farmer and to society. This dual assessment was a feature of all subsequent chapters.

Chapter 6 presented GIS-based models of timber yield. Our methodology allowed us to use the Forestry Commission's sub-compartment database, thus permitting a very substantial increase in sample size compared to previous studies. The GIS also allowed us to incorporate data taken from the Soil Survey and Land Research Centre's (SSLRC) LandIS database detailing the environmental characteristics of a site. The high quality and extent of these data facilitated the estimation of yield models which were more robust than those previously reported in the literature. Information from Chapter 5 allowed us to convert these yield estimates into maps of timber value for both our conifer and broadleaf species.

The yield model also provided the basis for our analysis of carbon sequestration in Chapter 7. Forestry Commission models of carbon storage in timber and carbon liberation from its products were combined with information concerning soil carbon flux to produce assessments of the net impact of planting trees upon the carbon cycle. A review of the literature on valuing carbon storage was used to provide a monetary evaluation of the results from this model which, as before, involved analyses for both of our selected tree species.

Chapter 8 shifted attention from woodland to agriculture. The GIS-based models of agricultural value presented utilise farm-level rather than parish or other aggregated data. This methodology permitted the inclusion of the environmental characteristics of individual farms as explanatory variables in the value functions. A cluster analysis was used to identify homogeneous sectors within the farm database and separate modelling exercises were conducted for the two principal sectors – sheep and milk production. Finally a shadow pricing exercise provided comparisons with estimated levels of farm-gate income.

All the preceding analyses were synthesised in Chapter 9 which provided a cost-benefit appraisal of converting land out of the two agricultural sectors considered and into either of the woodland types considered. Net benefits were calculated from both farm-gate and social perspectives. Comparison of predicted values with the actual very low numbers of conversions led us to conclude that sheep farms were using a risk-weighted discount rate of about 6 per cent. While this rate meant that the level of woodland grants and subsidies made conversion unattractive from the farmers' perspective, our analysis showed that conversion from sheep farming to conifer woodland would generate substantial net social benefits which would justify the relatively modest increase in grants and subsidies necessary to induce such conversion. The scope for conversion from sheep production to broadleaf woodland was reduced by the long rotations of such tree species although some conversion was still justified (see the discussion of this issue in the following section). A particularly important finding was that the optimal location for conversion out of sheep farming was not, as in general planting practice, in remote upland areas but, rather, near heavily populated, high accessibility, lowland locations. However, when we turned to consider milk farms we found little economic justification for conversion to either conifer or broadleaf woodland.

Problems, progress and plans

Prior to presenting our final conclusions it is essential that we draw the reader's attention to several problems and omissions in this research and highlight, in mitigation, certain ongoing work addressing some if not all of these problems.

This was a relatively ambitious project covering a wide range of analyses all of which have scope for improvement. One such area is the need for further consideration of the impact of statistical error in a multimodel system. In particular, while actual versus predicted tests were conducted on recreational demand and timber yield estimates, to date such a validation analysis has not been performed for our agricultural models.

A number of issues arise from our analysis of recreation values. One point, which is more of a finding than a criticism, is that our CV and TC studies have raised significant concerns over the impact of study design, implementation and data analysis upon resultant valuation estimates. While this is an interesting research finding it does raise questions regarding the use of such values in our subsequent cost-benefit analysis. We have attempted to address these issues by using upper- and lower-bound estimates in this analysis but feel that this is a less than ideal solution. In summary, more research into the understanding and control of design effects is necessary.

Another valuation issue concerns the limitations of the recreation benefits transfer analysis presented here. While the GIS-based definition of the variables used is reasonably sophisticated, encompassing factors such as population distribution and accessibility, other factors such as site characteristics were omitted. However, in mitigation, our most recent work (overviewed in Chapter 4) shows that these omitted factors do not radically alter the relative distribution recreation values away from that predicted by the simpler models used in this analysis. This suggests that our overall conclusions are not in error here.

A further issue is that, like most studies, the present analysis becomes dated even while it is under construction. This is particularly true of our agricultural model which relies upon data from the early 1990s. In Chapter 8 we reviewed the intervening period from then to the present day, noting that the latter half of the 1990s saw substantial falls in Welsh agricultural incomes. Although, as noted in Chapter 5, timber prices have also fallen during this period the overall effect seems likely to have been either neutral or shifting marginally in favour of timber. Such moves imply that our predictions of the economic potential for land use change out of agriculture and into multipurpose woodland can be defended as conservative estimates of the present-day position.

A final issue we would highlight is that, while our study attempts to significantly extend the analysis of costs and benefits, we have omitted certain items. Of these the more important omissions include sporting revenues (which in some locations may be highly significant; see McGilvray and Perman, 1991), livestock shelter, and externalities such as biodiversity and habitat value (Jenkins, 1984, 1986; Good, 1987; Good *et al.*, 1991; Peterken, 1993; Garrod and Willis, 1994; Woodhouse *et al.*, 2000; Cowling and Heijnis, 2001), acidification impacts and landscape amenity effects (Campbell and Fairley, 1991; Dillman and Bergstrom, 1991; Lavers and Haines-Young, 1993; Fleischer and Tsur, 2000). Some have argued that values associated with the benefit streams issues, such as biodiversity and habitat values, may be better incorporated into decision-making by attempting to harmonise CBA with non-economic appraisal systems such as multicriteria analysis (MCA) and some commentators have attempted to bring these approaches together (Turner *et al.*, 2000). We have not attempted such a harmonisation of appraisal approaches, partly because of time constraints, but principally because of the present lack of a consistent theoretical framework for such analyses.

Many of the concerns raised above are already the subject of ongoing research. Considering those externalities which are omitted from our analysis to date, one area of ongoing work is the assessment of landscape amenity. Funding from various authorities[1] has supported the development of a GIS-based hedonic pricing (HP) model of such values. The viewshed calculation capabilities of a GIS (which allow the analyst to measure the extent and type of view observed from any given point taking into account the natural terrain and man-made visual intrusions and obstacles) make it the ideal tool for compiling map databases of an area, thus obviating the need to rely on the crude distance-based measures typical of most HP models of landscape amenity. This work is now well advanced (see Lake *et al.*, 1998, 2000a,b; Bateman *et al.*, 2001a) and seems promising. A related development has been the increasing scope for creating realistic 3D visualisations of landscapes from GIS databases. Our initial research (Lovett *et al.*, 2001; Appleton *et al.*, 2002) leads us to believe that such techniques would be highly appropriate for enhancing contingent valuation, conjoint analysis and other expressed preference valuation techniques so that they might be more readily applied to the valuation of future and planned landscapes.

A further area of ongoing research examines the biodiversity and habitat values of woodland, and the implications for these values of implementing the optimal policy changes implied by the present study. This work combines our various datasets with those from the British Trust for Ornithology (BTO) to use certain bird species as flags for the wider biodiversity implications of policy change. This research is still under development but initial results (Bateman *et al.*, 1997c; Woodhouse *et al.*, 2000; Dolman *et al.*, 2001) and other papers using GIS techniques (Gurnell *et al.*,

---

[1] Including the Economic and Social Research Council (ESRC), Commission for the European Community (CEC), Ordnance Survey and the Scottish Executive.

1996; Swetnam *et al.*, 1998) suggest that this will provide a powerful tool for identifying the wider effects of the decision on which tree species to use in conversion schemes. Our findings confirm the expected superiority of broadleaves over conifers as providers of desirable biodiversity outcomes, a factor which has the potential to reverse the apparent economic superiority of softwoods over hardwoods observed in Chapter 9. As discussed in Chapter 8, an important complicating factor here is that recent decreases in agricultural incomes have been accompanied by an increase in stocking densities and consequent overgrazing and ecological damage across many areas of Wales. However, as noted previously, such trends will only serve to enhance the net benefits of conversion from conventional agriculture into multipurpose forestry, thus tending to make the results presented here appear somewhat conservative.

One area in which we have to date achieved little more than a review of the literature (Bateman, 1992) is the incorporation of the acidification effects of woodlands, particularly those composed of conifers. Here, while some evidence is contradictory, the general consensus is that conifers can cause acidification damage to watersheds. There is considerable scope for addressing this issue. First, the literature is extensive, particularly with reference to Wales (see, for example, the numerous papers contained in Edwards *et al.*, 1990). Second, there is a burgeoning literature concerning the valuation of acidification impacts.[2] Finally, a number of previous studies have shown that a GIS provides the ideal tool for catchment analysis (see, for example, Adams *et al.*, 1995). This should make the future analysis of acidification impacts reasonably tractable.

Conclusions

As discussed earlier this research has addressed a number of objectives. However, we choose to emphasise two general points as its principal features, one methodological, the other empirical.

Principal methodological feature

The principal methodological achievement of this research is, we believe, the improved incorporation of spatial and environmental variables into a variety of economic models through the medium of GIS. This enhances the researcher's ability to model spatial complexity within a variety of economic analyses (Lovett and Bateman, 2001).

---

[2] This includes two large ongoing studies, one led by Alan Krupnick at Resources For the Future (RFF) in Washington, D.C., the other conducted by the authors and others at CSERGE, UEA, as part of the CEC EMERGE project.

A number of examples of this methodology are presented here. For example, the GIS is employed to incorporate road infrastructure characteristics and the distribution of population in our model of woodland recreation demand. The software is also used to manipulate and integrate environmental data into our analysis of agricultural values. Similarly, the GIS provides an ideal medium for combining a variety of diverse data which had not previously been linked, such as the integration of SSLRC LandIS and Forestry Commission sub-compartment databases in our analysis of timber yields. A further feature of this methodology is that the resultant maps provide easily interpretable results which can readily be used by decision-makers to analyse the impact of policy changes, and they also provide information on the most appropriate sites for targeting policy initiatives.

The flexibility and analytical power of a GIS makes it, we feel, the ideal tool for incorporating and analysing the spatial complexity which is such an important part of the real world but is often so conspicuously absent from many economic analyses.

Principal empirical feature

This research presents a cost-benefit analysis of the agriculture/forestry trade-off in one large area of the UK. The results of this analysis have, we feel, important consequences for future policy. Accepting the caveats set out above, we feel that the research has highlighted the potential for generating substantial net social benefits by converting some sheep farms to multipurpose woodland. Furthermore, the identification of optimum conversion sites, facilitated by the methodological advances discussed above, indicates that planting policy to date has been diametrically opposed to that which is required to maximise economic benefits in that it has been concentrated in remote upland areas rather than accessible lowland locations. However, our analysis has also shown that levels of woodland grant and subsidy are insufficient to induce conversion (a result which reflects real-world observations). Nevertheless, our results indicate that only modest increases in these grants and subsidies would be necessary to create the financial incentive for land use conversion and thereby release the economic net benefits arising from such change.

In essence, our analysis has highlighted the marked difference between the market appraisal of the status quo and its social value. By including externalities in our analysis we have shown that the situation is one of poorly targeted government intervention leading to market failure, a situation which can readily be remedied by linking transfer payments to the total economic value of goods rather than to their market price.

Finally, while we recognise that the research presented in this volume is not fully comprehensive with respect to the full complexities of land use change, we do believe that it represents a significant improvement on the current state of decision analysis. Furthermore, we feel that the methodology developed here is readily amenable to extension and that future research may develop this into a practical decision support system of considerable assistance to policy- and decision-makers as well as being of interest to academics and users of the land alike.

References

Achen, C.H. (1982), *Interpreting and Using Regression*, Quantitative Applications in the Social Sciences No. 29, Sage, London.

Adams, R., Dunn, S.M., Lunn, R., Mackay, R. and O'Callaghan, J.R. (1995), Assessing the performance of the NELUP hydrological models for river basin planning, *Journal of Environmental Planning and Management*, 38(1): 53–76.

Adger, W.N. and Brown, K. (1994), *Land Use and the Causes of Global Warming*, John Wiley and Sons, Chichester.

Adger, W.N., Brown, K., Shiel, R.S. and Whitby, M.C. (1992), Carbon dynamics of land use in Great Britain, *Journal of Environmental Management*, 36: 117–33.

Adger, W.N., Pettenella, D. and Whitby, M. (eds.) (1997), *Climate Change Mitigation and European Land Use Policy*, CAB International, Wallingford, Oxon.

Adger, W.N. and Subak, S. (1996), Estimating above-ground carbon fluxes from UK agricultural land, *Geographical Journal*, 162(2): 191–204.

Adler, M.D. and Posner, E.A. (1999), Rethinking cost-benefit analysis, *Yale Law Journal*, 109(2): 165–249.

Aitken, M., Anderson, D., Francis, B. and Hinde, J. (1989), *Statistical Modelling in GLIM*, Clarendon Press, Oxford.

Ajzen, I. and Fishbein, M. (1977), Attitude–behaviour relations: a theoretical analysis and review of empirical research, *Psychological Bulletin* 84(5): 888–918.

Akabua, K.M., Adamowicz, W.L. and Boxall, P.C. (2000), Spatial non-timber valuation decision support systems, *Forestry Chronicle*, 76(2): 319–27.

Alberini, A. and Carson, R.T. (2001), Yea-sayers, nay-sayers or just plain confused? Mixture of populations in contingent valuation survey responses. Paper presented at the Eleventh Annual Conference of the European Association of Environmental and Resource Economists (EAERE), University of Southampton, 28–30 June 2001.

Allanson, P., Savage, D. and White, B. (1992), Areal interpolation of parish agricultural census data, in Whitby, M.C. (ed.), *Land Use Change: The Causes and Consequences*, ITE Symposium No. 27, HMSO, London.

Alston, J.E. (1986), An analysis of growth of US farmland prices 1963–82, *American Journal of Agricultural Economics*, 68: 1–9.

Altman, D.G. and Gardner, M.J. (1989), Calculating confidence intervals for regression and correlation, in Gardner, M.J. and Altman, D.G. (eds.), *Statistics with Confidence: Confidence Intervals and Statistical Guidelines*, British Medical Journal, London, pp. 34–49.

Anderson, K. and Tyers, R. (1991), *Global Effects of Liberalizing Trade in Farm Products*, Thames Essay No. 55, Harvester Wheatsheaf, Hemel Hempstead.

Appleton, K.J., Lovett, A.A., Sünnenberg, G. and Dockerty, T.D. (2002), Rural landscape visualisation from GIS databases: a comparison of approaches, options and problems, *Computers, Environment and Urban Systems*, 26: 141–62.

Arrow, K.J. Parikh, J. and Pillet, G. (with contributions from Babu, P.G., Beltratti, A., Chichilnisky, G., Fankhauser, S., Faucheux, S., Froger, G., Gassmann, F., Haites, E.F., Hediger, W., Hourcade, J-Ch., Morgan, M.G., Parikh, H., Pearce, D.W., Peck, S., Richels, R., Schubert, R., Suarez, C. and Wellenmann, U.) (1996), *Decision Making Framework to Address Climate Change*, report by IPCC Working Group III Writing Team II, Intergovernmental Panel on Climate Change, Geneva, Switzerland.

Arrow, K.J, Solow, R., Portney, P.R., Leamer, E.E., Radner, R. and Schuman, E.H. (1993), *Report of the NOAA Panel on Contingent Valuation*, Report to the General Counsel of the US National Oceanic and Atmospheric Administration, Resources for the Future, Washington, D.C.

Askew, G.P., Payton, R.W. and Shiel, R.S. (1985), Upland soils and land clearance in Britain during the second millennium BC, in Spratt, D. and Burgess, C. (eds.), *Upland Settlement in Britain: The Second Millennium BC and After*, British Archaeological Report: British Series, vol. 143: 5–33.

Aspinall, R. (1991), GIS and forestry, *Mapping Awareness*, 5(4): 12–14.

Atkinson, S.E., Crocker, T.D. and Shogren, J.F. (1992), Bayesian exchangeability, benefit transfer, and research efficiency, *Water Resources Research*, 28(3): 715–22.

Australian Bureau of Agricultural Economics (ABAE) (1985), *Agricultural Policies in the European Community: Their Origins, Nature and Effects on Production and Trade*, Government Publications Service, Canberra.

Ayres, R. and Walter, J. (1991), The greenhouse effect: damages, costs and abatement, *Environmental and Resource Economics*, 1: 237–70.

Azar, C. (1998), Are optimal CO_2 emissions really optimal? Four critical issues for economists in the greenhouse, *Environmental and Resource Economics*, 11(3–4): 301–15.

Backlund, K., Kriström, B., Löfgren, K.-G. and Samakovlis, E. (1995), Global warming and dynamic cost-benefit analysis under uncertainty: an economic analysis of forest carbon sequestration, mimeo, Department of Economics, University of Umeå, Sweden.

Baldock, D. and Conder, D. (eds.) (1987), *Removing Land from Agriculture*. Council for the Protection of Rural England and Institute for European Environmental Policy, London.

Baldwin, B. (1996), Spruce trees provoke turf war, Horticultural Information Service, Department of Horticulture, University of Saskatchewan.

Balkan, E. and Kahn, R. (1988), The value of changes in deer hunting quality: a travel-cost approach, *Applied Economics*, 20: 533–9.

Baron, J. and Maxwell, N.P. (1996), Cost of public goods affects willingness to pay for them, *Journal of Behavioural Decision Making*, 9(3): 173–83.

Barrow, P., Hinsley, A.P. and Price, C. (1986), The effect of afforestation on hydroelecticity generation, *Land Use Policy*, 3 (April):141–51.

Bateman, I.J. (1991a), Recent developments in the evaluation of non-timber forest products: the extended CBA method, *Quarterly Journal of Forestry*, 85(2): 90–102.

   (1991b), Placing money values on the unpriced benefits of forestry, *Quarterly Journal of Forestry*, 85(3): 152–65.

(1992), The United Kingdom, in Wibe, S. and Jones, T. (eds.), *Forests: Market and Intervention Failures*, Earthscan, London, pp. 10–57.

(1993), Valuation of the environment, methods and techniques: revealed preference methods, in Turner R.K. (ed.), *Sustainable Economics and Management: Principles and Practice*, Belhaven Press, London, pp. 192–265.

(1995), Environmental and economic appraisal, in O'Riordan, T. (ed.), *Environmental Science for Environmental Management*, Longman, Harlow, pp. 45–65.

(1996), An economic comparison of forest recreation, timber and carbon fixing values with agriculture in Wales: a geographical information systems approach, Ph.D. thesis, Department of Economics, University of Nottingham.

(1999), Environmental impact assessment, cost-benefit analysis and the valuation of environmental impacts, in Petts, J. (ed.), *Handbook of Environmental Impact Assessment*, vol. I: *Environmental Impact Assessment: Process, Methods and Potential*, Blackwell Science, Oxford, pp. 93–120.

Bateman, I.J., Brainard, J.S., Garrod, G.D. and Lovett, A.A. (1999a), The impact of journey origin specification and other measurement assumptions upon individual travel cost estimates of consumer surplus: a geographical information systems analysis, *Regional Environmental Change*, 1(1): 24–30.

Bateman, I.J., Brainard, J.S. and Lovett, A.A. (1995b), Modelling woodland recreation demand using geographical information systems: a benefit transfers study, CSERGE Global Environmental Change Working Paper 95–06, Centre for Social and Economic Research on the Global Environment, University of East Anglia and University College London.

(1998), Transferring multivariate benefit functions using geographical information systems, Nota di Lavoro 84.98, Fondazione Eni Enrico Mattei (FEEM), Milan.

Bateman, I.J., Carson, R.T., Day, B., Hanemann, W.M., Hanley, N., Hett, T., Jones-Lee, M., Loomes, G., Mourato, S., Ozdemiroglu, E., Pearce, D.W., Sugden, R. and Swanson, J. (2002), *Economic Valuation with Stated Preference Techniques: A Manual*, Edward Elgar, Cheltenham.

Bateman, I.J., Cole, M., Cooper, P., Georgiou, S., Hadley, D. and Poe, G.L. (2001c), Visible choice sets and scope sensitivity: an experimental and field test of study design effects upon contingent values, CSERGE Environmental Decision Making Working Paper EDM01–01, Centre for Social and Economic Research on the Global Environment, University of East Anglia.

Bateman, I.J., Day, B.H., Lake, I. and Lovett, A.A. (2001a), *The Effect of Road Traffic on Residential Property Values: A Literature Review and Hedonic Pricing Study*, The Stationery Office, Edinburgh and London.

Bateman, I.J., Diamand, E., Langford, I.H. and Jones, A.P. (1996b), Household willingness to pay and farmers' willingness to accept compensation for establishing a recreational woodland, *Journal of Environmental Planning and Management*, 39(1): 21–43.

Bateman, I.J., Dolman, P., Lovett, A.A. and Brainard, J.S. (1997c), Placing the biodiversity consequences of land use change within a wider context: developing a GIS/CBA methodology for assessing conversions from agriculture to farm forestry in Wales, in O'Riordan, T. (ed.), *Economics of Biological Resources and Biodiversity*. Proceedings of a DoE/CSERGE seminar, Department of Environment, London, 31 October 1996, published by the Centre for Social and Economic Research on the Global Environment, University of East Anglia and University College London, pp. 33–52.

Bateman, I.J., Ennew, C., Lovett, A.A. and Rayner, A.J. (1999d), Modelling and mapping agricultural output values using farm specific details and environmental databases, *Journal of Agricultural Economics*, 50(3): 488–511.

Bateman, I.J., Garrod, G.D., Brainard, J.S. and Lovett, A.A. (1996a), Measurement, valuation and estimation issues in the travel cost method: a geographical information systems approach, *Journal of Agricultural Economics*, 47(2): 191–205.

Bateman, I.J., Jones, A.P., Nishikawa, N. and Brouwer, R. (2001d), Benefits transfer in theory and practice: a review, CSERGE Global Environmental Change Working Paper GEC2000–25, Centre for Social and Economic Research on the Global Environment, University of East Anglia and University College London.

Bateman, I.J. and Langford, I.H. (1997a), Budget constraint, temporal and ordering effects in contingent valuation studies, *Environment and Planning A*, 29(7): 1215–28.

(1997b), Non-users' willingness to pay for a National Park: an application and critique of the contingent valuation method, *Regional Studies*, 31(6): 571–82.

Bateman, I.J., Langford, I.H., Jones, A.P. and Kerr, G.N. (2001b), Bound and path effects in multiple-bound dichotomous choice contingent valuation, *Resource and Energy Economics*, 23(3): 191–213.

Bateman, I.J., Langford, I.H., Munro, A., Starmer, C. and Sugden, R. (2000a), Estimating the four Hicksian measures for a public good: a contingent valuation investigation, *Land Economics*, 76(3): 355–73.

Bateman, I.J., Langford, I.H., Nishikawa, N. and Lake, I. (2000b), The Axford debate revisited: a case study illustrating different approaches to the aggregation of benefits data, *Journal of Environmental Planning and Management*, 43(2): 291–302.

Bateman, I.J., Langford, I.H. and Rasbash, J. (1999b), Willingness-to-pay question format effects in contingent valuation studies, in Bateman, I.J. and Willis, K.G. (eds.), *Valuing Environmental Preferences: Theory and Practice of the Contingent Valuation Method in the US, EU, and Developing Countries*, Oxford University Press, pp. 511–39.

Bateman, I.J., Langford, I.H., Turner, R.K., Willis, K.G. and Garrod, G.D. (1995a), Elicitation and Truncation Effects in Contingent Valuation Studies, *Ecological Economics*, 12(2): 161–79.

Bateman, I.J., Langford, I.H., Willis, K.G., Turner, R.K. and Garrod, G.D. (1993b), The impacts of changing willingness to pay question format in contingent valuation studies: an analysis of open-ended, iterative bidding and dichotomous choice formats, Global Environmental Change Working Paper 93–05, Centre for Social and Economic Research on the Global Environment, University of East Anglia and University College London.

Bateman, I.J. and Lovett, A.A. (1992), Modelling the potential impact of changing UK agro-forestry subsidies using GIS: a bioeconomic approach, in Rideout, T.W. (ed.), *Geographical Information Systems and Urban and Rural Planning*, The Planning and Environmental Study Group of the Institute of British Geographers, Edinburgh, pp. 100–15.

(1997), Modelling the yield and value of forestry over a large area: a GIS based model of Sitka spruce and beech yield in Wales, Information Paper, Department of Resource Management, Lincoln University, Canterbury, New Zealand.

(1998), Using geographical information systems (GIS) and large area databases to predict yield class: a study of Sitka spruce in Wales, *Forestry*, 71(2): 147–68.

(2000a), Modelling and mapping timber values using geographical information systems, *Quarterly Journal of Forestry*, 94(2): 127–38.

(2000b), Modelling and valuing carbon sequestration in softwood and hardwood trees, timber products and forest soils, *Journal of Environmental Management*, 60(4): 301–23.

Bateman, I.J., Lovett, A.A. and Brainard, J.S. (1999c), Developing a methodology for benefit transfers using geographical information systems: modelling demand for woodland recreation, *Regional Studies*, 33(3): 191–205.

Bateman, I.J. and Mellor, C. (1990), The UK timber market: an econometric model, *Oxford Agrarian Studies*, 18(1): 53–61.

Bateman, I.J., Munro, A., Rhodes, B., Starmer, C. and Sugden, R. (1997a), Does part-whole bias exist? An experimental investigation, *Economic Journal*, 107(441): 322–32.

(1997b), A test of the theory of reference-dependent preferences, *Quarterly Journal of Economics*, 112(2): 479–505.

Bateman, I.J. and Turner, R.K. (1993), Valuation of the environment, methods and techniques: the contingent valuation method, in Turner, R.K. (ed.), *Sustainable Environmental Economics and Management: Principles and Practice*, Belhaven Press, London, pp. 120–91.

Bateman, I.J., Turner, R.K. and Bateman, S.D. (1993a), Extending cost benefit analysis of UK highway proposals: environmental evaluation and equity, *Project Appraisal*, 8(4): 213–24.

Bateman, I.J. and Willis, K.G. (eds.) (1999), *Valuing Environmental Preferences: Theory and Practice of the Contingent Valuation Method in the US, EU, and Developing Countries*, Oxford University Press.

Bateman, I.J., Willis K.G. and Garrod, G.D. (1994), Consistency between contingent valuation estimates: a comparison of two studies of UK National Parks, *Regional Studies*, 28(5): 457–74.

Batterbee, R.W. (1984), Diatom analysis and the acidification of lakes, *Philosophical Transactions of the Royal Society of London: Series B*, 305: 451–77.

Batty, M. and Longley, P.A. (eds.) (1996), *Spatial Analysis: Modelling in a GIS Environment*, GeoInformation International, Cambridge.

Baumol, W.J. (1968), On the social rate of discount, *American Economic Review*, 58: 788–802.

Beauchamp, T.L. and Bowie, N.E. (1988), *Ethical Theory and Business*, 3rd edn. Prentice Hall, Englewood Cliffs, N.J.

Benson, J.F. and Willis, K.G. (1990), The aggregate value of non-priced recreation benefits of the Forestry Commission estate. Report to the Forestry Commission, Dept. of Town and Country Planning, University of Newcastle upon Tyne.

(1992), Valuing informal recreation on the Forestry Commission estate, *Forestry Commission Bulletin* 104, HMSO, London.

(1993), Implications of recreation demand for forest expansion in Great Britain, *Regional Studies*, 27(1): 29–39.

Bergen, V., Behrndt, M. and Pfister, G. (1992), Germany, in Wibe, S. and Jones, T. (eds.), *Forestry: Market and Intervention Failures*, Earthscan, London, pp. 127–64.

Bergh, van den, J.C.J.M., Button, K.J., Nijkamp, P. and Pepping, G.C. (1997), *Meta-Analysis in Environmental Economics*, Kluwer Academic Publishers, Dordrecht.

Bergland, O., Magnussen, K. and Navrud, S. (1995), Benefit transfer: testing for accuracy and reliability, Discussion Paper #D-03/1995, Agricultural University of Norway, Ås.

Berman, M.D. and Kim, H.J. (1999), Endogenous on-site time in the recreation demand model, *Land Economics*, 75(4): 603–19.

Berry, J.K. (1993), Cartographic modelling: the analytical capabilities of GIS, in Goodchild, M.F., Parks, B.O. and Steyaert, L.T. (eds.), *Environmental Modelling with GIS*, Oxford University Press, pp. 58–74.

Bhat, G. and Bergstrom, J.C. (1997), Integration of geographical information systems based spatial analysis in recreation demand analysis, Faculty Series 96–26, Department of Agricultural and Applied Economics, University of Georgia, Athens, Ga.

Billing, P. (1998), Towards sustainable agriculture: the perspectives of the common agricultural policy in the EU, in Dabbert, S., Whitby, M. and Dubgaard, A. (eds.), *The Economics of Landscape and Wildlife Conservation*, CABI International, Wallingford, Oxon.

Bishop, K.D. (1992), Assessing the benefits of community forests: an evaluation of the recreational use benefits of two urban fringe woodlands, *Journal of Environmental Planning and Management*, 35(1): 63–76.

Bjornstad, D.J. and Kahn, J.R. (eds.) (1996), *The Contingent Valuation of Environmental Resources: Methodological Issues and Research Needs,* Edward Elgar, Cheltenham.

Blakeway-Smith, J., Miller, D. and Quine, C. (1993), The use of geographic information systems in forest management, mimeo, Macaulay Land Use Research Institute, Aberdeen.

   (1994), An appraisal of the susceptibility of forestry to windblow using GIS. *Proceedings of the GIS Research UK 1994 Conference*, 11–13 April. Department of Geography, University of Leicester, Association of Geographical Information.

Blamey, R.K. (1995), Citizens, consumers and contingent valuation: an investigation into respondent behaviour, Ph.D. thesis, Australian National University.

   (1996), Citizens, consumers and contingent valuation: clarification and the expression of citizen values and issue-opinions, in Adamowicz, W.L., Boxall, P.C., Luckert, M.K., Phillips, W.E. and White, W.A. (eds.), *Forestry, Economics and the Environment*, CAB International, Wallingford, Oxon, pp. 103–33.

   (1998), Contingent valuation and the activation of environmental norms, *Ecological Economics*, 24(1): 47–72.

Bloom, B. (1988), Unlovely as a tree, *Financial Times*, 10 March, London.

Blunden, J. and Curry, N. (1985), *The Changing Countryside*, Croom Helm/Open University, London.

   (1988), *A Future For Our Countryside*, Blackwell, Oxford.

Blyth, J.F. (1974), Land capability assessment for forestry in north-east Scotland, Ph.D. thesis, University of Aberdeen.

Blyth, J.F. and MacLeod, D.A. (1981), Sitka spruce (*Picea sitchensis*) in north-east Scotland: 1. Relationships between site factors and growth, *Forestry*, 54: 41–62.

Bockstael, N.E., McConnell, K.E. and Strand, I.E. (1991), *Recreation*, in Braden, J.B. and Kolstad, C.D. (eds.), *Measuring the Demand for Environmental Quality*, North-Holland, Elsevier Science Publishers, Amsterdam, pp. 227–70.

Bockstael, N.E., Strand, I.E. Jr and Hanemann, W.M. (1987), Time and the recreational demand model, *American Journal of Agricultural Economics*, 69(2): 293–302.

Body, R. (1982), *Agriculture: The Triumph and the Shame*, Temple Smith, London.

Bohm, P. (1972), Estimating demand for public goods: an experiment, *European Economic Review*, 3: 733–6.

Bojö, J. (1985), *A Cost-Benefit Analysis of Forestry in Mountainous Areas: The Case of Valadalen*, Stockholm School of Economics.

Boulding, K. (1966), The economics of the coming Spaceship Earth, in Jarett, H. (ed.), *Environmental Quality in a Growing Economy*, Johns Hopkins University Press, Baltimore, pp. 3–14.

Bowers, J.K. (1985), Do we need more forests?, Discussion Paper 137, Department of Economics, University of Leeds.

(1987), Set-aside and other stories, in Baldock, D. and Conder, D. (eds.), *Removing Land from Agriculture*, Council for the Protection of Rural England and Institute for European Environmental Policy, London, pp. 5–18.

Bowers, J.K. and Cheshire, P. (1983), *Agriculture, the Countryside and Land Use*, Methuen, London.

Bowes, M.D. and Loomis, J.B. (1980), A note on the use of travel cost models with unequal zonal populations, *Land Economics*, 56: 465–70.

Bowler, I.R. (1985), *Agriculture under the Common Agricultural Policy: A Geography*, Manchester University Press.

Boxall, P.C., McFarlane, B.L. and Gartrell, M. (1996), An aggregate travel cost approach to valuing forest recreation at managed sites, *Forestry Chronicle*, 72: 615–21.

Boyle, K.J., Bishop, R.C. and Welsh, M.P. (1985), Starting point bias in contingent valuation surveys, *Land Economics*, 61: 188–94.

Bracken, I. and Martin, D.J. (1995), Linkage of the 1981 and 1991 UK Census using surface modelling concepts, *Environment and Planning A*, 27: 379–90.

Bradley, R.I. and Knox, J.W. (1995), The prediction of irrigation demands for England and Wales. *Proceedings of the GIS Research UK 1995 Conference*, 5–7 April. Department of Surveying, University of Newcastle upon Tyne, Association for Geographical Information.

Brainard, J.S., Lovett, A.A. and Bateman, I.J. (1997), Using isochrone surfaces in travel cost models, *Journal of Transport Geography*, 5(2): 117–26.

(1999), Integrating geographical information systems into travel cost analysis and benefit transfer, *International Journal of Geographical Information Systems*, 13(3): 227–46.

Brase, B.T. and La Due, E.L. (1989), Farmer investment behavior: a review of the literature, Discussion Paper 89/5, Department of Agricultural Economics, Cornell University.

Brennan, G. and Buchanan, J.M. (1984), Voter choice, *American Behavioral Scientist*, 28: 185–201.

Bridges, E.M. and Batjes, N.H. (1996), Soil gaseous emissions and global climatic change, *Geography*, 81: 155–69.

Britton, D. (1990), Recent changes and current trends, in Britton, D. (ed.), *Agriculture in Britain: Changing Pressures and Policies*, CAB International, Wallingford, Oxon, pp. 1–33.

Broadhurst, R. (2001), *Managing Environments for Leisure and Recreation*, Routledge, London.

Brookshire, D.S. and Coursey, D.L. (1987), Measuring the value of a public good: an empirical comparison of elicitation procedures, *American Economic Review* 77: 554–66.

Brookshire, D.S., d'Arge, R.C., Schulze, W.D. and Thayer, M.A. (1981), Experiments in valuing public goods, in Smith, V.K. (ed.), *Advances in Applied Economics*, vol. I, JAI Press, Greenwich, Conn.

Broome, J. (1992), *Counting the Costs of Global Warming*, White Horse Press, Cambridge.

Brouwer, F. and Lowe, P. (eds.) (2000a), *CAP Regimes and the European Countryside*, CABI Publishing, Wallingford, Oxon.

Brouwer, F. and Lowe, P. (2000b), CAP and the environment: policy development and the state of research, in Brouwer, F. and Lowe, P. (eds.), *CAP Regimes and the European Countryside*, CABI Publishing, Wallingford, Oxon, pp. 1–14.

Brouwer, R. and Bateman, I.J. (2000), A comparison of the social benefits of reducing sunbathing health risks in low and high risk countries: further empirical testing of the validity and reliability of benefits transfer, CSERGE Global Environmental Change Working Paper GEC2000–17, Centre for Social and Economic Research on the Global Environment, University of East Anglia and University College London.

Brouwer, R., Langford, I.H., Bateman, I.J. and Turner, R.K. (1999), A meta-analysis of wetland contingent valuation studies, *Regional Environmental Change*, 1(1): 47–57.

Brouwer, R. and Spaninks, F.A., (1999), The validity of environmental benefits transfer: further empirical testing. *Environmental and Resource Economics*, 14(1): 95–117.

Brown, C. (1999), Global Forest Products Outlook Study: thematic Study on plantations, Working Paper No. GFPOS/WP/03 (Draft), FAO, Rome.

Brown, P. (1998), *Climate, Biodiversity and Forests: Issues and Opportunities Emerging from the Kyoto Protocol*, World Resources Institute, Washington, D.C.

Brown, T.C. and Slovic, P. (1988), Effects of context on economic measures of values, in Peterson, G.L., Driver, B.L. and Gregory, R. (eds.), *Amenity Resource Valuation: Integrating Economics with Other Disciplines*, Venture State College, Penn., pp. 23–30.

Brown, W.G. and Nawas, F. (1973), Impact of aggregation on the estimation of outdoor recreation demand functions, *American Journal of Agricultural Economics*, 55(2): 246–9.

Brubaker, E. (1982), Sixty-eight percent free revelation and thirty-two percent free ride? Demand disclosures under varying conditions of exclusion, in Smith, V.L. (ed.), *Research in Experimental Economics*, vol. II, JAI Press, Greenwich, Conn., pp. 151–66.

Bryant, D., Nielsen, D. and Tangley, L. (1997), *The Last Frontier Forests*, World Resources Institute, Washington D.C.

Bucher-Wallin, I.K., Sonnleitner, M.A., Egli, P., Gunthardt-Georg, M.S., Tarjan, D., Schulin, R. and Bucher, J.B. (2000), Effects of elevated CO_2, increased nitrogen deposition and soil on evapotranspiration and water use efficiency of spruce–beech model ecosystems, *Phyton-Annales Rei Botanicae*, 40(4): 49–60.

Buckley, G.P. (ed.) (1989), *Biological Habitat Reconstruction*, Belhaven Press, London.

Buckwell, A. (1989), Economic signals, farmers' response and environmental change, *Journal of Rural Studies*, 5(2): 149–60.

Buckwell, A.E., Harvey, D.R., Thomson, K.J. and Parton, K.A. (1982), *The Costs of the Common Agricultural Policy*. Croom Helm, London.

Bureau of Transport and Communications Economics (BTCE) (1996a), Trees and greenhouse: costs of sequestering Australian transport emissions, Working Paper 23, Bureau of Transport and Communications Economics, Canberra.

Bureau of Transport and Communications Economics (BTCE) (1996b), *Transport Greenhouse: Costs and Options for Reducing Emissions*, Report 94, Bureau of Transport and Communications Economics, Canberra.

Burness, H.S., Cummings, R.G., Mehr, A.F. and Walbert, M.S. (1983), Valuing policies which reduce environmental risk, *Natural Resources Journal* 23: 675–82.

Burnham, P. (1985), A turning point in British land use policies, *Town and Country Planning*, June 1985.

Burrell, A. (1987), EC agricultural surpluses and budget control, *Journal of Agricultural Economics*, 38(1): 1–14.

Burrough, P.A. and McDonnell, R.A. (1998), *Principles of Geographical Information Systems*, Oxford University Press.

Burt, O.R. (1986), Econometric modeling of the capitalization formula for farmland prices, *American Journal of Agricultural Economics*, 68: 10–26.

Busby, R.J.N. (1974), Forest site yield guide to upland Britain, *Forestry Commission Forest Record* 97, HMSO, London.

Cabinet Office (2000), *Sharing the Nation's Prosperity: Economic, Social and Environmental Conditions in the Countryside*, a report to the Prime Minister by the Cabinet Office, Whitehall, London.

Campbell, D. and Fairley, R. (1991), Forestry and the conservation and enhancement of landscape, in *Forestry Expansion: A Study of Technical, Economic and Ecological Factors*, Paper No. 2, Forestry Commission, Edinburgh.

Cannell, M.G.R. and Cape, J. (1991), International environmental impacts: acid rain and the greenhouse effect, in *Forestry Expansion: A Study of Technical, Economic and Ecological Factors*, Forestry Commission, Edinburgh.

Cannell, M.G.R. and Dewar R.C. (1995), The carbon sink provided by plantation forests and their products in Britain, *Forestry*, 68: 35–48.

Cannell, M.G.R., Dewar, R.C. and Pyatt, D.G. (1993), Conifer plantations on drained peatlands in Britain: a net gain or loss of carbon? *Forestry*, 66: 353–69.

Cannell, M.G.R. and Milne, R. (1995a), Carbon pools and sequestration in forest ecosystems in Britain, in *Carbon Sequestration in Vegetation and Soils,* report to the Global Atmosphere Division of the Department of the Environment, Institute of Terrestrial Ecology, Penicuik, Edinburgh.

(1995b), Carbon pools and sequestration in forest ecosystems in Britain, *Forestry*, 68: 361–78.

Capstick, C.W. (1991), British agricultural policy under the CAP, in Ritson, C. and Harvey, D. (eds.), *The Common Agricultural Policy and the World Economy: Essays in Honour of John Ashton*, CAB International, Wallingford, Oxon.

Carson, R.T. (1998), Valuation of tropical rainforests: philosophical and practical issues in the use of contingent valuation, *Ecological Economics*, 24(1): 15–29.

Carson, R.T., Flores, N.E. and Hanemann, W.M. (1992), On the creation and destruction of public goods: the matter of sequencing, paper presented at the Third Annual Conference of the European Association of Environmental and Resource Economists, Cracow.

(1998), Sequencing and valuing public goods, *Journal of Environmental Economics and Management*, 36: 314–23.

Carson, R.T., Flores, N.E., Martin, K.M. and Wright, J.L. (1996), Contingent valuation and revealed preference methodologies: comparing the estimates for quasi-public goods, *Land Economics*, 72: 80–99.

Carson, R.T., Groves, T. and Machina, M.J. (1999), Incentive and informational properties of preference questions, plenary address at the Ninth Annual Conference of the European Association of Environmental and Resource Economists (EAERE), Oslo, June.

Carson, R.T. and Mitchell, R.C. (1995), Sequencing and nesting in contingent valuation surveys, *Journal of Environmental Economics and Management*, 28: 155–73.

Central Statistical Office (1991), *Regional Trends 1991*, HMSO, London.

(1993a), *Internal Purchasing Power of the Pound: March 1993*, HMSO, London.

(1993b), *Monthly Digest of Statistics: February 1993*, No. 566, HMSO, London.

Cesario, F.J. (1976), Value of time in recreation benefit studies, *Land Economics*, 55: 32–41.

Cesario, F.J. and Knetsch, J.L. (1970), Time bias in recreation benefit estimates, *Water Resources Research*, 6(3): 700–4.

(1976), A recreation site demand and benefit estimation model, *Regional Studies*, 10: 97–104.

Chambers, R.G. and Pope, R.D. (1994), A virtually ideal production system: specifying and estimating the VIPS model, *American Journal of Agricultural Economics*, 76: 105–13.

Champ, P.A., Boyle, K. and Brown, T.C. (eds.) (forthcoming), *A Primer on Non-market Valuation*, Kluwer, Dordrecht.

Chang, S.J. (1998), A generalized Faustmann model for the determination of optimal harvest age, *Canadian Journal of Forest Research*, 28(5): 652–9.

Cheshire, P.C. and Stabler, M.J. (1976), Joint consumption benefits in recreational site 'surplus': an empirical estimate, *Regional Studies*, 10: 343–51.

Christensen, J.B. (1985), An economic approach to assessing the value of recreation with special reference to forest areas, Ph.D. thesis, Department of Forestry and Wood Science, University College of North Wales, Bangor.

Cicchetti, C.J. and Freeman, A.M. III (1971), Optimal demand and consumer's surplus: further comment, *Quarterly Journal of Economics*, 85: 528–39.

Cieszewski, C.J., Turner, D.P. and Phillips, D.L. (1996), Statistical analysis of error propagation in national level carbon budgets, *Proceedings of the Second International Symposium on Spatial Accuracy Assessment in Natural Resources and Environmental Sciences*, USDA Forest Service, Fort Collins, Colo., pp. 649–58.

Cline, W.R. (1992a), *The Economics of Global Warming*, Institute for International Economics, Washington, D.C.

   (1992b), Optimal carbon emissions over time: experiments with the Nordhaus DICE model, mimeo, Institute for International Economics, Washington, D.C.

   (1993), Give greenhouse abatement a fair chance, *Finance and Development*, 30(1): 3–5.

Cloke, P., Milbourne, P. and Thomas, C. (1996), From wasteland to wonderland: opencast mining, regeneration and the English National Forest, *Geoforum*, 27(2): 159–74.

Cobb, R.N. (1993), The merging of agricultural and environmental policy – a study of farmers' responses to policy change, Ph.D. thesis, School of Environmental Sciences, University of East Anglia.

Colenutt, R.J. and Sidaway, R.M. (1973), Forest of Dean Day Visitor Survey, *Forestry Commission Bulletin* 46, HMSO, London.

Collins' Atlas of the World (1991), Collins, Edinburgh.

Colman, D. (1991), Land purchase as a means of providing external benefits from agriculture, in Hanley, N.D. (ed.), *Farming and the Countryside: An Economic Analysis of External Costs and Benefits*, CAB International, Wallingford, Oxon., pp. 215–29.

   (1993), Environmental economics and agricultural policy, in Rayner, A.J. and Colman, D. (eds.), *Current Issues in Agricultural Economics*, Macmillan, Basingstoke, pp. 205–23.

Commission of the European Communities (CEC) (1985a), *Perspectives for the Common Agricultural Policy*, COM(85)333, Commission of the European Communities, Brussels.

   (1985b), *The Agricultural Situation in the Community – 1984 Report*. Commission of the European Communities, Brussels.

   (1987), *The Agricultural Situation in the Community – 1986 Report*. Commission of the European Communities, Brussels.

   (1989), *The Agricultural Situation in the Community – 1988 Report*. Commission of the European Communities, Brussels.

(1990), *The Agricultural Situation in the Community – 1989 Report*. Commission of the European Communities, Brussels.

(1991), *The Development and Future of the Common Agricultural Policy: Proposals of the Commission of the European Communities*, COM(91)258, Commission of the European Communities, Brussels.

(1992a), *The Agricultural Situation in the Community – 1991 Report*, Commission of the European Communities, Brussels.

(1992b), *Towards Sustainability: A European Community Programme for Policy and Action in Relation to the Environment and Sustainable Development*, Commission of the European Communities, Brussels.

(1992c), *Council Regulation No. 1765/92 Establishing a Support System for Producers of Certain Arable Crops*, Commission of the European Communities, Brussels.

(1992d), *Council Regulation No. 2078/92 on Agricultural Production Methods Compatible with the Requirements of the Protection of the Environment and the Maintenance of the Countryside*, Commission of the European Communities, Brussels.

Common, M. (1973), A note on the use of the Clawson method, *Regional Studies*, 7: 401–6.

Common, M., Bull, T. and Stoeckl, N. (1999), The Travel Cost Method: an empirical investigation of Randall's difficulty, *Australian Journal of Agricultural and Resource Economics*, 43(4): 457–77.

Cooper, D.N. (1992), An analysis of the agricultural input industries, Ph.D. thesis, Department of Economics, University of Nottingham.

Cooper, J.C. (2000), Nonparametric and semi-nonparametric recreational demand analysis, *American Journal of Agricultural Economics*, 82(2): 451–62.

Corbett, J.D. and Carter, S.E. (1997), Using GIS to enhance agricultural planning: the example of inter-seasonal rainfall in Zimbabwe, *Transactions in GIS*, 1: 207–18.

Costanza, R. and Daly, H. (1992), Natural capital and sustainable development, *Conservation Biology* 6: 37–46.

Council for the Protection of Rural England (CPRE) (1992), *The Lost Land: Land Use Change in England 1945–90*, CPRE, London.

Countryside Agency (2001), *The State of the Countryside 2001*, Countryside Agency Publications, Wetherby.

Countryside Commission (1987), *Forestry in the Countryside, CCP245*, Countryside Commission, Cheltenham.

(1993), *The National Forest, CCP410*, Countryside Commission, Cheltenham.

Countryside Commission and Forestry Commission (1996), *Woodland Creation: Needs and Opportunities in the English Countryside*, Countryside Commission, Cheltenham.

Coursey, D.L., Hovis, J. and Schulze, W.D. (1986), The disparity between willingness to accept and willingness to pay measures of value, *Quarterly Journal of Economics*, 102: 679–90.

Cowling, R.M. and Heijnis, C.E. (2001), The identification of Broad Habitat Units as biodiversity entities for systematic conservation planning in the Cape Floristic Region, *South African Journal of Botany*, 67(1): 15–38.

Crabtree, B., Chalmers, N. and Barron, N. J. (1998), Information for policy design: modelling participation in a farm woodland incentive scheme, *Journal of Agricultural Economics*, 49(3): 306–20.

Cronin, F.J. and Herzeg, K. (1982), Valuing nonmarket Goods through contingent markets, cited in Cummings, R.G., Brookshire, D.S. and Schulze, W.D. (eds.),

Valuing Environmental Goods: A State of the Arts Assessment of the Contingent Method, Rowman and Allenheld, Totowa, N.J. (1986).

Cruikshank, M.M., Tomlinson, R.W., Devine, P.M. and Milne, R. (1995), Estimation of carbon stores and production of carbon density maps for Northern Ireland: progress in the use of data based on CORINE land cover, Soil Survey and the Peatland Survey, in *Carbon Sequestration in Vegetation and Soils,* report to the Global Atmosphere Division of the Department of the Environment, Institute of Terrestrial Ecology, Penicuik, Edinburgh.

Cummings, R.G., Brookshire, D.S. and Schulze, W.D. (eds.) (1986), *Valuing Environmental Goods: A State of the Arts Assessment of the Contingent Method*, Rowman and Allenheld, Totowa, N.J.

Cunningham, S. (1990), An economic analysis of depreciation and investment in UK agricultural machinery, Ph.D. thesis, Department of Economics, University of Exeter.

Daily, G.C., Ehrlich, P.R., Mooney, H.A. and Ehrlich, A.H. (1991), Greenhouse economics: learn before you leap, *Ecological Economics*, 4: 1–10.

Dake, K. (1991), Orienting dispositions in the perception of risk, *Journal of Cross-Cultural Psychology*, 22(1): 61–82.

Dalias, P., Anderson, J.M., Bottner, P. and Couteaux, M.M. (2001), Temperature responses of carbon mineralization in conifer forest soils from different regional climates incubated under standard laboratory conditions, *Global Change Biology*, 7(2): 181–92.

Daly, H. (1977), *Steady State Economics*, Freeman, San Francisco.
  (1995), On Wilfred Beckerman's critique of sustainable development, *Environmental Values*, 4(1): 49–55.

Daly, H. and Cobb, J. (1990), *For the Common Good*, Greenprint Press, London.

D'Arrigo, R., Jocoby, G.C. and Fung, I.Y. (1987), Boreal forests and atmosphere–biosphere exchange of carbon dioxide, *Nature*, 329: 321–3.

Davidson, D.A. (1991), Forestry and GIS, *Mapping Awareness*, 5(5): 43–5.

Davidson, D.A. and Grieve, I.C. (1995), Peat erosion in upland Scotland, in *Carbon Sequestration in Vegetation and Soils,* report to the Global Atmosphere Division of the Department of the Environment, Institute of Terrestrial Ecology, Penicuik, Edinburgh.

Davis, S. D., Heywood, V.H. and Hamilton, A.C. (1994), *Centres of Plant Diversity: A Guide and Strategy for their Conservation*, vol. I., World Wide Fund for Nature, Gland, Switzerland.

Deaton, A. and Muellbauer, J. (1980), *Economics and Consumer Behaviour*, Cambridge University Press.

Deegen, P. (2000), Concerning the interpretation of the Faustmann's formula as a complex behavioral model in forest economics, *Allgemeine Forst- und Jagdzeitung*, 171(5–6): 88–96.

Department for Environment, Food and Rural Affairs (DEFRA) (2002), *Agriculture in the United Kingdom*, HMSO, London.

Department for the Environment, Transport and the Regions (DETR) (2000), *Our Countryside: The Future. A Fair Deal for Rural England* (Rural White Paper), Cm 4909, HMSO, Norwich.

Department of the Environment (DoE) (1987), *Handling Geographic Information: Report of the Committee of Enquiry chaired by Lord Chorley*, HMSO, London.
  (1988), *Memorandum of Evidence Submitted to the House of Lords Select Committee on the European Communities Set-aside of Agricultural Land, 1987/88 session, 10th Report*, HMSO, London.
  (1991), *Policy Appraisal and the Environment*, HMSO, London.

Department of Transport (DoT), (1987), *Values for Journey Time Savings and Accident Prevention*, Department of Transport, London.

(1992), London traffic monitoring report 1992, *Transport Statistics Report*, Department of Transport, London.

(1993), Vehicle speeds in Great Britain 1992, *Statistics Bulletin*, 93 (30), Department of Transport, London.

Desvousges, W.H., Johnson, F.R. and Banzaf, H.S. (1998), *Environmental Policy Analysis With Limited Information: Principles and Applications of the Transfer Method*, Edward Elgar, Northampton, Mass.

Desvousges, W.H., Naughton, M.C. and Parsons, G.R. (1992), Benefit transfer: conceptual problems in estimating water quality benefits using existing studies, *Water Resources Research*, 28(3): 675–83.

Desvousges, W.H., Smith, V.K. and McGivney, M.P. (1983), A comparison of alternative approaches for estimating recreation and related benefits of water quality improvements. Report No. EPA-230-05-83-001, Office of Policy Analysis, US Environmental Protection Agency, Washington, D.C.

Dewar, R.C. and Cannell, M.G.R. (1992), Carbon sequestration in the trees, products and soils of forest plantations: an analysis using UK examples, *Tree Physiology*, 11: 49–72.

Diamond, P.A. and Hausman, J.A. (1994), Contingent valuation: is some number better than no number?, *Journal of Economic Perspectives*, 8(4): 45–64.

Diewart, W.E. (1973), Functional forms for profit and transformation functions, *Journal of Economic Theory*, 6: 284–316.

Dillman, B.L. and Bergstrom, J.C. (1991), Measuring environmental amenity benefits of agricultural land, in Hanley, N.D. (ed.), *Farming and the Countryside: An Economic Analysis of External Costs and Benefits*, CAB International, Wallingford, Oxon, pp. 250–71.

Dobbs, I.M. (1991), The individual travel cost method: estimation and benefit assessment with a discrete and possibly grouped dependent variable, Countryside Change Unit Working Paper 17, University of Newcastle upon Tyne.

Dobson, R. (1997), Four sheep for every Welshman, *The Independent on Sunday*, 27 July.

Dolman, P.M., Lovett, A.A., O'Riordan, T. and Cobb, R.N. (2001), Designing whole landscapes, *Landscape Research*, 26: 305–35.

Doran, A. (1979), Economics of forestry: a review and critical appraisal, Bulletin No. 168, Manchester University.

Dore, M., Kulshreshtha, S. and Johnston, M. (2001), An integrated economic–ecological analysis of land use decisions in forest–agriculture fringe regions of Northern Saskatchewan, *Geographical and Environmental Modelling*, 5(3): 159–75.

Downing, M. and Ozuna, T. (1996), Testing the reliability of the benefit function transfer approach, *Journal of Environmental Economics and Management*, 30: 316–22.

Dubourg, W.R., Jones-Lee, M.W. and Loomes, G. (1997), Imprecise preferences and survey design in contingent valuation, *Economica*, 64(256): 681–702.

Eade, J.D.O. and Moran, D. (1996), Spatial economic valuation: benefits transfer using geographical information systems, *Journal of Environmental Management*, 48: 97–110.

Eamus, D. and Jarvis, P.G. (1989), Direct effects of CO_2 increases on trees and forest in the UK, *Advances in Ecological Research*, 19: 1–55.

Economic Commission for Europe and the European Community (ECE) (1993), *Forest Condition in Europe – Results of the 1992 Survey*, UN/ECE, Geneva.

Edwards, N.T. (1975), Effect of temperature and moisture on carbon dioxide evolution in a mixed deciduous forest floor, *Soil Science Society of America Journal*, 39: 361–5.

Edwards, N.T. and Ross-Todd, B.M. (1983), Soil carbon in a mixed deciduous forest following clear-butting with and without residue removal, *Soil Science Society of America Journal*, 47: 1014–21.

Edwards, P.N. and Christie, J.M. (1981), Yield models for forest management, *Forestry Commission Booklet* 48, HMSO, London.

Edwards, R.W., Gee, A.S. and Stoner, J.H. (eds.) (1990), *Acid Waters in Wales*, Monographiae Biologicae, vol. LXVI, Kluwer, London.

Efron, B. and Tibshirani, R.J. (1993), *An Introduction to the Bootstrap*, Chapman and Hall, New York.

Egli, P., Maurer, S., Spinnler, D., Landolt, W., Gunthardt-Georg, M.S. and Korner, C. (2001), Downward adjustment of carbon fluxes at the biochemical, leaf, and ecosystem scale in beech–spruce model communities exposed to long-term atmospheric CO_2 enrichment, *Oikos*, 92(2): 279–90.

Elston, D.A., Jayasinghe, G., Buckland, S.T., Macmillan, D.C. and Aspinall, R.J. (1997), Adapting regression equations to minimise the mean squared error of predictions made using covariate data from a GIS, *International Journal of Geographical Information Science*, 11(3): 265–80.

Elvidge, C. D. *et al.* (1999), DMSP-OLS estimation of tropical forest area impacted by ground fires in Roriama, Brazil, cited in United Nations Development Programme (UNDP), United Nations Environment Programme (UNEP), World Bank and the World Resources Institute, *World Resources 2000–2001: People and Ecosystems, The Fraying Web of Life*, Elsevier Science, Amsterdam (2000).

Englin, J. and Mendelsohn, R. (1991), A hedonic travel cost analysis for valuation of multiple components of site quality: the recreation value of forest management, *Journal of Environmental Economics and Management*, 21: 275–90.

Environmental Systems Research Institute (ESRI) (1994), *Arc/Info Release 7: Network Analysis*, Environmental Systems Research Institute, Redlands, Calif.

Ernle, Lord (1919), *English Farming Past and Present*, Longman, Harlow.

European Commission and the United Nations Economic Commission for Europe (EC-UNECE) (1994), *Forest Condition in Europe: Results of the 1993 Survey*, EC-UNECE, Brussels.

European Economic Community (EEC) (1962), *Treaty Establishing the European Economic Community, Rome 1957, Article* 39, HMSO, London.
   (1987), *Changes to the EEC Market Organisation for Milk and Milk Products*. Green Europe, 220. European Economic Community, Luxembourg.

European Union (EU) (1992), *CORINE Land Cover Technical Guide*, part 1, European Commission, Directorate-General Environment, Nuclear Safety and Civil Protection, Brussels.

Evans, A. (1987), The growth of forestry and its effects upon rural communities in North East Scotland: the case of Strathdon, *Scottish Forestry*, 41: 310–13.

Evans, N. and Morris, C. (1997), Towards a geography of agri-environmental policies in England and Wales, *Geoforum*, 28(2): 189–204.

Everett, R.D. (1979), The monetary value of the recreational benefits of wildlife, *Journal of Environmental Management*, 8: 203–13.

Ewers, H.J. *et al.* (1986), Zur monetären Bewertung von Umweltschäden: methodische Untersuchung am Beispiel der Waldschäden, *Umweltbundesamt Bericht*, 4/86, Berlin.

Fankhauser, S. (1993), Global warming economics: issues and state of the art, CSERGE Working Paper GEC 93–28, Centre for Social and Economic Research on the Global Environment, University of East Anglia and University College London.

—— (1994a), Evaluating the social costs of greenhouse gas emissions, CSERGE Working Paper GEC 94–01, Centre for Social and Economic Research on the Global Environment, University of East Anglia and University College London.

—— (1994b), The social costs of greenhouse gas emissions: an expected value approach, *Energy Journal*, 15(2): 157–84.

—— (1995), *Valuing Climate Change: The Economics of the Greenhouse*, Earthscan, London.

Farm Business Survey (FBS) (1988), *Farm Business Survey in Wales: Statistical Results for 1987/88*, Department of Economics and Agricultural Economics, University of Wales, Aberystwyth.

—— (1989), *Farm Business Survey in Wales: Statistical Results for 1988/89*, Department of Economics and Agricultural Economics, University of Wales, Aberystwyth.

—— (1990), *Farm Business Survey in Wales: Statistical Results for 1989/90*, Department of Economics and Agricultural Economics, University of Wales, Aberystwyth.

—— (1991), *Farm Business Survey in Wales: Statistical Results for 1990/91*, Department of Economics and Agricultural Economics, University of Wales, Aberystwyth.

—— (1992), *Farm Business Survey in Wales: Statistical Results for 1991/92*, Department of Economics and Agricultural Economics, University of Wales, Aberystwyth.

Faustmann, M. (1849), Berechnung des Wertes welchen Waldboden sowie noch nicht haubare Holzbestände für die Waldwirtschaft besitzen. Originally published in *Allgemeine Forst Jagd*, translated by Linnard, W. in *Martin Faustmann and the evolution of the discounted cash flow*, Institute Paper No. 42, Commonwealth Forestry Institute, Oxford.

Fearn, H. (1990), Motivating farmers to plant trees, paper presented at the Forestry Commission's First Economics Research Conference, University of York, September.

Fearne, A. (1991), The history and development of the CAP, in Ritson, C. and Harvey, D. (eds.), *The Common Agricultural Policy and the World Economy: Essays in Honour of John Ashton*, CAB International, Wallingford, Oxon.

Feldstein, M. (1980), Inflation, portfolio choice and the prices of land and corporate stock, *American Journal of Agricultural Economics*, 62: 910–16.

Fennell, R. (1987), *The Common Agricultural Policy of the European Community*, 2nd edn, BSP Professional Books, Oxford.

Fishbein, M. and Ajzen, I. (1975), *Belief, Attitude, Intention and Behaviour: An Introduction to Theory and Research*, Addison-Wesley, Reading, Mass.

Fleischer, A. and Tsur, Y. (2000), Measuring the recreational value of agricultural landscape, *European Review of Agricultural Economics*, 27(3): 385–98.

Food and Agriculture Organization (FAO) (1997), *State of the World's Forests 1997*, FAO, Rome.

Forest Enterprise (2001), *Standing Sales Price Index and Competitive Softwood Log Index*, Edinburgh.

Forestry Commission (FC) (1979), *Forestry Facts and Figures*, Edinburgh.

—— (1985a), *65th Annual Report and Accounts*, Edinburgh.

—— (1985b), *Forestry Facts and Figures*, Edinburgh.

—— (1985c), *The Policy for Broadleaved Woodlands*, Policy Paper 5, Edinburgh.

—— (1987), Census of woodlands and trees 1979–82, *Forestry Commission Bulletin* 63, Edinburgh.

—— (1988a), *Forestry Facts and Figures*, Edinburgh.

(1988b), Woodland grant scheme (leaflet), Edinburgh.

(1989), *Forestry Facts and Figures*, Edinburgh.

(1990), *Forestry Facts and Figures*, Edinburgh.

(1991), Community woodland supplement (leaflet WGS 12/91), Edinburgh.

(1992), *Forestry Facts and Figures*, Edinburgh.

(1993), *Forestry Facts and Figures*, Edinburgh.

(1994a), *Forestry Facts and Figures*, Edinburgh.

(1994b), *Forestry Review: Highlights from the Forestry Commission Annual Report 1993/94*, Edinburgh.

(1996), *Forestry Facts and Figures*, Edinburgh.

(1997), *Forestry Facts and Figures*, Edinburgh.

(1998), *A New Focus for England's Woodlands: Strategic Priorities and Programmes*, Cambridge.

(2001a), 'Vital' woodlands can help rural economy, *says Deputy Rural Affairs Minister*, New Release No. 4155, 6 August 2001, Forestry Commission website (www.forestry.gov.uk).

(2001b), *A Woodland Strategy for Wales: Executive Summary of Consultation Responses*, Forestry Commission website (www.forestry.gov.uk).

(2001c), *Forestry Facts and Figures*, Edinburgh.

Forestry Industry Committee of Great Britain (FICGB) (1992), *The Forestry Industry Year-Book 1991–92*, London.

Foster, V., Bateman, I.J. and Harley, D. (1997), Real and hypothetical willingness to pay for environmental preservation: a non-experimental comparison, *Journal of Agricultural Economics*, 48(2): 123–38.

Franklin, M. (1988), *Rich Man's Farming – The Crisis in Agriculture*. Royal Institute of International Affairs, London.

Freeman, A.M., III (1979), *The Benefits of Environmental Improvement: Theory and Practice*, Johns Hopkins University Press, Baltimore.

(1993), *The Measurement of Environmental and Resource Values: Theory and Methods*. Resources for the Future, Washington, D.C.

Fromm, O. (2000), Ecological structure and functions of biodiversity as elements of its total economic value, *Environmental and Resource Economics*, 16(3): 303–28.

Fuller, R.J. (1996), Relationship between grazing and birds with particular reference to sheep in the British uplands, BTO Research Report No. 164, report to the Joint Nature Conservation Committee, British Trust for Ornithology, Thetford, Norfolk.

Fuller, R.J., Gregory, R.D., Gibbons, D.W., Marchant, J.H., Wilson, J.D., Baillie, S.R. and Carter, N. (1995), Population declines and range contractions among lowland farmland birds in Britain, *Conservation Biology*, 9: 1425–41.

Gale, M.F. and Anderson, A.B. (1984), High elevation planting in Galloway, *Scottish Forestry*, 38(1): 3–15.

Galinski, W. and Kuppers, M. (1994), Polish forest ecosystem: the influence of changes in the economic system on the carbon balance, *Climatic Change*, 27(1): 103–19.

Garrod, G.D. and Willis, K.G. (1991), Some empirical estimates of forest amenity value, Working Paper 13, Countryside Change Unit, University of Newcastle upon Tyne.

(1992a), The environmental impact of woodland: a two-stage hedonic price model of the amenity value of forestry in Britain, *Applied Economics*, 24: 715–28.

(1992b), Valuing goods' characteristics: an application of the hedonic price method to environmental attributes, *Journal of Environmental Management*, 34: 59–76.

(1992c), The amenity value of woodland in Great Britain: a comparison of economic estimates, *Environmental and Resource Economics*, 2: 1–20.

(1994), Valuing biodiversity and nature conservation at the local level, *Biodiversity and Conservation*, 3: 555–65.

Gatrell, A.C. and Naumann, I. (1992), Hospital location planning: a pilot GIS study, paper presented at the Mapping Awareness Conference, London, February.

Gemmell, F.M. (1995), Effects of forest cover, terrain, and scale on timber volume estimation with thematic mapper data in a Rocky Mountain site, *Remote Sensing Environment*, 51: 291–305.

Geoghegan, J., Wainger, L.A. and Bockstael, N.E. (1997), Spatial landscape indices in a hedonic framework: an ecological economics analysis using GIS, *Ecological Economics*, 23: 251–64.

Gilg, A.W. (1996), *Countryside Planning,* 2nd edn, Routledge, London.

Glass, G., McGaw, B. and Smith, M.L. (1981), *Meta-Analysis in Social Research*, Sage, Beverly Hills, Calif.

Global Environment Facility (GEF) (1998), *Valuing the Global Environment: Actions and Investments for a 21st Century*. Washington, D.C.

Goldstein, H. (1995), *Multilevel Statistical Models*, 2nd edn, Edward Arnold, London.

Good, J.E.G. (ed.) (1987), *Environmental Aspects of Plantation Forestry in Wales*, ITE Symposium No. 22, Institute of Terrestrial Ecology, Grange-over-Sands.

Good, J.E.G., Newton, I., Miles, J., Marrs, R., Greatorex-Davies, J.N. (1991), Forests as wildlife habitat, in *Forestry Expansion: A Study of Technical, Economic and Ecological Factors*, Paper No. 4, Forestry Commission, Edinburgh.

Goodchild, M.F. (1993), Data models and data quality: problems and prospects, in Goodchild, M.F., Parks, B.O. and Steyaert, L.T. (eds.), *Environmental Modelling with GIS*, Oxford University Press, pp. 94–103.

Goodin, R.E. (1982), Discounting discounting, *Journal of Public Policy*, 2: 53–72.

Goodpaster, K.E. (1978), On being morally considerable, *Journal of Philosophy*, 75: 308–325.

Goodwin, S. (1995), It's hard to get into the woods today, *The Independent*, 15 November.

Grace, J. (1977), *Plant Responses to Wind*, Academic Press, London.

Green, B. (1996), *Countryside Conservation*, 3rd edn, Spon, London.

Green, C.H. and Tunstall, S.M. (1991), The evaluation of river quality improvements by the contingent valuation method, *Applied Economics* 23: 1135–46.

Green, C.H., Tunstall, S.M., N'Jai, A. and Rodgers, A. (1990), The economic evaluation of environmental goods, *Project Appraisal* 5(2): 70–82.

Green, D., Jacowitz, K.E., Kahneman, D. and McFadden, D. (1998), Referendum contingent valuation, anchoring, and willingness to pay for public goods, *Resource and Energy Economics*, 20(2): 85–116.

Grieve, I.C. (2001), Human impacts on soil properties and their implications for the sensitivity of soil systems in Scotland, *Catena*, 42(2–4): 361–74.

Griffin, R.C. (1998), The fundamental principles of cost-benefit analysis, *Water Resources Research*, 34(8): 2063–71.

Grubb, M. (1992), The costs of climate change: critical elements, paper presented at the HASA workshop on Costs, Impacts and Possible Benefits of CO_2 Mitigation, Laxenburg, Austria, September.

Gum, R.L. and Martin, W.E. (1975), Problems and solutions in estimating the demand for and value of rural outdoor recreation, *American Journal of Agricultural Economics*, 57: 558–66.

Gurnell, J. Clark, M. and Feaver, J. (1996), Red squirrels in Thetford Forest: habitat modelling for better forestry, *Mapping Awareness*, 10(4): 36–8.

H.M. Government (1990), *Our Common Inheritance – Britain's Environmental Strategy*. HMSO, London.

H.M. Treasury (1972), *Forestry in Great Britain: An Interdepartmental Cost/Benefit Study*, HMSO, London.

   (1991), *Economic Appraisal in Central Government: A Technical Guide for Government Departments*, HMSO, London.

Haggett, P., Cliff, A.D. and Frey, A. (1977), *Locational Analysis in Human Geography*, vol. I: *Locational Models*, 2nd edn, Edward Arnold, London.

Hallett, S.H., Jones, R.J.A. and Keay, C.A. (1996), Environmental information systems developments for planning sustainable land use, *International Journal of Geographical Information Systems*, 10(1): 47–64.

Hammitt, J.K. and Harvey, C.M. (2000), Equity, efficiency, uncertainty, and the mitigation of global climate change, *Risk Analysis*, 20(6): 851–60.

Hanemann, W.M. (1999), Neo-classical economic theory and contingent valuation, in Bateman, I.J. and Willis, K.G. (eds.), *Valuing Environmental Preferences: Theory and Practice of the Contingent Valuation Method in the US, EU, and Developing Countries*, Oxford University Press, pp. 42–96.

Hanemann, W.M., Loomis, J. and Kanninen, B. (1991), Statistical efficiency of double-bounded dichotomous choice contingent valuation, *American Journal of Agricultural Economics* 73: 1255–63.

Hanley, N. (1989), Valuing rural recreation benefits: an empirical comparison of two approaches, *Journal of Agricultural Economics*, 40(3): 361–74.

   (1990), *Valuation of Environmental Effects: Final Report – Stage One*, Industry Department of Scotland and the Scottish Development Agency, Edinburgh.

   (2001), Cost-benefit analysis and environmental policy making, *Environment and Planning C*, 19: 103–18.

Hanley, N. and Common, M.S. (1987), Evaluating the recreation wildlife and landscape benefits of forestry: preliminary results from a Scottish study, *Papers in Economics Finance and Investment*, No. 141, University of Stirling, Scotland.

Hanley, N. and Ruffell, R.J. (1991), Recreational use values of woodland features, report to the Forestry Commission, University of Stirling.

   (1992), The valuation of forest characteristics, Working Paper 849, Institute for Economic Research, Queen's University, Kingston, Ontario.

Hanley, N. and Spash, C.L. (1993), *Cost Benefit Analysis and the Environment*, Edward Elgar, Cheltenham.

Hanley, N., Whitby, M. and Simpson, E. (1999), Assessing the success of agri-environmental policy in the UK, *Land Use Policy*, 16: 67–80.

Hanley, N., Wright, R.E. and Adamowicz, V. (1998), Using choice experiments to value the environment: design issues, current experience and future prospects, *Environmental and Resource Economics*, 11(3–4): 413–28.

Harriman, R. and Morrison, B.R.S. (1982), Ecology of streams draining forested and non-forested catchments in an area of central Scotland subject to acid precipitation, *Hydrobiologia*, 88: 251–63.

Harris, C.C. and Brown, G. (1992), Gain, loss and personal responsibility: the role of motivation in resource valuation decision-making, *Ecological Economics* 5: 73–92.

Harris, C.C., Driver, B.L. and McLaughlin, M.J. (1989), Improving the contingent valuation method: a psychological approach, *Journal of Environmental Economics and Management*, 17: 213–29.

Harris, S., Swinbank, A. and Wilkinson, G. (1983), *The Food and Farm Policies of the European Community*. John Wiley and Sons, Chichester.

Harrison, A. and Tranter, R.B. (1989), The changing financial structure of farming, Centre for Agricultural Strategy Report 13, University of Reading.

Harrison, A.F., Jones, H.E., Howson, G. and Garnett, M.H. (1995), Impacts of forestry on carbon balance in peats, in *Carbon Sequestration in Vegetation and Soils*, report to the Global Atmosphere Division of the Department of the Environment, Institute of Terrestrial Ecology, Penicuik, Edinburgh.

Harrison, A.R., Dunn, R., Brown, L. and Turton, P.J. (1991), The use of geographical information systems in the analysis of countryside data, final report to the Department of the Environment (research contract PECD 7/2/77), Department of Geography, University of Bristol.

Hart, C.E. (1987), *Private Woodlands: A Guide to British Timber Prices and Forestry Costings*, published by the author, Coleford, Dean, Gloucestershire.

(1990), Broadleaf planting costs, pers. comm., Chenies, Dean, Gloucestershire.

(1991), *Practical Forestry*, 3rd edn, Alan Sutton Publishing, Stroud.

Harvey, D.R. (1991a), Agriculture and the environment: the way ahead?, in Hanley, N.D. (ed.), *Farming and the Countryside: An Economic Analysis of External Costs and Benefits*, CAB International, Wallingford, Oxon., pp. 275–321.

(1991b), The agricultural demand for land: its availability and cost for forestry, in *Forestry Expansion: A Study of Technical, Economic and Ecological Factors: Paper No. 11*, Forestry Commission, Edinburgh.

Hasselmann, K. (1999), Intertemporal accounting of climate change – harmonizing economic efficiency and climate stewardship, *Climatic Change*, 41(3–4): 333–50.

Hausman, J.A. (1993), *Contingent Valuation: A Critical Assessment*, Elsevier Science Publishers, Amsterdam.

Healey, J.R., Price, C. and Tay, J. (2000), The cost of carbon retention by reduced impact logging, *Forest Ecology and Management*, 139(1–3): 237–55.

Heath, J., Kersteins, G. and Mansfield, T.A. (1995), Growth and physiological response of beech and oak seedlings to elevated atmospheric CO_2 concentration under two levels of mineral nutrient supply, in *Carbon Sequestration in Vegetation and Soils,* report to the Global Atmosphere Division of the Department of the Environment, Institute of Terrestrial Ecology, Penicuik, Edinburgh.

Henderson, N. and Bateman, I.J. (1995), Empirical and public choice evidence for hyperbolic social discount rates and the implications for intergenerational discounting, *Environmental and Resource Economics*, 5: 413–23.

Herriges, J.A. and Kling C.L. (eds.) (1999), *Valuing Recreation and the Environment: Revealed Preference Methods in Theory and Practice*, Edward Elgar, Cheltenham.

Hill, B.E. (1984), *The Common Agricultural Policy – Past, Present and Future*. Methuen, London.

(1990), Incomes and wealth, in Britton, D. (ed.), *Agriculture in Britain: Changing Pressures and Policies*, CAB International, Wallingford, Oxon., pp. 135–60.

Hill, M.J. and Aspinall, R.J. (eds.) (2000), *Spatial Information for Land Use Management*, Gordon and Breach Science Publishers, Amsterdam.

Hodge, I. (1990a), The changing place of farming, in Britton, D. (ed.), *Agriculture in Britain: Changing Pressures and Policies*, CAB International, Wallingford, Oxon., pp. 34–44.

(1990b), The future public pressures on farming, in Britton, D. (ed.), *Agriculture in Britain: Changing Pressures and Policies*, CAB International, Wallingford, Oxon., pp. 119–34.

(1990c), Conflict or consensus over agricultural and countryside issues, in Britton, D. (ed.), *Agriculture in Britain: Changing Pressures and Policies*, CAB International, Wallingford, Oxon., pp. 94–104.

(1990d), Land use by design?, in Britton, D. (ed.), *Agriculture in Britain: Changing Pressures and Policies*, CAB International, Wallingford, Oxon., pp. 105–18.

Hodge, S.J. (1995), *Creating and Managing Woodlands Around Towns*, Forestry Commission, Edinburgh.

Hoehn, J.P. and Randall, A. (1987), A satisfactory benefit cost indicator from contingent valuation, *Journal of Environmental Economics and Management* 14(3): 226–47.

Hoevenagel, R. (1990), The validity of the Contingent Valuation method: some aspects on the basis of three Dutch studies, paper presented at the First Annual Meeting of the European Association of Environmental and Resource Economists (EAERE), Venice, 17–20 April.

Hornung, M. and Adamson, J. (1991), The impacts on water quality and quantity, in *Forestry Expansion: A Study of Technical, Economic and Ecological Factors*, Forestry Commission, Edinburgh.

Houghton, J.T., Callander, B.A. and Varney, S.K. (eds.) (1992), Supplement, in *Climate Change 1992: The Supplementary Report to the IPCC Scientific Assessment*, Cambridge University Press, pp. 1–22.

House of Lords (1992), *Select Committee on the European Communities: The Implementation of the Reform of the Common Agricultural Policy, 1992/93 Session, 9th Report*, HMSO, London.

Howarth, R.B. (1996), Discount rates and sustainable development, *Ecological Modelling*, 92(2): 263–70.

Howarth, R.W. (1985), *Farming for Farmers?*, Institute of Economic Affairs, London.

Hubbard, L. and Ritson, C. (1991), The reform of the CAP, in Ritson, C. and Harvey, D. (eds.), *The Common Agricultural Policy and the World Economy: Essays in Honour of John Ashton*, CAB International, Wallingford, Oxon.

Hufschmidt, M.M., James, D.E., Meister, A.D., Bower, B.T. and Dixon, J.A. (1983), *Environment, Natural Systems and Development: An Economic Valuation Guide*, Johns Hopkins University Press, Baltimore.

Innes, J.L. (1987), Air pollution and forestry, *Forestry Commission Bulletin* 70, Edinburgh.

Intergovernmental Panel on Climate Change (IPCC) (1992), *Global Climate Change and the Rising Challenge of the Sea: Supporting Document for the IPCC Update 1992*, WMO and UNEP, Geneva.

(1996a), *Climate Change 1995 – Impact, Adaptation and Mitigation of Climate Change – Scientific-Technical Analysis. Contribution of Working Group II to the Second Assessment Report of the Intergovernmental Panel on Climate Change*, Cambridge University Press.

(1996b), *Climate Change 1995 – Economic and Social Dimensions. Contribution of Working Group III to the Second Assessment Report of the Intergovernmental Panel on Climate Change*, Cambridge University Press.

(2000), *Land Use, Land Change, and Forestry*, Cambridge University Press.

(2001a), *Climate Change 2001: The Scientific Basis. Contribution of Working Group I to the Third Assessment Report of the Intergovernmental Panel on Climate Change*, Cambridge University Press.

(2001b), *Climate Change 2001: Impacts, Adaptation and Vulnerability. Contribution of Working Group II to the Third Assessment Report of the Intergovernmental Panel on Climate Change*, Cambridge University Press.

Jarvis, N.J. and Mullins, C.E. (1987), Modelling the effects of drought on the growth of Sitka spruce in Scotland. *Forestry*, 60: 13–30.

Jenkins, D. (ed.) (1984), *Agriculture and the Environment*, ITE Symposium No. 13, Institute of Terrestrial Ecology, Cambridge.

(1986), *Trees and Wildlife in the Scottish Uplands*, ITE Symposium No. 17, Institute of Terrestrial Ecology, Monks Wood.

Jenkinson, D.A. (1971), *The Accumulation of Organic Matter on Soil Left Uncultivated*, Rothamsted Experimental Station, Harpenden.

(1988), Soil organic matter and its dynamics, in Wild, A. (ed.), *Russell's Soil Conditions and Plant Growth*, Longman, London.

Johansson, P.-O. (1987), *The Economic Theory and Measurement of Environmental Benefits*. Cambridge University Press.

Johnson, B.M. (1966), Travel time and the price of leisure, *Western Economic Journal*, 4: 135–45.

Johnson, J.A. and Nicholls, D.C. (1991), The impact of government intervention on private forest management in England and Wales, *Occasional Paper* 30, Forestry Commission, Edinburgh.

Johnson, J.A. and Price, C. (1987), Afforestation, employment and depopulation in the Snowdonia National Park, *Journal of Rural Studies*, 87(3): 195–205.

Johnston, D.R., Grayson, A.J. and Bradley, R.T. (1967), *Forest Planning*, Faber, London.

Jones, P.J., Rehman, T., Harvey, D.R., Tranter, R.B., Marsh, J.S., Bunce, R.G.H. and Howard, D.C. (1995), Developing LUAM (Land Use Allocation Model) and modelling CAP reforms, *Centre for Agricultural Strategy Paper* 32, University of Reading.

Jones, R.J.A. and Thomasson, A.J. (1985), *An Agroclimatic Databank for England and Wales*, Technical Monograph No. 16, Soil Survey of England and Wales, Harpenden.

Josling, T. (1993), Agricultural policy reform in the USA and the EC, in Rayner, A.J. and Colman, D. (eds.), *Current Issues in Agricultural Economics*, Macmillan, Basingstoke, pp. 32–61.

Just, R.E., Hueth, D.L. and Schmitz, A. (1982), *Applied Welfare Economics and Public Policy*, Prentice Hall, Englewood Cliffs, N.J.

Kahn, J.R. (1995), Square pegs and round holes: can the economic paradigm be used to value the wilderness?, *Growth and Change*, 26(4): 591–610.

Kahneman, D. (1986), Comments, in Cummings, R.G., Brookshire, D.S. and Schulze, W.D. (eds.), *Valuing Environmental Goods: A State of the Arts Assessment of the Contingent Method*, Rowman and Allenheld, Totowa, N.J.

Kahneman, D. and Knetsch, J.L. (1992), Valuing public goods: the purchase of moral satisfaction, *Journal of Environmental Economics and Management*, 22(1): 57–70.

Kahneman, D., Slovic, P. and Tversky, A. (eds.) (1982), *Judgement Under Uncertainty: Heuristics and Biases*, Cambridge University Press.

Kahneman, D. and Tversky, A. (1982), The psychology of preferences, *Scientific American*, January, pp. 2136–41.

(1984), Choices, values and frames, *American Psychologist*, 39: 341–50.

Kaiser, K., Kaupenjohann, M. and Zech, W. (2001), Sorption of dissolved organic carbon in soils: effects of soil sample storage, soil-to-solution ratio, and temperature, *Geoderma*, 99(3–4): 317–28.

Kanninen, B.J. (1995), Bias in discrete response contingent valuation, *Journal of Environmental Economics and Management*, 28(1): 114–25.

Kauppi, P.E., Mieliköinen, K. and Kuusela, K. (1992), Biomass and carbon budget of European forests, 1971 to 1990, *Science*, 256: 70–4.

Kazmier, L.J. and Pohl, N.F. (1987), *Basic Statistics for Business and Economics*, McGraw-Hill, Singapore.

Kellomaki, S., Karjalainen, T. and Vaisanen, H. (1997), More timber from boreal forests under changing climate?, *Forest Ecology and Management*, 94(1–3): 195–208.

Kilpatrick, D.J. and Savill, P.S. (1981), Top height growth curves for Sitka spruce in Northern Ireland. *Forestry*, 54: 63–73.

King, G.M. (2000), Land use impacts on atmospheric carbon monoxide consumption by soils, *Global Biochemical Cycles*, 14(4): 1161–72.

Kirchhoff, S., Colby, B. G. and LaFrance, J. T. (1997), Evaluating the performance of benefit transfer: an empirical inquiry, *Journal of Environmental Economics and Management*, 33: 75–93.

Klimowicz, Z. and Uziak, S. (2001), The influence of long-term cultivation on soil properties and patterns in an undulating terrain in Poland, *Catena*, 43(3): 177–89.

Kliskey, A.D. (2000), Recreation terrain suitability mapping: a spatially explicit methodology for determining recreation potential for resource use assessment, *Landscape and Urban Planning*, 52(1): 33–43.

Kneese, A.V. and Schulze, W.D. (1985), Ethics and environmental economics, in Kneese, A.V. and Sweeney, J.L. (eds.) *Handbook of Natural Resource and Energy Economics*, vol. I, Elsevier Science Publishers, Amsterdam, pp. 191–220.

Kolchugina, T.P. and Vinson, T.S. (1993), Carbon sources and sinks in forest biomes of the Soviet Union. *Global Biogeochemical Cycles* 7: 291–304.

Kraak, M.J. and Ormeling, F.J. (1996), *Cartography: Visualization of Spatial Data*, Longman, Harlow.

Kriström, B. (1990), W. Stanley Jeavons (1988) on option value, *Journal of Environmental Economics and Management*, 18: 86–87.

Krutilla, J.V. and Fisher, A.C. (1975), *The Economics of Natural Environments: Studies in the Valuation of Commodity and Amenity Resources*, Johns Hopkins University Press, Baltimore.

Kurz, W.A., Apps, M.J., Beukema, S.J. and Lekstrum, T. (1994), 20th century carbon budget of Canadian forests, *Tellus*, 47B: 170–7.

Kurz, W.A., Apps, M.J., Webb, T.M. and McNamee. P.J. (1992), *Informative Report. The Carbon Budget of the Canadian Forest Sector: Phase I*, NOR-X-326, Forestry Canada, Edmonton.

Laidler, D. and Estrin, S. (1989), *Introduction to Microeconomics*, 3rd edn, Philip Allan, New York.

Lake, I. R., Bateman, I.J., Day, B.H. and Lovett, A.A. (2000b), Improving land compensation procedures via GIS and hedonic pricing, *Environment and Planning C*, 18: 681–696.

Lake, I.R., Lovett, A.A., Bateman, I.J. and Day, B. (2000a), Using GIS and large-scale digital data to implement hedonic pricing studies, *International Journal of Geographical Information Systems*, 14(6): 521–41.

Lake, I.R., Lovett, A.A., Bateman, I.J. and Langford, I.H. (1998), Modelling environmental influences on property prices in an urban environment, *Computers, Environment and Urban Systems*, 22(2), 121–36.

Langford, I.H., Bateman, I.J. and Langford, H.D. (1996), A multilevel modelling approach to triple-bounded dichotomous choice contingent valuation, *Environmental and Resource Economics*, 7(3): 197–211.

Langford, I.H., Georgiou, S., Bateman, I.J., Day, R.J. and Turner, R.K. (2000), Public perceptions of health risks from polluted coastal bathing waters: a mixed methodological analysis using cultural theory, *Risk Analysis*, 20(5): 691–704.

Laurini, R. and Thompson, D. (1992), *Fundamentals of Spatial Information Systems*, Academic Press, London.

Lavers, C. and Haines-Young, R. (1993), The use of landscape models for the prediction of the environmental impact of forestry, in Haines-Young, R., Green, D.R. and Cousins, S.H. (eds.), *Landscape Ecology and GIS*, Taylor and Francis, London, pp. 273–81.

Lavers, G.M. (1969), *The Strength Properties of Timbers*, Forest Products Research Bulletin 50, 2nd edn, HMSO, London.

Laxton, H. and Whitby, M.C. (1986), Employment in forestry in the Northern Region, report to the Countryside Commission, University of Newcastle upon Tyne.

Layard, P.R.G. and Walters, A.A (1978), *Microeconomic Theory*, McGraw-Hill, Maidenhead.

Lean, G. (1996), Where have all the woods gone?, *The Independent on Sunday*, 16 June.

Lean, G. and Rosie, G. (1988), Forests of money, *The Observer Magazine*, 14 February.

Leigh, J.A. and Randall, A.G. (1981), *Timber Trade Practice*, 4th edn, Macmillan, London.

Leopold, A. (1949), *A Sand County Almanac and Sketches Here and There*, Oxford University Press.

Lewis, F. (1988), Broadleaf planting costs, pers. comm., Kerswell, Exeter.

Lewis-Beck, M.S. (1980), *Applied Regression: An Introduction*, Quantitative Applications in the Social Sciences Series, Paper No. 22, Sage Publications, Beverly Hills, Calif.

Lind, R.C. (ed.) (1982a), *Discounting for Time and Risk in Energy Policy*, Johns Hopkins University Press, Baltimore.

Lind, R.C. (1982b), A primer on the major issues relating to the discount rate for evaluating national energy options, in Lind, R.C. (ed.), *Discounting for Time and Risk in Energy Policy*, Johns Hopkins University Press, Baltimore, pp. 21–94.

(1982c), Introduction, in Lind, R.C. (ed.), *Discounting for Time and Risk in Energy Policy*, Johns Hopkins University Press, Baltimore, pp. 1–19.

Liston-Heyes, C. (1999), Stated vs. computed travel data: a note for TCM practitioners, *Tourism Management*, 20(1): 149–52.

Little, I.M.D. and Mirlees, J.A. (1974), *Project Appraisal and Planning for Developing Countries*, Heinemann, London.

Lloyd, T. (1993), Testing a present value model of agricultural land prices, paper presented at the *Agricultural Economics Society 1993 Conference*, Department of Economics, University of Nottingham.

Lloyd, T., Watkins, C. and Williams, D. (1995), Turning farmers into foresters via market liberalisation, *Journal of Agricultural Economics*, 46(3): 361–70.

London Research Centre (1992), *SASPAC User Manual*. Reprinted by Manchester Computing Centre, Manchester.

Longley, P.A., Goodchild, M.F., Maguire, D.J. and Rhind, D.W. (eds.) (1999), *Geographical Information Systems*, John Wiley and Sons, New York.

Longley, P.A., Goodchild, M.F., Maguire, D.J. and Rhind, D.W. (2001), *Geographical Information Systems and Science*, John Wiley and Sons, Chichester.

Loomis, J.B. (1990), Comparative reliability of the dichotomous choice and open-ended contingent valuation techniques, *Journal of Environmental Economics and Management* 18(1): 78–85.

(1992), The evolution of a more rigorous approach to benefit transfer: benefit function transfer, *Water Resources Research*, 28(3): 701–705.

(1996), Measuring general public preservation values for forest resources: evidence from contingent valuation surveys, in Adamowicz, W.L., Boxall, P.C., Luckert, M.K.,

Phillips, W.E. and White, W.A. (eds.), *Forestry, Economics and the Environment*, CAB International, Wallingford, Oxon.

Loomis, J.B., Gonzalez-Caban, A. and Gregory, R. (1994), Do reminders of substitutes and budget constraints influence contingent valuation estimates?, *Land Economics*, 70(4): 499–506.

Loomis, J.B., Roach, B., Ward, F. and Ready, R. (1995), Testing transferability of recreation demand models across regions: a study of Corps of Engineers reservoirs, *Water Resources Research*, 31(3): 721–30.

Lovett, A.A. (2000), GIS and environmental management, in O'Riordan, T. (ed.), *Environmental Science for Environmental Management*, 2nd edn, Prentice Hall, Harlow, pp. 267–85.

Lovett, A.A. and Bateman, I.J. (2001), Economic analysis of environmental preferences: progress and prospects, *Computers, Environment and Urban Systems*, 25: 131–9.

Lovett, A.A., Brainard, J.S. and Bateman, I.J. (1997), Improving benefit transfer demand functions: a GIS approach, *Journal of Environmental Management*, 51: 373–89.

Lovett, A.A. and Flowerdew, R. (1989), Analysis of count data using Poisson regression, *Professional Geographer*, 41: 190–8.

Lovett, A.A., Kennaway, J.R., Sünnenberg, G., Cobb, R.N., Dolman, P.M., O'Riordan, T. and Arnold, D.B. (2001), Visualising sustainable agricultural landscapes, in Fisher, P. and Unwin, D. (eds.), *Virtual Reality in Geography*, Taylor & Francis, London, pp. 102–30.

Lowe, P. and Baldock, D. (2000), Integration of environmental objectives into agricultural policy making, in Brouwer, F. and Lowe, P. (eds.), *CAP Regimes and the European Countryside*, CABI Publishing, Wallingford, Oxon., pp. 31–52.

Lupien, A.E., Moreland, W.H. and Dangermond, J. (1987), Network analysis in geographic information systems, *Photogrammetric Engineering and Remote Sensing*, 53: 1417–21.

Lynch, T.D. (1989), *The Taxation of Woodlands in the United Kingdom*, Green and Son, Edinburgh.

MacFarlane, R. (2000), Managing whole landscapes in the post-productive rural environment, in Benson, J.F. and Roe, M.H. (eds.), *Landscape and Sustainability*, Spon Press, London, pp. 129–56.

MacKenzie, D. (1990), Europe's agricultural policy 'destroys the environment', *New Scientist*, 126 (1714): 20–2.

Maclaren, J.P. (1996a), *Environmental Effects of Planted Forests in New Zealand*, Bulletin No. 198, Forest Research Institute, New Zealand.

(1996b), New Zealand's planted forests as carbon sinks, *Commonwealth Forestry Review*, 75(1): 100–3.

Maclaren, J.P. and Wakelin, S.J. (1991), *Forestry and Forest Products as a Carbon Sink in New Zealand*. (Bulletin No. 162, Forest Reasearch Institute, New Zealand) Ian Bryce, Rotorua, New Zealand.

Maclaren, J.P., Wakelin, S. and Te Morenga, L. (1995), Plantation forestry in New Zealand – concepts, methodologies and recent calculations, *Proceedings of the 1995 Invitation Symposium of the Australian Academy of Technological Sciences and Engineering*, Parkville, Australia, pp. 217–36.

Macmillan, D.C. (1991), Predicting the general yield class of Sitka spruce on better quality land in Scotland, *Forestry*, 64(4): 359–72.

MacNeill, J. (1990), Sustainable development: meeting the growth imperative for the 21st century, in Angell, D.J.R., Comer, J.D. and Wilkinson, M.L.N. (eds.), *Sustaining Earth: Response to the Environmental Threats*, Macmillan, London, pp. 191–205.

Maddala, G.S. (1988), *Introduction to Econometrics*, Macmillan, New York.

Makundi, W., Sathaye, J. and Masera, O. (1992), Carbon emission and sequestration in forest: case studies from seven developing countries, vol. 1: Summary. Report No. LBL-32199, Lawrence Berkeley Laboratory, University of California, Berkeley, Calif.

Malcolm, D.C. (1970), Site factors and the growth of Sitka spruce, Ph.D. thesis, University of Edinburgh.

Malcolm, D.C. and Studholme, W.P. (1972), Yield and form in high elevation stands of Sitka spruce and European larch in Scotland, *Scottish Forestry*, 26(4): 296–308.

Mann, H.B. and Whitney, R. (1947), On a test of whether one of two random samples is stochastically larger than the other, *Annals of Mathematical Statistics*, 18: 50–60.

Markandya, A. and Pearce, D.W. (1994), Natural environments and the social rate of discount, in Weiss, J. (ed.), *The Economics of Project Appraisal and the Environment*, Edward Elgar, Cheltenham.

Marland, G. and Marland, S. (1992), Should we store carbon in trees? *Water, Air and Soil Pollution*, 64: 181–95.

Marques, M.C., Gravenhorst, G., and Ibrom, A. (2001), Input of atmospheric particles into forest stands by dry deposition, *Water, Air and Soil Pollution*, 130 (1–4), part 2: 571–6.

Marris, C., O'Riordan, T. and Langford, I. (1996), Integrating sociological approaches to public perceptions of environmental risks: detailed results from a questionnaire survey, CSERGE Working Paper GEC 96–07, Centre for Social and Economic Research on the Global Environment, University of East Anglia.

Marsh, J.S. and Swanney, P.J. (1980), *Agriculture and the European Community*. George Allen and Unwin, London.

Martin, D.J. (1990), A suite of programs for socioeconomic surface modelling, Technical Report in Geo-Information Systems, Computing and Cartography No. 28, Wales and South West Regional Research Laboratory, Cardiff.

(1996a), *Geographic Information Systems: Socioeconomic Applications*, Routledge, London.

(1996b), An assessment of surface and zonal models of population, *International Journal of Geographical Information Systems*, 10: 973–89.

Marwell, G. and Ames, R.E. (1981), Economists free ride, does anyone else? Experiments on the provision of public goods, part 4, *Journal of Public Economics* 15: 295–310.

Mather, A.S. (1998), The changing role of forests, in Ilbery, B. (ed.), *The Geography of Rural Change*, Longman, London, pp. 106–27.

Matthews, E. and Hammond, A. (1999), *Critical Consumption Trends and Implications: Degrading the Earth's Ecosystems*, World Resources Institute, Washington, D.C.

Matthews, E., Payne, R., Rohweder, M. and Murray, S. (2000), *Pilot Analysis of Global Ecosystems: Forest Ecosystems*, World Resources Institute, Washington, D.C.

Matthews, G. (1993), The carbon content of trees, *Technical Paper* 4, Forestry Commission, Edinburgh.

Matthews, R.W. (1991), Biomass production and carbon storage by British forests, mimeo, Mensuration Branch, Forestry Commission, Alice Holt Lodge Research Station, Farnham.

(1992), Forests and arable energy crops in Britain: can they help stop global warming? in *Wood, Fuel for Thought*, Conference Proceedings, Harwell Laboratories, Oxfordshire.

(1993), Towards a methodology for the evaluation of the carbon budget of forests, mimeo, Mensuration Branch, Forestry Commission, Alice Holt Lodge, Farnham.

(1995), The influence of carbon budget methodology on assessments of the impacts of forest management on the carbon balance, Proceedings of the NATO Advanced Research Workshop, March 1995, available from author, Forestry Commission, Alice Holt Lodge, Farnham.

Mauldin, T. and Platinga, A.J., (1998), An econometric analysis of the costs of reducing atmospheric carbon dioxide concentrations through afforestation, paper presented at the World Congress of Environmental and Resource Economists, Isola di San Giorgio, Venice, Italy, 25–27 June (available at www.feem.it/gnee/).

Mayhead, G.J. (1973), The effect of altitude above sea level on the yield class of Sitka spruce, *Scottish Forestry*, 27: 231–7.

McConnell, K.E. (1975), Some problems in estimating the demand for outdoor recreation, *American Journal of Agricultural Economics*, 57(2): 330–4.

(1992a), On-site time in the demand for recreation, *American Journal of Agricultural Economics*, 74(4): 918–25.

(1992b), Model building with judgement: implications for benefit transfers with travel cost models, *Water Resources Research*, 28(3): 695–700.

(1999), Household labor market choices and the demand for recreation, *Land Economics*, 75(3): 466–77.

McConnell, K.E. and Strand, I. (1981), Measuring the cost of time in recreation demand analysis: an application to sport fishing, *American Journal of Agricultural Economics*, 63(1): 153–6.

McGilvray, J. and Perman, R. (1991), Sporting recreational use of land, in *Forestry Expansion: A Study of Technical, Economic and Ecological Factors*, Forestry Commission, Edinburgh.

McGrath, S.P. and Loveland, P.J. (1992), *The Soil Geochemical Atlas of England and Wales*, Blackie Academic and Professional, London.

McInerney, J. (1986), Agricultural policy at the crossroads, in Gilg, A. (ed.), *Countryside Planning Yearbook 1986*, Geobooks, Norwich, pp. 44–75.

Medley, G. (1992), Nature, the environment and the future, presented at The University of the Third Age at Cambridge: 1992 International Symposium, *The Challenges of the Future*, 13–18 September, King's College, Cambridge.

Melichar, E. (1979), Capital gains versus current income in the farming sector, *American Journal of Agricultural Economics*, 61: 1085–92.

Mendelsohn, R., Hof, J., Peterson, G. and Johnson, R. (1992), Measuring recreation values with multiple destination trips, *American Journal of Agricultural Economics*, 24(4): 926–33.

Mendenhall, W., Reinmuth, J.E., Beaver, R. and Dunhan, D. (1986), *Statistics for Management and Economics*, 5th edn, Duxbury Press, Boston.

Mill, J.S. (1863), Utilitarianism, in Smith, J.M. and Sosa, E. (eds.) (1969), *Mill's Utilitarianism: Text and Criticism*, Wadsworth, Belmont, Calif.

Milne, R. and Brown, T.A. (1997), Carbon in the vegetation and soils of Great Britain, *Journal of Environmental Management*, 49: 413–33.

Ministry of Agriculture, Fisheries and Food (MAFF) (1987a), *Farm Woodland Scheme*, A consultation document by the Agriculture Departments and the Forestry Commission, London and Edinburgh.

(1987b), *Farming UK*. HMSO, London.

(1990), *Pilot Nitrate Scheme – Nitrate Sensitive Areas: Explanatory Leaflet*, London.

(1992a), Increased incentives for farm woodlands: joint announcement by Agriculture Departments of the UK and the Forestry Commission, News Release 36/92, 31 January, London.

(1992b), *The Farm Woodland Premium Scheme: Rules and Procedures*, London.

(1992c), *Farm Woodlands: A Practical Guide*, London.

(1992d), *Arable Area Payments: Explanatory Booklet*, London.

Minitab (1992) *Minitab Version 9.1: Reference Manual*, Minitab Inc., State College, Penn.

(1994) *MINITAB Reference Manual*, Minitab Inc., Rosemont, Penn.

Mitchell, R.C. and Carson, R.T. (1989), *Using Surveys to Value Public Goods: The Contingent Valuation Method*, Resources for the Future, Washington, D.C.

Mitlin, D.C. (1987), Price–size curves for conifers, *Forestry Commission Bulletin* 68, HMSO, London.

Morris, C.N. (1980), The Common Agricultural Policy, *Fiscal Studies*, 1: 17–35.

Motha, J. and Heyhoe, E. (1998), Road improvements and greenhouse gas emissions, paper presented at the Eighth World Conference on Transport Research, Antwerp, 16 July, Bureau of Transport Economics, Canberra, Australia.

Moxey, A. (1996), Geographical information systems and agricultural economics, *Journal of Agricultural Economics*, 47(1): 115–16.

Moxey, A. and Allanson, P. (1994), Areal interpolation of spatially extensive variables: a comparison of alternative techniques, *International Journal of Geographical Information Systems*, 8(5): 479–87.

Moxey, A. and White, B. (1998), Interdisciplinary modelling of agri-environmental problems: lessons from NELUP, in Dabbert, S., Dubgaard, A., Slangen, L. and Whitby, M. (eds.), *The Economics of Landscape and Wildlife Conservation*, CAB International, Wallingford, Oxon., pp. 231–8.

Moyer, H.W. and Josling, T.E. (1990), *Agricultural Policy Reform: Politics and Process in the EC and US*, Harvester Wheatsheaf, Hemel Hempstead.

Murray, M.B., Leith, I.D. and Friend, A.D. (1995), Growth and nutrition of Sitka spruce and beech seedlings grown at three relative nutrient addition rates under ambient and elevated CO_2 concentration, in *Carbon Sequestration in Vegetation and Soils*, report to the Global Atmosphere Division of the Department of the Environment, Institute of Terrestrial Ecology, Penicuik, Edinburgh.

Myers, N. (1990), Tropical forests, in Leggett, J. (ed.), *Global Warming: the Greenpeace Report*, Oxford University Press, pp. 372–99.

National Assembly for Wales (1999) *Woodland for Wales*, Consultation Document, Cardiff.

(2000), *Welsh Agricultural Statistics 2000*, Cardiff.

(2001a), *Woodlands for Wales: The National Assembly for Wales' Strategy for Trees and Woodlands*, Forestry Commission (on behalf of the National Assembly for Wales), Aberystwyth.

(2001b), *Draft Document on the Future of Agriculture*, Cardiff.

(2001c), *Farming Facts and Figures, Wales 2001*, Cardiff.

National Audit Office (NAO) (1986), *Review of the Forestry Commission's Objectives and Achievements*, report by the Comptroller and Auditor General, HMSO, London.

National Farmers Union (NFU) (1992), Memorandum of evidence submitted to the House of Lords Select Committee on the European Communities. *The Implementation of the Reform of the Common Agricultural Policy*. 1992/93 Session, 9th Report, HMSO, London.

Nature Conservancy Council (NCC) (1977), *Nature Conservation and Agriculture*, London.

(1984), *Nature Conservation in Great Britain*, Shrewsbury.

Navrud, S. (1989a), Estimating social benefits of environmental improvements from reduced acid depositions: a contingent valuation survey, in Folmer, H. and van

Ierland, E., (eds.), *Valuation Methods and Policy Making in Environmental Economics*, Elsevier, Amsterdam.

(1989b), *The Use of Benefits Estimates in Environmental Decision Making: Case Study on Norway*, OECD, Paris.

(1991), Willingness to pay for preservation of species: an experiment with actual payments, paper presented at the Second Annual Conference of the European Association of Environmental and Resource Economists, Stockholm, 11–14 June.

Neff, J.C. and Asner, G.P. (2001), Dissolved organic carbon in terrestrial ecosystems: synthesis and a model, *Ecosystems*, 4(1): 29–48.

Nelson, J.P. (1977), Accessibility and the value of time in commuting, *Southern Economic Journal*, 43(3): 1321–9.

Neville, W. and Mordaunt, F. (1993), *A Guide to the Reformed Common Agricultural Policy*, Estates Gazette Ltd, London.

Neville-Rolfe, E. (1990), British agricultural policy and the EC, in Britton, D. (ed.), *Agriculture in Britain: Changing Pressures and Policies*, CAB International, Wallingford, Oxon.

Nisbet, T.R. (1990), Forests and surface water acidification, *Forestry Commission Bulletin* 86, Forestry Commission, Edinburgh.

Noel, J.F., O'Connor, M. and Sang, J.T.K. (2000), The Bouchereau woodland and the transmission of socio-ecological economic value, *Ecological Economics*, 34(2): 247–66.

Nordhaus, W.D. (1991a), The cost of slowing climate change: a survey, *Energy Journal*, 12(1): 37–65.

(1991b), A sketch of the economics of the greenhouse effect, *American Economic Review, Papers and Proceedings*, 81(2): 146–50.

(1991c), To slow or not to slow: the economics of the greenhouse effect, *Economic Journal*, 101(407): 920–37.

(1992a), The DICE model: background and structure of a dynamic integrated climate economy model of the economics of global warming, *Cowles Foundation Discussion Paper* 1009, New Haven, Conn.

(1992b), An optimal transition path for controlling greenhouse gases, *Science*, 258: 1315–19.

Norman, C., Potter, C. and Cook, H. (1994), Using GIS to target agri-environmental policy, in Worboys, M. (ed.), *Innovations in GIS*, vol. I, Taylor and Francis, London, pp. 251–62.

North, J. (1990), Future agricultural land use patterns, in Britton, D. (ed.), *Agriculture in Britain: Changing Pressures and Policies*, CAB International, Wallingford, Oxon.

Norusis, M.J. (1985), *SPSS-X: Advanced Statistics Guide*, McGraw-Hill, New York.

Nowak, D.J. (1993), Atmospheric carbon reduction by urban trees, *Journal of Environmental Management*, 37: 207–17.

Nozick, R. (1974), *Anarchy, State and Utopia*, Johns Hopkins University Press, Baltimore.

O'Callaghan, J.R. (1995), NELUP: an introduction, *Journal of Environmental Planning and Management*, 38(1): 5–20.

(1996), *Land Use: The Interaction of Economics, Ecology and Hydrology*, Chapman and Hall, London.

O'Riordan, T. (1976), *Environmentalism*, Pion Press, London.

Oglethorpe, D.R. and O'Callaghan, J.R. (1995), Farm-level economic modelling within a river catchment decision support system, *Journal of Environmental Planning and Management*, 38(1): 93–106.

Oldfield, S., Lusty, C. and MacKiven, A. (1998), *The World List of Threatened Trees*, World Conservation Press, Cambridge.

Olson, D.M. and Dinerstein, E. (1998), The Global 2000: a representation approach to conserving the earth's most biologically valuable ecoregions, *Conservation Biology* 12(3): 502–15.

Openshaw, S. (1984), The modifiable areal unit problem, *Concepts and Techniques in Modern Geography (CATMOG)* 38, Environmental Publications, Norwich.

Opschoor, J.B. and Pearce, D.W. (eds.) (1991), *Persistent Pollutants: Economics and Policy*, Kluwer Academic Publishers, Dordrecht.

Ordnance Survey (1987), *Gazetteer of Great Britain*, Macmillan, London.

Organisation for Economic Cooperation and Development (OECD) (1987), *National Policies and Agricultural Trade*, Paris.

(1991), *Environmental Policy: How to Apply Economic Instruments*, Paris.

(1992), *Tables of Producer Subsidy Equivalents and Consumer Subsidy Equivalents 1978–1991*, Paris.

Orne, M.T. (1962), On the social psychology of the psychological experiment, *American Psychologist*, 17: 776–89.

Page, G. (1970), Quantitative site assessment: some practical applications in British forestry, *Forestry*, 43: 45–56.

Page, T. (1977), *Conservation and Economic Efficiency*, Johns Hopkins University Press, Baltimore.

Parry, M.L. (1993), Climate change and the future of agriculture, *International Journal of Environment and Pollution*, 3(1–3): 13–30.

Parry, M.L. (ed.) (2000), *Assessment of Potential Effects and Adaptations for Climate Change in Europe*, The Europe ACACIA Project, Jackson Environment Institute, University of East Anglia.

Parton, W.J., Schmiel, D.S., Cole, C.V., Ojima, D.S. (1987), Analysis of factors controlling soil organic matter levels in Great Plains grassland, *Soil Science Society of America Journal*, 51: 1173–9.

Pearce, D.W. (1986), *Cost-Benefit Analysis*, 2nd edn, Macmillan, Basingstoke.

(1991), Assessing the returns to the economy and to society from investments in forestry, in *Forestry Expansion: A Study of Technical, Economic and Ecological Factors, Paper No. 14*, Forestry Commission, Edinburgh.

(1993), *Blueprint 3*, Earthscan, London.

(1994), Assessing the social rate of return from investment in temperate zone forestry, in Layard, R. and Glaister, S. (eds.), *Cost-Benefit Analysis*, 2nd edn, Cambridge University Press, pp. 464–90.

(1998), Cost-benefit analysis and environmental policy, *Oxford Review of Economic Policy*, 14(4): 84–100.

Pearce, D.W. and Barbier, E.B. (2000), *Blueprint for a Sustainable Economy*, Earthscan, London.

Pearce, D.W., Barbier, E.B. and Markandya, A. (1990), *Sustainable Development: Economics and Environment in the Third World*, Earthscan, London.

Pearce, D.W. and Markandya, A. (1989), *The Benefits of Environmental Policy*, Organisation for Economic Cooperation and Development, Paris.

Pearce, D.W. and Markandya, A. (undated) An analysis of real prices of UK timber, mimeo, University College London.

Pearce, D.W., Markandya, A. and Barbier, E.B. (1989), *Blueprint for a Green Economy*, Earthscan, London.

Pearce, D.W. and Turner, R.K. (1990), *The Economics of Natural Resources and the Environment*, Harvester Wheatsheaf, Hemel Hempstead.

Pearce, D.W. and Ulph, D. (1995), *A social discount rate for the United Kingdom*, CSERGE GEC Working Paper 95–01, Centre for Social and Economic Research on the Global Environment, University of East Anglia and University College London.

(1998), A social discount rate for the United Kingdom, in Pearce, D.W. (ed.), *Economics and Environment: Essays on Ecological Economics and Sustainable Development*, Edward Elgar, Cheltenham, pp. 268–85.

Pearce, D.W. and Warford, J.J. (1993), *World Without End*, Oxford University Press.

Peck, S.C. and Teisberg, T.J. (1992a), CETA: a model for carbon emissions trajectory assessment, *Energy Journal*, 13(1): 55–77.

(1992b), *Global Warming Uncertainties and the Value of Information: an Analysis using CETA*, Electric Power Research Institute, Palo Alto, Calif.

Perman, R., Ma, Y. and McGilvray, J. (1996), *Natural Resource and Environmental Economics*, Longman, Harlow.

Perman, R., Ma, Y., McGilvray, J. and Common, M. (1999), *Natural Resource and Environmental Economics*, 2nd edn, Longman, London.

Peterken, G. (1993), *Woodland Conservation and Management*, 2nd edn, Chapman and Hall, London.

Peterson, G.L., Brown, T.C., McCollum, D.W., Bell, P.A., Birjulin, A.A. and Clarke, A. (1996), Moral responsibility effects in valuation of WTA for public and private goods by the method of paired comparison, in Adamowicz, W.L., Boxall, P.C., Luckert, M.K., Phillips, W.E. and White, W.A. (eds.), *Forestry, Economics and the Environment*, CAB International, Wallingford, Oxon.

Peterson, R.W. and Boyle, K.J. (forthcoming), Out of sight, out of mind? Using GIS to incorporate visibility in hedonic property value models, *Land Economics*, in press.

Peyron, J.L., Terreaux, J.P., Calvet, P. and Guo, B. (1998), Main economic management criteria for forests: a review, *Annales des Sciences Forestieres*, 55(5): 523–51.

Philip, M.S. (1976), The impact of policies and fiscal measures on forest investment, in Grayson, A.J. (ed.), *Evaluation of the Contribution of Forestry to Economic Development*, Bulletin 56, Forestry Commission, Edinburgh, pp. 79–85.

Pigou, A.C. (1932), *The Economics of Welfare*, 4th edn, Macmillan, London.

Pollock, S. (1999), Discounting the future – the cost of global warming, *Interdisciplinary Science Reviews*, 24(3): 195–201.

Post, W.M., Peng, T.H., Emanuel, W.R., King, A.W., Dale, V.H. and De Angelis, D.L. (1990), The global carbon cycle, *American Scientist*, 78: 310–26.

Potter, C. (1988), Environmentally sensitive areas in England and Wales: an experiment in countryside management, *Land Use Policy* 5(3): 301–12.

(1990), Conservation under a European farm survival policy, *Journal of Rural Studies*. 6(1): 1–7.

Potter, C., Burnham, P., Edwards, A., Gasson, R. and Green, B. (1991), *Diversion of Land – Conservation in a Period of Farming Contraction*, Routledge, London.

Powe, N.A., Garrod, G.D., Brunsdon, C.F. and Willis, K.G. (1997), Using a geographic information system to estimate an hedonic price model of the benefits of woodland access, *Forestry*, 70(2): 139–49.

Price, C. (1983), Evaluation of congestion and other social costs: implications for systems of recreation parks, *Sistemi Urbani*, 1: 119–39.

(1987a), Does shadow pricing go on for ever?, mimeo, School of Agricultural and Forest Sciences, University College of North Wales, Bangor.

(1987b), *The Theory and Application of Forest Economics*, Blackwell, Oxford.

(1993), *Time, Discounting and Value*, Blackwell, Oxford.

(1997a), Twenty-five years of forestry cost-benefit analysis in Britain, *Forestry*, 70(3): 171–89.

(1997b), Analysis of time profiles of climate change, in Adger, W.N., Pettenella, D. and Whitby, M. (eds.), *Climate-Change Mitigation and European Land-Use Policies*, CAB International, Wallingford, Oxon., pp. 71–88.

(2000), Valuation of unpriced products: contingent valuation, cost-benefit analysis and participatory democracy, *Land Use Policy*, 17(3): 187–96.

Price, C., Christensen, J.B. and Humphreys, S.K. (1986), Elasticities of demand for recreation site and recreation experience, *Environment and Planning A*, 18: 1259–63.

Price, C. and Dale, I. (1982), Price predictions and economically affordable area, *Journal of Agricultural Economics*, 33(1): 13–23.

Priha, O., Grayston, S.J., Hiukka, R., Pennanen, T. and Smolander, A. (2001), Microbial community structure and characteristics of the organic matter in soils under *Pinus sylvestris, Picea abies* and *Betula pendula* at two forest sites, *Biology and Fertility of Soils*, 33(1): 17–24.

Rackham, O. (1976), *Trees and Woodland in the British Landscape*, Dent, London.

Ragg, J.M., Jones, R.J.A. and Proctor, M.E. (1988), The refinement and representation of spatial data in an information system using statistical and DBMS procedures and trend surface analysis, *Geologische Jahrbuch*, A104: 295–308, Hanover.

Ramsey, F.P. (1928), A mathematical theory of saving, *Economic Journal*, 38: 543–59.

Randall, A. (1987), The total value dilemma, in Peterson, G.L. and Sorg, C.F. (eds.), *Toward the measurement of total economic value*, General Technical Report RM-148, United States Department of Agriculture: Forest Service, Rocky Mountain Forest and Range Experimental Station, Fort Collins, Colo., pp. 3–13.

(1994), A difficulty with the travel cost method, *Land Economics*, 70(1): 88–96.

Randall, A. and Hoehn, J.P. (1992), Embedding effects in contingent valuation: implications for natural resource damage assessment, Staff Paper 92 14, Department of Agricultural Economics, Michigan State University.

(1996), Embedding in market demand systems, *Journal of Environmental Economics and Management*, 30: 369–80.

Rasse, D.P., Longdoz, B. and Ceulemans, R. (2001), TRAP: a modelling approach to below-ground carbon allocation in temperate forests, *Plant and Soil*, 229(2): 281–93.

Ravenscraft, D.J. and Dwyer, J.F. (1978), Reflecting site attractiveness in travel cost-based models for recreation benefit estimation, Forestry Research Report 78-6, Dept. of Forestry, University of Illinois at Urbana-Champaign.

Rawls, J. (1972), *A Theory of Justice*, Oxford University Press.

Reed, W.J. and Haight, R.G. (1996), Predicting the present value distribution of a forest plantation investment, *Forest Science*, 42(3): 378–88.

Repetto, R., Magrath, W., Well, M., Beer, C. and Rossini, F. (1989), *Wasting Assets: Natural Resources in the National Income Accounts*, World Resources Institute, Washington, D.C.

Revesz, R.L. (1999), Environmental regulation, cost-benefit analysis, and the discounting of human lives, *Columbia Law Review*, 99(4): 941–1017.

Rhind, D.W. (1990), Global databases and GIS, in Foster, M.J. and Shand, P.J. (eds.), *The Association for Geographic Information Yearbook 1990*, Taylor & Francis, London, pp. 218–23.

Ritson, C. (1991a), Introduction to the CAP, in Ritson, C. and Harvey, D. (eds.), *The Common Agricultural Policy and the World Economy: Essays in Honour of John Ashton*, CAB International, Wallingford, Oxon.

(1991b), The CAP and the consumer, in Ritson, C. and Harvey, D. (eds.) *The Common Agricultural Policy and the World Economy: Essays in Honour of John Ashton*, CAB International, Wallingford, Oxon.

Robbins, L. (1935), *An Essay on the Nature and Significance of Economic Science*, 2nd edn, Macmillan, London.

Roberts, K.J. and Thompson, M.E. (1983), An empirical application of the contingent valuation method to value marine resources. Reprinted in Cummings R.G., Brookshire, D.S. and Schulze, W.D. (eds.), *Valuing Environmental Goods: A State of the Arts Assessment of the Contingent Method*, Rowman and Allenheld, Totowa, N.J.

Roberts, K.J., Thompson, M.E. and Pawlyk, P.W. (1985), Contingent valuation of recreational diving at petroleum rigs, Gulf of Mexico, *Transactions of the American Fisheries Society*, 114: 155–65.

Robinson, G.M. (1990), *Conflict and Change in the Countryside*. Belhaven Press, London.

Röling, N. (1993), Agricultural knowledge and environmental regulation: the Crop Protection Plan and the Koekoekspolder, *Sociologia Ruralis*, 33: 212–31.

   (1994), Platforms for decision-making about ecosystems, in Fresco, L.O., Stroosnijder, L., Bouma, J. and van Keulen, H. (eds.), *The Future of the Land: Mobilising and Integrating Knowledge for Land Use Options*, John Wiley and Sons, Chichester, pp. 385–93.

Rollins, K. and Lyke, A. (1998), The case for diminishing marginal existence values, *Journal of Environmental Economics and Management*, 36(3): 324–44.

Rollston, H. (1988), *Environmental Ethics*, Temple University Press, Philadelphia.

Roningen, V.O. and Dixit, P.M. (1989), Economics implications of agricultural policy reforms in industrial market economics, Staff Report No. AGES 89–36, Agriculture and Trade Analysis Division, Economics Research Service, United States Department of Agriculture.

Rosenberger, R.S. and Loomis, J.B. (2000), Using meta-analysis for benefit transfer: in-sample convergent validity tests of an outdoor recreation database, *Water Resources Research*, 36(4): 1097–107.

Rosenblatt, J., Mayer, T., Bartholdy, K., Demekas, D., Gupta, S. and Lipschitz, L. (1988), The Common Agricultural Policy of the European Community: principles and consequences, *Occasional Paper* 62, International Monetary Fund, Washington, D.C.

Rosenthal, D.H., Donnelly, D.M., Schiffhauer, M.B. and Brink, G.E. (1986), *User's Guide to RMTCM: Software for Travel Cost Analysis*, General Technical Report RM-132, United States Department of Agriculture: Forest Service, Rocky Mountain Forest and Range Experimental Station, Fort Collins, Colo.

Rowe, R.D., d'Arge, R. and Brookshire, D. (1980), An experiment on the economic value of visibility. *Journal of Environmental Economics and Management* 7: 1–19.

Rowe, R.D., Schulze, W.D. and Breffle, W. (1996), A test for payment card biases, *Journal of Environmental Economics and Management*, 31: 178–85.

Royal Society for the Protection of Birds (RSPB) (1987), Forestry in the flows of Caithness and Sutherland, *Conservation Topic Paper No. 17*, Sandy, Bedfordshire.

   (1988), Memorandum of evidence submitted to the House of Lords Select Committee on the European Communities. Set aside of Agricultural Land. 1987/88 Session, 10th Report, HMSO, London.

Rudeforth, C.C., Hartnup, R., Lea, J.W., Thompson, T.R.E. and Wright, P.S. (1984), *Soils and Their Use in Wales*, Bulletin No. 11, Soil Survey of England and Wales, Harpenden.

Saarinen, T.F. (1966), *Perception of the Drought Hazard on the Great Plains*, University of Chicago Press.

Sagoff, M. (1988), *The Economy of the Earth*, Cambridge University Press.

Sampson, R.N. (1992), Forestry opportunities in the United States to mitigate the effects of global warming, *Water, Air and Soil Pollution*, 64: 157–80.

Samuelson, P. (1954), The pure theory of public expenditure, *Review of Economics and Statistics*, 36: 387–9.

Schkade, D.A. and Payne, J.W. (1994), How people respond to contingent valuation questions: a verbal protocol analysis of willingness to pay for an environmental regulation, *Journal of Environmental Economics and Management*, 26: 88–109.

Schulze, W.D., Brookshire, D.S., Walther, E.G., MacFarland, K.K., Thayer, M.A., Whitworth, R.L., Ben-David, S., Malm, W. and Molenar, J. (1983), The economic benefits of preserving Visibility in the national parklands of the south-west, *Natural Resources Journal* 23: 149–73.

Schumpeter, J.A. (1952), *Ten Great Economists: From Marx to Keynes*, George Allen and Unwin, London.

Sedjo, R.A. (1989), Forests: a tool to moderate global warming?, *Environment*, 31(1): 14–20.

Sedjo, R.A., Sampson, R.N., and Wisniewski, J. (eds.) (1997), *Economics of Carbon Sequestration in Forestry*, CRC Press, New York.

Sedjo, R.A., Wisniewski, J., Sample, A.V. and Kinsman, J.D. (1995), The economics of managing carbon via forestry: assessment of existing studies, *Environmental and Resource Economics*, 6: 139–65.

Seip, K. and J. Strand (1990), Willingness to pay for environmental goods in Norway: a contingent valuation study with real payments, paper presented at the First Annual Conference of the European Association of Environmental and Resource Economists, 17–20 April, Venice.

Selman, P. (1997), The role of forestry in meeting planning objectives, *Land Use Policy*, 14(1): 55–73.

Sen, A. (1982), Approaches to the choice of discount rates for social benefit-cost analysis, in Lind, R.C. (ed.), *Discounting for Time and Risk in Energy Policy*, Johns Hopkins University Press, Baltimore, pp. 325–53.

(1987), *On Ethics and Economics*, Blackwell, Oxford.

Shaw, W.D. (1992), Searching for the opportunity cost of an individual's time, *Land Economics*, 68(1): 107–15.

Shaw, W.D. and Feather, P. (1999a), Estimating the cost of leisure time for recreation demand models, *Journal of Environmental Economics and Management*, 38(1): 49–65.

(1999b), Possibilities for including the opportunity cost of time in recreation demand systems, *Land Economics*, 75(4): 592–602.

Shoard, M. (1980), *The Theft of the Countryside*. Maurice Temple Smith, London.

Shogren, J.F., Tschirhart, J., Anderson, T., Ando, A.W., Beissinger, S.R., Brookshire, D., Brown, G.M., Coursey, D., Innes, R., Meyer, S.M. and Polasky, S. (1999), Why economics matters for endangered species protection, *Conservation Biology*, 13(6): 1257–61.

Sinclair, J. and Whiteman, A. (1992), Price–size curve for conifers, Forestry Commission Research Information Note 226, Forestry Commission, Edinburgh.

Singer, P. (1993), *Practical Ethics*, 2nd edn, Cambridge University Press.

Sjöberg, L. (1995), Explaining risk perception: an empirical and quantitative evaluation of cultural theory, RHIZIKON Risk Research Reports No. 22, Center for Risk Research, Stockholm School of Economics.

Skidmore, A.K., Ryan, P.J., Dawes, W., Short, D. and O'Loughlin, E. (1991), Use of an expert system to map forest soils from a geographical information system, *International Journal of Geographical Information Systems*, 5(4): 431–45.

Smith, M. (1996), Where have all the woods gone?, *The Independent: Weekend*, 25 May.

Smith, M.J. (1990), *The Politics of Agricultural Support in Britain: The Development of the Agricultural Policy Community*. Dartmouth, Aldershot.

Smith, R.J. and Kavanagh, N.J. (1969), The measurement of benefits of trout fishing: preliminary results of a study at Grafham Water, Great Ouse Water Authority, Huntingdonshire, *Journal of Leisure Research*, 1: 316–32.

Smith, V.K. (1992), On separating defensible benefit transfers from 'smoke and mirrors', *Water Resources Research*, 28(3): 685–94.

Smith, V.K. and Desvousges, W.H. (1986), *Measuring Water Quality Benefits*, Kluwer-Nijhoff, Boston.

Smith, V.K. and Kaoru, Y. (1990), Signals or noise? Explaining the variation in recreation benefit estimates, *American Journal of Agricultural Economics*, 72(2): 419–33.

Söderstern, B. (1980), *International Economics*, Macmillan, London.

Soil Survey of England and Wales (SSEW) (1983), *Legend for the 1:250,000 Soil Map of England and Wales: A Brief Explanation of the Constituent Soil Associations*, Rothamsted.

Solow, R.M. (1974a), Intergenerational equity and exhaustible resources, *Review of Economic Studies*, 41: 29–46.

(1974b), The economics of resources or the resources of economics, *American Economic Review*, 64(2): 1–14.

(1992), An almost practical step toward sustainability, invited lecture on the occasion of the fortieth anniversary of Resources for the Future, Washington, D.C.

Spash, C.L. (1997), Ethics and environmental attitudes with implications for economic valuation, *Journal of Environmental Management*, 50(4): 403–16.

Squire, L. and van der Tak, H. (1975), *Economic Analysis of Projects*, Johns Hopkins University Press, Baltimore.

Steinkamp, R., Butterbach-Bahl, K. and Papen, H. (2001), Methane oxidation by soils of an N limited and N fertilized spruce forest in the Black Forest, Germany, *Soil Biology and Biogeochemistry*, 33(2): 145–53.

Stern, N. (1977), The marginal valuation of income, in Artis, M.J. and Nobay, A.R. (eds.), *Studies in Modern Economic Analysis*, Blackwell, Oxford, pp. 209–54.

Sturgess, I. (1996), Interpretation and execution of measures of farm income: discussion group guidelines, Agricultural Economics Society annual conference, University of Newcastle, March 1996.

Sugden, R. (1999a), Public goods and contingent valuation, in Bateman, I.J. and Willis, K.G. (eds.), *Valuing Environmental Preferences: Theory and Practice of the Contingent Valuation Method in the US, EU, and Developing Countries*, Oxford University Press, pp. 131–51.

(1999b), Alternative theories of choice, in Bateman, I.J. and Willis, K.G. (eds.), *Valuing Environmental Preferences: Theory and Practice of the Contingent Valuation Method in the US, EU, and Developing Countries*, Oxford University Press, pp. 152–80.

Swetnam, R.D., Ragou, P., Firbank, L.G., Hinsley, S.A. and Bellamy, P.E. (1998), Applying ecological models to altered landscapes: scenario-testing with GIS, *Landscape and Urban Planning*, 41: 3–18.

Tahvonen, O. (1999), Forest harvesting decisions: the economics of household forest owners in the presence of in situ benefits, *Biodiversity and Conservation*, 8(1): 101–17.

Takahashi, A., Sato, K., Wakamatsu, T. and Fujita, S.I. (2001), Atmospheric deposition of acidifying components to a Japanese cedar forest, *Water, Air and Soil Pollution*, 130 (1–4), part 2: 559–64.

Talheim, D.R. (1978), A general theory of supply and demand for outdoor recreation and recreation system, manuscript, Department of Agricultural Economics, Michigan State University.

Tanzi, V. (1980), Inflationary expectations, economic activity, taxes and interest rates, *American Economic Review*, 70: 12–21.

Tarrant, J.R. (1980), *Food Policies*. John Wiley and Sons, Chichester.

The Times (1988), Lords speech for Prince on tax forests, *The Times*, 13 February.

Thompson, D.A. and Matthews, R.W. (1989a), CO_2 in trees and timber lowers greenhouse effect, *Forestry and British Timber*, October: 19–22.

—— (1989b), The storage of carbon in trees and timber, Research Information Note 160, Forestry Commission, Alice Holt Lodge, Farnham.

Thompson, J. (1990), Forest employment survey 1988–89, *Occasional Paper* 27, Forestry Commission, Edinburgh.

Thompson, W.A., van Kooten, G.C. and Vertinsky, I. (1997), Assessing timber and non-timber values in forestry using a general equilibrium framework, *Critical Reviews in Environmental Science and Technology*, 27(SI): S351–S364.

Thornley, J.H.M. and Cannell, M.G.R. (2000), Managing forests for wood yield and carbon storage: a theoretical study, *Tree Physiology*, 20(7): 477–84.

Thunen, J.H. von (1826), *Der Isolierte Staat in Beziehung auf Landwirtschaft und Nationalökonomie*, Hamburg.

Tiessen, H., Stewart, J.W.B. and Bettany, J.R. (1982), Cultivation effects on the amounts and concentration of carbon, nitrogen and phosphorus in grassland soils, *Agronomy Journal*, 74: 831–5.

Tolley, G.S. and Randall, A., with Blomquist, G., Fabian, R., Fishelson, G., Frankel, A., Hoehn, J., Krumm, R. and Mensah, E. (1983), *Establishing and Valuing the Effects of Improved Visibility in the Eastern United States*, interim report to the U.S. Environmental Protection Agency.

Toman, M.A. (1992), The difficulty of defining sustainability, *Resources*, 106: 3–6.

Tranquillini, W. (1979), *Physiological Ecology of the Alpine Treeline – Tree Existence at High Altitudes with Special Reference to the European Alps*, Springer-Verlag, Berlin.

Tucker, C. J. and Townsend, J.R.G. (2000), Strategies for monitoring tropical deforestation using satellite data. *International Journal of Remote Sensing* 21(6): 1461–72.

Tunstall, S., Green, C.H. and Lord, J. (1988), The evaluation of environmental goods by the contingent valuation method, report by the Flood Hazard Research Centre, Middlesex Polytechnic.

Turner, D.P., Koerper, G.J., Harmon, M.E. and Lee, J.J. (1995), A carbon budget for forests of the conterminous United States, *Ecological Applications*, 5(2): 421–36.

Turner, D.P., Lee, J.J., Koerper, G.J., and Barker, J.R., (eds.) (1993), The forest sector carbon budget of the United States: carbon pools and flux under alternative policy options, EPA/600/3-93/093, United States Environmental Protection Agency, Environmental Research Laboratory, Corvallis, Oreg.

Turner, R.K. (1992), Speculations on weak and strong sustainability, CSERGE Global Environmental Change Working Paper 92–96, Centre for Social and Economic Research on the Global Environment, University of East Anglia and University College London.

—— (1999), The place of economic values in environmental valuation, in Bateman, I.J. and Willis, K.G. (eds.), *Valuing Environmental Preferences: Theory and Practice of the Contingent Valuation Method in the US, EU, and Developing Countries*, Oxford University Press, pp. 17–41.

Turner, R.K., Bateman, I.J. and Pearce, D.W. (1992), United Kingdom, in Navrud, S. (ed.), *Valuing the Environment: The European Experience*, Scandinavian University Press, Oslo, pp. 150–76.

Turner, R.K. and Brooke, J.S. (1988), A benefits assessment for the Aldeburgh Sea Defence Scheme, Environmental Appraisal Group, University of East Anglia.

Turner, R.K. and Pearce, D.W. (1993), Sustainable economic development: economic and ethical principles, in Barbier, E.B. (ed.), *Economics and Ecology: New Frontiers and Sustainable Development*, Chapman and Hall, London, pp. 176–94.

Turner, R.K., Pearce, D.W. and Bateman, I.J. (1994), *Environmental Economics: An Elementary Introduction*, Harvester Wheatsheaf, Hemel Hempstead.

Turner, R.K., Perrings, C. and Folke, C. (1995), Ecological economics: perspective or paradigm? CSERGE Global Environmental Change Working Paper 95–17, Centre for Social and Economic Research on the Global Environment, University of East Anglia and University College, London.

Turner, R.K., van den Bergh, J.C.J.M., Soderqvist, T., Barendregt, A., van der Straaten, J., Maltby, E. and van Ierland, E.C. (2000), Ecological-economic analysis of wetlands: scientific integration for management and policy, *Ecological Economics*, 35(1): 7–23.

Tversky, A. and Kahneman, D. (1981), The framing of decisions and the psychology of choice, *Science*, 211: 453–8.

Tyers, R. and Anderson, K. (1987), Liberalising OECD agricultural policies in the Uruguay round: effects on trade and welfare, Working Papers in Trade and Development No. 87/10, Department of Economics, Australian National University, Canberra.

United Kingdom Parliament (1988), House of Commons Official Report: Written Answers, 23 March 1988, *Weekly Hansard*, Issue 1443: Cols. 137–9.

United Nations Development Programme (UNDP), United Nations Environment Programme (UNEP), World Bank and the World Resources Institute (2000), *World Resources 2000–2001: People and Ecosystems, The Fraying Web of Life*, Elsevier Science, Amsterdam.

United Nations Population Division (UNPD) (1998), *World Population Prospects: The 1998 Revision – 1*, New York.

Updegraff, K., Bridgham, S.D., Pastor, J., Weishampel, P. and Harth, C. (2001), Response of CO_2 and CH_4 emissions from peatlands to warming and water table manipulation, *Ecological Applications*, 11(2): 311–26.

van der Ploeg, J.D. (1993), Rural sociology and the new agrarian question: a perspective from the Netherlands, *Sociologia Ruralis*, 33: 240–60.

van Kooten, G.C. and Bulte, E.H. (1999), How much primary coastal temperate rain forest should society retain? Carbon uptake, recreation, and other values, *Canadian Journal of Forest Research*, 29(12): 1879–89.

Varian, H.R. (1987), *Intermediate Microeconomics*, 2nd edn, Norton, New York.

Vaughan, W.J. and Russell, C.S. (1982), *Freshwater Recreational Fishing: The National Benefits of Water Pollution Control*, Resources for the Future, Washington, D.C.

Vaughan, W.J., Russell, C.S. and Hazilla, M. (1982), A note on the use of travel cost models with unequal zonal populations: comment, *Land Economics*, 58(3): 400–7.

Waggoner, P.E. (1983), Agriculture and a climate changed by more carbon dioxide, in *Changing Climate: Report of the Carbon Dioxide Assessment Committee*, National Academy Press, Washington, D.C., pp. 383–418.

Walsh, R.G., Johnson, D.M. and KcKean, J.R. (1992), Benefits transfer of outdoor recreation demand studies, 1968–1988, *Water Resources Research*, 28(3): 707–13.

Walter, J. and Ayres, R. (1990), Global warming: damages and costs, mimeo, International Institute for Applied Systems Analysis, Laxenburg, Austria.

Ward, J.H. (1963), Hierarchical grouping to optimize an objective function, *Journal of the American Statistical Association*, 58: 236–44.

Warr, K. and Smith, S. (1993), *Science Matters: The Changing Climate*, Open University Press, Milton Keynes.

Watson, P.M. and Wadsworth, R.A. (1996), A computerised decision support system for rural policy formulation, *International Journal of Geographical Information Systems*, 10(4): 425–40.

Watson, R., Dixon, J., Hamburg, S., Janetos, A. and Moss, R. (1998), *Protecting Our Planet, Securing Our Future*, UN Environment Programme, US Aeronautics and Space Administration, The World Bank, Washington, D.C.

Watson, R.A. (1979), Self-consciousness and the rights of non-human animals, *Environmental Ethics*, 1(2): 99.

Weisbrod, B.A. (1964), Collective-consumption services of individual-consumption goods, *Quarterly Journal of Economics*, 78: 471–7.

Welsh Office (1989a), *Cambrian Mountains Environmentally Sensitive Area: Guidelines for Farmers*, Agricultural Department, Welsh Office, Llandrindod Wells.

(1989b), *Cambrian Mountains Environmentally Sensitive Area* (leaflet), Agricultural Department, Welsh Office, Llandrindod Wells.

(1992a), *Lleyn Peninsula Environmentally Sensitive Area: Guidelines for Farmers*, Agricultural Department, Welsh Office, Aberystwyth.

(1992b), *Lleyn Peninsula Environmentally Sensitive Area*, Agricultural Department, Welsh Office, Aberystwyth.

Whitby, M. (1991a), The CAP and the countryside, in Ritson, C. and Harvey, D. (eds.), *The Common Agricultural Policy and the World Economy: Essays in Honour of John Ashton*, CAB International, Wallingford, Oxon.

(1991b), The changing nature of rural land use, in Hanley, N.D. (ed.), *Farming and the Countryside: An Economic Analysis of External Costs and Benefits*, CAB International, Wallingford, Oxon., pp. 12–25.

Whitehead, D.C., Buchan, H. and Hartley, R.D. (1975), Components of soil organic matter under grass and arable cropping, *Soil Biology and Biochemistry* 7: 65–71.

Whiteman, A. (1990), Price–size curves for conifers, Forestry Commission Research Information Note 192, Forestry Commission, Edinburgh.

(1991), An analysis of forest visitor numbers using household surveys 1987–1991, Research Information Note (draft), Forestry Commission, Edinburgh.

(1995), The supply and demand for timber, recreation and community forest outputs in Great Britain, Ph.D. thesis, University of Edinburgh.

Whiteman, A., Insley, H. and Watt, G. (1991), Price–size curves for broadleaves, *Occasional Paper* 32, Forestry Commission, Edinburgh.

Whiteman, A. and Sinclair, J. (1994), The costs and benefits of planting three community forests: Forest of Mercia, Thames Chase and Great North Forest, Policy Studies Division, Forestry Commission, Edinburgh.

Whittington, D., Mu, X. and Roche, R. (1990), Calculating the value of time spent collecting water: some estimates for Ukunda, Kenya, *World Development*, 18(2): 269–80.

Wibe, S. (1992), Sweden, in Wibe, S. and Jones, T. (eds.), *Forestry: Market and Intervention Failures*, Earthscan, London.

Wigley, T.M.L. and Raper, S.C.B. (1992), Implications for climate and sea level of revised IPCC emissions scenarios, *Nature*, 357: 293–300.

Wilcoxon, F. (1945), Individual comparisons by ranking methods, *Biometrics*, 1: 80–3.

Williams, D., Lloyd, T. and Watkins, C. (1994), Farmers not foresters: constraints on the planting of new farm woodland, Working Paper 27, Department of Geography, University of Nottingham.

Willis, K.G. and Benson, J.F. (1988), A comparison of user benefits and costs of nature conservation at three nature reserves, *Regional Studies*, 22: 417–28.

(1989), Values of user benefits of forest recreation: some further site surveys, report to the Forestry Commission, Department of Town and Country Planning. University of Newcastle upon Tyne.

Willis, K.G., Benson, J.F and Whitby, M.C. (1988), Values of user benefits of forest recreation and wildlife, report to the Forestry Commission, Department of Town and Country Planning, University of Newcastle upon Tyne.

Willis, K.G. and Garrod, G.D. (1991a), An individual travel-cost method of evaluating forest recreation, *Journal of Agricultural Economics*, 42(1): 33–42.

(1991b), Landscape values: a contingent valuation approach and case study of the Yorkshire Dales National Park, Countryside Change Initiative Working Paper 21, Department of Agricultural Economics and Food Marketing, University of Newcastle upon Tyne.

(1993), Valuing landscape – a contingent valuation approach, *Journal of Environmental Management*, 37 (1): 1–22.

Wilman, E.A. (1980), The value of time in recreation benefit studies, *Journal of Environmental Economics and Management*, 7: 272–86.

Wilson, B.R. (1991), The nature and pattern of soils under ancient woodland in Southern England, Ph.D. thesis, Reading University; cited in R. Matthews (1993).

Winter, M. (1996), *Rural Politics: Policies for Agriculture, Forestry and the Environment*, Routledge, London.

Winters, L.A. (1993), The political economy of industrial countries' agricultural policies, in Rayner, A.J. and Colman, D. (eds.), *Current Issues in Agricultural Economics*, Macmillan, Basingstoke, pp. 11–31.

Wolf, F.M. (1986), *Meta-analysis: Quantitative Methods for Research Synthesis*, Quantitative Applications in the Social Sciences No. 07-059, Sage, Beverly Hills, Calif.

Woodhouse, S. (2002), The effects of agricultural change on Welsh farmland birds: analyses at different spatial scales and implications for conservation, Ph.D. thesis, University of East Anglia.

Woodhouse, S., Lovett, A., Dolman, P. and Fuller, R. (2000), Using a GIS to select priority areas for conservation, *Computer, Environment and Urban Systems* 24: 79–93.

World Bank (1996), Looking back to look forward: the World Bank's global warming backcasting exercise, *Environment Matters*, Summer 1996, World Bank, Washington, D.C., pp. 12–13.

(1999), *World Development Indicators 1999*, Washington, D.C.

World Commission on Environment and Development (WCED) (1987), *Our Common Future*, Oxford University Press.

World Commission on Forests and Sustainable Development (WCFSD) (1999), *Our Forests, Our Future*, Winnipeg.

World Resources Institute (1994), *World Resources 1994–95*, Oxford University Press.

Worrell, R. (1987a), Geographical variation in Sitka spruce productivity and its dependence on environmental factors, Ph.D. thesis, Department of Forestry and Natural Resources, University of Edinburgh.

(1987b), Predicting the productivity of Sitka spruce on upland sites in northern Britain, *Forestry Commission Bulletin* 72, HMSO, London.

Worrell, R. and Malcolm, D.C. (1990a), Productivity of Sitka spruce in northern Britain: 1. The effects of elevation and climate, *Forestry*, 63(2): 105–18.

(1990b), Productivity of Sitka spruce in northern Britain: 2. Prediction from site factors, *Forestry*, 63(2): 119–28.

Young, M.D. (1992), *Sustainable Investment and Resource Use*, Parthenon Publishing, Carnforth, Lancs and UNESCO, Paris.

Zecca, A. and Brusa, R.S., (1997), A critical review of the scientific basis of projected global warming, in Adger, W.N., Pettenella, D. and Whitby, M. (eds.), *Climate-Change Mitigation and European Land-Use Policies*, CAB International, Wallingford, Oxon., pp. 49–58.

Ziemer, R., Musser, W.N. and Hill, R.C. (1980), Recreational demand equations: functional form and consumer surplus, *American Journal of Agricultural Economics*, 62: 136–41.

Zobeck, T.M., Parker, N.C., Haskell, S. and Guoding, K. (2000), Scaling up from field to region for wind erosion prediction using a field-scale wind erosion model and GIS, *Agricultural Ecosystems and Environment*, 82(1–3): 247–59.

Index